Trafficking Data

Trafficking Data

How China Is Winning the Battle for
Digital Sovereignty

AYNNE KOKAS

OXFORD
UNIVERSITY PRESS

Oxford University Press is a department of the University of Oxford. It furthers the University's objective of excellence in research, scholarship, and education by publishing worldwide. Oxford is a registered trade mark of Oxford University Press in the UK and certain other countries.

Published in the United States of America by Oxford University Press
198 Madison Avenue, New York, NY 10016, United States of America.

CIP data is on file at the Library of Congress
ISBN 978–0–19–762050–2

DOI: 10.1093/oso/9780197620502.001.0001

1 3 5 7 9 8 6 4 2

Printed by Sheridan Books, Inc., United States of America

For Aynne Zazas, whose name I am honored to share

Contents

Acronyms

AI	artificial intelligence
ATM	automated teller machine
BGI	Beijing Genomics Institute
BRI	Belt and Road Initiative
CAC	Cyberspace Administration of China
CCP	Chinese Communist Party
CCPA	California Consumer Privacy Act
CDA 230	Communications Decency Act Section 230
CEIEC	China National Electronics Import and Export Corporation
CEO	chief executive officer
CES	Consumer Electronics Show
CFIUS	Committee on Foreign Investment in the United States
CIA	Central Intelligence Agency
CISA	Cybersecurity and Infrastructure Security Agency
CLIA	Clinical Laboratory Improvement Amendments
CMS	Centers for Medicare and Medicaid
COPPA	Children's Online Privacy Protection Act
DHS	Department of Homeland Security
DJI	SZ DJI Technology Co., Ltd.
DNA	deoxyribonucleic acid
DoD	Department of Defense
DSR	Digital Silk Road
EDM	electronic dance music
ESG	environmental, social, and corporate governance
EU	European Union
FBI	Federal Bureau of Investigation
FCC	Federal Communications Commission
FCPA	Foreign Corrupt Practices Act
FDA	Food and Drug Administration
FHSS	frequency-hopping spread spectrum
FINSA	Foreign Investment and National Security Act of 2007
FIRRMA	Foreign Investment Risk Review Modernization Act
FTC	Federal Trade Commission
GAN	generative adversarial networks
GDPR	General Data Protection Regulation

GFW	Great Firewall of China
GGE	United Nations Group of Governmental Experts on Developments in the Field of Information and Telecommunications in the Context of International Security
GPS	Global Positioning System
HGR	human genetic regulations
HIPAA	Health Insurance Portability and Accountability Act of 1996
HMO	health maintenance organization
ICT	information and communication technology
IEEE	Institute of Electrical and Electronics Engineers
IETF	Internet Engineering Task Force
IGF	Internet Governance Forum
IIA	Information Industry Association
IoT	Internet of Things
IP	intellectual property
IPO	initial public offering
IT	information technology
ITU	International Telecommunication Union
M&A	mergers and acquisitions
MMORPG	massively multiplayer online role-playing game
NIST	National Institute for Standards and Technology
NSL	national security law
NYSE	New York Stock Exchange
OEWG	Open-Ended Working Group
OPM	Office of Personnel Management
PBOC	People's Bank of China
PLA	People's Liberation Army
PRC	People's Republic of China
RNA	ribonucleic acid
SCO	Shanghai Cooperation Organization
SEC	Securities and Exchange Commission
SOE	state-owned enterprise
TPP	Trans-Pacific Partnership
UN	United Nations
VPN	virtual private network
WoW	World of Warcraft

Acknowledgments

This book has been the product of conversations, talks, meetings, reviews, and fellowships occurring over more than ten years, so it is impossible to thank all of those who contributed to it, but I will try to do my best here. The first thanks need to go out to Sera Hill, Ryan Adams, and Tony Luce for inviting me to work in the offices of their proxy server company, VPNinja, in Shanghai when I was finishing my Fulbright fellowship in 2009. They showed me why my project on Chinese media was a project on the Chinese tech sector. During my 2012–2014 postdoctoral fellowship at Rice University's Chao Center for Asian Studies, Dan Wallach, Anhei Shu, Peiyou Song, and Chris Bronk warmly welcomed me to the world of cybersecurity research, for which I will be forever grateful.

Fellowship funding from several generous benefactors was integral to the completion of this book. These include the the Abe Fellowship, the Kluge Center at the Library of Congress, the National Endowment for the Humanities, the National Committee for US-China Relations, the Mellon Foundation, and the Woodrow Wilson Center for International Scholars.

At the Library of Congress's Kluge Center, Andrew Breiner, Janna Deitz, Travis Hensley, John Haskell, David Konteh, Michael Stratmoen, and Dan Turello provided remarkable support. Feedback from Caitlin Campbell, Carla Freeman, Andrew Hammond, Susan Lawrence, Kenneth Pomeranz, Constanze Steltzenmüller, Yuwu Song, and others helped to shape the direction of the project.

The Woodrow Wilson Center provided extensive support for this work. During my time as a Wilson Fellow in 2017–2018, Robert Litwak, Robert Daly, Ambassador Stapleton Roy, Sandy Pho, and Rui Zhong offered a richly supportive atmosphere to advance my policy knowledge. Liz Stanley, Liz Newbury, Amy Austin Holmes, and Irene Wu offered detailed comments on drafts and ideas, as did many of the other fellows at the Center during my residency. Meg King and the participants of the Congressional Cybersecurity Fellowship were instrumental in helping me think through how Congress navigates challenging questions of cybersecurity oversight. Kim Conners, and Lindsay Collins ensured that our experience as residential scholars was rich and interactive, something that has become even more precious with the passage of time. As a Wilson China Fellow, I was lucky to work with Abraham Denmark, Lucas Meyers, and Shihoko Goto, and learn from a fantastic group of fellows including Michael Beckley, Ling Chen, Joseph Torigian, and Jack Zhang.

The National Committee on US-China Relations Public Intellectual's Program (PIP) supported by the Corporation of New York was essential to this project. The National Committee supported field visits to China's Guizhou National Big Data (Guizhou) Comprehensive Pilot Zone, two trips to meet with policymakers in Beijing, and site visits in Hangzhou and Qingdao organized by Jan Berris and Sarah Jessup and in conjunction with other members of PIP. My colleagues in the Public Intellectuals Program also were central to shaping the ideas in this book; Matthew Erie, Scott Kastner, Scott Moore, and Johanna Ransmeier all helped me to test the intellectual framing for the project. This book also benefitted greatly from my being able to travel to China as part of a National Committee Congressional Staff Delegation to China.

The Mellon Foundation offered transformative resources for the book's early development through a grant to the University of Virginia's Institute of Humanities and Global Cultures. Colleagues Samhita Sunya, Ricardo Padron, Paul Dobryden, Natasha Heller, and others asked crucial questions during Mellon workshops. Debjani Ganguly, Bruce Holsinger, and Anne Gilliam capably guided the Center to ensure our success on Mellon grant. The grant also funded a book workshop led by Shirley Syaru Lin and Silvia Lindtner, where Philip Howard, Min Jiang, Florian Schneider, Irene Wu, and Sheena Chestnut Greitens shepherded the project to completion through their expert guidance.

The National Endowment for the Humanities made it possible to complete this book. The NEH's Object Lessons Fellowship helped me hone the book's framework under Ian Bogost and Christopher Schaberg's guidance. Support from the NEH Fellowship allowed me to spend a year focusing on writing.

Funding from the Abe Fellowship provided time and resources for me to explore how this subject matter extends far beyond the US-China relationship. The diligent work of Seio Nakajima, Nicole Restrick Levit, Linda Grove, Wakaba Kurata, and Briyanna Brinson, and colleagues at Waseda University ensured that pandemic-constrained travel to Japan eventually happened.

Two working groups that were convened around issues of technology, China, and the nation offered helpful insights into the constraints faced by businesspeople and policymakers in working with China. Kara Frederick, Martijn Rasser, and the Center for New American Security Digital Freedom Forum members were instrumental in exploring questions of US government policymaking solutions and understanding the risks presented by data transfer from the United States. The Schmidt Futures/Young Professionals in Foreign Policy US-China Futures Program brought together Sino-US relations experts from across a wide range of sectors to address questions of US-China tech governance. I am thankful to Adam Segal, Ian Wallace, Jason Matheny and Ali Wyne for their leadership. Anna Ashton, Alexander Bowe, Rachael Burton, Dahlia Petersen, Graham Webster, and others shared expertise that informed this book.

Many experts generously shared their insights with me. I am particularly grateful to Christopher Ali, Hector Amaya, Rick Carew, Wenhong Chen, Martin Chorzempa, Meredith Clark, Nick Couldry, Nancy Damon, Elizabeth Ellcessor, Roslyn Layton, David Nemer, Camilla Fojas, Aswin Punethambekar, Lana Swartz, and Siva Vaidhyanathan, all of whom provided consequential feedback on early drafts of the book. I am also indebted to the anonymous reviewers of this manuscript, and to peer feedback on articles in the *Journal of Asian Studies, Information, Communication, and Society*, and *Television and New Media*.

Andrea Press, Ira Bashkow, and the University of Virginia Field Methods Research Workshop offered transformative early guidance for the project. My current and former colleagues at the Miller Center, Bill Antholis, Evan Feigenbaum, Harry Harding, David LeBlang, Shirley Lin, Chris Lu, and Brantly Womack at UVA, fostered lively discussions about issues of Sino-US relations and issues of governance. At the UVA East Asia Center, Dorothy Wong, Charles Laughlin, Brian Murphy, and others provided support in the field of area studies. My now-colleague and former Chinese teacher Hsin-Hsin Liang spurred me on by requesting that I complete this book before her retirement. My UVA media studies department colleagues Wyatt Andrews, Aniko Bodroghkozy, Francesca Borrione, Andre Cavalcante, Anna Katherine Clay, Shilpa Davé, Mamadou Dia, Kevin Driscoll, Sean Duncan, Elizabeth Ellcessor, Keara Goin, Jack Hamilton, William Little, Lori Morimoto, Andrea Press, Pallavi Rao, Lana Swartz, Siva Vaidhyanathan, and Bruce Williams have made it a pleasure to come to work while writing this book.

My term and life membership at the Council on Foreign Relations have been central to testing out the claims of this book with both industry and policy audiences. I am grateful to Richard Haas, Meaghan Fulco, Patrick

Costello, Carrie Bueche, and Sam Dunderdale for the chance engage with the Council membership and the policy community in Washington, DC. There are many other CFR members I would like to thank here, but their names will be lost to posterity in adherence to Chatham House Rules.

Conference panels tested and strengthened the book's claims. Scott Wallsten, Ambassador David Gross, Samm Sacks, Miriam Sapiro, and Fiona Alexander shared important insights through the Aspen Institute Technology Policy Forum. Talks and Q&A sessions hosted by the the the Center for New American Security, the George Washington University School of Media and Public Affairs, the Hong Kong Forum, the Library of Congress, Rice University's Baker Institute, the University of Hawai'i at Manoa, the University of Michigan's Center for Ethics, Science, and Computing and Lieberthal-Rogel Center for Chinese Studies, the University of Pennsylvania's Center for Advanced Research in Global Communication, the University of Texas–Austin, and the University of Tokyo, all contributed to this work. Great questions and comments at conferences like the Association for Asian Studies, the International Communication, Association, the Society of Cinema and Media Studies, and TPRC along with innumerable conversations with friends and colleagues were essential for the book's development.

Many people shared their guidance on how to write this book. I would like to thank Tom Boellstorff, Joe Calamia, Justin Kehoe, Marwan Kraidy, Raina Polivka, Sharmila Sen, and Eric Zimmer, who tightened the book's structure through generous guidance in our conversations. Laura Portwood-Stacer and the Manuscript Workers offered invaluable assistance in drafting the book proposal. Seamane Flanagan, Emily Hamilton, and Mary Child helped to clarify my writing. Dina Dineva crafted a clear and tight index. Allison Van Deventer used her vision to transform the structure of the book. I remain in awe of Allison's ability to coax wild ideas into coherent arguments.

Oriana Skylar-Mastro offered dedicated weekly feedback and guidance throughout the writing process, as well as a regular dose of inspiration and motivation. Patricia Kim, Angilee Shah, and Maria Repnikova helped me navigate book-writing and the complexities of researching about China amid the US-China tech war paired with necessary perspective. I am grateful to the Medic Writing Group, and especially Josh Braun, Andrea Guzman, Valerie Belair-Gagnon, Alison Novak, Emily West, Matthew Crain, Seth Lewis, Jen Schradie, and Rodrigo Zamith for their continuous support. Amy Zimmerman and John Bultman made sure that I am literally stronger after writing this book than when I began it.

Trafficking Data would not exist in its current form without my amazing agent, Tisse Takagi and my superb Oxford University Press editor, Angela Chnapko. Tisse honed the project with me, worked tirelessly to find the right home for the book, and offered steady support during uncertain moments. Angela provided thorough guidance on every stage of the book-writing process. Her expert feedback constantly pushed me to think of new ways I could incisively convey the book's ideas.

At Oxford University Press, Alexcee Bechthold marshaled the project through to production. Amy Whitmer worked with me on Tokyo time to navigate getting the book in print. Amy Packard Ferro and Erin Cox diligently worked to ensure the book would find its audience. I could not have hoped for a better team with which to work.

Throughout the project, I was privileged to work with a team of talented research assistants. Angela Deng, Benjamin Guggenheim, Matthew Ichida-Marsh, Joshua Jensen, Noelle Mendelson, Yuqing Sun, Wei Li, Taylor Walshe Yule Wang, Yunchu Wang, and Michael Xiao all toiled to bring the best, freshest research to the page. Maryann Xue took on every task that came her way with incredible dedication and attention to detail. Will Yuyang Chu brought the best in contemporary Chinese tech analysis to the project. Xiaona Guo helped with sourcing and citing in ways that made my jaw drop on a weekly basis. Aileen Zhang was my ride or die on this project for three years, from the Before Times through shutdowns, national protests, contested elections, and more. This book would not have happened without Aileen's fearless persistence.

Finally, I could not have written this book without the support of my loving husband, supportive family, and amazing friends. Thank you for your care while I wrote this book, but even more for your enduring love.

Preface

In 2009, on a muggy summer day in Shanghai, my proxy server stopped working, again. I was a Fulbright scholar in Shanghai doing research for my first book, *Hollywood Made in China*. My spotty internet access was just one tiny aspect of a larger phenomenon shaping China's digital landscape. That same year, the Chinese government heightened blackouts of US tech platforms as China tested out its digital borders, giving Chinese tech firms room to grow safe from foreign competition. My neighbors in Shanghai's former French Concession ran a now-defunct consumer-focused VPN start-up called VPNinja that circumvented the China's internet censorship, where they generously invited me to write in their offices, with reliable Internet access to sites I needed for my work.

At first, working at the VPN company was a merely fun and convenient way to work on my project about China's relationship with Hollywood. But one conversation changed things. I was trying to write about the possibility of Netflix in China, and my friend Tony Luce at VPNinja made the point that Netflix's issue in China was not its content but its data.

When I began my postdoctoral fellowship at Rice University's Chao Center for Asian Studies in 2012, serendipity once again intervened. My office was around the corner from the Rice Computer Science Department. I had started research for this book, planning to look at streaming platforms operating between the United States and China. Cybersecurity expert Dan Wallach and his team helped me see the flow of digital entertainment as a spigot of data, one the Chinese government was turning off and the United States was turning on. As I began to dig through the consumer platforms and products around me, it became clear that the movement of data to China extended into most aspects of life, from the mundane to the intimate. What began as curiosity about why US entertainment firms were being prevented from gathering data in China became a much bigger question of how the Chinese government was now influencing the US tech sector.

On December 7, 2018, Canadian authorities arrested Huawei chief financial officer Meng Wanzhou in Vancouver. US authorities sought her extradition on charges of conspiracy to commit bank fraud and wire fraud related to violation of US sanctions. Chinese authorities arrested Canadians Michael Spavor and Michael Kovrig in retaliation shortly after.

That week I was researching Shanghai's ICT infrastructure at the Shanghai Municipal Government's cadre training school as part of a field visit supported by the American Mandarin Society. For four tense days after Meng's arrest, I continued my work within the walls of the residential training facility. With each passing day, it became more evident how consequential the US-China tech competition would be not just for the tech sector, but for the US relationship with China as a whole.

Huawei's global expansion has drawn attention because of its role in the growth of 5G infrastructure and its potential to serve as a Chinese government surveillance and control tool. The Meng case made plain the stakes of the tech relationship between China and liberal democracies surrounding control of the data and infrastructure of the digital economy. Nearly three years later when Canadian authorities released Meng from house arrest in her Vancouver home, the Chinese government then released the two Canadians from their prison cells in China.

Despite the increasingly high profile of tensions in the US-China relationship, the lived impacts of data gathering by Chinese tech firms remain opaque to many users. In April 2019, I spoke about data trafficking with a group of state and local officials with China-related portfolios at the National Committee for US-China Relations Sub-National Symposium at the University of Michigan. This group included staffers for governors and mayors in swing states. Over half of the officials in the audience had no data security protocols in place for their offices concerning possible data gathering by Chinese tech firms, including when those officials traveled to China. I received worried requests for basic data security protocols because local government leadership had ignored these issues due to budgetary or time constraints. This was in the pre-COVID era, so people worked in their offices. When people work from home, the challenge is more significant as, without the benefit of corporate or government networks, they work with a host of other personal devices concurrently gathering data in their homes.

While I was working on this book, the Chinese government data gathering and storage practices that initially seemed far away became central to daily existence. With the COVID-19 pandemic, life moved online. Beijing-based social platform TikTok moved from a fringe teen app to a primary mode of communication for people across generations. The

Chinese government subjected the firm's algorithm to national security controls. Gaming platforms owned by Chinese tech firm Tencent moved from a site for hobbyists to a hub for social gatherings like concerts and after-school socializing for children in remote learning environments. Zoom, previously a niche business communication platform, became a verb and a lifestyle where activists, students, and businesspeople connected between the United States and China. Even sex went remote. Cam girls and cam boys deploy remote sex tech following the explosion of online sex work, and pandemic-distanced couples experiment with remote sex toys. While this book beganby exploring hypothetical risks, it then became a journal chronicling the new challenges of our online lives as shaped by the pandemic.

As this book describes, examples abound of data security risks that users may not even know they are taking. State and local officials are only part of this more extensive risk portfolio. The data gathered about us has exploded since I first began this research. However, user protections have not kept up. My sense of urgency in writing this book builds upon decades of observing the US-China media and technology relationship firsthand. I have spent more than twenty years doing research and work in the US and Chinese media and tech sectors, in both English and Mandarin; I have been a market entry strategy consultant for small, medium, and large firms in the United States and China in the media and tech sectors. This includes delivering testimony in both chambers of Congress, advising multiple executive commissions and trade officials in the United States, and meeting with trade and foreign affairs officials in China.

Beginning with Chinese president Xi Jinping's ascent to power in 2012, the politics of access to China for international scholars have shifted dramatically. When schools in the United States moved to online learning during the COVID-19 pandemic, my colleagues in the field of Chinese studies and I began having discussions about what the extraterritoriality of Hong Kong's national security law might mean for us. After all, anyone who teaches about China will likely refer to Tiananmen Square at some point, and possibly the more politically contentious topics of Taiwan, Tibet, Hong Kong, and Xinjiang. Such risks pale in comparison to those faced by researchers with family in China or colleagues based in China. Thus, for this book, questions of research methodology and access have become entwined with the subject matter. As Chinese government laws overseeing online conduct become more stringent and extraterritorial, they constrain how researchers can safely conduct their work.

Trafficking Data explains how the US tech sector set a standard for exploiting user data that makes it difficult for everyday people—and governments around the world—to protect against data exfiltration to China. By contrast, the Chinese government's sophisticated tech-focused industrial policy has precise (if not always realized) goals for using data gathered from the United States. These goals span product development, education, health, military modernization, intelligence gathering, and more. I hope that this book will help explain how the US tech innovation system's problems aid the Chinese government's efforts at global tech expansion and even perhaps inspire efforts toward data stabilization.

1

The Data Trafficking Dilemma

On May 31st, 2020, activists from the US-based human rights group Humanitarian China hosted an online event commemorating the violent crackdown on civilian protests in Tiananmen Square in 1989. Participants from both the United States and China, including "Tiananmen Mothers," women who lost children when the People's Liberation Army (PLA) quashed the demonstrations, joined the meeting. The Chinese government has long censored June 4th anniversary events, but this time it influenced international remembrance of the infamous day via Zoom, a US-based firm.

Zoom terminated the accounts of activists who hosted the event, as well as other Tiananmen remembrance events that included Chinese nationals, according to the firm' website. The United States Department of Justice charged a now former China-based Zoom employee for terminating the meetings but the company itself faced no charges.[1] When asked about its actions, Zoom responded to critics in the United States by stating that it was following local laws in China.[2] A necessity due to the COVID-19 pandemic, Zoom grew despite this controversy, with a year-over-year revenue increase of 326 percent from the beginning of 2020 to the beginning of 2021.[3] The company's behavior in this incident reflects its sensitivity to Chinese regulations. With more than 700 engineers based in China, the firm depends on access to the Chinese market.[4] Zoom adjusted its corporate oversight policies following the June 4th-related incidents. However, the United States' response to Zoom—which amounted to investigations across a patchwork of government agencies only after the incident attracted widespread public attention—reveals a lack of systematic user data protection in an increasingly connected world.

The Tiananmen commemoration case demonstrates the vulnerability of US consumer protections to Chinese government demands. Tech firms operating in both countries must balance their corporate interests against the possibility of Chinese government pressure. Penalties can include market bans, incitement of consumer boycotts, and invasive and expensive national security reviews, as well as civil and criminal liability.

In the United States, by contrast, firms enjoy limited government oversight. Only a piecemeal system of user protections exists. The power of the US tech sector has transformed it into a tool to expand US influence, further complicating efforts to regulate it.

Why Data Trafficking Matters

In this book, I argue that the movement of data from tech firms in the United States to China threatens digital sovereignty around the world. The term digital sovereignty (along with the related Chinese concept of cyber sovereignty) refers to a country's control over its national digital infrastructures, technologies, and data.[5] In prioritizing growth, US regulators have taken a laissez-faire approach to digital sovereignty by permitting opaque and often predatory data-gathering practices.[6] The Chinese government builds on US-based tech firms' long tradition of exploiting the public for commercial gain. It amplifies its national power through tech corporations that depend on access to the Chinese market. Together, the US and Chinese approaches to data security increase the odds that citizens' data will be moved across international borders without those citizens' consent. In response, some countries have developed digital borders to protect their users.[7] Many have not, however, leaving them open to exploitative corporate practices and unexpected government surveillance. To better navigate this challenge, I introduce the concept of data trafficking, the commercial extraction of consumer data to support a government outside the legal system users consented to have protect them.

Chinese laws enshrine direct government access to corporate data, both domestically and internationally. Thus, the failure to regulate data gathering by tech firms operating in the United States not only exploits consumers but empowers the Chinese government. To be clear, China's role as a global data extractor is a Chinese government process grounded in the exploitative data-gathering practices that built Silicon Valley.

Although data trafficking occurs around the world, I focus on data transfers from the United States to China in this book. As the two largest global economies and major trading partners, the United States and China are central to international trade. When investing in technology, most countries choose between buying products from the United States and buying them from China.

The lack of systemic data governance in the United States—a historic cata-lyst for tech industry growth—enables widespread data trafficking. As com-pared to other developed democracies like the EU and Japan, for example, tech firms in the United States face much looser standards surrounding con-sumer data extraction and international data transfer. Meta's rampant user data-gathering, Google's vast data monetization, data security firm Palantir's monitoring, and other such practices have all established the global identity of the US tech sector as one defined by exploitative practices. US firms mon-etize user data generated when corporations monitor their behavior online, in what author Shoshana Zuboff dubs "surveillance capitalism."[8] In this way, the flexible regulatory environment of the US tech sector has given US tech firms the gift of global dominance across a wide range of consumer apps and technologies.

US government agencies can and do gain access to limited amounts of user data in the United States. Edward Snowden revealed that secret Foreign Intelligence Surveillance Act (FISA) courts siphoned user data from US platforms for the US government. The FISA abuses, however, did not stem from standardized government data access requirements, but rather as spe-cific cases of egregious consumer data collection.

By contrast, the Chinese government allows companies to access the Chinese market only if they submit to formal centralized oversight of all corporate data as a condition of their presence in the Chinese market. The Chinese government further exercises control by underwriting tech "national champions," which come from the private sector but also advance and ben-efit from state policies. Common examples include the "BAT firms": Baidu, Alibaba, and Tencent. Chinese government policies allow regulators to maintain an iron grip both at home and abroad on these firms and their data.

The Chinese government also fosters the growth of Chinese tech firms by placing restrictions on foreign firms. The government follows a model of *cyber sovereignty*: it defines and protects the country's digital borders by con-trolling data and tech infrastructure. The framework extends government control over any sector Chinese tech firms touch upon. Because of its size, scale, and trade protections, China's domestic market excels at developing global tech products. The social media platform WeChat, for example, be-came essential to people in China and their contacts after filling the void left by the forced exit of US social media platforms from China. By restricting for-eign firms' access to the domestic market and supporting local alternatives, the Chinese government has fueled the global expansion of Chinese firms.

This government support, however, comes with increased oversight. Since the 2010 white paper on the internet in China, which formed the foundation of Chinese cyber sovereignty principles, the Chinese government has increased its control over the tech sector.[9] Expanded Chinese government supervision covers everything from national security data audits to civil and criminal penalties to extraterritorial enforcement of Chinese laws. Chinese firms face extensive, vaguely-defined national security reviews of all of the data they generate.[10] Chinese or foreign firms operating in China must legally store their data in Chinese-government-run servers.[11] In addition, China's military–civil fusion strategy, which allows the Chinese military to use all Chinese consumer technologies, supports nationalizing specific data, algorithms, and artificial intelligence tools for warfare.[12]

Since 2010, increased control of China's domestic tech sector has been extended to include corporations operating outside of China. The 2020 Hong Kong national security law applies Chinese law extraterritorially. This means that Chinese and non-Chinese firms, along with individuals, are now subject, upon entering Hong Kong, to Chinese government punishment for crimes against Chinese national security committed anywhere in the world. China's 2021 Data Security Law strengthens the grip, imposing legal penalties—including fines, the forced suspension of business operations, and the revocation of business licenses—for handling data outside of China that the Chinese government deems harmful to the PRC's national security. The Data Security Law's vagueness chills the behavior of firms wishing to limit their legal exposure.[13]

Zoom, Apple, Alibaba, Tencent, and others that depend on both the US and Chinese markets must balance their interests in the US and Chinese tech regulatory systems. In the US tech sector, firms have every incentive to only meet the minimum US government requirements because of their power relative to the government. By contrast, China's opaque system of cyber sovereignty encourages firms, both Chinese and international, to exceed the minimum oversight requirements as a precaution against banishment from the market.

Any critique of the relationship between the US tech sector and China's system of cyber sovereignty demands acknowledgment of the historical pattern of anti-Asian discrimination stemming from US policies related to Asia.[14] Criticism of Chinese investment in the United States evokes the moral panic over Japanese tech investment in the United States during the 1980s.[15] The "China threat" discourse, which characterizes China's reemergence on the global stage as an existential risk to the United States, emerged in the early 1990s in parallel with discussions about "China's rise."[16] Australian political scientist Chengxin Pan argues that the idea of a "China threat" is a self-fulfilling prophecy.[17] The modern idea of the "China threat" leverages fear about China's growth and development as a tool for US policymaking, which further inflames public sentiment.

When we foreground Asian American experiences in analyzing US-China tech relations, however, the complexity of the US-China tech relationship becomes clearer. For example, Chinese government actors have promulgated stories of anti-Asian hate narratives in the United States on the Chinese-owned platform WeChat to delegitimize critiques of the Chinese government.[18] Asian Americans in the United States—from Uyghur Muslims to Hong Kong democracy advocates to Tiananmen activists—face disproportionate threats of tech-enabled monitoring and censorship by the Chinese government.[19] This book seeks to examine the factors and influences that are creating "gridlock" on the road to a solution for data trafficking. Anthropologist Pardis Mahdavi has identified gridlock as the entanglement of international and domestic political, economic, and social phenomena that shape lives, communities, and governments.[20] In doing so, this book argues that it is the interactions between China and the United States that weaken digital protections around the world, rather than strictly the actions of one country.

The Risks of Data Trafficking

Data trafficking presents three levels of risk—personal, economic, and national security. First, and most immediate, data trafficking impacts individual users, who face violations of privacy or risk surveillance. Personal risk stems not just from the data that a person shares with one platform but also from the information that this user's data can generate when combined with other data sources.

Insights gleaned from combining multiple sources of data exemplify the idea of *mosaic theory*, also known as *compilation theory*. In its Freedom of Information Act guidelines, the United States Department of the Navy defines mosaic theory as "the concept that apparently harmless pieces of information, when assembled together could reveal a damaging picture."[21] In one striking example of mosaic theory, Target sent coupons for maternity-related products to a teenage girl, thereby exposing her pregnancy to her parents before she notified them.[22] In an environment in which Chinese commercial tech firms face government pressure to share user data and the Chinese state is credibly identified as sponsoring the hacking of major US corporate and government databases, data trafficking can produce rich profiles of individual users. This individual-level risk feels unnerving. It is not, however, the most serious risk posed by data trafficking. Most people are simply not exciting intelligence targets.

Data trafficking also poses a threat to companies'—and countries'—economic competitiveness. Large data sets generated by consumers are used to train machine learning algorithms that support the development of artificial intelligence. Technologist Cory Doctorow compares the risks presented by data gathering to those presented by climate change, where threats loom large and over a long time horizon.[23] Advances in artificial intelligence offer a path to long-term economic dominance, where improved data gathering leads to better products, which in turn leads to market control. Such pathways are developed through US tech firms' monopolistic practices, which advance predatory US corporate data-gathering methods. Tech trade with China amplifies such concerns. When exploitative data gathering meets expansive Chinese government data controls, as described above, the result is that Chinese firms gain long-term economic advantages.

The social media firms TikTok and WeChat, for instance, have built their economic might by following the path made by Silicon Valley's social platforms, operating with opaque algorithms that can elevate disinformation and gather reams of consumer data under the radar. Because the platforms are essential to today's communications and beloved by many users, such risks are increasingly pervasive. With each new user, the platforms become more attractive. Increasing popularity expands not just their current reach but their growing interdependence with politicians and government agencies. Because their parent companies are based in China, the firms also bolster China's intelligence-gathering efforts, censor content deemed sensitive to the Chinese government, and improve not just their own algorithms but the rich mosaic of user data accessible to the Chinese government.

The bulk of the content on TikTok poses little concern on its own. But the claim that its data gathering presents no risk to individual users misses the point. The app collects a wide range of user data and reserves the right to share any data it collects with its parent company, Beijing-based ByteDance. A class-action lawsuit in California argues that TikTok harmed its users by sending personally identifiable information to China without their consent.[24] In China, intelligence professionals have the ability to integrate TikTok data with data obtained from Chinese government hacks to create detailed profiles.

In the online gaming industry, massive platforms at the intersection of networked social life, financial transactions, and play have turned data trafficking into a way of life, particularly during the isolation of the COVID-19 pandemic. The Chinese firm Tencent, a leader in global surveillance and a close ally of the Chinese government, leads the global gaming industry as an investor in popular games like Fortnite. Tencent, along with Alibaba affiliate Ant Group, is also a major player in payment apps. Chinese payment apps extend the power of China's nonconvertible currency, the *renminbi* (RMB). The data they gather support China's emergence as a leader in the global financial industry by building models to predict consumer behavior and credit risk. Weak data security standards for the consumer products industry bring data trafficking into the most intimate of spaces. By permitting pervasive data gathering, they also sap consumers' will to resist such invasions of their privacy. Social media platforms, online games, and payment apps, as well as a wide range of connected devices and infrastructure, can produce enhanced data sets accessible to the Chinese government that synthesize everything from video to speech and beyond. Applications in artificial and augmented intelligence, surveillance, bioengineering, and a host of other emerging technologies lay the foundation for long-term economic power.

Health security is another area in which data gathering poses significant risks. Thanks to its data-gathering abilities, the Chinese government can develop advanced precision medicine in a research environment that lacks the individual protections present in the United States. And, as China's coronavirus vaccine development efforts have demonstrated, emerging medical treatments are an area of intense Sino-US competition.

Economic competition paves the way for security risks. Chinese tech platforms serve as a vehicle for economic statecraft, or the strategic use of economic power to advance foreign policy goals.[25] China's tech sector undergirds the state's economic power while also strategically countering US power.[26] The Chinese government gives Chinese firms a global competitive advantage by privileging domestic investment in this sector, providing a guaranteed market. Chinese firms' investment in critical infrastructure overseas supports new products and the building of new markets. In telecommunications, agriculture, and smart-city sectors, Chinese government involvement presents both economic and security risks by creating dependence on critical infrastructure manufactured by firms with close government ties. In space, satellite infrastructure offers data that advances both economic and national security. Data-driven medical therapies can be a tool for economic competitiveness or a strategic resource accessible only to certain preferred countries.

By forcing companies to store data locally and requiring national data audits, the Chinese government blurs the lines dividing private digital spaces and national information resources. Chinese consumer data gathering in the United States presents opportunities for surveilling US elites, advancing misinformation on popular US platforms, and modeling US communities to gather insights for advanced product development (something that US firms cannot do in China). Refining dual-use consumer technologies such as virtual reality, augmented reality, and artificial intelligence further strengthens the tools available to the Chinese military.

Chinese government efforts to control the country's domestic tech sector thus have a global impact. Each sector presents its own data-trafficking risks. Taken together, the data they gather create a mosaic, in the sense described above, composed not just of the life of one person but of an entire community's political beliefs, health risks, and economic vulnerabilities.

For ordinary US consumers, data trafficking is part of life. Nothing about the way data is collected, compiled, stored, processed, mined, and interpreted is transparent. Users wishing simply to scroll through funny videos, attend school during a COVID-19 quarantine, play video games with their friends, map their family tree, or clean their floors with a robot vacuum are drawn into a transnational cycle that they neither understand nor have the power to influence. But the uses of such data present risks to individuals, economic competitiveness, and national security—not just in the present but for decades to come.

Defining Data Trafficking

While the discussion above has suggested various aspects of the impacts of data trafficking, it is worth more closely examining the term and its parameters for the purpose of this study. Data trafficking extracts national resources including, but not limited to, everything from consumer insights to proprietary commercial machine-learning tools gleaned through corporate data gathering. This process reflects a symbiosis between nation-states, tech corporations, and users, part of what media and communications scholar Iginio Gagliardone calls "technopolitical regimes."[27] "Trafficked" data crosses national boundaries to become subject to new forms of control that further alienate it from any existing protections.

Pardis Mahdavi's book *From Trafficking to Terror* notes that Euro-American trafficking discourses often replicate racialized tropes by defining some groups as victims in need of rescuing and others as villains.[28] Mahdavi highlights the struggle of how to discuss trafficking without reinforcing caricatures or stereotypes. I hope to use the concept of data trafficking to complicate our understanding of how corporate and government actors in both the United States and China exploit the data of users, while also acknowledging that the Chinese government has developed a uniquely expansive legal apparatus to gather and control user data.

What Is Data?

Understanding data trafficking requires understanding data. Data underpins twenty-first century trade, but it is by no means a self-evident category. Researchers in information science distinguish between data, information, and knowledge, describing *data* as raw material, *information* as data taken in context to gain insight, and *knowledge* as information that operates within a system of thinking.

Three metaphors came to prominence in the early 2000s to help users and investors understand the role of data in economic life.[29] The metaphor "data as the new oil," suggesting a rich, unprocessed crude resource, came into use in the early 2000s.[30] The idea of "data as infrastructure" appeared in the 2010s as the economic role of data increased.[31] The third metaphor, "data as an asset," emerged in response to corporations' monetization of data.[32] While these phrases speak to the type of information contained within large data resources, with a focus on its economic and security value, they do not clarify what data does.

Thinking of data as oil, infrastructure, and an asset does not capture the full power of the personal and social data culled through mass data-gathering. While data, like oil, can be a productive resource, data can include proprietary information and be used to the detriment of persons, communities and countries. Technology that monitors your heart rate, allows you to watch your children while they sleep, or provides genetic information on your unborn child, can also feed data to third parties. Media studies and science and technology studies scholars argue that human systems create data. When firms store, manipulate, or transmit data, they are gathering important personal insights; more importantly, those systems have power over us. Media historian Lisa Gitelman and literature scholar Virginia Jackson note, "If data are somehow subject to us, we are also subject to data."[33] Such data is important because it operates as "systems of power," according to information studies scholars Silvia Lindtner, Ken Anderson, and Paul Dourish.[34] *Trafficking Data* examines how corporate data collection empowers nation-states by mapping our lives.

Yet as user data becomes more powerful, users feel less empowered to manage it. Corporations cultivate "digital resignation," or "the condition produced when people desire to control the information digital entities have about them but feel unable to do so."[35] The insecurity of data, data centers, and data movement exceeds the capacity to practice digital hygiene at an individual level, to say nothing of managing how user data functions in asserting national sovereignty.

What Is Trafficking?

Corporate practices, national laws, and consumer exploitation are linked between the United States and China in ways that enable data trafficking. Legal scholar Jessica Elliott argues that trafficking consists of three elements: the "action," the "means," and the "purpose."[36] Potential actions include "recruitment, transportation, transfer, harbouring or receipt."[37] Means include "threat or use of force or other forms of coercion, of abduction, of fraud, of deception, of the abuse of power or of a position of vulnerability or of the giving or receiving of payments or benefits to achieve the consent."[38] The purpose is the reason the trafficking occurred.

The term *trafficking* evokes questions of consent for access, from sexuality to DNA, reflecting the increasingly close connection between the human body, the human experience, and the data gathered about them. Data trafficking includes all these elements, from recruiting confidential data to collecting and transferring it. Similarly present are the abuse of power and positions of vulnerability, the trading of benefits to achieve consent, and coercion and deception. Without systemic data reform, inequities render individual agency a farce in the context of larger social and economic pressures.

What Are the Elements of Data Trafficking?

Armed with the basic definitions of 'data' and 'trafficking,' we can proceed, in the following sections, to explore more closely the elements of data trafficking that come together to produce cross-border exploitation. The idea of data trafficking combines three uses of the word *traffic*. First, Hector Amaya's framing of drug trafficking suggests the erosion of national sovereignty as part of a system of trade that crosses legal boundaries.[39] Trafficking drugs produces a mobile, multilayered system of trade that exists on the margins of the law and produces violence, in addition to rich personal and financial benefits for individual users, groups, and corporations. Second, from research on human trafficking, I draw the idea that users enter into an exploitative labor agreement, or bargain, when they share their data.[40] Consumers, in essence, "work" for corporations when generating data through their use of consumer platforms. The third use of the word relates to tech-sector tools to monetize data. The term *traffic* refers to a metric for data movement.[41] Measurements of the amount of data flowing onto a platform, or its traffic, reveal the popularity of a given product. High traffic demonstrates high consumer engagement, which also correlates with profitability. Combined, these three uses of the term synthesize elements of border transgressions, the intimacy of our user data, and the networked systems that produce and transfer it.

Data transfers challenge national boundaries. Consent mechanisms, particularly in the United States, have evolved much more slowly than the technologies to which they apply. US users encounter opaque agreements with complex language that fail to inform them of the risks they face.[42] The European General Data Protection Regulation (GDPR), to counter such practices, monitors user consent and provider accountability in depth.[43]

Most terms of service in the United States fail to make it clear that the user is consenting to let their data be moved to a different jurisdiction. Indeed, companies' terms of service—which are not usually designed to be read by users—often obscure the ways the companies manage their data. In 2020, TikTok's parent company, ByteDance, disclosed that it moved TikTok's data storage centers to Singapore and the United States but failed to share that its engineering facilities in Beijing were still processing user data.[44] Citizens cannot consent to involvement in a system they do not understand. Such practices erode national sovereignty by making legal borders fuzzy.

Data trafficking also builds on what scholars identify as a "labor paradigm," wherein workers agree "to severely exploitative labor practices."[45] In thinking of consumers as workers, media theorist Dallas Smythe characterizes free time as a commodity sold in the "consciousness industry," in which individuals sell advertisers their consciousness and time by paying attention to something.[46] Online participation often takes the form of "playbour," a mechanism that encourages users to engage in unpaid labor, such as online gaming or posting on social media, that generates data for firms.[47] Users submit to surveillance to digital services in what media studies scholar Mark Andejevic calls "the work of being watched."[48] Surveillance on social media platforms and online gaming communities such as TikTok and Fortnite gave way to similar practices on social payment platforms such as Venmo and Alipay. Consumers produce media content and take on the role previously played by workers.[49] They generate data with everything they do, in areas ranging from finances to health to sex.

To further explore how data trafficking undermines consent, consider revenge porn, the nonconsensual disclosure of intimate photos or videos. This occurs, for example, when an individual posts erotic photos or videos of a former romantic partner on a porn site, either for sale or for free. For women, people of color, LGBTQ+ individuals, and other marginalized populations subject to increased online violence, weak consent to consumer data gathering elevates the security risks they already face.[50] Sharing an intimate photo with a partner can be an expression of affection. When the partner shares that photo with another party without the subject's consent, they violate that individual's trust and in some circumstances commit a crime. When a company uses that photo based on their terms of service, they exploit their labor bargain with the user. When sharing that photo with a foreign government under the same exploitative terms, the company erodes digital sovereignty.

Finally, data trafficking evokes the metric for data movement—traffic. Data generates value when transferred, aggregated, or processed, not when static. On social media platforms, traffic predicts firm equity value.[51] High traffic generates user data, which correlates with improved financial outcomes for senior executives and shareholders.[52] For example, TikTok users generate traffic on the app. That traffic improves its algorithm by drawing on a greater volume of user data. An improved algorithm better engages users, further improves traffic flow, and thereby increases value.

Better products lead to improved consumer engagement (and financial outcomes), but the utility of data gathering transcends financial enrichment.[53] Data traffic provides mechanisms for states to surveil at scale. Software developer Dmytri Kleiner and computer security expert Jacob Appelbaum argue that consumer data creates maps—of relationships, speech, location, biological measurements.[54] From the sociocultural to the spatial, maps are, as geographer J. B. Harley argues, central to accruing and maintaining national influence.[55] Like Harley, Anthony Giddens associates such insights with dominance. He refers to surveillance as the collation and supervision of information relevant to state control.[56] Data trafficking enables the mapping of consumer data in a way that shifts the contours of global power.

What Is Not Data Trafficking?

To fully understand the nature of data trafficking, we must also recognize what data trafficking is *not*. Data trafficking, which denies consent through obfuscation and structural inequalities, stands in stark contrast to transparent data flows, or data migration.

Data migration is the nonambiguous, deliberate, procedure-driven process of selecting, preparing, extracting, and transferring data from one storage system to another in an information technology (IT) context.[57] A legal, systematic, rules-based approach to data movement constitutes data migration, such as the systematic movement of data within the European Union, which views privacy as a social right and individual value. At present, neither US nor Chinese laws allow for reliable, transparent migration of user-generated data. By contrast, the EU and Japan have established mutual standards of data adequacy that allow individuals to track where their data goes and how to remove it.[58] Data trafficking and data migration differ because data trafficking involves unclear data storage, governance, and integration processes and, as discussed above, confusing consent agreements through corporate terms of service.

Data trafficking also differs from data theft. Whereas data trafficking relies on obfuscation, the veneer of legality disintegrates altogether in cases of data theft. Examples include the 2015 hacking of the Office of Personnel

Management (OPM) involving the exfiltration of the US government's security clearance data.[59] Also in 2015, hackers allegedly affiliated with the PRC's Ministry of State Security attacked the health insurer Anthem, accessing an estimated 78.8 million people's medical records.[60] In 2017, PLA-affiliated hackers were identified as infiltrating the US credit reporting firm Equifax, gathering the financial data of approximately 145 million Americans.[61] In 2018, a data breach of the international hotel chain Marriott, gathering travel information for roughly 500 million guests around the world, was linked to hackers working on behalf of China's Ministry of State Security.[62] The OPM, Anthem, Equifax, and Marriott database hacks augment data trafficking by increasing the information available to the Chinese government. Data trafficking and data theft complement each other: national laws and corporate incentives in the Chinese market drive data trafficking, and government-sponsored hacking makes the trafficked data even more useful.

How the US-China Tech Relationship Destabilizes Global User Data

Emerging technologies have long destabilized sovereignty. The age of exploration redefined maritime borders, paving the way for colonialism. Aviation gave rise to the concept of airspace.[63] Oil exploration ushered in mineral rights.[64] The space race created a new contest for planetary exploration.[65] The internet led to the concept of sovereignty over data.[66]

In their work on data colonialism, Nick Couldry and Ulises A. Mejias refer to the United States and China as two poles of colonial power in the global internet. Couldry and Mejias use the term *data colonialism* to argue that extracting data relates to historical practices of colonialism.[67] While data colonialism presents an invaluable way to reflect upon the United States and China as extractors and colonial powers with respect to other nations, it raises the question of what happens when these two global powers engage in trade with each other.[68]

The two countries are economically enmeshed, with a trade volume exceeding US$500 billion.[69] Whoever controls each nation's data shapes international trade between global hegemons. After all, as media studies scholar Stefano Calzati notes, "Behind the scenes, these two poles of interests often find an agreement when it comes to the very basic principle of surveillance through data."[70] China and the United States both strip citizens' control of personal data via unclear consent agreements, labyrinthine corporate partnerships, and government policies that privilege corporate access to data over citizens' rights.[71] In China, laws prioritize mass government data aggregation and control at the national level, while the United States relies heavily on corporate data management in a system of fragmented regulations. China's policies then magnify the risks embedded within the US approach to data governance.

US tech firms congratulate themselves on their ability to "move fast and break things," but by prioritizing time to market over security, companies make users vulnerable not just to nonstate hackers but also to other governments.[72] Corporations harvest videos of religious ceremonies and babies sleeping in their cribs, among countless other private moments, as data.[73] Once collected, intimate moments transform into valuable resources that secure corporate debt.[74] They become algorithms that support new products, including entertainment, weapons systems, and health care.[75] In the Sino-US case, customer data becomes both a financial and an intelligence asset.

The governing systems of the United States and China have differing views on individual rights. However, despite their political differences, both the United States and China leverage the combined power of government and corporate influence to alienate citizens from their data.[76] The exploitative US tech sector started a race to the bottom for user data security; Chinese government data access requirements have accelerated it.

Why the US Tech Ecosystem Makes
Data Trafficking a Problem

The twenty-first century US economy grew from corporate data gathering. Fragmented government oversight and processes that prioritize time to market over user safety allow US firms to aggregate data with impunity, with a few exceptions (such as individual health data, financial data in New York, and certain consumer data in California).[77] The US tech giant Google pioneered the process of data gathering with its unprecedented surveillance of human life through a suite of "free" services, including the email client Gmail, the file storage service Google Drive, the web browser Google Chrome, and other applications that mine and integrate individual user data.[78] Google paved the way for the extensive data-gathering practices of other firms like Amazon, Apple, and Meta.[79]

In parallel with US Department of Defense funding for the internet in the 1970s and 1980s, the US government advocated for the emergence of a multistakeholder system of global digital governance which, by including corporate perspectives, provided those firms a voice in international tech standards-setting.[80] The combination of corporate governance and multistakeholderism laid the framework for much of the current global digital regulatory landscape.[81]

In many parts of the world, US-based tech firms can drive policy to suit their economic interests. The most egregious instances of abuse by US tech firms—from promoting genocidal rhetoric against the Rohingya people in Myanmar to amplifying popular misinformation in the 2016 US presidential election—emerge from their mercenary reliance on profit-generating algorithms .[82] At the US-Mexico border, an alliance between the US tech sector and the US government extends oppressive US government surveillance, but US corporations retain more power in such relationships than their Chinese counterparts.[83] Balancing US-China competition with tech sector growth complicates digital policymaking. As political scientist Syaru Shirley Lin argues, contested politics make prioritizing interests in economic policy difficult.[84]

Surveillance capitalism in the tech sector undermines the rights that users enjoy in other sectors of the economy. Computer security expert Bruce Schneier argues that US tech firms lure their users into a sort of digital feudalism, with users pledging fealty to noninteroperable corporate tech ecosystems from firms such as Google, Apple, and Microsoft.[85] Amid such digital feudalism, firms keep proprietary commercial data from one another and the US government to preserve their competitive advantage. The power of these warring corporate fiefdoms limits the scale and scope of liberal democratic norms within the platforms.

US liberal democracy, though fragile, relies on free and fair elections and a rule of law that protects basic liberties.[86] Political liberalism depends on civil rights, equal opportunities, free markets, secular government, and political representation.[87] The twenty-first century brought with it an onslaught of challenges to US liberalism against the backdrop of the USA Patriot Act and a fractious Congress, including contested election outcomes, and the assault on executive branch norms.

Incidents such as Edward Snowden's disclosures of FISA court abuses, and the Cambridge Analytica scandal, have revealed how the tech sector amplifies illiberalism within the United States.[88] Legal scholar Samuli Seppänen argues that illiberalism undermines both legal processes and the protection of individual rights.[89] The lack of transparency around data gathering by US tech firms, paired with the monopolistic tendencies of digital feudalism, drove illiberal practices in the US tech sector. As discussed above, proprietary corporate algorithms and opaque terms of service mask how corporations gather user data. FISA courts conceal corporate practices through hidden procedures of data gathering and enforcement at the government level.

Groups of US citizens have organized to advocate for improved data security. However, like climate change, data security presents a chronic but often imperceptible risk—at least until a major disaster occurs.[90] It therefore tends to draw less attention than immediate, acute policy issues such as economic and public health crises.[91] Just as in environmental protection, where US companies exploit, rather than care for, national resources, firms care little to promote, and indeed often undermine, the rights of individuals over corporations.[92]

Network effects—the idea that the more populous a network, the greater its value—form the foundation of data trafficking. When platforms, devices, or civic infrastructure reach an economy of scale, users have difficulty extricating themselves because platforms reconstitute social ties and boundaries.[93] Online network affiliations have become integral, vital even, to our daily social and economic functioning. Many community groups and churches stream meetings and services.[94] A generation of students has now participated in online classes, which required them to log on regularly to the platform to access their education. Purchasing goods online, a practice that only grew during the COVID-19 pandemic, not only offers convenience, but improves the product recommendations that draw from large networks of users.[95] In each of these cases, expansive networks make users more dependent on platforms and increase the likelihood they will continue to share their data, even in the face of security concerns.

Data gathered from a wide range of industries offers the chance to aggregate large-scale consumer and industrial behavior insights. In addition to social media platforms, many other kinds of firms gather user data, using it to shape global decision-making on everything from how to spend advertising dollars to insurance underwriting decisions. Commercial data gathering enables data trafficking and the cross-border integration of commercial and government data.

How Trade with China Amplifies US Tech Illiberalism

China's model of cyber sovereignty, what Sarah McKune and Shazeda Ahmed call "the regime's absolute control over the digital experience of its population," represents a new dimension of centralized sovereignty.[96] The Chinese system of cyber sovereignty operates under what communications scholar Min Jiang refers to as "authoritarian informationalism," a blending of capitalism, authoritarianism, and Confucianism through which the Chinese government balances social control and efforts to preserve political legitimacy.[97] Chinese government regulations prioritize Party control over legal transparency.[98] Political scientist Rachel Esplin Odell argues that China's illiberalism is rooted in "a deep-seated insecurity about the Party's ability to effectively maintain and exercise power as it seeks to reform China's economy in order to ensure long-term growth."[99] Efforts to enhance corporate autonomy or individual rights would only exist insofar as they align with Party efforts to retain national control.

Illiberal Chinese government tech oversight can therefore extend to tech firms with global influence. The COVID-19 pandemic, for example, allowed the Chinese government to increase its domestic digital surveillance. However, after developing domestically, the new surveillance practices have diffused globally.[100]

Chinese tech regulations highlight two key features of US illiberalism. First, they call attention to the fragility of open markets. Tech firms from China and US-based tech firms have similar access to the United States market, despite different relationships with their national governments. Second, and more significantly for this book, they underscore the inadequacy of digital protections. As political scientist Qingming Huang puts it, trade with China "exposes the contradictions in the dominant Western model."[101] Users face not only exploitation by Silicon Valley but also the extension of illiberal Chinese government oversight of the tech sector.

US firms pioneered data trafficking, but the Chinese party-state refined the legal frameworks that allow the state control over transnational tech corporations and have turned them into a feature of twenty-first century sovereignty. In China, the government permits the growth only of firms that advance national strategic interests.[102] Trade barriers, including extensive joint venture requirements, labyrinthine regulations, and strategic bans on foreign investment in certain industries, protect Chinese firms from foreign competitors seeking to enter the market.[103] China's consumer data oversight now influences global norms, in much the same way that US-led intellectual property rights battles shifted the global tech landscape in the 1990s and 2000s.[104] In parallel, Chinese government oversight of Chinese firms grew via capital controls, anti-corruption campaigns targeting leading entrepreneurs, and national security reviews of corporate data-gathering practices.[105]

Of course, this system faces challenges. Fragmented authoritarianism, or the uneven application of laws by China's different national bureaucracies and stakeholders, presents one such challenge.[106] In the tech sector, the siloing of data weakens Chinese government surveillance efforts. Chinese agencies compete for access to valuable data.[107] China's social credit system, for example, synthesizes a wide range of surveillance tools with varying levels of reach and convergence. Two points are important to note here. First, as in the case of the social credit system, China's data regulations have coalesced over time, which suggests that siloed Chinese policies are likely to converge. Second, Chinese tech firms that push back face progressively more centralized oversight from regulators, as in the crackdowns on Chinese tech firms like fintech leader Ant Group and the rideshare app DiDi.

China's growing influence in the tech sphere propagates illiberal digital practices. The potential effects of digital technologies include surveillance and repression facilitated by Chinese tech platforms.[108] In describing the dynamic between Chinese firms and the Chinese government, political scientist Lizhi Liu raises concerns about "commitment problems" relating to big data in China. Liu asserts the following: "(1) multinational firms cannot credibly commit to not sharing personal data with their home government; and (2) the home government cannot commit to not abusing personal data for surveillance or for other political purposes that encroach on individual liberty."[109] When China's illiberalism spreads abroad via digital tools, it further weakens user protections on US tech platforms.

Without the indigenous tech power of the United States or China, democracies around the world have tried to constrain US and Chinese data gathering through new legal frameworks. These countries include US allies and China's Indo-Pacific neighbors Korea, Japan, India, and Australia, all of which have developed laws to address the expansive reach of Chinese and US government tech oversight.[110] European allies have also sought to bolster domestic consumer data protections relative to China and the United States.[111] However, most places remain mired in the system of surveillance capitalism pioneered by the United States and refined by the Chinese government.

Why Preventing Data Trafficking Is Difficult

As noted throughout this chapter, US regulations remain fragmented across different agencies and industrial sectors that prioritize corporate governance while Chinese government data-access policies are expanding. The value of users' data further increases tech firms' financial stake in preserving the status quo in consumer-data-gathering practices. With more robust US data protections in place, perhaps the Tiananmen activists' online commemorations would have been protected from the outset, rather than being subject to Chinese government review and corporate shutdown by Zoom.

How is user data protected? Where is it stored? These might seem like technical questions, unworthy of the average person's attention. Global data flows between the United States and China, however, make issues of consumer data protection not just a national matter but also an international one that shapes US-China relations.

When corporations in democratic nations conceal how they manage consumer data, they disempower not only users but also the nations that provide them with a stable business environment. Political scientist Allison Stanger sagely argues that opaque algorithms threaten self-government by turning individuals into abstractions.[112] Protecting the rights of individuals becomes an even greater challenge when citizen and consumer identities conflict in the production of the precious resource. Chinese firms face multiple Chinese government pressure points—plus the pressure to return value to shareholders. US-based corporations are beholden to shareholder value, not liberal democracy.

Data trafficking emerged from profiteering on the human experience in a world of geopolitical competition. US and Chinese tech firms play a central role because their products form the foundation of tech ecosystems for countries around the world. Despite political pressure on both sides to decouple, their economic entanglements mean the two countries' data security systems will continue to interact for the foreseeable future. Thanks to the conflict between the US market-driven data economy and the Chinese party-state's push for extraterritorial control, this tension will persist between the two countries and with their mutual trade partners.

Identifying how weak data protections corrode digital sovereignty is the first step. Stabilizing data flows in a technology-driven world shaped by the United States and China must be the next. Despite their efforts to protect national data security, the EU, Japan, Canada, and other countries still trade with both the United States and China.[113] Other countries around the world lack the technology, capital, and expertise to enact domestic data security regulations. The solution is straightforward but challenging—empowering consumers, holding firms accountable, and building international consensus, not only between the United States and China but around the world. As the following chapters show, in areas ranging from social media and games to agriculture and health, data trafficking is becoming a pervasive part of our human experience.

2

What Happens in Vegas Stays in China

Fragmented US Tech Oversight

Outside the 2019 Consumer Electronics Show (CES) in Las Vegas, Nevada, the leading global consumer appliance showcase, Apple shamed its competitors with a gigantic billboard proclaiming, "What Happens on Your iPhone, Stays on Your iPhone."[1] But Apple's user data protection differs in China. Since the 2017 enactment of China's Cybersecurity Law, which requires all data generated in China to be stored on Chinese-government-run servers, the firm has stored the data for its China-based accounts at sites controlled by Chinese government-affiliated firms. Apple's ad campaign demonstrates how market power and government pressure shift norms—in this case, norms regarding privacy and government access to data. In startling contrast to Apple's commitment to personal privacy on its US iPhones, the firm shares Chinese iCloud with the Chinese government through its normal daily business operations.

Firms like Apple have grown out of a US consumer data protection system where corporations enjoy significant self-governance. Apple's statement in Vegas was designed to make the company stand out from its competitors, tech platforms that shape the use of consumer data in the United States through opaque notice and consent practices and predatory data gathering. Apple has long been a leader in privacy and consumer data protection in the United States. But now, like all tech companies operating between the United States and China, the company must balance its interests and exposure and consider the risk that the Chinese government will limits its access to the world's largest potential market. China's legal demands for access to its attractive market are much more intensive than those made by the US government. As a result, corporations have a clear incentive to adhere to Chinese legal requirements while tailoring voluntary responses in the US market to the more flexible US policymaking environment. This approach enables the Chinese government to drive global standards-setting.

In this chapter, I argue that the United States fails to protect its consumer data from data trafficking because of its reliance on a patchwork of US data oversight practices in a world where the Chinese government financially pressures global firms to follow Chinese laws. Fragmented data oversight presents the first challenge. In large states such as California and New York, state-level data security laws compete with and extend national-level efforts. Lack of long-term data governance presents the second key limitation. Shifts in policy between administrations and congressional sessions create an inconsistent environment for policymaking, which requires a long-term, stable direction to be effective. Finally, any efforts to limit data gathering must balance US economic and security interests. Restricting the data-gathering sector prevents data trafficking, but it also constrains US tech sector growth, and the influence that comes with it.

Data trafficking emerged from limitations in the US model of tech industry development. Historical reliance on corporate leadership, paired with the prioritization of growth over security, encouraged the expansion of US innovation. Following US government investment in the technologies that formed the foundation of the internet, corporate leadership of US tech governance enabled the growth of Silicon Valley's firms. Those same tech firms served as an engine of US influence around the world. The model worked so long as the United States was the global commercial leader, and other countries maintained faith in US technology firms and government. However, the United States' retreat from global leadership and the exploitative practices of US tech firms have diminished the country's dominance.

The US data security landscape nevertheless laid the groundwork for data trafficking by creating a system that supports data extraction. As Chapter 1 discussed, this landscape has conditioned tech product consumers to ignore the question of where their data goes and mindlessly agree to obscure terms of service. This conditioned inattention has yielded the commodification of personal data for profit, what Shoshana Zuboff calls "surveillanc capitalism."[2] With government pressure on Chinese firms to gather and transport data to China, such data feeds information to the Chinese state sector.

Digital Sovereignty in the United States

When countries have divergent conceptions of sovereignty, the competitive relationships between corporations and governments shape the movement of data into and out of a country. In this section, I illustrate how governments enable data trafficking, paying particular attention to the US system, by examining the different ways that China, the United States, and other countries conceptualize the relationship between data and sovereignty.

Today, growing nationalism is driving countries to police their terrestrial borders more carefully. In the United States, we have seen crackdowns on immigration. In Europe, an increase in immigration from the Middle East has severely tested the freedom of movement across borders guaranteed by European Union member states. In China, assertive efforts to define China's possession of water and land through its contested nine-dash line (a maritime sovereignty claim) in the South China Sea have led to tense confrontations during freedom-of-navigation exercises by the United States and other militaries. The policing of terrestrial borders has intensified in parallel with the assertion of new technology-driven boundaries. Government and consumer data likewise present countries with a strategic national resource[3], as they inform new artificial intelligence technologies, offer intelligence assets, and provide a strategic economic advantage.[4]

To understand this situation, we can think about other technologies that have forced the creation of new national borders. The aviation industry drove countries to think differently about their airspace. Petroleum exploitation motivated countries to think in new ways about the rights to their minerals. Now, amid a great new game, countries are exploring how to control their digital resources.

Global differences in the relationship between the state and the market in this competitive context complicate data gathering and use. Who, in each country, controls the most data? Who influences how the control of this data evolves? In the United States, both the data itself and the infrastructure that stores it are part of private sector networks. Yet much of the data comes from citizens unaware of the long-term risks of data sharing who offer it to corporations via ambiguous consent procedures.

The seminal court ruling defining the relationship between digital boundaries and territorial boundaries was issued in the 1997 case *Digital Equipment Corp. v. Altavista Technology*. Judge Nancy Gertner, who presided over the United States District Court for the District of Massachusetts, asserted, "The Internet has no territorial boundaries. To paraphrase Gertrude Stein, as far as the Internet is concerned, not only is there perhaps 'no there there,' the 'there' is everywhere where there is Internet access."[5] *Digital Equipment Corp.*

v. Altavista Technology established a US legal standard for the internet's expansiveness beyond national borders.

Of course, the broader philosophical approach to data a-territoriality has exceptions. Communications scholar Milton Mueller has argued that the concept of data sovereignty in the United States dates to the USA Patriot Act, in which the United States post-9/11 framed digital assets as sovereign territory without explicitly using the term.[6] The CIA has long monitored certain foreign allies' and adversaries' encrypted messages through Crypto AG, a joint venture between US and West German intelligence, among other approaches.[7] While deeply concerning for privacy advocates, this effort still exists within the fragmented US regulatory system, as contrasted to China's more systematic efforts.

One way to understand the current data landscape is to view the world as being made up of evolving closed and open systems of internet sovereignty. In his book *The Open Society and Its Enemies* (1945), Karl Popper contends that democratic societies protect their existence through openness. This openness, however, leads to the system's eventual failure because it also makes the system vulnerable to authoritarian control.[8] Popper refers to this concept as the "paradox of tolerance," where the very characteristics that make a democratic system stable are also those that lead to its decline.[9] Although Popper wrote his book in the context of World War II, his argument applies to contemporary US-China tech relations.

The US system's openness offers both power and vulnerability vis-à-vis China. In the United States, the private sector holds between 80 and 90 percent of critical infrastructure, a figure that varies according to how each source defines "critical infrastructure."[10] This means that private corporations' needs and interests predominantly shape the US technical infrastructure. However, the US government does not benefit from corporate interests to the same degree it once did. In the twentieth century, the US government and corporations aligned in their goal of serving the US market while also defining sovereignty through new technologies. The Convention on International Civil Aviation established air rights, while the Outer Space Treaty influenced the current structure of sovereignty in space.[11] Institutions such as the Defense Advanced Research Projects Agency relied on the industry to continue to advance US power in the tech sector.

The privatization of data emerged from the technology industry's "techno-libertarianism," a principle that prioritizes individual and technical systems over bureaucracy and political oversight.[12] The US system prioritizes commercial interests in the development of new technologies while building these techno-libertarian ideals. It also faces renewed threats amid the devolution of tech sector oversight, from election interference and vaccine misinformation to data trafficking.

Between the competing impulses of control and openness, the definition of sovereignty over US digital territory remains unclear. Critical areas of discussion include what to govern, who will govern it, and whether military, civilian, or private sector leadership (or any combination thereof) will assume responsibility for oversight. Competing priorities yield a system in which powerful groups, particularly US corporations, have opposing loyalties. National interests play against corporate interests and firms' fiduciary responsibility to maximize shareholder value. China still offers one of the largest untapped markets for the US tech sector. However, access has become markedly more difficult, testing US tech firms' willingness to comply with local laws to maintain access.

The US system's openness has clear benefits: a welcoming environment for capital investment and innovation from around the world. The system's central problem is not openness—rather, it is openness paired with the three key limitations of the US system: regulatory fragmentation, inconsistent policymaking, and the difficulty balancing between corporate profitability and data security. The US tech sector does not need to become more like China's, with strict government data security audits and forced military-civil fusion. Instead, improved outcomes would come with consistent US-China cybersecurity regulations, long-term planning for long-term challenges, and the requirement that firms operating in the United States not participate in forced data sharing with other countries. Openness means preserving interoperability, not enabling exploitative behavior.

In the following sections, I discuss how the United States governs data while relying on an extractive system. I explain how this fragmented system reflects a failure to conceive of a national role in managing our data, even as that data forms the core of the future of emerging industries, personal identity, and national defense.

Regulatory Fragmentation

Data security oversight in the United States is piecemeal because it comprises overlapping, disjointed, and at times conflicting policies generated by the federal government, states, and the private sector. Regulatory fragmentation divides oversight across agencies, sectors, and jurisdictions in the United States. The diffusion of authority over the nation's data emerged from the checks-and-balances system, through which individual government branches oversee different domains. This prevents one branch from gaining too much power, thereby minimizing the likelihood of a national government data monopoly. Such a system also prevents the development of comprehensive data regulations that would prioritize citizens' rights to their data and safeguard user data from exploitative corporate practices.

Another challenge of this approach is the competition between different legal jurisdictions in the United States. Individual states with robust tech sectors, such as California and Virginia, have enacted their own data privacy regulations, which only increases fragmentation. Strategic sectors such as health care and finance have data security requirements, but such requirements largely apply only to legacy institutions such as hospitals and banks. Separate military and civilian oversight further balkanizes the structure of US data regulation.

Military Oversight

In the United States, the Department of Defense (DoD) wields the most power over national strategy development regarding data storage and security of all government agencies. The US Defense Advanced Research Projects Agency was a driving force behind the internet's development in the 1970s.[13] The Omnibus Trade and Competitiveness Act of 1988 drove the United States to focus on encouraging both private and public investment and on opening emerging markets in the tech sector.[14] This approach set the stage for massive cyber defense budgets that overtook spending on maintenance to protect user data. The DoD has a department-wide strategy that considers consumer vulnerabilities for its soldiers.[15] It shapes cyber norms because of its extensive role in global technology procurement. To the extent that the United States has a coordinated vision for data storage and security, that strategy emerges from the DoD via its annual National Defense Strategy. The 2018 National Defense Strategy, which guides the DoD 2019–2023 fiscal defense budgets, focuses on cyberspace as a battleground for both state and nonstate actors. It also prioritizes investments in military technologies that create resilient networks and information ecosystems, implying careful data control.

However, competing strategies for data security exist even within the US military. Each military branch has its own cybersecurity team, with proprietary resources and priorities, and competes against the others to acquire top cybersecurity talent. The US Cyber Command, one of the DoD's combatant commands, directs US cyberspace actions, including the reinforcement of DoD cyberspace capabilities. Cyber Command controls a leading global cyber military operation that can execute international exploits capable of bringing down power grids and nuclear programs. However, the inattention to mundane noncombatant data, such as medical and personnel records, weakens the nation's digital borders. This dearth of resources to protect individual user data outside of a combat environment characterizes the entire US system—from extractive corporate data practices to the absence of meaningful penalties for consumer data breaches.

The US government's focus on new cyber weapons capabilities creates a stunning asymmetry between different parts of the US government's tech infrastructure and its ability to maintain legacy technology, particularly in areas of the DoD outside the realm of weapons systems. At the 2019 CXO Tech Forum in Arlington, Virginia, Adrian Monza, then US Citizenship and Immigration Services cyber defense branch chief, celebrated his success in finally discarding some 1970s legacy machines at his agency. Notably, Monza moved to Amazon Web Services the next year. Air Force chief information security officer Wanda Jones-Heath explained the risks posed by "brownouts" of equipment that still had data but were not suitable for regular use by the Air Force. The DoD has massive resource capabilities, but these resources are distributed unevenly because of differing missions. While new weapons systems come online, unmaintained legacy tech systems across the US government create data trafficking risks. Compared to the resources the DoD has for oversight of technical systems, civilian technical infrastructure faces even greater resource constraints.

Civilian Oversight

In the National Security Council, the National Economic Council, and other parts of the executive branch, the United States has talented experts who serve in the difficult capacity of technology policymaking. However, these organizations must coordinate across a wide range of agencies whose mandates are distant from data security. The 2015 hacking of the Office of Personnel

Management allegedly by agents affiliated with the Chinese government—which exposed the security clearance data of 22.1 million US citizens (including 4 million current and former federal employees)[16]—represents a central challenge of regulatory fragmentation. The agency tasked with managing such sensitive data lacked sufficient data security systems to protect it. The following figure offers an overview of key US data oversight regulations from 1996 to 2020.

Multiple government branches have official oversight over civilian cybersecurity through the Department of Homeland Security (DHS), the Federal Trade Commission (FTC), the Federal Communications Commission (FCC), and other such agencies. Within the US House of Representatives, the Committee on Energy and Commerce and the Committee on Homeland Security share (or compete for) jurisdiction over cybersecurity matters. The Department of Commerce enforces trade regulations that limit which international firms can operate in the United States based upon their corporate practices. The Commerce Department's Entity List restricts trade in the United States by individuals and other entities. Under a June 2021 Biden executive order, the Department of Commerce also serves a coordinating function for data security oversight practices across US industries.[17] Although these organizations address overlapping concerns, as this section demonstrates, the United States government lacks an industrial and defense policy unified by issues of data gathering and integration that can span a long time period or all branches of government. Even with the Department of Commerce's coordinating role for international data security in the United States, enforcement via executive order faces limitations. A policy response from a single branch of government that can be immediately rescinded with a change in administration limits the breadth of enforcement and time horizon of international corporate data security oversight in the United States.

Interagency oversight offers one way to draw expertise from multiple sources but presents new challenges for coordination not just between individual agencies but also within the interagency committee itself. These challenges become particularly apparent in the US-China context. The US Department of the Treasury chairs the Committee on Foreign Investment in the United States (CFIUS). Representatives from sixteen US government departments and agencies also serve on the committee, which is one of the leading actors overseeing data security concerns related to Chinese firms.[18]

Major Developments in US Data Governance

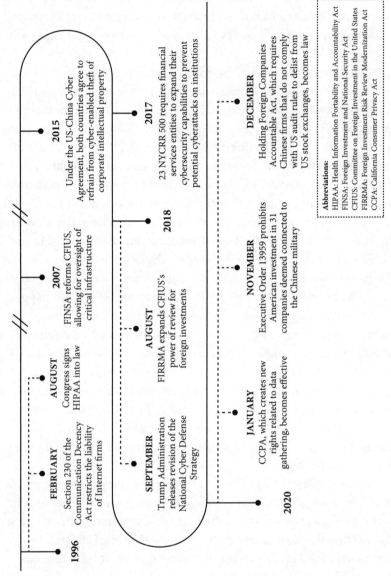

1996

FEBRUARY
Section 230 of the Communication Decency Act restricts the liability of Internet firms

AUGUST
Congress signs HIPAA into law

2007
FINSA reforms CFIUS, allowing for oversight of critical infrastructure

2015
Under the US-China Cyber Agreement, both countries agree to refrain from cyber-enabled theft of corporate intellectual property

2017
23 NYCRR 500 requires financial services entities to expand their cybersecurity capabilities to prevent potential cyberattacks on institutions

SEPTEMBER
Trump Administration releases revision of the National Cyber Defense Strategy

AUGUST
FIRRMA expands CFIUS's power of review for foreign investments

2018

JANUARY
CCPA, which creates new rights related to data gathering, becomes effective

NOVEMBER
Executive Order 13959 prohibits American investment in 31 companies deemed connected to the Chinese military

DECEMBER
Holding Foreign Companies Accountable Act, which requires Chinese firms that do not comply with US audit rules to delist from US stock exchanges, becomes law

2020

Abbreviations:
HIPAA: Health Information Portability and Accountability Act
FINSA: Foreign Investment and National Security Act
CFIUS: Committee on Foreign Investment in the United States
FIRRMA: Foreign Investment Risk Review Modernization Act
CCPA: California Consumer Privacy Act

Figure 2.1 Major Developments in US Data Governance from 1996–2020

CFIUS was established in 1975 by Executive Order 11858.[19] The Foreign Investment and National Security Act of 2007 (FINSA) then transformed CFIUS into the backbone of economic national security oversight of critical infrastructure in the United States. The Homeland Security Act of 2002 defined critical infrastructure as "publicly or privately controlled resources essential to the minimal operation of the economy and government" for seventeen sectors, including public health and health care, banking and finance, IT, and telecommunications.[20] However, during the Obama, Trump, and Biden administrations, CFIUS took on a role of increasing importance: the oversight of investment from China.

Several more recent developments, however, have hampered the CFIUS oversight process. In August 2018, then-president Donald Trump signed into law the John S. McCain National Defense Authorization Act for Fiscal Year 2019.[21] The act included the congressional consensus version of the 2018 Foreign Investment Risk Review Modernization Act (FIRRMA), a bipartisan effort to modernize CFIUS that expanded the committee's power of review for foreign investment in the United States. In 2018, FIRRMA was passed by Congress to expand US government oversight of foreign acquisitions to include "critical infrastructure" and "homeland security" as broad categories of review.[22] CFIUS reviews require significant resources. They also evaluate transactions on a case-by-case basis. Both of these features of the process preclude more systematic oversight of the US economy and investment trends. The CFIUS review process has blocked only a few Chinese technology acquisitions and does not apply to a wide range of transactions.

CFIUS actions take time. Data gathering in the US tech sector, by contrast, accelerates each day. For example, US government scrutiny of TikTok began in 2018, but as of June 2022, the firm was still gathering data in the United States.[23] Beijing-based ByteDance retained control as its parent company. Despite efforts to shore up oversight over technology acquisitions, limited oversight capacity strains the US government's capacity to manage data flows.

The scope of data gathering is growing apace. Consumer sectors including games, finance, health, consumer goods, and more are identifying new ways to acquire user data. Regulators must keep up not just with existing industries but also with new sectors that offer opportunities to monetize consumer behavior. In short, tracking the practices of US-based firms presents a challenge. But understanding how Chinese corporations share their data with Chinese government regulators increases the difficulty of such oversight.

The limitations of CFIUS oversight highlight another challenge in US private-public interactions in the tech sector: secrecy. CFIUS is a black box—it reports its cases' final outcomes but provides no public listing of companies currently under committee review. When I contacted CFIUS employees, from lawyers to interns, the message came through clearly that the committee's activities were to be kept private, even in an off-the-record setting.

The committee has limited resources to deal with powerful stakeholders. Private corporations in the United States do not have to report the sources of their investments. And popular products are difficult to purge from the market for economic reasons. TikTok's role in the US advertising and marketing world, paired with its loyal user base, has rendered it too big to ban, despite political efforts to the contrary. The range of financial instruments available to US investors makes tracking the provenance of money and influence difficult, not just for domestic investments but also for foreign ones.

CFIUS must also contend with potentially competing actions by the Office of the President. Executive orders, which are presidential directives designed to manage US federal government operations, present a targeted option for tech oversight—such as the Trump administration's August 2020 TikTok ban, which the Biden administration subsequently overturned. The TikTok case underscores the central thesis of this chapter, and a major focus of this book: that inconsistent, piecemeal efforts to manage Chinese consumer data gathering in the United States reveal the US tech regulatory system's frailty.

Congress also has tools for regulating US data. However, the challenge of building consensus in Congress yields data oversight that, like executive data oversight, focuses on a few specific cases, with the potential for competing action on highly publicized cases. On August 6, 2020, a bill that Senator Josh Hawley cosponsored with Senator Rick Scott passed in the Senate, prohibiting the use of TikTok on government devices. It passed on the same day the (now inactive) executive order banning TikTok was issued, a coincidence that exposes both the haphazardness and the duplication of effort in the US data regulatory context. Rather than enacting broad data security regulations, both the executive and legislative branches issued narrow laws targeting a single firm that had already gathered extensive data in the United States and shared that data with its parent company in China, where the government treated it as a national security asset.

Civilian tech oversight operates in an environment that limits its ability to succeed, given broad responsibilities, limited resources, rivalry from other government entities, and competing corporate interests. Competition within and between different branches of government, illustrated in this section, complicates oversight decisions, creating inefficiencies in the national data governance landscape even in widely publicized US-China trade cases.

Fragmentation by Sector

Regulatory fragmentation shaped the US data governance system. Since the 1990s, Congress has introduced bills that limit the oversight of data-generating platforms. Section 230, Part C, of the Communications Decency Act (CDA 230), which is often credited as the founding law of the modern US consumer internet, restricts the liability of firms that make information available on the internet and explicitly treats them not as publishers of information but rather as conduits of information. In *Reno v. ACLU*, the US Supreme Court affirmed that the antipornography restrictions outlined in CDA 230 constrained speech.[24] Although part of this ruling was a reaction to the restrictions' vagueness, it further limited firms' legal liability on the internet.

Other congressional data protections only target specific industries or demographics. Huge swaths of the economy have no consumer data security protection at all. The Health Insurance Portability and Accountability Act of 1996 (HIPAA), which protects oral, written, and electronic medical records, offers an example of sector-specific national legislation.[25] However, health tech products—such as fitness trackers—do not need to follow HIPAA. Further complicating matters, HIPAA health data protection stops where jurisdiction ends. The Department of Health and Human Services lacks meaningful enforcement capabilities outside the United States.

Children's data has some limited protections thanks to the Children's Online Privacy Protection Act (COPPA), which requires parental consent for self-disclosure of information by children under thirteen.[26] The law also has serious limitations—it protects children under thirteen only when they, rather than an adult, share their personal information.[27] It also protects them only on sites that are designed for children under thirteen, not sites for adults that they happen to visit.[28] Once a parent consents to the child's self-disclosure, sites can freely collect any shared information.[29] Moreover, the law does not appear to cover household-level (rather than individual-level) data, which might include that of children under thirteen—such as that collected by Google Home and Amazon Alexa devices.[30] The omnipresence of consumer technology erodes the privacy rights of children.

Enforcement of user privacy through the FTC, the major US consumer protection bureau, consists of manageable fines applied to only the most egregious cases. The FTC's record-breaking penalty for Facebook in 2019 was US$5 billion on revenue of US$70.7 billion; the firm deceived users about their ability to control personal information.[31] The firm overpaid the settlement by US$4.9 billion more than the maximum fine under the statute to allow Mark Zuckerberg and Sheryl Sandberg to avoid having to give sworn testimony.[32] A suit by the firm's investors seeking to claw back the excess payment quotes FTC commissioner Rohit Chopra on the egregious exchange of money for political coverage:[33] "The government essentially traded getting more money, so that an individual did not have to submit to sworn testimony and I just think that's fundamentally wrong."[34] Because of limited resources, regulators face even greater constraints in pursuing actions against more diffuse or small-scale offenders.[35] The gaps in sector-by-sector oversight demonstrate the US regulator system's fundamental weaknesses. However, sector-based data security does have national reach. Other US data security laws, as examined in the following section, apply only in certain jurisdictions.

Fragmentation by Locality

Conflicts between state and federal regulations also complicate US data security frameworks. Without national data security regulation, the responsibility for managing complicated, technical enforcement falls to the states—even though the federal government possesses a stronger technical capacity to both investigate and enforce these issues.

States can act independently, which increases fragmentation. Historically, state laws have provided users only limited protection from data breaches. Forty-eight states and most territories require that consumers be notified if hackers breach user data, but until recently courts have interpreted this requirement as applying only to unencrypted data.[36] The following figure shows the key state-level regulations in relation to national oversight practices.

Large, wealthy states such as New York and California have attempted to build out privacy regulations. New York has comparatively robust data protections in place for financial data. The 2017 New York Department

Data Regulations on a National and State Level

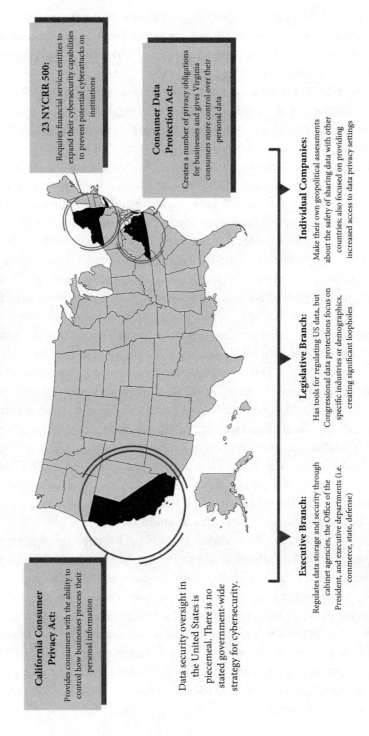

23 NYCRR 500:

Requires financial services entities to expand their cybersecurity capabilities to prevent potential cyberattacks on institutions

Consumer Data Protection Act:

Creates a number of privacy obligations for businesses and gives Virginia consumers more control over their personal data

California Consumer Privacy Act:

Provides consumers with the ability to control how businesses process their personal information

Data security oversight in the United States is piecemeal. There is no stated government-wide strategy for cybersecurity.

Executive Branch:

Regulates data storage and security through cabinet agencies, the Office of the President, and executive departments (i.e. commerce, state, defense)

Legislative Branch:

Has tools for regulating US data, but Congressional data protections focus on specific industries or demographics, creating significant loopholes

Individual Companies:

Make their own geopolitical assessments about the safety of sharing data with other countries; also focused on providing increased access to data privacy settings

Figure 2.2 Examples of US Data Regulations on the National and State Level

of Financial Services Cybersecurity Regulation requires financial services entities to expand their cybersecurity capabilities to prevent potential cyberattacks on institutions operating in New York State.[37] The regulation does not give individuals more access to their data or the ability to control it.[38] However, it does establish more transparent standards for how that data should be stored and secured. Ultimately, this regulation provides de facto support for data localization by raising the bar for risk management of corporate and consumer financial data.

The California Consumer Privacy Act (CCPA) took effect in January 2020, creating new rights for California residents related to data gathered about their online behavior.[39] These rights include the ability to request the deletion of data, information about the sharing of data, and access to data. The act also guides businesses on how to comply with the law. It has, however, proven particularly challenging to enforce. State regulation offers an opportunity to experiment with data security regulation, but its effects remain limited because of budgetary challenges and a lack of federal support.

State-level comprehensive data regulation has become a hot issue, with an increasing number of states considering it. Virginia passed state data privacy legislation in 2021.[40] Texas is considering passing such a law, amid significant partisan debate.[41] However, state data privacy legislation is still in its infancy; as of 2020, forty-seven states still had little or no privacy regulation.[42] Notably, larger states with active tech sectors are the ones considering such legislation, given its vast cost and human capital needs. The difference in state-level resources reflects the disparity in access to technical talent for monitoring and oversight within the United States. A state-by-state approach magnifies the existing digital divide between states with more urban populations and those with more rural populations.

The fragmentation of US digital oversight, as argued throughout this chapter, presents a significant challenge in responding to the broad instances of data gathering in the United States. Competing agendas within the public sector prioritize certain types of data over others. Military-industrial partnerships create vulnerabilities as US defense contractors navigate their relationship with the federal government, in parallel with their commercial relationships around the world. Consumer data oversight faces the limitations of sector- and jurisdiction-based regulation that fails to account for the holistic growth of consumer-data-driven products across a wide range of industries and localities.

Short-Term Policymaking

The second major limitation of the US data regulatory system is short-term policymaking. The US military IT infrastructure links the openness of the system to its long-term vision. In September 2018, the Trump administration released its National Cyber Strategy, the first revision of the policy since 2003.[43] The strategy presents the goal of "expand[ing] American influence abroad to extend the key tenets of an open, interoperable, reliable, and secure internet."[44] However, the five-year time frame of the US National Defense Strategy limits its planning process.

This time horizon fails to consider how technology develops over ten, twenty, or even thirty years. A time frame of five years fails to envision other mid- and long-range opportunities that could emerge from current significant data gathering, especially those that fall outside the domain of "battle" in cyberspace. If organizations steward data well, that data can create a foundation for technologies and intelligence that will be useful within not just the next five years but also the next twenty. In much the same way that a US exchange program to Iowa in 1985 offered Terry Branstad, a future US ambassador to China, a chance to get to know a young visitor named Xi Jinping, social data gathered today promises insight into future world leaders.[45] Consumer data provide a rich resource for understanding and manipulating populations not just over the near term but for decades to come. However, the challenge of short-term policymaking does not just complicate national defense strategy. It also emerges in three other key areas: abandoned bilateral and multilateral agreements, lack of leadership continuity, and conflicting policy-planning goals.

Abandoned Agreements

Short-term solutions to long-term challenges are a hallmark of US technology policymaking. Perhaps the most vivid example of short-term shifts on long-term policy issues can be found in the abandoned agreements that frequently accompany changes in US government leadership. One key Obama-era agreement later abandoned by the Trump Administration was the landmark 2015 US-China Cyber Agreement, in which the US and Chinese governments agreed that neither would hack foreign corporate interests.[46] The governments' decision to "refrain from conducting or knowingly supporting cyber-enabled theft of [corporate] intellectual property [IP]" was designed to mitigate Chinese government interference in US corporations and vice versa.[47] One element required that foreign firms participate in joint ventures to access the Chinese market. Chinese companies would manage international data, thereby giving Chinese regulators the power to oversee it. The agreement left significant issues unaddressed, however. For example, its definitions of IP typically cover the structural design of databases but not necessarily the privacy of the user-generated data within those databases, rendering the agreement minimally effective, even with both parties' compliance.

Most significantly, the US-China Cyber Agreement applied only to foreign corporations in each country, so partially owned companies or joint ventures complicate the question of who owns a firm's intellectual property. As a result, proving that a theft has occurred can be difficult. Increased Chinese acquisitions and partial acquisitions of US firms render much of the agreement moot by shifting the ownership structure of firms. These kinds of mergers and joint ownership structures transfer IP to foreign firms, and thus out of US jurisdiction, except for what is covered by the bilateral agreement.

The agreement ultimately fell apart in the lead-up to and aftermath of the 2016 US presidential election. Its brief implementation and eventual failure underscores the challenge that US policymakers face in aligning short-term US election cycles with long-term Chinese policies.

Inconsistency in Leadership

The policies of the US Department of Homeland Security illuminate US data policymaking's fundamental weakness: erratic shifts that lead to loss of staff in competitive areas such as government IT. The DHS has a mandate to manage domestic public security, which includes the oversight of national digital interests. Yet this mandate contends with the same obstacles the US government encounters in planning for a world of digital borders. Resource constraints hamper DHS government and civilian data infrastructure oversight both domestically and overseas. Furthermore, inconsistent policymaking makes the agency even less attractive to in-demand talent from the tech sector.

The Trump administration, for instance, grabbed headlines for firing the DHS Cybersecurity and Infrastructure Security Agency (CISA) head Chris

Krebs. Counter to Trump's claims of a "rigged election," Krebs asserted that the 2020 presidential election was "the most secure election in American history."[48] What most reports failed to note was that Krebs's role had expanded far beyond simply overseeing election security. As head of CISA, Krebs had the daunting task of managing the threats to US critical digital infrastructure across both the public and private sectors. He had already proven himself through a successful tenure, which included securing the US elections after allegations of Russian interference in the 2016 election. At an October 2019 Washington, DC, event titled "CyberScoop CyberTalks," speakers lauded Krebs as the unique type of public servant who had taken a pay cut to serve, despite having highly valued private sector expertise. Krebs's firing demonstrates the competing interests within US tech policy that undermine comprehensive national data protection efforts. Even when the US government secures industry talent for top tech jobs, retaining talent proves difficult. The changing political winds in Washington further imperil the continuity of US tech oversight.

Conflicting Policy Planning

Inconsistent policy planning—when long-term tech governance plans from one agency get jettisoned in the transition between administrations, for example—poses a third challenge. The process of introducing and retracting policies is resource-intensive. It also precludes the opportunity to implement plans over a five-, ten-, or twenty-year time period, as needed for global competition and alliance building. Despite its international scope, the State Department has not historically been heavily involved in global data governance issues. Competition from the private sector and within the government, such as from the DoD and the intelligence community, further limits the State Department's ability to lead on tech policy.[49] Changing stances on data security practices between administrations present a particular challenge because the State Department must navigate relationships with other countries that have stabler, longer-term strategies.

In August 2020, the State Department introduced its Clean Network Initiative, an effort to build relationships between like-minded countries to create what the United States deemed a "secure and trusted" network worldwide.[50] The lack of clarity about what constituted a "secure and trusted network," however, complicated which standards the United States would adopt.

In another example of the US system's internal conflicts, the Clean Network Initiative website was archived by the State Department when President Joe Biden took office in January 2021.

Even when such guidelines remain in place for years, shared policy-making, such as that proposed by the Clean Network Initiative, lacks the enforcement mechanisms available through the legal frameworks of other efforts to manage data security. The Trans-Pacific Partnership (TPP), a landmark trade agreement for the Indo-Pacific region, excluding China, is one such agreement; the United States negotiated it during the Obama administration but withdrew from it during the Trump administration.[51] Other countries involved in the agreement moved forward without the United States, signing the Comprehensive and Progressive Agreement for Trans-Pacific Partnership.

Competing Financial and Security Priorities

Fragmented data security oversight in the United States presents a problem for US national security, whereas corporations have a clear incentive to advocate for limited oversight. Because massive data collection drives the creation of new products and services that firms can capitalize on, firms benefit from the status quo.

At a November 2019 lunch event held by a US tech investment think tank in New York City, I witnessed members of the US military and investors at leading US funds nearly come to blows when the topic of Chinese tech investment arose. The military personnel accused the investors of putting their personal financial interests ahead of the country's interests and of profiteering from companies that undermine US national security. In response, the investors accused the military officials of failing to understand how the country stays afloat—namely, through Wall Street's ability to attract and grow capital. The disagreement was never resolved; as the lunch continued, the participants sat in stony silence, reflecting the intractable conflict between US investment and national security sectors as they relate to the Chinese tech industry. By contrast, Mark Zuckerberg invited President Xi to name his firstborn child—an honor Xi promptly rejected—as a gambit to induce the Chinese leader to take a favorable view of his company's activities in China.[52]

The US corporate sector shapes the national data sovereignty landscape through its influence on multistakeholder organizations, capital markets, corporate governance, joint ventures, and mergers and acquisitions (M&A, the process of combining and purchasing firms). US capital markets have a financial incentive to welcome the world's largest and most profitable firms to raise capital, regardless of those firms' political interests. And US corporations have a financial incentive to operate in as many markets as possible to increase shareholder value. Because of the US political structure, US firms do not have to consider risks to US national security unless the fragmented regulatory system explicitly requires it. This creates one of the fundamental conflicts enabling the data trafficking examined across this book—the tension between US national security efforts to control Chinese tech investment and US corporate efforts to maximize growth.

Multistakeholder Organizations

A key feature of the US system is the phenomenon known as *multistakeholderism*, which communication scholars Mark Raymond and Laura DeNardis define as "two or more classes of actors engaged in a common governance enterprise concerning issues they regard as public in nature."[53] Multistakeholderism includes the joint participation of states, corporations, and civil society organizations in establishing tech standards.[54] Multistakeholderism allows US corporations to shape standards not only in international organizations but also in domestic organizations with broad international influence. Relying on multistakeholder organizations has long benefited the United States. Historically, multiple US firms and government organizations represented US interests in standards-setting.[55] However, this system then devolved, as reflected in the refrain I kept hearing from US agencies, into the US government relying on US firms to represent US interests.[56]

Multistakeholderism contrasts with what political scientist John Ruggie influentially characterized as *multilateralism*.[57] Through multilateralism, national governments (rather than individuals or nonstate actors) coordinate policy action on areas of common concern. China favors multilateralism because its government funds participants in international standards-setting, rather than relying on corporate influence in multistakeholder organizations, as has long been the US approach.

The devolution of US data oversight to global corporations that need Chinese market access demonstrates the fundamental weakness of relying on US firms to shape long-term data governance in the national interest. The National Institute of Standards and Technology (NIST), the US Department of Commerce's standards-setting body, comprises several low-lying office parks in the DC area. The October 22, 2019, "Cybersecurity Innovation at NIST . . . and Beyond" meeting at the National Cybersecurity Center of Excellence stands out as emblematic of the tension between the US government and industry standards-setting.

In the meeting, NIST officials deferred to experts from Microsoft. Representatives from US companies were in attendance to help NIST design its future tech standards, which have assumed global influence thanks to the US tech economy's outsized importance. NIST employees soaked up advice from Microsoft's experts. However, Microsoft must balance its interests in the United States with its financial survival around the world, including in China. The United States faces a crisis in domestic tech standards: US firms have financial incentives to develop tech standards that support their global interests over those of US national security.

One way of grasping multistakeholderism's role is to examine where it fails to work. In June 2017, I had a discussion with US-China experts at the Department of Commerce headquarters about the challenges the United States faces in relation to tech trade with China. When I brought up the fact that the number of Chinese government and corporate representatives in key global tech policymaking entities had grown over the years, I received what would become a common refrain in both on-the-record and off-the-record conversations throughout my research for this book: US corporations, rather than the US government, drive US tech policy because the US model relies on private sector leadership. Policymakers argue that US companies have the financial resources to attend these meetings and shape outcomes that serve their interests.

Facial recognition standards-setting provides an excellent example of the weakness of this approach. For example, in the International Telecommunication Union (ITU), a branch of the UN, China has taken the lead in developing new standards for facial recognition technology. Industry leaders who, according to the framework used by the Department of Commerce and other agencies, should take the lead in setting facial recognition standards counter that doing so would require them to share their new technology publicly. Such revelations would put them at a disadvantage vis-à-vis China. US firms risk revealing the tech behind new products and losing market share; Chinese tech firms, by contrast, have built-in government support and a closed domestic market.

Capital Markets

The US market's regulatory patchwork creates comparative flexibility for firms seeking to raise capital or expand investments in the market. Capital markets offer Chinese firms the chance to raise funds from US investors. US capital markets thus magnify the influence of Chinese technology platforms by underwriting Chinese firms interested in raising capital, despite a lack of reciprocity for foreign direct investment. The initial public offering (IPO) process, in which corporations raise capital by selling shares to institutional and retail investors, allows firms to expand their operations. Investment banks, which underwrite this process, assess each company's appeal as an investment prospect. Suppose that capital markets and the investment banks underwriting IPOs do not perceive data trafficking as an investment risk; firms can continue to raise money despite data-trafficking activity (or even because of it). Without consequences in the capital markets for data gathering, they have little reason to change their practices.

Alibaba, a Chinese tech "national champion" (a firm that the Chinese government both supports and draws from to build its tech sector), raised US$25 billion on the New York Stock Exchange (NYSE) in the largest-ever IPO in the United States.[58] At the same time, funding from US capital markets extends the reach of Chinese firms beholden to Chinese market access for their continued existence. Such firms face extensive, formalized data oversight by the Chinese government. US capital markets empower the Chinese state by bankrolling the expansion of these firms, even as they also serve as an important engine of American economic growth.

Publicly traded Chinese firms listed on US exchanges have long presented a challenge to US auditors because of a lack of transparency in accounting data. On December 18, 2020, Congress passed the Holding Foreign Companies Accountable Act, requiring Chinese firms that do not fully comply with US audit rules to delist from US stock exchanges.[59] Yet this seemingly severe penalty does not impede noncompliant firms from raising capital in the United States through venture capital or M&A, or otherwise operating in the market.[60] Congressional leaders introduced the bill only because Chinese companies have been disregarding other US financial laws for decades.[61] Further complicating the issue, the Chinese government controls the export of algorithms, has national security oversight over corporate data, and maintains special government shares of key firms.

Capital markets are also designed to monitor corporate behavior after an IPO. Public corporations in the United States must release annual and quarterly reports to comply with Securities and Exchange Commission (SEC) regulations. Earnings reports, particularly those that reference earlier earnings predictions, often influence a company's stock price. Some companies also hold earnings calls, during which corporate leaders present forecasts for the firm and typically conduct a question-and-answer session. At present, corporations are not required to disclose their data storage strategies, nor is such disclosure a significant component of investor decision-making. By neglecting to account for the data security risk inherent in rampant data trafficking, capital market regulators ultimately permit firms to traffic data.

Major Chinese internet firms such as Alibaba, Tencent, and Baidu have historically listed their stocks on US stock exchanges rather than Chinese ones.[62] This strategy has enabled Chinese companies to become significant global competitors that benefit from a broader shareholder base, foreign expertise, and access to additional capital.[63] Even if Chinese firms delist from US capital markets, they have already received infusions of both cash and legitimacy to advance their global growth.

The asymmetry created by the lack of reciprocity for foreign direct investment and technology in China particularly impacts platforms that handle consumer data. Private users have fewer resources than corporations and governments to redress international data breaches abroad. Chinese platforms that gather consumer data also extend Chinese soft power through the growth of attractive international products like TikTok. Firms also increase their influence through IPOs in the United States, which embed these firms in both financial and consumer markets.[64]

Shareholders also pressure US firms to introduce or expand their Chinese offerings. The interplay of financing, regulatory oversight, and technological development in the funding of Chinese technology firms offers valuable insight into the leverage the Chinese government and US capital markets have in the growth of the Chinese technology industry. Chinese firms currently draw capital from and produce profits for US-based financial institutions. This arrangement benefits the US financial industry but provides Chinese firms with preferential access to US consumers; and, as underscored above, the Chinese government does not reciprocate for US firms.

Corporate Governance

The asymmetry in the US and Chinese financial markets echoes a similar asymmetry in the corporate governance practices of US and Chinese firms. As China outlines its long-term technology development goals, US CEOs have repeatedly demonstrated that they are willing to provide Chinese government officials with access to their platforms in exchange for market access. For example, Meta's Mark Zuckerberg and Apple's Tim Cook took meetings with China's former internet czar Lu Wei.[65] Microsoft worked with a Chinese military university on artificial intelligence development.[66] The OpenPOWER Foundation, a nonprofit organization with leadership from IBM and Google executives, established a collaboration between IBM, Chinese firm Semptian, and US chip manufacturer Xilinx, to advance Semptian's data-intensive internet surveillance.[67] US CEOs have demonstrated little willingness to push back against the Chinese government's corporate policy demands, especially if such pushback would affect their potential to operate and thrive in the market.[68]

Companies have come together voluntarily on key issues to address shared concerns, as in the case of the Christchurch Call. An outgrowth of the 2019 mass shooting that targeted the Muslim community of Christchurch, New Zealand, the initiative produced a voluntary series of commitments by governments, civil society, and tech corporations to fight misinformation and online terrorism. The value of such efforts is that it allows corporations to engage at a level that is economically viable while also protective of users in the tech sector. Such solutions have significant value, but they are not sufficient in a global framework where the Chinese government has both a large, desirable market and the ability to pressure Chinese and foreign firms to hand over their data.

In response to concerns about user data exploitation, firms like Zoom and TikTok have developed corporate transparency reports that disclose how they use data they gather from consumers. However, as long as these reports are the result of voluntary disclosure practices, there is a key difference between what the firms choose to disclose in the United States and what they must disclose in China. To put it more plainly, the lack of disclosure requirements in the United States gives the firms flexibility in what they reveal about their engagement with China.

Public relations messaging about operations for the same country often reveals more than it conceals about how user data is used or stored. For example, Elon Musk, cofounder and CEO of Tesla, which has data storage facilities for its vehicles in China, noted in a speech to the China Development Forum that "there is a very strong incentive to be confidential with information."[69] However, Tesla's head of communication and government affairs, Grace Tao, pointed out that the firm would follow all Chinese laws and that its data would be stored in China.[70] Unlike Musk's vaguer statement about the importance of confidentiality, following all relevant Chinese laws would require Tesla to both store its data on Chinese-run servers and be subject to national security data audits. The challenge with a system of voluntary reporting is that, as in the case of Tesla, the firm must balance its interest in appeasing investors who may be concerned about data privacy issues with legal requirements for market access set by the Chinese government.

Individual companies make their own geopolitical assessments about the safety of sharing data with other countries. This practice ultimately devolves the work of international affairs agencies to tech companies. This presents conflicts of interest, as those same firms benefit financially by ignoring data security abuses in certain countries when operating there enhances shareholder value.

A fundamental feature of the system is that users are responsible for managing their own security on billion-dollar platforms. Instead, platforms could enhance user security by limiting access to nonencrypted data. Federated models of data storage do not transfer information to a central repository, yet they are technically challenging and expensive to implement. Thus, the current system privileges corporate profitability over user safety.

Companies treat information sharing in joint ventures and across borders as an internal corporate matter whenever possible, which results in IP or data privacy violations. US companies in the tech sector form joint ventures with Chinese firms as a Chinese government requirement for market entry to increase the Chinese government's access to data.[71] As Chapter 1 notes, China's 2017 Cybersecurity Law requires that all critical information (broadly defined) be stored on Chinese-owned servers.[72] Meanwhile, US government oversight fails to set standards for how US firms share data with China. By structuring its laws to increase the amount and type of data stored in Chinese-owned data centers, China has augmented the data under its government jurisdiction and the range of firms affected by the laws. As a result, the cybersecurity risk incurred by US technology companies with a significant presence in China has grown.

Mergers and acquisitions are another weak point in the US system because they can give Chinese firms access to data from US-based firms. Cybersecurity assessments of M&A activities are still in their infancy. Until recently, Chinese firms that acquired only a partial stake in a US company were not subject to CFIUS review, meaning that their efforts to access or move corporate data did not come under scrutiny. Now that partial acquisitions are subject to CFIUS oversight, those prior acquisitions must be unwound at a high cost to the market, a cost that the government is often unwilling to impose on investors. A cautionary M&A tale is that of the Chinese firm Beijing Kunlun Tech Co., Ltd. (now Kunlun Tech Co. Ltd.), which purchased the LGBTQ+ dating app Grindr in 2018 after a major investment in 2016 and was forced to divest it in 2020 because of a CFIUS investigation.[73] Even after the divestment, questions about data security did not fully resolve themselves.

US capital markets have clear motives to forge ahead with Chinese firms to raise capital. Joint ventures, mergers, and acquisitions complicate data security regulations, with US firms not only sharing their data with Chinese partners but also merging into a combined corporate entity. Chinese firms face the same challenges, in addition to an activist Chinese government that conducts regular data audits and requires local storage of data and algorithms.

The competing economic and security priorities in multistakeholder organizations, capital markets, and corporate governance, as this books seeks to illuminate, are difficult to balance. US investment banks and venture capital funds seeking to expand their exposure to Chinese firms advocate for Chinese firms, despite concerns about Chinese government overreach on the part of both investors and regulators. US tech firms benefit from autonomy in data governance because it enables them to develop new data-driven products. Those same regulations enable Chinese firms to gather data in the United States that is accessible to the Chinese government, a phenomenon I will discuss at greater length in Chapter 3. A wide range of joint venture, merger, and acquisition tools allow all kinds of US firms to benefit from local partnerships in China. Although US corporations are the beneficiaries in the short and medium terms, Chinese firms and the Chinese government gain a long-term strategic advantage.

Conclusion

Technology regulation in the United States has emerged through a patch-work of frameworks intended to guide corporations and the government in storing consumer data. Although data security has long been a simmering issue in the United States, it has taken on increased urgency as the Chinese and US digital economies become more entwined. Now, rather than being concerned solely about the conflicts of interest entrenched in relationships between US policymakers and US companies, tech consumers in the United States must consider the same issues among a wide range of interdependent constituencies, including private US and Chinese companies, Chinese state-owned enterprises (SOEs), capital markets, policymakers, regulators, and consumers and investors in both countries. As this chapter has illustrated, the layers of relationships involved in data gathering far exceed the current system's capability to manage complexity and are rife with potential for abuse.

The US strategy of deferring to Silicon Valley in technology policymaking and supporting disruption while limiting regulation spurs domestic innovation in the United States.[74] However, it also leaves both US companies and global consumers vulnerable to the Chinese government's efforts to control global data through export controls on algorithms generated by consumer data, national security oversight of Chinese corporate data, and the treatment of Chinese firms' data as a strategic national asset.[75] In other words, China influences the worldwide circulation and security of commercial data by taking advantage of the gaps in US regulation. The financing of Chinese technology firms via US-based capital markets magnifies the risks to US user data produced by minimal regulatory oversight, as does Chinese technology policy, including acquisitions and expansion. PRC-based technology companies encounter a comparatively open digital environment in the United States and many other markets around the world. This chapter has described how Chinese firms can raise capital by selling shares and listing IPOs on US capital markets, but US firms cannot do the same in China.[76] Chinese social media, video, and payment platforms are accessible in the United States, whereas US firms face operational bans in China. Even though such policies result from national-level decisions in both countries, they have global consequences for the international tech industry and local impacts on individual consumers.

The oversight of Chinese tech investment in the United States raises several problems. It fails to address the systemic issues related to US capital markets' funding of a wide range of Chinese firms. Rapid regulation with no industry feedback injects uncertainty into the US tech sector, which harms both Chinese and US companies. Most importantly, oversight that singles out individual companies neglects systemic issues that allow corporations to exploit loopholes in the US tech investment landscape. Executive actions give the illusion that someone is remedying this large problem. Nevertheless, as the TikTok ban illustrates, such partial solutions to rampant data trafficking tend to distract from less glamorous, more systematic government efforts.

This industrial structure minimizes legal liability for tech firms.[77] The US approach, with its tendency to avoid holding US platforms legally liable for data breaches, differs dramatically from the Chinese approach, which subjects platforms to government oversight and partial ownership in the private sector.[78] As more and more US corporations rely on consumer data, the need to enact stronger oversight over consumer data gathering increases.

Continued reliance on regulations that prioritize corporate interests means that the United States is failing to meet the challenges of building, maintaining, and protecting its digital sovereignty. At the same time, as underscored throughout this book, because of this openness and lack of sufficient guardrails, US firms with operations in China and Chinese firms operating in the United States are expanding the Chinese government's data oversight not just in the United States, but globally. Firms dependent on the Chinese market will continue to extract commercial data and share it with the Chinese government if US corporate and government leaders continue to allow the tech industry's financial interests to direct policy.

The fragmentation of digital regulations in the United States gives corporations flexibility in how and with whom they share data. While this relative openness has made the US tech innovation ecosystem possible, it also presents a significant challenge to anyone seeking to control the movement of data into or out of the country in a comprehensive way. Regulators encounter entrenched interests with clear financial motives to maintain the status quo for US corporations' profitability. Chinese firms and the Chinese government have increased incentives to extract data from the US system as that data becomes an ever more valuable commodity. These parallel trends present a conundrum that requires the United States to shift the relationship between tech investment and national security in response to China's rise.

By contrast, the Cyberspace Administration of China (CAC) has released a series of personal data protections. The protections further limit the type of data corporations can gather and share in the United States. They expand the Chinese government's efforts to control how Chinese firms raise capital, partner with other firms, and, in many cases, operate in the United States.

Appreciating how the Chinese government approaches data reveals why consumer data protection supports long-term US competitiveness. The Chinese government considers data nationalization to be part of its vision to strengthen China's economy, military power, and national security. In Chapter 3, I explain how the Chinese government structures its relationship between consumer data and national interests.

3

Becoming a Cyber Sovereign

China's Politics of Data Governance

On July 4, 2021, the Cyberspace Administration of China pulled the DiDi app from China's app store. DiDi, China's leading rideshare platform, had listed on the New York Stock Exchange just days before, on June 30. The CAC's move caused DiDi's share price to tank. Days later, regulators in China revealed that they had sought to prevent DiDi's IPO because of concerns that the firm's NYSE listing failed to fully comply with Chinese data security laws and regulations.[1] Investors lost US$15 billion in market value when the share price dropped from its initial stock offering of US$14 to US$12.49 per share, and it saw a dramatic decline over the following months.[2] On American Independence Day, the CAC demonstrated leverage over a powerful US sector by enforcing data security regulations abroad.

Shortly after the DiDi IPO, reports began to emerge that the firm might enter into a new data-sharing agreement with Chinese regulators. The state-owned Beijing Tourism Group, an influential state-owned enterprise, and other SOEs would acquire a stake in the firm, a board seat, and "golden shares," giving the investment consortium power over the firm's charter.[3] In June 2022, DiDi delisted from the NYSE under Chinese government pressure. The DiDi case occurred in the context of a larger People's Republic of China (PRC) data oversight system that gives the government a clear advantage in asserting data security standards over global firms.[4] US companies are not immune. Many disclose data in China that they would be unwilling to share with the US government. For example, as the previous chapter notes, to operate in China, Tesla must store its data on government-run servers.[5] How companies choose to share data with local governments ultimately shifts the global balance of power.[6]

In this chapter, I provide a framework for thinking about how Chinese government policies leverage corporate economies of scale to maximize global data gathering and influence global data governance. China's conception of data is transforming global power structures: it empowers Chinese

technology firms and gives the Chinese government access to other countries' information. Such practices also create incentives for companies
around the world to follow Chinese standards in the development of new
technologies. Market incentives, combined with Chinese government activism in global standards-setting bodies, create a feedback loop that further
shifts power dynamics in the global tech sector.

Literature on "fragmented authoritarianism" in China, a bureaucratic
system characterized by an unequal application of policies by different political entities, demands skepticism about the evenness of China's long-term
application of tech policies.[7] Indeed, the siloing of information in different
bureaucracies has presented practical challenges to the implementation of
surveillance technologies on a large scale.[8] The Chinese government's overarching framework for cyber sovereignty, however, offers an unprecedented
vision of the role of data and the state. The size, scale, and intention behind
China's digital governance framework mean that even iterative or uneven
applications of China's digital power structures have already begun to transform the global order.

Cyber sovereignty is extended through government oversight of
corporations, government control of data, long-range policy planning,
and global institutional leadership. Tech firms that operate in the Chinese
market thus must take their cues from government-determined notions of
what constitutes the state's property. In addition to asserting China's national
boundaries, each of these practices enhances the Chinese government's
ability to influence, and even control, digital domains beyond the country's
current national borders—to become a global cyber sovereign.

China's Approach to Cyber Sovereignty

China's national data governance system expands the range of China's sovereign territory to make the country what the Theoretical Studies Center Group
of the CAC terms a "cyber superpower."[9] Political scientist Yuen Yuen Ang
characterizes the Chinese state as a polity with extensive control over social
and political life, including the media, internet, and education.[10] In parallel,
China's economy involves both market-based practices and strong state control in key industrial sectors.[11] The Chinese government has developed the
idea of cyber sovereignty to establish that a country's national borders extend
to the data gathered within its terrestrial borders, by its military, and—in an

increasing number of circumstances—by corporations headquartered on its land.

China was among the earliest countries to assert a tightly closed system of internet sovereignty in its military and commercial spaces. It articulated its policy of cyber sovereignty in its landmark 2010 White Paper on the Internet in China, which defined the scope of its internet. Only now are the full implications of that white paper becoming apparent. The paper features questions of sovereignty:

> The internet sovereignty of China should be respected and protected. . . . China maintains that all countries have equal rights in participating in the administration of the international resources of the internet and a multilateral and transparent allocation system should be established based on the current management mode, so as to allocate those international resources of the internet, and a multilateral and transparent allocation system should be established on the basis of the current management mode, so as to allocate those resources in a rational way and to promote the balanced development of the global internet industry.[12]

This definition clarifies several points about China's position on how the state and the market should guide the digital economy, naming internet sovereignty as a central feature. China acknowledges the importance of multistakeholder agreements (that is, agreements that consider the demands of the private sector, nongovernmental organizations, and governments) in this earliest articulation of its cyber sovereignty, yet it also argues for a balance of digital power that prioritizes state control. This argument centers on the state by framing the issue in terms of multilateral relations rather than multistakeholder relations.

Several related terms have emerged as a constellation around the idea of internet sovereignty in China. At the 2015 Wuzhen World Internet Conference, China's major annual internet conference, President Xi Jinping asserted the importance of the "shared construction" of cyberspace, a vision that, in practice, reflects strong Chinese leadership rather than collective global decision-making.[13] Two days later, the *China Daily*, China's state-run English-language newspaper of record, interpreted Xi's words for a global public.[14] He articulated a vision of cyber sovereignty, translated from the Chinese phrase *wangluo zhuquan*.[15] This vision of cyber sovereignty underscored the importance of following each country's laws within the domain of cyberspace.[16] It is China's answer to digital sovereignty, a term that has come to prominence in the West to reflect the idea of national power—primarily, though not exclusively—over digital resources and infrastructure.[17] Yet while digital sovereignty offers a comparatively narrow vision of following existing territorial boundaries, the Chinese-language definition of cyber sovereignty put out by the CAC in 2014 presents a more expansive view, one that includes not just the enforcement of national laws but the protection of a country's very existence.[18] The CAC document argues that cyber sovereignty is essential for development and security, and that each country must implement laws to advance its own interests.[19] The cyber sovereignty framework forms the foundation of China's vision for a digital domain.

User data is part of China's broad vision of cyber sovereignty. Business scholar Lizhi Liu argues that in parallel with its discourse on cyber sovereignty, the Chinese government is asserting data sovereignty, or *shuju zhuquan*, through suites of laws that control how data generated in China can be stored, used, and moved.[20] China's 2021 Data Security Law offers a strategic vision for the role of data in relation to national borders.[21] Indeed, many of China's policies that shape its digital terrain influence not just the digital world and not just China's sovereign territory. Rather, they reflect how data networks create a web of influence that extends beyond established territorial boundaries.

One of the most astonishing features of China's cyber sovereignty framework is the pace and unpredictability with which it has unfolded. As this chapter outlines, the Chinese government has moved quickly to redefine what constitutes the data of the state, from the beginning of the Great Firewall of China (GFW, formerly known as the Golden Shield Project) in 2000, to early conceptions of cyber sovereignty in 2010, to expansive national security audits for all data generated by Chinese companies in 2021. These steps, as well as the other intermediate regulations establishing state control of data, all occurred with limited transparency about the full scope of government power they offered. As Félix Boudreault, managing director of Sustainable Market Strategies (an environmental, social, and corporate governance [ESG] investment research group) put it, Chinese media and tech companies are "extremely vulnerable to the strike of a pen from a Chinese bureaucrat."[22]

The Chinese government's broad assertion of cyber sovereignty is at the foundation of what I term a national *data corpus*, a connected system that builds a national digital domain by gathering and integrating consumer, corporate, and government data. In this chapter, I use the concept of the data corpus to explain how and why China's data domain coheres and expands. The idea of the data corpus builds on Black studies scholar Simone Browne's conceptualization of digital "epidermalization," wherein the body is made biometric. In this case, however, we are talking not just about one body but about a population of many.[23]

The concept of the data corpus draws on the idea that cross-platform data gathering extends the aggregate of information that governments and corporations have about individuals. So it involves accumulating not merely each individual platform's data but also the data generated across multiple communities and then integrated into a digital polity. China shapes its data corpus by defining the relationship between individuals, corporations, and the nation in the context of national security.

The term *data corpus* is particularly useful for understanding the aggregation of national and corporate data in China for three key reasons. First, as *corpus* is a Latin and Middle English term for the body, it recalls the human origins of consumer data. Second, the word *corpus*, which can refer to a collection of written texts on a particular subject, incorporates the vastness and completeness of data that is gathered through platforms and then cumulated by the Chinese government. Finally, the corpus evokes the body politic. This medieval metaphor frames the nation, its people, and its resources. Indeed, *corpus* is the Latin root of the term *corporation*. In Mandarin, *tishen* means "body." One of its homonyms is the word *tishen* 替身, which means "stand-in" or "substitute body." In this case, the digital double evokes the body. The term *data corpus* reflects the transition from the extraction of raw data to the genesis of a social body of data that represents the digital embodiment of the state. The data corpus is thus part of the nation itself, and national sovereignty relies on control of user data.

Building the data corpus also creates strategic national resources, through corporations with unique access to data, a government empowered to obtain corporate data, and highly trained algorithms for governance and prediction. The Chinese government thus not only establishes new standards for what constitutes citizenship, but also generates opposition to the compulsory surrender of individual privacy. Science and technology studies scholar Ruha Benjamin has referred to this as "biodefection"—the resistance to "technoscientific conscription, or the forced integration of one's biodata into the state."[24]

China has already developed versions of a social credit system or *shehui xinyong tixi,* a suite of public and private sector tools that gather user data for domestic governance decisions. A pilot program began in 2014 to evaluate Chinese citizens based on such information as travel history, school records, government positions, and even dating app data.[25] The COVID-19 pandemic Health Code system developed by Alipay and WeChat expanded health surveillance.[26] More of a strategic vision drawing upon multiple sources, the social credit system relies on data from companies operating in China and extends the cyber sovereignty model to the body politic.[27] The system's purpose is to collect data on citizens' activities, including everything from traffic violations to tax payments. By shaping how individuals can function within Chinese society, it also constitutes what it means to be a citizen.[28] The social credit system is just one part of China's larger data corpus.

What makes the development of China's data corpus distinctive is the colossal global influence of Chinese tech firms and the Chinese market.[29] This domestic advantage, in turn, guides future industrial development. It helps China to develop corporate tech tools earlier and more efficiently than other countries, tools that they then export to other nations. The shift in industrial development influences which countries can accrue soft power through the next generation of data-driven products. With more access to data, the Chinese government, in conjunction with Chinese firms, can also influence new standards for international organizations in critical technologies such as facial recognition, surveillance, artificial intelligence (AI), telecommunications infrastructure, and networked consumer products. Thus, such participation in the global corporate technology marketplace and regulatory landscape not only affects China's domestic economy, but also complicates the operations of major multinational firms. The firms must either standardize their terms of service to suit the Chinese market or, at a minimum, have terms for the Chinese market that contradict the ones used for other countries. The following figure offers an overview of the strategies the Chinese government uses to assert digital boundaries.

With extensive government support and a massive domestic market, and by working within international standards-setting bodies, Chinese regulators are influencing the standards for the global data trade. These tools shape how the global technology landscape will look in the future. Although US tech firms pioneered the approach of leveraging market power and influence over international organizations, the Chinese government has refined it by incorporating much more systematic government control of corporations

Government oversight of corporations

Oversight through nationalization of private sector firms, civil-military fusion, partial state ownership of private sector firms, and defining the roles of data through laws, principles, specifications, politics, and plans

Government control of innovation through institutional development

Oversight over global consumer platforms through standards building, participation in international organizations, and overseas direct investment

Internationally:
Shaping the global data management environment through building digital infrastructures and leadership in global standard setting

China asserts digital boundaries in four key areas.

Domestically:
Building out its data corpus through principles, plans, standards, laws, and technology firms' growth with government access to data

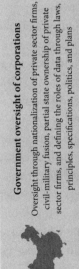

Government control of data

Direct control of structuring sovereignty through largescale efforts to control and manage the data generated in the PRC, including the CAC, "Great Firewall of China," and 2017 Cybersecurity Law

Global network development

Leadership in international organizations that set multistakeholder standards, including growing influence in the United Nations International Telecommunication Union

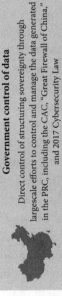

Figure 3.1 How China Asserts Digital Boundaries

and their data. In much the same way that satellites extend sovereignty by expanding the footprint of access beyond territorial boundaries, the impact of the Chinese market extends its influence over the tech sector through the reach of Chinese corporations. In the following sections, I examine how oversight of corporations and their data, policy planning, and institutional leadership extend the Chinese government's control over user data beyond the territorial bounds of the state.

Government Oversight of Corporations

The Chinese government's oversight of technology corporations takes multiple forms. These include the ownership or threat of ownership of corporations, the control of data, pressure from the Chinese military, the influence of the Chinese Communist Party (CCP), the leveraging of legacy governance structures on the tech sector, and, paradoxically, the delegation of tech oversight power to corporations. Together, these practices present carrots and sticks to Chinese tech firms seeking to operate within China's complex market landscape.

The Chinese government has demonstrated a willingness to take over strategically significant or imperiled firms. China's nationalization of private-sector firms such as Anbang Insurance Group Co., Ltd., which had a substantial technology, media, and telecommunications business, suggests a clear breach in the already highly permeable border between the private and state sectors in China.[30] In 2017, the Chinese government proposed rules to take a small stake in the tech companies Alibaba, Tencent, and Weibo Corp. as a way of controlling the liberalization of the tech sector.[31] I spoke with Malcolm Lee, then managing director and head of policy for international government affairs at Alibaba, shortly after the *Wall Street Journal* reported that the PRC government planned to take special management shares of Alibaba. He categorically denied it would happen. However, China's legal system empowers the government to extend the use of oversight powers in wide-ranging ways that are often not enumerated clearly by Chinese laws. In addition to nationalizing old-economy Chinese firms, the Chinese government has established an important new precedent for the partial state ownership of private-sector firms. One form of this state ownership is the above-mentioned special management shares, which are stocks that allow government control in private-sector media and technology firms.[32] These shares differ from other shares floated by Chinese firms in that only the Chinese government can own them. The November 12, 2013, "Decision of the Central Committee of the Communist Party of China on Some Major Issues Concerning Comprehensively Deepening the Reform," adopted at the Third Plenary Session of the 18th Central Committee of the Communist Party of China, established the foundation for the special management shares.[33] It defines the continuing relationship between the state and for-profit cultural institutions as follows:

> We will continue to transform state-owned for-profit cultural institutions into business enterprises, and adopt for them corporate systems or share-holding systems at a faster pace. We will experiment in carrying out a system of special management shares in important state-owned media enterprises that have been transformed according to regulations.[34]

This approach has manifested as special management share ownership by the Chinese government in several technology firms in addition to Alibaba.[35] Reporting has pointed to two Chinese tech start-ups as test cases for this approach. The military and defense e-commerce site Beijing Tiexue Tech Co. Ltd., a privately held Chinese tech firm, is one example.[36] Perhaps more intriguing are the special management shares the Chinese government acquired in the news and media aggregator Yidian Zixun. NYSE-traded Phoenix Media has a 42 percent stake in Yidian Zixun, entwining the special management shares with a firm that is publicly traded in the United States.[37] The special management shares acquired in Yidian Zixun demonstrate the intimate connection between Chinese-owned, state-run firms and publicly traded firms. This partial nationalization of firms with financial links to publicly traded firms extends the scope of China's sovereign digital territory. Although only a few have been nationalized, the move underscores the permeability of private- and public-sector control of data in China.

China's current data governance landscape is distinctive not merely because of its large market size but also because of the relationship between the military and private sectors. *Military–civil fusion* refers to the principle that any property built by Chinese firms is subject to Chinese government control.[38] What this means in practice is that the government can assert its right to corporate data, including user data, for military use. This prerogative exists separately from national security data audits, through which the government can fully access corporate data for regulatory purposes. Firms operating in

China—both Chinese firms and foreign firms with Chinese partners—are subject to this principle. The military is at the foundation of China's party-state, the closely entwined relationship between the Chinese Communist Party and the nation.[39] These complementary national and defense innovation strategies allow China to leverage its technological developments as part of a broader national and military development strategy.[40]

In addition to the relationship between the military and the tech sector, the Communist Party's role in the private sector has grown since China's 2001 accession to the World Trade Organization. The framework of the party-state is an area of scholarly debate.[41] The precise closeness of the Party and the state differs over time and under different leaders.[42] Following Jiang Zemin's Three Represents Campaign, which brought capitalists into the Party fold, the Party has taken on a much more powerful role in private-sector enterprises. China's leading entrepreneurs, including Alibaba's founder Jack Ma, are Party members.[43] Party committees play a prominent role in the corporate culture of private-sector Chinese tech firms and foreign joint ventures, where the formal and informal power of Party officials shape both state- and privately owned enterprises.[44]

The Chinese government defines data as a national asset through laws, principles, specifications, policies, and plans. However, corporate data governance is an area of back-and-forth negotiation between the Chinese government and corporations based in China. Companies have a financial need to maximize their data gathering, but the leaders of corporations operating in China, often have tense relationships with government leaders as they negotiate how the corporate control of data will play out.

For example, when Chinese multinational tech firm ByteDance was in negotiations to divest TikTok's US operations, the Chinese government instituted a new national security review for the export of algorithms.[45] The review jeopardized the potential deal because it prevented ByteDance from moving TikTok's engineering operations outside of China.[46] Ultimately, actions by US courts and the Biden administration enabled ByteDance to continue its operations in Beijing while operating in the US market.[47] However, the move demonstrates the power the Chinese government wields over tech firms seeking to operate internationally.

The relationship between the state and digital sectors allows for more significant government influence, as more and more legacy industries enter the tech sector. In the United States, when the technology sector interacts with other sectors, the resulting friction frequently leads to "disruption" of the preexisting sector.[48] However, in China, this phenomenon works slightly differently with deeply entrenched, state-owned industries. The state can leverage control over the legacy business to gain greater control over its emergent technologies. Thus, rather than eroding borders, the phenomenon deepens state cyber sovereignty by extending the range of state firms.

One key example is the interaction between the financial and the tech sectors. China is a global leader in the mobile payments arena, with platforms such as Alipay and WeChat Pay.[49] Both are mobile payment systems that link to the dominant Chinese social media platform WeChat.[50] Alipay and WeChat Pay are ubiquitous in China. The Chinese government supported the growth of fintech platforms as part of its social credit system and also as a way of liberalizing credit in the Chinese financial sector.[51] Most airlines and many vendors no longer accept cash.[52] ATMs are increasingly difficult to find on the streets of major Chinese cities because of the prevalence of mobile payments.[53] Via WeChat, users can easily send funds from their Alipay and WeChat Pay accounts to their contacts anywhere in the world.[54]

At first glance, this setup appears to be precisely the type of borderlessness promised by the internet. However, the state determines the sovereignty of the apps. Both Alipay and WeChat Pay require users to have a Chinese bank account unless they receive a financial gift from a Chinese user. New bank accounts in China are available only to Chinese nationals and people living in China with a residence permit associated with their employment.[55] Thus, to open and fund an Alipay or WeChat Pay account, one must be under the Chinese state's sovereign control. As the government enacts this control at the intersection of the digital and legacy economies, it shapes the borders of China's sovereign through the capital movement of its citizens and residents online.

Payment platforms are also a critical site at which the Chinese government can assert its cyber sovereignty by using the surveillance tools embedded in the social credit system. In fact, China can access the data of its citizens around the world. Alipay has an opt-in function to use Zhima Credit, a system that tracks bill payments, spending habits, friends' social credit scores, and other personal information to algorithmically produce an individual's social credit score.[56] Elements of the social credit system (like payment platforms) monitor Chinese citizens not just in China but also in their digital interactions with others outside the country. Popular platforms such as WeChat, Sina Weibo, and QQ that Chinese citizens use globally might at some point form the backbone of China's social credit system. Citizens' various social media accounts could therefore be integrated into a nationwide platform. Users can make payments with Alipay around the world, and Zhima Credit can gather data globally.[57] Thus, China has a mechanism for expanding its data corpus internationally using Chinese technology products.

The relationship between China's financial sector and the tech sector is ultimately a leading indicator of how the state sector can shape the tech sector to transition legacy businesses into the digital economy. Multiple layers of linked institutions conjoining the government and the tech sector enhance the government's control. For example, the banking system connects with payment apps, which connect to phone numbers. Establishing a social media account on WeChat requires a cellphone number, which requires government approval to obtain. When requesting a new phone number, individuals must be photographed and share biometric data, which is then linked with the number.[58] One's number and the payment platform connect with one's social media account.[59] And all this information is accessible by government officials.[60]

China's "borderless" payment platforms operate within a closed financial system. Thus, by controlling corporations such as banks that interact with Chinese fintech firms, the government can control the activity of the firms themselves. The Chinese government thereby determines which companies can supply its tech firms' financial services and participate in the system.

While regulations facilitate government control of corporations, the devolution of government control to tech sector firms offers a parallel form of governance. By putting Chinese tech firms in charge of tech oversight, the Chinese government encourages a distinctively conservative tech regulatory environment with high levels of buy-in from the firms.[61] Companies depend on their licenses and contacts with government officials to maintain profitability. As a result, they have a financial incentive to be overly cautious in their application of Chinese government tech policies.[62] In some ways, these intimate connections in cyber governance between Chinese firms and the Chinese government echo the channels through which the US government outsources internet governance to US firms. The crucial difference is that in China, the government has a comprehensive vision of what constitutes national data governance.

Chinese firms pay for their unique control over user data. while Chinese government regulations related to national security review constrain ambitious entrepreneurs. "Anti-corruption" campaigns against individuals, paired with antitrust regulations against corporations, offer the Party numerous tools with which to constrain what it perceives as excessive private-sector power.[63] Increasing global concerns about the Chinese government's efforts to gather data via Chinese corporations have driven scrutiny of Chinese firms operating in foreign markets.[64] For example, the United States has blocked certain Chinese tech firms from operating in the US market by placing them on the Department of Commerce's Entity List of trade restrictions. Increased review of Chinese firms has also decreased receptivity to Chinese capital investment in some parts of Silicon Valley's innovation ecosystem.[65] However, the gains allow for the integration of government oversight and corporate data at an unprecedented level. Intensive local investment in education, business development, and next-generation technologies helps developing technologies leapfrog into the market. The Chinese government's strategic efforts to block foreign corporations from gathering extensive data in China also benefit Chinese companies. As Chinese policies limit access to the largest market in the world, Chinese firms can develop products at scale for Chinese consumers. Thus, despite the high cost they pay, Chinese corporations benefit significantly from China's efforts to build a national data corpus.

Government Control of Data

Oversight of corporations is just one way of structuring sovereignty. China's development of a data-driven economy relies heavily on the government's capacity to gather extensive data in a domestic context. Accordingly, in the past decade, China's digital surveillance apparatus has bloomed like fungi after a rainstorm. However, population surveillance in China has a long history. Premodern imperial ledgers of merit and demerit during the Ming and Qing periods monitored people's deeds to advance or preserve social status. After the 1949 founding of the People's Republic of China, unrelated groups of citizens in Beijing watched each other across the centers of the city's courtyard houses.[66] China's Communist Party instituted robust citizen surveillance during its rise to power. From the Mao era onward, personal dossiers, or *geren dangan*, have followed urban residents; they include a wide range of personal information, from family background and mental health status to educational and professional progress.[67]

Even now, those legacy surveillance systems persist in some compounds. Residents' committees observe building occupants' behaviors, and in the case of the COVID-19 pandemic, they both provided supplies for community members and surveilled the health status of residents.[68] Guards watch to see who enters and exits the compounds. Much of the media coverage of China's successful COVID-19 response highlights how the country leveraged digital monitoring apps to control the virus's spread. However, reporters have documented that community oversight was equally, if not more, important in maintaining effective quarantines.[69] With these surveillance systems already in place, there is a lack of corresponding legal protections relating to privacy or the gathering and aggregation of individual data.[70] Although China's social credit system, which synthesizes data about everything from online posts to creditworthiness, has captured imaginations outside of China, we should remember that Communist work units, where individuals lived, toiled, and studied together, formed the system's foundation.[71]

The social credit system vision underscores that these surveillance structures, while comprising real technology, are part of the national imaginary. Competing government-run and private-sector-run versions of the social credit system exist as trials to integrate national data. Alibaba and Huawei both have "smart city" solutions that combine data gathered through citywide systems, including payment platforms.[72] By conducting simultaneous trials across cities, China is building on its modernization efforts of the 1980s, in which Shenzhen, Shanghai, and Wenzhou offered new models for Chinese economic liberalization.[73] Like those early models, current national data governance practices operate unevenly across the country. In wealthy cities such as Beijing, Shanghai, Hangzhou, and Shenzhen, municipal resources, paired with private funding and technical infrastructure, advance the rate of urban data integration.[74] Conversely, the Xinjiang Uyghur Autonomous Region faces intense technical surveillance focused on colonizing minority populations through voice recognition, facial recognition, and smartphone tracking.[75]

The PRC government, unlike the United States government, has a clear mandate to control the country's national technology landscape.[76] The CAC oversees large-scale efforts to control and manage the data generated within the PRC. It develops long-term policies for China's data governance. China maintains its national sovereignty and protects the nation's borders through increasing surveillance and AI oversight of the Chinese population. Government estimates placed the number of surveillance cameras in the country at 176 million in 2018, with projected growth to 1 billion globally, half of which were expected to be in China by the end of 2021.[77] Such estimates are notoriously difficult to verify externally, but they underscore the scale and scope of the planned growth.

China has long had a policy of controlling the information that enters the country. Its information control system extends to a system colloquially known as the Great Firewall of China, which comprises proxy servers at Chinese internet entry points that limit information distribution throughout the country.[78] The system also tampers with internet addresses and domain names, blocks websites, and filters keywords to restrict the flow of data.[79]

Online content regulations also structure China's data corpus. The 2016 Online Publishing Services Management Rules explicitly advocate promoting China's core socialist values (*shehui zhuyi hexin jiazhiguan*) in content distributed by online platforms.[80] These twelve values range from prosperity to geniality and encourage Chinese citizens to behave in prosocial and prostate ways at the national, social, and individual levels.[81] Regulators have even used the phrase "core socialist values" in nationalizing the data storage facilities of foreign corporations through China's 2017 Cybersecurity Law.[82]

Another set of guidelines for China's data corpus was established by China's 2019 Provisions on the Governance of the Online Information Content Ecosystem.[83] They impose criminal or civil penalties for producing or distributing "unhealthy" content and limit what people can access and post online. In addition, they have a punitive element that allows the monitoring of content and, by extension, data that users attempt to upload. This practice establishes clear digital borders around what can be part of the official Chinese data corpus by disciplining and excising parts of the national digital body.

Beyond online user content, corporations face restrictions that prevent them from privately storing the data they generate. China's 2017 Cybersecurity Law asserted that all "critical information" should be controlled by Chinese state-owned data centers, thus structuring it as part of the national security apparatus.[84] The law required the transfer of all such data, both government and commercial, to Chinese-government-run servers.[85]

Almost immediately following the Cybersecurity Law's enactment, the Chinese government sued Apple for violating it.[86] Apple then announced that it would move its data to the Chinese provincial-government-run cloud services provider Guizhou Yunshang, demonstrating that regardless of the policy's wisdom, it was effective in enabling government access to corporate data.[87]

China's 2021 Data Security Law offers an overarching national security strategy for the management of data generated by Chinese corporations.[88] Affirming the principles of military-civil fusion and the 2017 Cybersecurity Law, the Data Security Law formalizes government access to data. According to the law, corporations must be willing and able to make their data available for national security review at any time.[89] It also subjects companies to national data gathering, linking corporate data with data gathered by the nation.

China's Personal Information Security Specification, which took effect November 1, 2021, outlines how companies can share an individual's personal information (though not generalized data).[90] They limit consumer data gathering and sharing at the corporate level but do not restrict government surveillance of that data. The specification's data standards do offer valuable consumer recourse against corporations. They prevent the bundling of individual personal information across different parts of a business, a protection not afforded to US consumers.[91] Users must actively consent to the use of their personal information for a specific business function. If a company ceases to need a specific type of data for that business function, the firm must discontinue its data collection.[92] However, despite increasing restrictions on corporations, data would still be subject to government access for national security review.[93] So while the Personal Information Security Specification grants Chinese consumers greater control over how corporations use their data, it also reinforces the Chinese government's role as the arbiter of information flows into and out of the country. The following figure offers an overview of some of China's key data governance regulations from 1995 to 2021, a period of significant transition in the country's expanded global tech influence.

Many of China's data security regulations have extraterritorial implications. The Data Security Law, for example, as mentioned above, provides extraterritorial enforcement of the country's data oversight mechanisms.[94] However, Article 38 of Hong Kong's 2020 national security law drives home the fact that the Chinese government is establishing a national data corpus with extraterritorial enforcement even covering violations committed "outside the region by a person who is not a permanent resident of the region."[95] The law is deeply troubling in that it asserts jurisdiction over essentially everyone on the planet for national security reasons. China's online content regulations and its data laws and stipulations also rely on national security as a justification, fleshing out the implications of Article 38 for the tech sector. While

Major Developments in Chinese Data Governance

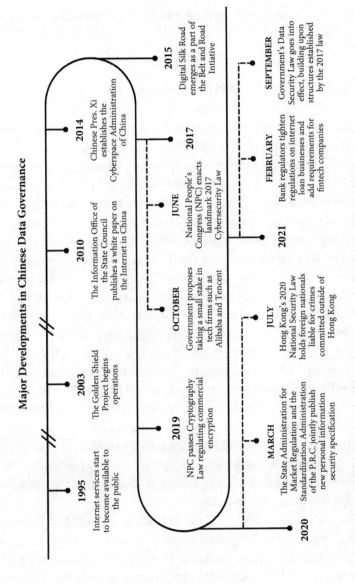

Figure 3.2 Major Developments in Chinese Data Governance from 1995 to 2021

the national security law's long-term implications will depend on its implementation, the law sends a clear message that global data oversight is subject to Chinese government law. Ultimately, wide-reaching laws enable vast government oversight of data. This approach is not haphazard, but rather the result of decades of careful policy planning toward the nationalization of global data oversight.

Policy Planning

Policy plans that outline goals for domestic technological development bolster China's cyber sovereignty framework. Western governments, corporations, and researchers have paid significant attention to China's efforts to become a leader in such technologies as AI, facial recognition, hyperloops, and advanced bioengineering.[96] China's policy planning presents an ambitious vision to build China's domestic data corpus through improved infrastructure for gathering, storing, and using data. Public, government, and academic databases connect with one another, and by extension, private firms that have exposure to these sectors also interconnect. Focusing on control of the overarching data corpus allows China to maintain domestic autonomy within the technology sector and key related sectors, such as media and manufacturing.

The country's policy planning in the technology sector takes three forms: five-year plans, sector-specific plans, and long-term national goal setting. Since the PRC's founding, the government has created industrial development plans at five-year intervals. As of the 11th Five-Year Plan (2006–2010), the tech sector has been a primary focus. The 11th and 12th (2011–2015) Five-Year Plans emphasized the development of "next-generation IT," a moving target that has required progressively increasing amounts of data. The 13th Five-Year Plan (2016–2020) focused on building out tech sectors in biopharmaceuticals, aviation, and robotics. It also dedicated an entire section to digital infrastructure development.[97]

Building on the 13th Five-Year Plan and Made in China 2025, China's government released a five-year plan on national informatization on December 27, 2016, expanding the country's data corpus using several key strategies.[98] The plan focuses on developing domestic IT resources, including 5G wireless systems, cloud computing, smart manufacturing, and the Internet of Things, to assert greater control over China's tech sector.[99] It outlines the need for integrated national databases for the government, public sector, academic institutions, and other spheres, and emphasizes the need to build information infrastructure in rural and remote regions.[100] Improving information infrastructure in small communities is a particularly significant element of the government's effort to increase its capacity to gather national data because digital oversight requires sufficient bandwidth.[101] Finally, the plan lays out a substantial effort to develop China's thirty-five-satellite BeiDou Navigation System, which can provide uplink and downlink services.[102]

China's 14th Five-Year Plan (2021–2025) doubled down on indigenous innovation. This effort seeks to make the PRC's innovation ecosystem independent from external trade pressures by funding domestic science and technology research.[103] The plan focuses further on enhancing data protection, including expanded cybersecurity review, new domestic standards, and increased influence in international standards-setting bodies, to safeguard national interests.[104]

In addition to the standard five-year-plan process, China has introduced longer-term planning mechanisms for developing the tech industry. The Made in China 2025 industrial policy aims to move China's economy further from low-end consumer goods to high-end tech manufacturing.[105] Like the 13th Five-Year Plan, Made in China 2025 focuses on data-intensive industries such as robotics, aviation, biopharmaceuticals, "next-generation IT," and advanced medical devices.[106] These targeted industrial policies work in concert with President Xi Jinping's pursuit of what he terms *wangluo qiangguo*, or "strong internet power."[107]

Scholars debate whether an exportable "China model" of governance exists. The nuances of Chinese political culture, in which even national leaders refer to their domestic leadership as "socialism with Chinese characteristics," or *zhongguotese shehui zhuyi*, suggest the uniqueness of China's system.[108] However, China offers a model of policy planning that can be adapted by other countries.[109] China's Digital Silk Road (DSR) plan offers a template for exporting the country's approach to cyber sovereignty. The DSR first emerged as a consensus term in roughly 2017, the year of Beijing's first Belt and Road Initiative (BRI) Forum, though use of the term dates back to 2015.[110] China's BRI is a trade and investment scheme designed to advance Chinese investment in the nation's territorial and maritime neighbors (broadly defined) focused on the acquisition of ports, railways, and other trade and transportation hubs. The DSR is central to China's plans to leverage investment to increase the country's global influence. President Xi's speech at the 2017 BRI Forum urged China to pursue "innovation-driven development and intensify cooperation in frontier areas such as digital economy, artificial intelligence, nanotechnology and quantum computing, and advance the development of big data, cloud computing and smart cities so as to turn them into a digital silk road of the 21st century."[111] The speech highlighted the importance of *hulian hutong*, which can be translated as "mutual connectivity," but for standards-setting is better translated as "cyberspace interoperability."[112] The first word, *hulian*, can be translated as "interconnected" or even "networked," underscoring how linkages between physical and digital infrastructure leverage digital investments to extend government oversight over physical infrastructure, and vice versa.

The DSR's engagement in the global technology trade is an extension of efforts to build a trade network that favors Chinese companies and standards across sectors. A notable twist of this export plan is that successful adoption of the model requires adopting Chinese tech—and, by extension, being enveloped into China's data corpus. Through the DSR, Chinese technology firms such as Huawei and ZTE introduce their corporate standards (which align with Chinese government standards) to digital technology infrastructure throughout China's trading relationships.[113] Both firms have expanded their footprint as providers of telecommunications equipment around the world and offer the potential for extensive Chinese government data gathering through backdoor access to their technology.[114] Chinese digital and physical infrastructure, paired with government investment, constitutes a foundation on which to build China's data corpus not just domestically but also internationally.

Institutional Leadership

China is also expanding its oversight of global consumer platforms through leadership in international organizations. Public policy forums such as the Internet Governance Forum (IGF) and China's World Internet Conference help spread the influence of China's standards.[115] The Chinese government takes advantage of the growing power of Chinese platforms in these organizations to influence global trade, exporting internet governance standards while Chinese platforms such as Alipay and WeChat become international players.[116] This approach has evolved so that China is now leveraging alternative strategies like institution-building and norms-setting to build power.[117]

These are not new strategies. The United States has long guided international technology governance organizations to advance its own strategic interests. Representatives from US firms and the US government have advocated for technology standards in line with US government and corporate interests. Multistakeholder governance structures benefit countries without large industrial entities that take a seat at the negotiating table for major institution-building efforts.

However, China has been proactive in consensus building. The Chinese government advocates for multilateral norms to protect national cyber sovereignty. Regional multilateral organizations, in particular, are useful in establishing norms for data governance without the influence of international corporations or civil society.

China has set out regional data principles through the Shanghai Cooperation Organization (SCO), a political, economic, and security alliance that includes China, Kazakhstan, Kyrgyzstan, Russia, Tajikistan, and Uzbekistan. Members announced its creation on June 15, 2001, in Shanghai, China. The organization's name underscores the central leadership role that China has played in the growth and development of international standards-setting[118]

As early as 2009—predating China's cybersecurity white paper—the SCO outlined principles establishing the relationship between data and the nation.[119] The SCO advanced the idea of the internet as a sovereign space to be governed with an eye to protecting national security. Shared standards agreements formed the backbone of this protection.[120] China even shared standards for cyberspace with the United Nations in 2011 and 2015, offering an alternative code of conduct for international information security.[121]

The first time SCO members released collaborative guidelines was in September 2011, immediately after the digital activism of the Arab Spring toppled governments throughout the Middle East and North Africa. In response, these countries asserted an International Code for Information Security.[122] Notably, the document draws a clear connection between information security and sovereignty, as did the 2010 White Paper on the Internet in China, and reaffirms "that policy authority for Internet-related public issues is the sovereign right of States, which have rights and responsibilities for international internet-related public policy issues."[123] The document goes on to reassert the relationship between critical information infrastructures and national sovereignty.

Following pushback from the United Nations over the first set of guidelines, SCO members revised and resubmitted their suggestions in 2015. The revised framework reflected an increased interest in issues of cyber sovereignty, and permanent representatives from Kazakhstan and Kyrgyzstan joined the group's original sponsors.[124] The SCO, with Chinese policy as its inspiration, established a multilateral alternative to the multistakeholder approach, which incorporates both corporate and nongovernmental organization perspectives and is favored by many developed democracies in Europe, North America, and Asia.

In addition to asserting the importance of regional governance organizations, the Chinese government uses leadership in international organizations that set global multistakeholder standards to expand China's global data grip. China's growing influence in the International Telecommunication Union, the UN's telecommunications regulator, offers a notable example of China's impact on global technology governance organizations. In recent years, Chinese bureaucrats have taken leadership roles in the organization. At the 2018 ITU Plenipotentiary, a quadrennial meeting of the ITU's supreme decision-making body, members reelected China's Houlin Zhao to a second four-year term as ITU secretary-general.[125] Before originally being elected secretary-general in 2014, he served two consecutive four-year terms as ITU deputy secretary-general.[126] Notably, Zhao's first leadership experience at the ITU was as director of the ITU Telecommunications Standardization Bureau, a role he held for two terms.[127] As a former leader in China's information and communication technology (ICT) standardization sector and a current ITU leader, Zhao presents an interesting contradiction. Before joining the ITU, he was a leading Chinese government official, participating in China's ICT standards-setting and national planning as part of the Chinese government's cyber sovereignty efforts.[128] He has also been involved in UN standards-setting for the past two decades. Zhao's many roles demonstrate how Chinese telecommunications officials are able to model global telecommunications standards on Chinese bureaucratic standards.

Zhao's ITU involvement has foregrounded Chinese strategic interests. In an unprecedented move, Zhao, as ITU secretary-general, responded to allegations of potential security risks to other nations posed by Chinese firm Huawei's 5G statement was notable for its very existence. Previous ITU heads have refrained from weighing in on bilateral trade issues, particularly those involving firms with close state ties. Moreover, instead of remaining neutral, Zhao dismissed Washington's concerns about the possible security risks embedded in Huawei's 5G infrastructure as a "loser's attitude."[129]

China's role in the ITU also intersected with other Chinese efforts to drive standardization through industrial dominance. Chinese firms and individuals have taken substantive leadership roles in 5G standards-setting in the ITU. According to the US-China Economic and Security and Review Commission, former Chinese government officials hold eight of the thirty-nine available leadership positions in the ITU's 5G-related standards-setting bodies. Richard Li, chief scientist at Futurewei Technologies (Huawei's US research branch), is the head of an ITU Emerging Tech and 5G Infrastructure Group.[130] Li's leadership exemplifies how Chinese tech leaders are now engaging in corporate influence tactics that have long been used by US firms. However, Chinese firms have much closer ties to their government than US firms because of national data audit and storage requirements.[131][132]

China's multitiered influence over global standardization demonstrates how the country's government, military, and corporate interests are leveraging global data regulations. It also highlights how China's national and international ICT governance positions contradict each other, as China's domestic laws and practices become more self-contained. Ultimately, these parallel attempts to seize global power and domestic control are building China's data corpus. In brief, China leads in international standards-setting but keeps local data at home.

Conclusion

China structures its national data corpus, the country's government-accessible private and public sector data, through legal mechanisms that define the relationship between data and national security. This chapter has focused on the ways this aggregated data extends the nation both within and beyond its borders. National boundaries materialize through a wide range of laws, specifications, and guidelines that frame data gathering and circulation as national security processes. Cybersecurity laws restrict where information is stored and how individuals, corporations, and the Chinese government can access it. Cryptographic standards protect the confidentiality of data that is transmitted and stored on networks. Data security laws dictate how and when the government can access user data. Together, these laws, standards, and provisions structure China's national data corpus. Specifications are arteries directing the flow of data, and cryptographic standards act as bones that shield and insulate it. Thus, the Data Security Law, as this chapter has explained, offers a comprehensive vision of what the national body of data might include. Combined, these approaches animate the nation's data corpus.

Chinese national industrial policy encourages Chinese firms to store data locally, whether they operate within or outside the country. Sweetheart deals for data center real estate reduce storage costs. The threat of national security crackdowns prevents firms from sending too many data assets outside of China.[133] Such an approach pays dividends for government oversight and product development. In China, government and consumer data can be aggregated in ways that are illegal in other countries.[134]

Beyond its borders, China is shaping the global data management environment. Laws require international corporations to use domestic Chinese digital infrastructure for international corporations to access Chinese markets. Domestic Chinese and multinational corporations face the potential of global data security audits related to activities conducted in China. Chinese-led international standards-setting bodies are growing. As outlined in the previous section, former Chinese government officials are also taking leadership in global standards-setting bodies, and efforts to set standards for global firms are expanding China's domestic data corpus to include international data. The next chapter demonstrates how Chinese corporations augment the country's data corpus by leveraging Chinese government laws and principles abroad. As it develops access to technical infrastructure abroad, the Chinese government is operationalizing its cyber sovereignty model globally.

No other country has adopted the Chinese model wholesale, though many have adopted elements of it as part of what legal scholars Matthew S. Erie and Thomas Streinz term the "Beijing Effect," through "push" and "pull" factors supplying emerging markets with digital infrastructure.[135] Indeed, certain countries have consulted with the Chinese government on how to optimize data-gathering practices both for improved municipal management and for more intensive government control.[136] Officers from the People's Liberation Army trained Sri Lankan officials to use website-filtering technologies.[137] China's Ministry of Public Security helped the Cambodian National Police install surveillance cameras in the capital city, Phnom Penh. Vietnam took its cue from China in developing a system of data localization for foreign firms.[138] Tanzania is learning from Chinese government officials how to establish national data centers.[139] The China National Electronics Import and Export Corporation (CEIEC) managed the installation of digital security infrastructure in both Venezuela and Ecuador.[140] State-owned Chinese firms have conducted digital espionage on buildings they have built, as in the Addis Ababa–based African Union headquarters.[141] Chinese private-sector firms have installed surveillance cameras with facial recognition in more than a hundred cities globally.[142]

US-based tech firms offer development tools and form the backbone of current global technological infrastructure. However, the United States has stepped back from technical leadership in recent years as the Chinese government has actively pursued involvement in global standards-setting. Moreover, Silicon Valley has shown—through such incidents as Facebook's enabling of the Myanmar genocide and the exposure of inhumane conditions for workers at device-manufacturing companies in China—that its products can come with political, social, and environmental costs.[143]

China's approach to data governance, steeped in the principles of the surveillance state, offers an attractive model for national oversight and control for certain countries around the world.[144] It offers clear benefits to places that have close geopolitical ties to China, active Chinese firms, and high crime rates.[145] With activism in global regulatory bodies, trade pressure on global firms to use Chinese standards, and the worldwide expansion of Chinese tech platforms, China is advancing its cyber sovereignty interests not just through domestic laws and powerful Chinese tech firms but with the assistance of the same regulatory loopholes that supported the growth of the US tech sector.

In this chapter, I have focused on the role the Chinese government plays in asserting control over corporate data. However, as underscored throughout these chapters, the Chinese tech industry entices users around the world to share their data with Chinese firms and by extension with the Chinese government. Through the combined power of Chinese corporations and the Chinese government's data governance regulations, China exerts a level of control over users that Silicon Valley can only imagine. In Chapter 4, I examine products ranging from agricultural tools to telecommunications networks to demonstrate how Chinese firms erode digital sovereignty in the United States.

4

From Farms to Outer Space

How China Networks Sovereignty in the United States

On July 2nd 2020, democracy activist Nathan Law announced that he had fled Hong Kong out of concern for his safety under the Hong Kong national security law (NSL).[1] Article 38 of the NSL penalizes actions against the mainland government, not just in Hong Kong, and not just by Hong Kong citizens, but by anyone, anywhere in the world.[2] The NSL's pernicious global reach, with the latter type of offenders subject to criminal prosecution upon entry to Hong Kong, is a harbinger of the ambitions of the People's Republic of China regarding individual human rights. Equally damaging, though much less obvious, is that Article 43 of the law signals for the control of critical infrastructure through its provisions for private corporations, allowing the search and seizure of assets—including a firm's data.[3] Although the law is technically for Hong Kong, it extends the reach of the PRC government's national security enforcement globally, for individuals as well as for corporations that rely on data to provide critical infrastructure.

Chinese tech investment in the United States poses the risk that China will exert coercive control over established critical infrastructure in the United States. In this chapter, I demonstrate how that risk functions in such sectors as telecommunications, agriculture, space, and municipal management. Unlike the sectors discussed in later chapters of this book, critical infrastructure comes with established oversight practices regarding data gathering. While US critical infrastructure is subject to the illiberal trends of tech sector oversight, protections drawn from long-established legal precedents also exist. In this chapter, I focus on these areas to demonstrate that the illiberal creep of tech oversight is occurring even in areas with established regulations. As data becomes vital to the functioning of the global economy, critical infrastructure with enhanced data-gathering capabilities is becoming a progressively more important to national power.

The concept of critical infrastructure, which has historically been an area of national security concern, emerged during the Cold War to define the role of US industrial systems as a strategic resource during targeted nuclear attacks.[4] Over the years, the practice of defining critical infrastructure became a process of asserting national boundaries.[5] As data-driven systems have multiplied, the need for oversight of such systems has increased.[6] The erosion of critical infrastructure security undermines national boundaries, enabling data trafficking. While mainland Chinese tech investment in the United States presents specific risks in individual corporate transactions, it also presents systemic risks because of its potential to shape the way critical infrastructure is managed.

Three key threats emerge from dependency in critical infrastructure. The first threat is to economic competitiveness, stemming from asymmetric data gathering in emerging industries. This imbalance disadvantages the country that falls behind in a key critical infrastructure sector.

The second threat is to infrastructure security. Even if a security risk is likely but not certain, removing and replacing existing critical infrastructure or installing new protocols for evaluating security in response to the threat of a risk carries an economic cost. Firms that provide critical infrastructure become essential to national security. When another country can revoke access to that critical technology, data, or service via its private-sector firms, it can also inflict significant harm. There is also the threat that external national actors will gain backdoor (secret) access to critical infrastructure. Although backdoor access is the threat most frequently discussed by international governments and industry experts, often in relation to firms like the Chinese telecommunications giant Huawei, it is only part of the risk with respect to the relationship between national security and the private sector.

The third key threat emerges from nature of the data itself. A firm or country that gains access to critical data can develop a cutting-edge understanding of markets and trends. *Data integration*, the process of synthesizing data from different sources to transform it into meaningful information, amplifies this risk. Advanced data access opens the door to potential market manipulation, or the identification and control of specific strategic bottlenecks, as well as improved counterintelligence capabilities.

US firms have long engaged in predatory data gathering, but the role of the Chinese government in the Chinese tech sector's pursuit of cyber sovereignty is distinct. First, because of the Chinese market's scale, domestic firms, while they may wish to, do not need to expand their business globally. On the flip side, this dependence on the domestic market gives the Chinese government unique leverage over Chinese firms. Second, pressure from shareholders tends to drive US firms toward China in search of market growth. Finally, Chinese government practices are aimed at doing far more than just supporting Chinese firms: they undergird a vision of global digital oversight.

The growth of Chinese national champions abroad in areas of critical infrastructure ultimately has the effect of extending China's influence by integrating Chinese firms into global critical infrastructure. I argue in this chapter that cyber sovereignty is not just a claim to controlling national data and technical infrastructure, but also a process of deepening global dependence on essential technical networks based in China. While the term *wangluo zhuquan* is most commonly translated into English as "cyber sovereignty," some scholars also translate the term as "network sovereignty."[7] This offers a fresh way to think about how China's efforts to imprint its digital footprint on global critical infrastructure is both a goal and a process—the achievement of network sovereignty and the process of networking sovereignty. To demonstrate what networking sovereignty looks like, I examine Chinese corporate influence in the critical technical infrastructure areas identified above—telecommunications, agriculture, space, and smart cities—to demonstrate both the potential and already realized risks of systemic data trafficking.

Networking Sovereignty

Anne Marie Slaughter popularized the idea of networked sovereignty as an alternative to the Westphalian ideal of a sovereign state in which political control maps directly onto territorial control. She suggests instead that international organizations, and the relationships between nations, shape sovereignty.[8] Information studies scholar Maria Elena Duarte, in her work on indigenous infrastructure in the United States, connects the idea of networked sovereignty to the independence of technical systems in her work.[9] Duarte explains that true sovereignty includes network sovereignty, which is control over technical systems.[10] The idea of network sovereignty aligns with the network effects of technologies; the more users that participate in a networked technology, the more powerful it becomes. Thus, networking increases China's sovereign footprint. Indeed, networking sovereignty is not something that is established in discrete moments when states meet on official occasions, but rather something that happens every day through the use of technology. This is not Westphalian sovereignty in the sense of explicit government control over territory. Rather, it is akin to the way, in the words of international affairs scholar Gerard Toal, "certain technological paradigms and systems enable new forms of territorialization and territoriality."[11] Media studies scholar Lana Swartz, in her study of networked financial technologies, refers to this phenomenon as "transactional communities the size and scope of the nation."[12]

To network sovereignty, and thus augment national power, China relies on digital network effects. Chinese president Xi Jinping refers to this idea as *shuzi wenming*, often translated as "digital civilization."[13] In his speech at the 2021 World Internet Forum, President Xi articulated a vision of a world in which digital spaces "create a community of common destiny," a phrase Xi has used in other contexts to make the case for China's global leadership.[14] The idea of *shuzi wenming* underscores how China has accrued power in ways that obscure its transformation into a dominant global force, operating as what international relations scholar Oriana Skylar Mastro terms a "stealth superpower."[15] Mastro argues that China's efforts to extend economic influence drive foreign financial dependence on Beijing's resources. That is, China is taking advantage of ambiguous global regulations in the tech sector to advance its interests.[16]

In this chapter I discuss networking sovereignty rather than the Chinese government's preferred term, *cyber sovereignty*—national control over nationally affiliated digital resources—because the former term centers on how data movement enables control. However, the idea is more expansive than that. Chinese firms' global digital networks shape the country's capacity for national control of data. President Xi's vision of *shuzi wenming* has built on an increasingly clear Chinese regulatory focus beyond national borders.[17] Yet as we know, despite increasing government scrutiny, China continues to attract corporate investors willing to trade access to their data for access to China's vast market. Networking sovereignty leverages digital economies of scale to build a foundation for coercive control over critical infrastructure, building across the global tech sector what political scientist Sheena Chestnut Greitens calls "low-intensity forms of repression."[18]

As mentioned earlier, Chinese leaders have historically used information management practices to assert sovereignty over China's borderlands. Imperial gazettes and early tomes categorizing land and community populations enlarged the scope of Chinese authority into Xinjiang, Tibet, and Inner Mongolia during the premodern period. During the Mao era, the Chinese Communist Party documented ethnic minority communities in Tibet and Xinjiang to bolster contested claims of sovereignty.[19] In the Xi era, data management has emerged as a central tactic for exerting domestic authority.[20] For example, the Chinese government uses Tencent's WeChat to track Uyghur dissidents.[21] The COVID-19 era has demonstrated how platforms can enable state surveillance for everything from preventing disease to controlling population movement.[22]

As shown in previous chapters, data trafficking gives the Chinese government extensive access to data gathered by Chinese firms worldwide (including in the United States) and by foreign firms operating in China. These firms' platforms also build on analog modes of population surveillance, such as Communist Party committees that meet in the workplaces of state- and privately-owned firms in China; these meetings require overlapping appointments for both Party and corporate personnel, plus Party supervision of corporate personnel.[23] The tech sector's strategic importance renders tech firms vulnerable to pressure to accept government oversight, even informally and when not officially required. In fact, legal scholars Curtis Milhaupt and Wentong Zheng found that Party influence over corporate actions depended less on whether the state owned part or all of the enterprise and more on the sector's importance to the Party.[24]

The Chinese government uses its authority over the domestic market to force policy changes outside of China. In 2018, the Civil Aviation Administration of China instructed more than thirty international airlines, including Delta, United, and American, to refer to destinations in Taiwan as being in located in China if they wanted access to the Chinese market.[25] While the airlines demurred at first, they circumvented the problem by dropping the country name from their destinations entirely.[26] That same year the hotel chain Marriott faced similar pressures to remove Taiwan as an independent destination.[27] In 2021, the actor John Cena experienced such swift backlash after referring to Taiwan as a country that he immediately apologized profusely on social media, even before any official government involvement.[28] The Chinese social media platform WeChat censors content according to government standards even for users outside of China.[29] Such instances demonstrate China's ability to broaden its sovereignty footprint globally.

Networking sovereignty extends national influence. International relations scholar Pak Nung Wong asserts that international boundaries could face an onslaught of "digital statecraft," which relies on data to conduct state affairs and to shape international competition, including through "non-human agency."[30] Pak defines nonhuman agency as data-driven processes that occur when artificial intelligence analyzes data, eventually evolving into a self-learning "neural network" that adapts to the situation at hand, and later into "super intelligence," surpassing that of humans.[31] Networking sovereignty builds a foundation for coercive control over critical infrastructure through technical systems. Perhaps the most troubling in this regard is what communications scholars Nora Draper, Philip M. Napoli, and others have demonstrated: that the regulation of technology lags behind its use, thus making it particularly difficult to roll back present or future gains made by China's network of sovereignty via tech platforms.[32]

One high-profile area in which China has imprinted its "digital footprint" on critical infrastructure is telecommunications. In the following section, I examine how that sector contributes to China's data-trafficking capabilities and the practice of networking sovereignty.

Telecommunications Infrastructure

Communications networks are an important part of critical infrastructure and, by extension, national security.[33] The United States has long been a leading global provider of communications infrastructure, using the growth of its tech sector to constrain Chinese competitors.[34] The global Chinese telecommunications firm Huawei has challenged that dynamic and advanced its technology as the global standard for this new industry.[35] Huawei provides both 5G internet infrastructure and low-cost broadband infrastructure. Established in 1987 by former PLA engineer Ren Zhengfei, it is the largest global manufacturer of telecommunications equipment.[36] Huawei executives and Chinese government officials assert that its use of products to drive industrial standardization merely follows the US industries' model of providing high-quality products that are in high demand in the rest of the world. However, in 1996 the Chinese government dubbed Huawei a "national champion," a firm that both receives preferential policy consideration and advances national interests.[37] The company's below-market prices stem from what NATO researchers Kadri Kaska, Tomáš Minárik, and Henrik Beckvard argue are "more likely an outcome of China's domestic policy than its fundamental technological superiority over competitors."[38] The US corporate sector subsidizes the industrial competition of unprofitable firms through venture capital investment, while the Chinese government not only subsidizes firms but also explicitly directs national investment priorities.

Huawei was not state-run when it was founded. In 1997, the firm hired IBM to support its international expansion, and it has since emerged as a major global leader in broadband infrastructure development, especially for 5G.[39] Despite not having emerged directly from the state sector, Huawei has a long-standing relationship with the Chinese government. One of the firm's early slogans, which *Harvard Business Review* credits partially for the firm's success, evokes Ren's military background: "We shall drink to our heart's content to celebrate our success, but if we should fail, let's fight to our utmost until we all die."[40] Technology firms must share data with the Chinese government on demand, though legal scholars Milhaupt and Zheng note that compliance with government regulations is usually also in the firms' financial interest.[41] British cybersecurity researcher Nigel Inkster argued in 2018, "While Huawei seeks to present itself as a normal private-sector company, the reality is that in China no company is in a position to refuse cooperation with the state."[42] Inkster's statement has become only more apparent with forced data audits, per China's 2021 Data Security Law, and extraterritorial national security enforcement action against corporations, per Hong Kong's 2020 NSL.

Because of the firm's close relationship with the Chinese government and related concerns that Huawei's technology functions as a conduit for Chinese government data gathering, several countries including the United States, Australia, New Zealand, Japan, and Czech Republic have restricted the use of Huawei technologies. The United Kingdom and other countries have repeatedly revised their stance on the use of Huawei technology in their grid.[43] Germany allows the adoption of Huawei 5G infrastructure but only with careful guardrails. At the same time, other EU nations, such as Romania, Sweden, and Poland, have banned the Chinese tech giant from supplying equipment, thereby setting the stage for a long-term security battle within the EU about Chinese tech.[44]

Though the US market began limiting Huawei's investment in 2008, the firm was banned only after it had already installed its technology in the United States.[45] Huawei operates eighteen cell towers in cost-sensitive communities in Nebraska, primarily in the state's rural western areas.[46] In 2019, then-president Donald Trump and the Department of Commerce added Huawei and one hundred fourteen other companies to its Entity List for being involved "in the activities contrary to the national security or foreign policy interests of the United States."[47] In August 2020, the United States banned Huawei from obtaining items made with US technology or software, and added thirty-eight additional affiliates to the Entity List.[48]

Underfunded localities around the United States that installed Huawei tech had to then request financial support from the federal government to "rip and replace" Huawei information and communications technology infrastructure. Concerns about the infrastructure's economic competitiveness, infrastructural security, and data access date back to at least 2017.[49] However, local providers who removed the telecommunications equipment did not receive full funding for the undertaking until amendments to the Secure and Trusted Communications Networks Reimbursement Program were passed in 2020.

Huawei's involvement in US communications infrastructure has demonstrated the threat that Chinese corporate investment poses in data-driven US sectors. "Ripping and replacing" Huawei and ZTE infrastructure imposed estimated costs of approximately US$1.8 billion on local governments already facing financial strain.[50] Additionally, the vast amount of time spent on the effort delayed the development of functional, modern communications systems in rural areas of the United States. In other words, Huawei's relationship with the Chinese government has already undermined the development of critical infrastructure in vulnerable communities.[51]

In 2021, the United States Congress passed a US$65 billion bill for broadband deployment, access, and affordability to make broadband universally available throughout the United States at a low cost.[52] However, building out high-speed broadband requires an extensive long-term infrastructure investment of more than US$100 billion.[53] It also requires subsidies for trusted technology providers to construct affordable broadband infrastructure.[54]

Communications scholar Min Tang contends that China's policy positions, paired with government support for indigenous innovation, challenge US leadership in global communications infrastructure.[55] Indeed, Huawei's presence in the US communications market as a Chinese-government-subsidized, low-cost broadband provider allowed it to compete against firms from other countries, crowd them out of the market, and create economies of scale.[56] Countries with concerns about Huawei's infrastructure were thus at a disadvantage because the firm's market dominance left few feasible alternatives, particularly in rural areas where installing such infrastructure would be unprofitable.[57]

The communications giant's involvement in the US market is both an economic and security risk not only because of its current business practices but also because of the long-term implications of its relationship with the Chinese government. Critical infrastructure destabilization—due to "rip and replace" campaigns, anticompetitive behavior in essential technologies, and data audits—underscores the real risks posed to critical telecommunications infrastructure.[58] Such complexity is a prime example of the gridlock presented by the challenge of US data governance as it relates to China. There are both concrete concerns and hyperbolic threats. Carefully sorting through the risks is essential to both the credibility of policymakers and the protection of users. While significant in the context for telecommunications infrastructure, such issues also present a serious risk in food production.

Agriculture

Telecommunications infrastructure has received significant attention in the context of critical tech infrastructure, but it is just the tip of the iceberg. Chinese tech firms now also play an essential role in managing food production. In addition to providing digital infrastructure for communities, data serves as the foundation for precision agriculture, a technologically advanced practice that uses crop data to optimize yields. The National Research Council defines precision agriculture as "the application of modern information technologies to provide, process and analyze multisource data of high spatial and temporal resolution for decision making and operations in the management of crop production."[59] Thus, precision agricultural data is important not only with respect to what it reveals about farming communities but also because it affects the sustainability of the US food system.

The use of precision agriculture plays a prominent role in data trafficking. Precision agriculture offers a rich target for data trafficking because it relies on telecommunications infrastructure. AgriEdge Excelsior, a tool that manages farm-related data, from crop yields to finances, offers an illuminating example of the complicated web of connections that make a sector vulnerable to data trafficking.[60]

Syngenta, one of precision agriculture's major players, distributes AgriEdge.[61] The Swiss firm, which gathers and integrates agricultural data, was acquired in 2017 by ChemChina, the state-owned China National Chemical Corporation, for US$43 billion.[62] As of 2022, Syngenta represented the largest-ever foreign acquisition by a Chinese firm. It is also the top pesticide seller in North America.[63]

Complementing its pesticide and agrochemical sales, Syngenta collects data via drones and satellites to help farmers manage crop yields.[64] It licenses AgriEdge to provide precision agriculture to farmers, and sells seeds, fertilizers, and pest management services to AgriEdge users at a discount. In 2021, AgriEdge covered 10.5 million acres of arable US land, with more than 95 percent of growers using whole-farm management systems from Syngenta, suggesting an affinity for, if not a dependence on, the product.[65] AgriEdge has become integrated into the US agricultural landscape. Even the Ram, a popular ffarm vehicle that holds a greater than 25 percent share of the US truck market, now offers packages that include AgriEdge.[66]

Syngenta illustrates the importance of both national standards for data gathering and international collaboration on data acquisition practices. Based in Switzerland, the firm is not subject to oversight by the Committee on Foreign Investment in the United States. It already had a significant presence in the United States before its acquisition by ChemChina. Given the agricultural sector's prominence in US-China trade tensions, US farmers who depend on tech products from Chinese state-owned enterprises present an important area of concern.

The Syngenta acquisition makes a large segment of US agricultural data subject to a Chinese government firm. Such a dynamic presents a risk to the US agricultural system on an economic and security level. As in the case of telecommunications infrastructure, perceived insecurity can present almost as much of a challenge as actual risk. Just as the Huawei case demonstrated, even heightened risk perception or tensions between the two can lead to costly, widespread industrial disruption. Already vulnerable US farmers face the risk of being held liable for the costs of replacing the equipment. From a large-scale economic standpoint, the firm provides leverage for sanctions against the US food system. From a security standpoint, Syngenta's data collection via drones and satellites, though for farmers, presents an area of asymmetric data gathering between China and the United States (US firms cannot operate agricultural drones or satellites in the Chinese market).

The datafication of agricultural food production is a prime example of how security issues can emerge rapidly in a sector with no history of data security oversight, either internally or at the federal government level. Reliable food production is essential to survival. Data vulnerabilities in the food production system present an existential threat that is currently masked by the rapid technological evolution and globalization of the US agricultural sector. Such a high-impact, swiftly evolving data security issue underscores how frail the US data security system is, as well as the potential for a foreign party to control US agricultural infrastructure.

Outer Space

Systematic data gathering occurs in industries other than agriculture and fixed communications infrastructure. Access to outer space plays a transformative role in US economic competitiveness and critical infrastructure. Reliable access to satellites is the foundation for such crucial technologies as GPS, weather prediction, ridesharing platforms, and ATMs.[67] From an infrastructural security standpoint, space access makes nuclear advance warning systems possible, and grants the capacity to defend ourselves against a wide range of high-impact weapons systems. US Space Force Lieutenant General Nina Armagno has noted that the loss of control of space would dramatically diminish competitiveness with China.[68]

The Chinese government, for its part, views space power as enabling US dominance.[69] International relations scholar Carla Freeman argues that China's bids for dominance in segments of the global commons like space are dependent on strategic interest.[70] Reflecting China's strategic interest in space, some Chinese military experts argue that Chinese sovereignty extends from its airspace through outer space, absent a more thorough agreed-upon global definition.[71]

The satellite industry, which sits at the intersection of space and digital sovereignty, thus poses long-term challenges for preventing data trafficking from happening in space, complicating notions of what constitutes sovereign territory. Communications scholar Lisa Parks explains that satellite footprints are a "territorializing gesture that represents the power to regulate and alter the kinds of signals that move across it and the practices that occur within it."[72] Parks contends that through data uplinks and downlinks, satellites "represent the power to transform, redefine, and hybridize nations, territories, and cultures in a most material way."[73] Her analysis of the territorializing effects of satellite infrastructure demonstrates how networking sovereignty works. Data-driven technologies strengthen China's commercial space industry but also offer ways for government involvement in that sector to increase China's influence globally.

In her analysis, Parks considers how satellites complicated national boundaries in the former Soviet Union, but similar principles are at play in China. According to President Xi's "space dream," China aspires to be the leading global space power by 2045.[74] Xi's 2014 "Document 60" policy directive advanced the need for private enterprise investment in strategic national interest areas, including civil telecommunications and space infrastructure.[75] The policy presents telecommunications and satellite data gathering as central goals for China's long-term national interest. In parallel with Huawei's global growth in the telecommunications sector, China's commercial space industry has grown significantly since 2014. In November 2020, China had more than 160 commercial space corporations, half of which entered the market after 2014.[76] Globally, the country's deep space network has ground stations for satellite operations in Chile, Kenya, Kiribati, Namibia, Argentina, and Pakistan.[77] Also, between 2016 and 2020, China launched satellites on behalf of Algeria, Argentina, Belarus, Ethiopia, Indonesia, and Pakistan. Venture capital funding for Chinese space firms was roughly US$516 million in 2018, though this number pales in comparison to the US$2.2 billion US firms raised that same year.[78] Still, the industry has grown dramatically during the Xi era.

Mixed public–private ventures are prevalent in the Chinese commercial space industry, as is ownership by state-owned enterprises, even ones with broad global reach.[79] State-owned China Satcom (China Satellite Communications Co. Ltd.), for example, is a subsidiary of China Aerospace Science and Technology Corporation, which reports directly to the Ministry of Industry and Information Technology.[80] The company specializes in communications and broadcasting services and operates sixteen satellites with footprints in Australia, Southeast Asia, Europe, the Middle East, and Africa.[81] State-owned Chinese satellites and those with mixed ownership have global reach, but they also present a moderate to high risk of competition with US space systems for control of data.[82]

The Chinese commercial space industry and the Chinese military are closely connected. China's airspace is heavily militarized, meaning that parsing commercial and state investment in space is even more challenging than it is in most other sectors.[83] The Chinese government's advocacy for growing a commercial space program competes with its overarching military–civil fusion strategy (also referred to as military–civil integration), which requires private companies to share strategic assets with the military.[84] Within Chinese jurisprudence, the lack of clear legal jurisdiction in space further complicates any efforts by China's trade partners to discern the depth of the Chinese government's involvement in private space-related enterprises.

Chinese military–civil fusion in space presents several key commercial and security challenges. First, extensive Chinese military access to outer space threatens the long-term competitiveness of US commercial interests in the industry.[85] From a security standpoint, the growth of Chinese firms in the commercial space sector enhances the Chinese military's access to tools that can be used for satellite-driven cyber attacks.

US tech firms have also become heavily involved in the commercial space industry, challenging Chinese ambitions in space. However, the two countries have significantly different points of leverage because of the US tech sector's openness to Chinese investment and its exposure to the Chinese market. For example, NASA's US$2.9 billion contract with entrepreneur Elon Musk's commercial aerospace firm SpaceX exists in parallel with Musk's 22 percent stake in the electric car maker Tesla, for whom the Chinese market is its second-largest, accounting for roughly one-third of its revenue.[86] Space start-up Blue Origin, established by Amazon founder Jeff Bezos, also depends on the Chinese market. Despite no longer being an e-commerce platform in the Chinese market, Amazon sees a new product listing from China uploaded every 1/50th of a second.[87] Therefore, Chinese government or corporate entities interested in collaborating with Blue Origin could use access to the Chinese market as a bargaining tool.[88] Yet again, the dependence of US tech entrepreneurs on the Chinese market gives the Chinese government leverage over a key US commercial sector—this time, that of outer space.

Smart Cities

China's expansion into "smart city" technology gives the nation another opportunity to engage in commercial data gathering beyond its borders. Smart cities use cameras, sensors, and other electronic methods to gather data and manage urban resources and services. Smart-city surveillance models have emerged in established cities like Hangzhou, with Alibaba's commercial Hangzhou "city brain," and Shanghai, via private-sector "Citizen Cloud," which aggregates access to government services.[89] Related commercial technologies also track Muslims in China's Xinjiang Uyghur Autonomous Region, a practice anthropologist Darren Byler refers to as "terror capitalism."[90]

Smart-city efforts have been designed to increase data gathering about individuals in China, with some elements being developed for export to other cities. These include the use of sensors and connected devices to track everything from individuals' eating habits to their movement.[91] The competing private- and public-sector models demonstrate the sectors' combined efforts to construct data-gathering infrastructure at the city level. The types of data collected through such smart-city infrastructure tools as cameras and sensors raise questions about data traffic and consent. Facial recognition technology, which is rapidly becoming more prevalent in China, generates massive databases of logged images with alarming accuracy: faces with eyes open and shut, with and without masks.[92] This enables sophisticated tracking of individuals who merely set foot in the city.

Chinese firms have not yet exported smart-city technology to the United States, but cities around the globe have adopted the systems. Surveillance technology is perhaps the most widely analyzed form of such infrastructure; it includes police body cameras, facial recognition systems, license plate recognition systems, and wide-ranging video capture and management systems. Within the scope of data management, firms such as Alibaba, Huawei, and Tencent export data centers, servers, and cloud networks to other countries, including Tanzania, Malaysia, and Germany.[93] While the countries have jurisdiction over the data the digital infrastructure generates, the effectiveness of their oversight depends on their technical capacity to manage and govern mass amounts of data. Likewise, if countries have the capacity to construct their own critical infrastructure, they are less vulnerable to predatory practices. For example, the Chinese government funded the construction of Ethiopia's African Union headquarters, but installed surveillance technology throughout the building without the African Union's knowledge or consent.[94]

Integrated city management platforms—which are more commonly considered smart-city technology—include emergency response systems, command centers, and dispatch systems from Huawei, ZTE, Alibaba, and Dahua. They appear in Malaysia, Ecuador, Kenya, and Germany, among other countries.[95] Fintech infrastructure and energy systems, though less widely adopted, are also on the menu of services Chinese tech national champions offer for smart-city export. Chinese firms sell municipal services systems such as smart parking, traffic management systems, bus systems, smart streetlights, and smart waste management, to Malaysia, Kenya, Germany, and the United Kingdom.[96]

Municipal technical infrastructure is an important, yet underresourced area for data protection.[97] It forms the foundation of a functioning society, from law enforcement to fire and disaster management. Individual municipal systems can connect to larger city infrastructure in strategic areas such as voting and identity verification. The risks of data trafficking in a municipal system, therefore, threaten the core of functional, secure governance.

The risks for the smart-city sector mirror the "rip and replace" challenges seen with Huawei's broadband infrastructure installation. Merely the threat of Chinese government control over Chinese commercial infrastructure in cities produces significant cost and security implications. Cities must choose between spending resources to monitor their infrastructure, and facing the security risk that their subcontractors comply with data-sharing requests without their knowledge. Should Chinese government control over corporate practices intensify and, unlike in the Huawei case, the munipalities lack sufficient funds to replace vulnerable technical systems, they could be stuck with compromised infrastructure.

Data trafficking by firms dependent on the Chinese market threatens US power over domestic critical infrastructure through systems of dependency and financial rewards. Discussion of the risks posed by Chinese government policies requires careful acknowledgment of "China threat" literature, which complicates conversations about legitimate concerns around the Chinese government's ability to exercise control over the United States.

"China threat" literature, which characterizes the reemergence of China on the global stage as an existential risk to the United States, as discussed in Chapter 1, appeared in the early 1990s in parallel with the idea of "China's rise,"[98] emerging from what some scholars like Chengxin Pan argue to be self-fulfilling prophecies about China as a "threatening other."[99] Understanding how this threat is used to motivate US foreign policy is important because of the long-standing tradition of orientalist and white-supremacist "yellow peril" framing in US foreign policy.

However, a parallel risk exists: that critiques of "China threat" discussions may obscure the Chinese government's growing influence via Chinese firms. Specific concerns, such as those about serious risks related to the widespread control of critical infrastructure, may be subsumed by the broader idea of a "threat." The threat literature ratchets up tensions between the United States and China while often preventing targeted concerns from being heard. Hyperbolic "China threat" discourse creates gridlock that makes it even more important to consider the specific mechanisms through which China is using data to enlarge its sovereign footprint.

Conclusion

In this chapter, I have demonstrated how critical infrastructure, ranging from agricultural systems to communications equipment, empowers Chinese firms to exert coercive power over key resources in the United States. Each of these systems is critical on its own, but they also reinforce one another. For example, as communications scholar Christopher Ali explains, the political economy of rural broadband and the political economy of agriculture are intertwined.[100] Similarly, smart cities rely on telecommunications infrastructure, and satellites operate as such. Each of these types of critical infrastructure relies on data. Their power stretches far beyond any individual industry because of the data they gather. Chinese firms' capacity to influence US technical systems in a manner favorable to the Chinese government presents a serious risk to digital sovereignty.

Most critical infrastructure sectors have systems of oversight already in place. In emerging technologies, the same economic and national security threats exist, but without the regulatory protections found in sectors such as space, agriculture, fixed telecommunications infrastructure, and municipal building codes. Although such regulations fail to consider the challenges presented by new data-driven technologies, at least some protections—albeit imperfect ones—are in place in the form of established agencies tasked with managing the sectors. In an ideal world, new technologies would spur the development of bespoke protections for their intended users. Instead, amid an illiberal environment for tech sector oversight, users depend on the emergence of new laws and protections, which have been slow to come, have a limited impact, or, in the worst case, never materialize.[101]

Digital footprints are growing. As this occurs, what constitutes "critical" infrastructure broadens to include systems that gather user data through entertainment, payments, health care, and home appliances. There is a pronounced gap, however, between critical infrastructure (as traditionally conceptualized) and consumer infrastructures in terms of security aware-ness and risk.[102] The threat of control of a portion of the agricultural sector presents an economic and political challenge. Influence over the parent com-pany of a firm like TikTok also offers economic and political power and the ability to exert authority and offer financial rewards, while also gathering unique personal information about US society.

For example, when a social media platform recommends content based on a user's prior searches or content consumption, that is an instance of data integration. Data integration sends information about what you searched for online to a pop-up ad on your social media. This strategy also tracks users' locations, actions, beliefs, and other personal insights far beyond their pre-ferred running gear. Data integration transforms data into a social, political, and economic resource. The term *integration* emphasizes the lack of agency on the part of the data's original owners.

Data integration allows platforms, as well as a wide range of devices and infrastructure, to gather key intelligence by tracking everything from video and speech to online communities. These capabilities increase by the day with applications in artificial intelligence, surveillance, bioengineering, and a host of other emerging technologies. Cross-border data integration with government access and without user consent is data trafficking.

Improved user insights enhance competitiveness in industries from cosmetics to pharmaceuticals, providing an advantage to any country that controls the data involved.[103] Financial institutions already use data as collateral in asset-based corporate finance deals, something that a secured lender can sell in the event of default.[104] Personality insights based on how a user and their followers interact allow algorithms, automation, and human curation to spread disinformation and manipulation campaigns that build on established user biases, generating what communication scholars Samuel Woolley and Philip N. Howard term "computational propaganda."[105] The platforms then can "manufacture consensus," seeking to drive particular policy responses online by creating a bandwagon ef-fect.[106] Troves of consumer images, videos, and voice data can also en-hance synthetic media development, helping machine learning to create convincing fakes.

Examining data vulnerabilities in areas commonly regarded as critical in-frastructure uncovers the risks that data gathering presents even in sectors with extensive historical regulations. In emergent tech, which has few regulations in the United States, the risks are even greater. In the following chapters, my focus moves to emerging industries ranging from social media platforms to connected devices that offer case studies on how this shift in power operates when data trafficking occurs across the US and Chinese tech industries.

5

Social Media

The Algorithm as National Security Asset

The WeChat Users Alliance filed suit against the Trump administration in the Northern District of California on September 19, 2020, in response to the administration's effort to ban the platform by executive order.[1] If implemented, the mandate would have blocked the use of the Chinese app WeChat in the United States. Called an "app for everything," WeChat allows users to share voice and video messages, play video games, pay for goods and services, engage in videoconferencing, and use other services, including disease monitoring.[2] WeChat is a subsidiary of Tencent, one of China's tech "national champions," which is involved in data-driven product development in entertainment, fintech, health care, municipal management, cloud services, and more.[3] Because of WeChat's unique role as the only means for individuals to reliably communicate with others in China, the app constitutes an essential form of communication. Magistrate Judge Laurel Beeler of the US District Court for the Northern District of California ruled that blocking its use would violate users' First Amendment rights.[4] In response, the Biden administration eventually replaced the Trump ban with an executive order prioritizing greater oversight of data-gathering platforms in the United States.[5] But the lawsuit demonstrated that WeChat's network effects had transformed the platform into a critical communications infrastructure in the United States.[6]

Network effects, as I show in this chapter, enable monopolistic tech sector behavior that affects both the United States and China. WeChat is hardly the only offender. Popular platforms like TikTok and Grindr have used their powerful networks to gather data in the United States while owned by Chinese companies. Even after corporate or policies or practices change, trafficked data remains part of China's data corpus. Paired with the normalization of exploitative data-gathering practices in the United States and with extensive Chinese government data-gathering practices, this chapter shows how network effects on social media form a critical foundation for data trafficking.

Social data generates tools that corporations and individuals use—and abuse—for social and political purposes. Platforms that optimize their algorithms through mass data collection accrue tremendous power over users.[7] US social media platforms are notorious for misuse, ranging from the rise of damaging surveillance campaigns by platforms headquartered in Silicon Valley to Facebook's distribution of COVID-19 vaccine disinformation.[8] Meanwhile, the Chinese government controls user data gathered from social media platforms with operations in China, using tools such as civil and criminal penalties, forced data localization, and national security audits.

As social media platforms become increasingly necessary, they become critical infrastructure. Communications scholar Megan Finn argues that social media platforms have become central to the information order, a system characterized by different infrastructures, institutions, technologies, and practices that shape how societies share important insights.[9] While Finn's work underscores how social media platforms operate in the context of acute disasters such as earthquakes, challenges such as the COVID-19 pandemic, and election interference highlight the importance of social media in managing chronic problems. Communications scholar Elizabeth Ellcessor observes that firsthand accounts of emergencies posted on social media, what she terms "testimony," are foundational not just to how we share information about crises but also to how we even know or understand what they are.[10] Yet despite the ever more critical role of social media platforms, the US tech sector's illiberal bent allows all firms operating in the United States to gather and exploit data with impunity.[11] At the same time, dependence on social platforms turns users against regulators who attempt to shape the social media landscape.[12]

Chinese social media platforms widen the range of surveillance tools available to the Chinese government for gathering intelligence, expanding global market share, and accruing soft power. Social platforms offer source material that can be used to generate fake images, carry out blackmail, and manipulate messaging to key constituencies.[13] The photos, videos, and sounds shared on social platforms also facilitate the development of other strategic tools for intelligence gathering, including digital forensics, sentiment analysis, phishing, and profiling.[14] And of course, they provide a social, cultural, and technical map that can be used for understanding and exploiting weaknesses in the US system.

Data trafficking by Chinese social platforms is asymmetrical: the US innovation system generates data resources for China, but the United States does not benefit equally from China in return. The Chinese government has banned US social media platforms such as Facebook and Twitter since 2009.[15] Judge Beeler's ruling notes that WeChat's singular importance as communications infrastructure between the United States and China emerged because of prohibitions on US tech firms in China. US firms have little opportunity to access Chinese users' data. While US companies lack access to China's social media market, Chinese firms are free to grow their market share in the United States. WeChat's critical role did not develop in a vacuum. This dynamic grants Chinese firms operating in the United States a distinct advantage in developing technology built on US social data. WeChat, TikTok, and other social media platforms owned by Chinese companies that are operating or have operated in the United States leverage the tech industry's confusing user consent practices to gather data widely. US- and Chinese-owned platforms alike collect and integrate data based on the thinnest of consent agreements. Chinese platforms also face additional economic and legal pressure from the Chinese government to share the data they gather abroad with Chinese regulators.

Exploitative social media practices become an even greater threat when data moves between political systems that differ in the relationship between data, users, and the state. Differences in the US-China context empower the Chinese government to leverage data gathered in the United States as an intelligence asset. In fact, the extraterritorial reach established by Hong Kong's National Security Law and China's Data Security Law subject US-based users to potential Chinese legal enforcement actions. The first arrest of a US citizen for Chinese national security crimes outside of mainland China has already occurred in Hong Kong, and the extraterritorial application of Chinese government censorship practices has increased on platforms such as TikTok and WeChat.[16]

In this chapter, I examine three social platforms that have been shaped by China's data governance practices. Tech conglomerates with headquarters in China currently own TikTok and WeChat. Similarly, a Chinese firm previously controlled Grindr. The platforms serve as critical infrastructure in specific contexts but are regulated only loosely in the United States. The combination of their important function and loose oversight makes them an appealing target for data trafficking.

Most people are familiar with TikTok as one of the most popular social platforms in the United States and around the globe, especially among young adults, teens, and tweens. Fewer users know that it is controlled by

Beijing-based ByteDance, much less understand the implications of that ownership. Furthermore, Grindr, the world's largest LGBTQ+ social media platform, was owned by Chinese firm Beijing Kunlun Tech Co. Ltd. (now Kunlun Tech Co. Ltd.), before a US government-forced sale to San Vicente Acquisition LLC in 2020.[17] The platform serves as a critical form of communication infrastructure for the LGBTQ+ community.

These three platforms' networks make them critical communication infrastructure. Not only is WeChat the most effective means of communicating with people in China, thanks to the Chinese government's constraints on US social media platforms in the country, but it also plays an essential role in marketing, communications, and payments for US companies operating in China. TikTok's network effects have generated legions of adoring fans willing to advocate for the network. During Russia's invasion of Ukraine, the White House briefed TikTok influencers about the conflict because of their outsized role in informing the public.[18] Because of Grindr's economic heft and important social community, rather than shutting it down, the US government waited for Kunlun Tech Co. Ltd. to sell the platform to a suitable buyer. Using these three cases, I show below how Chinese-owned social media platforms traffic sounds, images, videos, and networked social relationships. I also explore how firms based in China exploit the data of US-based consumers, leveraging network effects to preserve access to the US market. Such practices emerge from the toxic combination of loose US data regulatory policy and intensive Chinese government data oversight.

Social Platforms as Critical Infrastructure

In discussing how social media platforms take on critical infrastructure characteristics, communications scholars Jean-Christophe Plantin, Carl Lagoze, Paul N. Edwards, and Christian Sandvig identify two key threads in the field of infrastructure studies.[19] One focuses on large technical systems and another, highlighted in this chapter, focuses on how infrastructure shapes communities, nations, and life worlds. Internet historian Kevin Driscoll expresses the idea well: "Digital communication networks are the infrastructures through which we keep in touch with family, argue about politics, find romantic connection, look up health information, and seek emotional support."[20] By influencing how people participate in their communities, nations, and lifeworlds, social platforms are infrastructure not just for communication but also, more broadly, for social participation.

TikTok, a major global cultural force with over one billion users worldwide,[21] has grown famous for user-generated content and parody videos. It was during the COVID-19 pandemic, however, that the platform became a central feature of social life around the world.[22] Apart from Facebook, only TikTok has succeeded in reaching 3 billion global downloads.[23] TikTok is particularly influential in shaping young people's lives, communication systems, and worldviews.[24]

By banning financial transactions with TikTok, the Trump administration's August 6, 2020, executive order attempted a de facto ban of the platform. In response, TikTok sued the administration, generating documents demonstrating that the platform and its users see it as critical infrastructure. The authors of a memorandum in support of *TikTok v. Trump* refer to TikTok as a "virtual town square" where millions of individuals engage in speech.[25] The same document also likens TikTok to a "news wire feed" that electronically transfers news to the public and other media and is therefore not subject to oversight by presidential executive orders.[26] After the Biden Administration rescinded the TikTok ban in 2021, the platform's role in communication became even more critical.

Despite these characterizations, TikTok publicly presents itself as a platform that does not engage in political speech. Yet its stance has little bearing on how users use it or on its potential political impacts.[27] The complex politics of the social media were on full display when K-pop fans mobilized en masse to claim, but not use, free tickets to the Trump rally in Tulsa, Oklahoma.[28] In this case, the network effect of TikTok's user base turned the platform into a form of critical political communications infrastructure. More broadly, TikTok illustrates how a platform originally designed to offer light entertainment can transform into critical communications infrastructure for a massive global community.

Grindr, the social networking app for the LGBTQ+ community, presents another striking example. On its website, Grindr claims that it has "millions of daily users who use . . . location-based technology in almost every country in every corner of the planet."[29] Grindr's utility far outstrips its reputation as a hookup app. Public health and policy scholar Sam Miles notes that social platforms such as Grindr do more than provide access to queer male spaces; they increasingly constitute them.[30] Historian Andrew D. J. Shield asserts that Grindr's "semi-public profiles and private exchanges" operate as "valuable sites for understanding not only sexuality, but also social cultures of a primarily gay space."[31] Indeed, the platform is so dominant that critics argue that it reinscribes existing hierarchies of whiteness, nationality, and economic status through its pervasive hold on queer male social culture in many of the countries where it operates.[32]

Similarly, communications scholar Jean-Christophe Plantin and ethnologist Gabriele de Seta contend that WeChat is not just a social media platform but one of the "critical infrastructures of everyday life."[33] WeChat ranked as the fifth-largest social media platform in the world in 2021 and the largest in China.[34] Overseas Chinese communities make up a large portion of WeChat's user base in the United States.[35] It has more than 1 billion active monthly users worldwide.[36] China's bans on other social media platforms cemented WeChat's role as the country's go-to communications platform.[37] But WeChat's ability to operate in the Chinese market depends on its willingness to conform to Chinese laws.

How Tech Firms Traffic User Data

As in the case of critical infrastructure, US regulatory fragmentation enables cross-border data-gathering on social media. Because managing emerging data products would place a significant burden on regulators and corporations, the result is primarily a system of industrial self-governance. There are stronger incentives for resource extraction than for safety and national security. A similar phenomenon occurred in the US energy industry. Longtime practices of industrial self-governance aligned with the US market's leading-edge demand for petroleum. Financial incentives to ignore climate change enabled short-term economic gains but undermined long-term US national security interests in preserving a stable climate. Data presents a similar challenge in which short-term economic interests and mid- to long-term interests diverge. As with fossil fuels, damage from data extra extraction is permanent.

The US investment environment, which welcomes outside capital, supports a system wherein other countries can invest in US technologies, learn from them, and grow.[38] US companies such as Meta, Google, and Apple use this permissive regulatory landscape to develop new products based on social data collected via their platforms.[39] When this system works, it introduces new products, services, and industries.[40] But algorithms and data-gathering practices are competitive tools for firms. Opening themselves up to further regulation of their data-gathering or outside investment chafes against free-market growth principles. Even if companies voluntarily submitted to increased oversight, the US government lacks the technical capacity to comprehensively perform such a massive undertaking.

Users often do not fully understand what they share when they use a service. For example, the data and methodology that Cambridge Analytica built out through its Facebook personality test experiments allowed the firm to "micro-target" specific voters to receive disinformation in the 2016 election.[41] Chinese spies leverage US-based platforms such as LinkedIn and Facebook to legally gather intel and share disinformation.[42] On August 27, 2019, Edward Wong of *The New York Times* reported that Chinese spies were using LinkedIn to mine information about users.[43]

Despite such concerns, US government officials have found it challenging to monitor the data storage and security practices of firms in the United States. After all, these companies offer some of the most generous donations to their campaign coffers and increase US wealth through stock market gains.[44] Federal Trade Commission antitrust efforts, which focus on specific platforms, place pressure on tech firms to avoid acting as what media studies scholar Siva Vaidhyanathan terms "antisocial media," or media that undermines the social contract and good governance.[45] Yet current US regulations are straining under the pressure to provide comprehensive oversight. Demanding transparent consent agreements, data storage locations, and national data regulations for any markets where data will be shared, as well as other security measures, requires more resources and authority than US regulators currently possess.

TikTok's privacy policy provides limited specifics, apart from some wording about restrictions on the movement of data beyond rhe European Economic Area. It also includes an email address individuals can use to request the removal of personal information stored on the platform. My repeated queries to this address received no response. Further, the privacy policy notes that such requests do not ensure "complete or comprehensive removal of the material" unless the user is under 18 years of age and located in California.[46] Thus, the app's security infrastructure allows data to be gathered and moved with consideration only for the European Economic Area's General Data Protection Regulation and, to a limited degree, the California Consumer Privacy Act.[47] TikTok's privacy policy also notes that the app can share any data it gathers with its corporate group, ByteDance. A class-action lawsuit in California, settled for US$92 million, one of the largest payouts in the history of privacy lawsuits, contended that the app sends private, personally identifiable data and biometric data to China without user consent.[48] TikTok's privacy policy fails to explicitly protect users from data trafficking.[49]

TikTok's US privacy policy offers conflicting information about its information-sharing practices. The firm contends that it processes user data only in the United States and third countries such as Singapore.[50] Complicating matters, TikTok's engineering teams remain in the PRC, necessitating access to global user data. Rather than ensuring a firewall between its operations in China and global user data, the company states that it seeks to "minimize" ByteDance's data access.[51] According to its US privacy policy, the firm reserves the right to share user data with its parent company and with law enforcement officials.[52] Such data includes sensitive biometric information that far exceeds the type of data users might expect to share with a global entertainment platform.[53]

TikTok made global efforts to enhance transparency with respect to its data handling after the Committee on Foreign Investment in the United States launched an investigation into the firm on November 1, 2019.[54] But these efforts obscure as much as they reveal. In its Transparency Reports, TikTok discloses to the public which countries request its data but conceals how it aggregates that data. The company offers no insight into whether it aggregates data in individual countries or at the corporate level. TikTok's data security policies comply with data security regulations to the extent required by law, which means that even if a national government has exploitative policies, TikTok will assent to them. The company did respond to specific inquiries from the executive branch via CFIUS, as well as to related inquiries from the United States Congress.[55] Yet the absence of any formal reporting requirements limits disclosures on how the company moves data, what ByteDance does with aggregated data insights, and the degree to which the Chinese government has access.

TikTok clearly states that it complies with different regulations around the world. Cambodia, Hong Kong, Indonesia, Laos, Philippines, Singapore, Thailand, Japan, Korea, Taiwan, Vietnam, Malaysia, and Macau are reviewing or have restricted the use of the app.[56] In response to TikTok's data-gathering practices, countries worldwide have been limiting access to the platform. India has banned the app entirely, and Pakistan imposed temporary restrictions on the app four separate times.[57] Australia forbids the app on devices owned by its Department of Defence, and Japan is said to be considering a ban.[58] The variance in the platform's standards according to local law highlights how national regulations shape its data-gathering and extraction processes. Chinese government oversight of the data that Chinese firms gather thus depends not exclusively on China's policies but on the local environment as well.

The US government has taken small steps to respond to TikTok's data gathering in a characteristically piecemeal fashion, including executive orders, congressional hearings, and CFIUS oversight. TikTok has a strategic partnership with the US tech firm Oracle, in which Oracle would become a "trusted tech partner," that would permit TikTok to operate in the United States after the Trump administration's August 6 executive order.[59] However, the ambiguity of the term "trusted tech partner" underscores the US government's lack of tools with which to enforce new data relationships on firms operating in the United States.

The Biden administration's executive order revoking the TikTok ban empowered the US Department of Commerce and other agencies to evaluate the risk of "connected software applications designed, developed, manufactured, or supplied by persons owned or controlled by, or subject to the jurisdiction or direction of, a foreign adversary."[60] This important first step toward centering data in policymaking still must contend with the limitations of US federal power. On June 17, 2022, BuzzFeed News' Emily Baker-White reported that China-based employees have repeatedly accessed non-public TikTok data, even as the company was undergoing CFIUS review. While the company has pushed back against Baker-White's reporting in the media, the fact that these accusations are playing out in the court of public opinion underscores the difficulty of regulating tech firms. Furthermore, the company's responses to inquiries about the BuzzFeed report from a Federal Communications Commissioner and Republican Senators underscore the ad hoc nature of tech regulation in the United States. The company's assurances are carefully-worded, voluntary promises to improve the app's security, a much less restrictive standard than the mandatory national security audits parent company ByteDance faces in China.[61] Ultimately, efforts to exercise oversight over TikTok face the same types of roadblocks from corporate advocates that constrain regulation of the US tech sector. This illustrates the type of gridlock that confounds an effective resolution to data trafficking.

TikTok is not the only social platform that has gathered extensive images and videos and then moved that data to China. Some of the most intimate examples of Sino-US data trafficking occur via dating platforms, on which physical and emotional intimacy creates a rich trove of personal data, including text, images, and video. The trafficking of personal data from dating platforms such as the LGBTQ+ dating app Grindr offers a particularly evocative space in which to explore the intimate violations of data trafficking.

The Grindr case stands out because it underscores the impossibility of rectifying the damage caused by gathering and moving sensitive data. Beijing Kunlun Tech Co., Ltd. acquired 60 percent of Grindr in 2016, then wholly acquired it in 2018.[62] From 2016 to 2020, Grindr collected a wide range of personal data about its users, from HIV status and sexual preference to shared images and videos.[63] Following China's 2017 Cybersecurity Law, Grindr was required to store data on Chinese-government-run servers.[64] It also ran engineering facilities in China from 2016 to 2018.[65] CFIUS, following concerns expressed by US senators Edward Markey and Richard Blumenthal, called on Beijing Kunlun to divest itself of Grindr because of concerns about US national security.[66] Even though San Vicente Acquisition Partners, based in West Hollywood, California, bought Grindr from Beijing Kunlun in 2020,[67] the Chinese parent company's temporary ownership enabled data trafficking.

Grindr emerged in the popular imagination as a hookup site with a repository of nude images of men. Informatics scholar Amanda Karlsson contends that such photos are an essential form of communication that can convey humor, harass, or seduce.[68] Film scholar Evangelos Tziallas posits that the nude images and erotic chat reward users for being on the platform, underscoring the importance of the network.[69] Users revel in their sexuality under presumed anonymity. Meanwhile, the platform gathers extensive intimate information about individuals, such as their likes, looks, and health information.

Grindr's community standards enumerate how users can keep themselves physically safe on the app. By contrast, its privacy policy, posted on a different page, obscures how the platform exploits user data. Notably, it advises users to not share any information they would not want to end up in the hands of a third-party contractor.[70] But users received little other warning as the firm shared not just information about users' HIV status but also other highly sensitive data with third-party apps through April 2018.[71]

Grindr's privacy policy muddled the risks that data aggregation can pose to users. When owned by Beijing Kunlun Tech Co. Ltd., the privacy policy gavethe rights to individual user data to the following entities: "our parent company, any subsidiaries, joint ventures, or other companies under common control."[72] It went on to state, "If another company acquires our company, business, or our assets, that company will possess the Personal Data collected by us and will assume the rights and obligations regarding your Personal Data as described in this Privacy Policy."[73] Users therefore had only minimal protections from third-party firms and no protection from data acquisition by other companies that are related to Grindr or that might buy it. Further, the privacy policy stated explicitly that local laws might not protect user data. The company's original privacy policy read as follows:

> Your Personal Data may be processed in the country in which it was collected and in other countries, including the United States, where laws regarding Personal Data may be less stringent than the laws in your country. Therefore, in some circumstances, you might be left without a legal remedy in the event of a privacy breach. By submitting your Personal Data, you agree to this transfer, storage and/or processing, including all associated risks.[74]

Nowhere did the policy state that Grindr's parent company (which, again, had access to all user data) stored data in a country with government access to data centers. The policy left users vulnerable to data acquisition and mismanagement by Beijing Kunlun and by the government agencies that store the firm's data in China. In addition, it underscored that US data security policies offer less protection than those of many nations around the world.

Even with FIRRMA requirements for corporate acquisitions, considerable gaps in oversight remain. CFIUS faces resource constraints. How corporations store and transfer user data becomes more complex with each passing year. The Grindr case demonstrates how data trafficking can occur. Beijing Kunlun Tech Co. Ltd. committed no illegal acts, but it transferred huge amounts of data.

The Grindr divestment strongly echoes the TikTok debacle: in forcing, or attempting to force, the sale of a Chinese-owned tech firm, the US government failed to fully resolve concerns about international data gathering. Following San Vicente's acquisition of Grindr, the framing of the app's data gathering shifted. The firm updated its privacy policy, and the new text foregrounds the data security risks users accept when they store their data in the United States:

> **Grindr LLC is a U.S.-based Company.** By using the Grindr Services, you are transmitting information to the United States. If you are a resident of

another country, note that the United States may not afford the same privacy protections as your country of residence.[75]

As a result, Grindr users now are vulnerable to the commercial data brokering of the US system, rather than (as before) to weaknesses in both the US and Chinese data security systems. Perhaps even more importantly, the status of trafficked user data underscores that action after an issue has been identified is helpful, but does not resolve the issue. Much like regulations on carbon released into the atmosphere, they only address future issues, not the consequences of previous actions.

The US government's efforts to restrict Chinese corporate access to sensitive data such as individuals' HIV status and sexual orientation demonstrates the link between data sovereignty and national security. While CFIUS ultimately forced Beijing Kunlun to sell Grindr,[76] the sale failed to prevent the firm's data from being used by the firm to generate new AI tools or intelligence-gathering tools.

As TikTok and Grindr demonstrate, the absence of clear-cut US government data management guidelines allows companies to avoid revealing what they do with their users' data. Social data available from such platforms complement other sensitive data acquired via Chinese government hacks, such as security clearance information, travel records, and credit ratings. These cases shed important light on how the lack of concrete data regulations permits, and even facilitates, data trafficking both in the United States and abroad.

How Network Effects Enable Data Trafficking

Because social media, like other critical infrastructure such as food production and telecommunications, pose significant risks to national security, it is worth delving deeper into how their distinctive networks enable data trafficking. Such platforms have superpowers for gathering information about their users, including location, screen time usage, content choices, phone hardware, installed apps, network, and countless other insights.[77] When the Trump administration attempted to force the sale of TikTok to a US company, China's Ministry of Commerce updated its list of "forbidden or restricted technology exports" to include "personalized information recommendation services based on data analysis."[78] The ministry did not ban the export of TikTok's algorithm outright. But it did require central government approval to export the algorithm. Requiring export controls reflects the Chinese government's determination that TikTok's algorithm is a national security asset.

ByteDance developed TikTok both by protecting its Chinese sister company Douyin from competition and exploiting the open US tech innovation ecosystem. TikTok's parent company acquired the US-based short-form video app Musical.ly in November 2017. Musical.ly, on which users could create and post lip-synch video of popular songs, merged with the TikTok app on August 2, 2018.[79] TikTok's status as a dominant app globally drives ByteDance's rich user data acquisition.[80]

TikTok's addictive algorithm forms the foundation of its rich network. From a technical standpoint, large quantities of social data improve algorithms to drive user engagement and downloads. They can also sharpen the accuracy of surveillance technologies such as facial and voice recognition. While we know that network effects have a positive feedback loop where more users enhance the algorithm's accuracy at targeting users, permissive US corporate governance practices make it difficult to know precisely how TikTok uses its network to grow.

ByteDance's status as a private firm presents a challenge for monitoring how it uses data from TikTok's US operations. Few mechanisms exist through which the US government can fully assess how private firms use data, beyond what they voluntarily share. ByteDance has tried to separate its TikTok business unit from its Chinese operations. The firm's headquarters are in China, but its legal corporate domicile is officially the Cayman Islands. However, TikTok's privacy policy allows it to share data with other parts of its "corporate group." When Senator Ted Cruz questioned TikTok's representative about their privacy policy at a US Senate hearing, the firm's representative argued that it maintained "no affiliation" with Beijing ByteDance Technology (renamed Beijing Douyin Information Service Limited in May 2022), the arm of parent company ByteDance responsible for Chinese social media platforms Douyin and Toutiao.[81] However, TikTok's position as the subsidiary of a private firm operating in the United States makes it difficult to verify such a claim.

ByteDance's Beijing headquarters location amplifies the range of tools the Chinese government can use to access the firm's data, from national security audits to military access requests.[82] The Chinese government acquired a 1 percent stake in the firm along with the right to one of three board seats in April 2021.[83] The asymmetrical access to information for US regulators versus Chinese regulators about a Chinese-run platform operating in the United States offers a stunning example of how government policies shift access to powerful data sets.

US policymakers are in a difficult position—given the app's place in the US consumer landscape, and its widespread economic integration—and limited regulations exist on social media platforms in the United States. The tech landscape supports the platform's growth in the United States. However, the US government lacks the capacity to rein in or, frankly, even accurately assess TikTok's data trafficking because of its market power.

TikTok took advantage of its corporate influence in the US system as a member of the US tech lobbying group NetChoice, a trade organization that pushes back against tech company critics.[84] Founded in 2001, the group advocates for "light touch" internet regulation, embodying the extractive ethos that gave rise to the contemporary US tech landscape. The organization contends that "consumers know best the products and services they need."[85] The statement emphasizes the demand-side structure of the US digital economy, though it ignores how the supply side of the business works. Namely, to attract users, companies obscure their data-gathering, integration, and transfer practices.[86] In joining with other corporations operating in the United States, TikTok benefitted from a long tradition of advocacy for corporate financial interests regardless of the national security conflicts those interests represent.

WeChat similarly enables data trafficking through its network effects. For individual users, WeChat enables connection that is unavailable on other platforms, combining the functionality of Facebook, Instagram, Twitter, and PayPal, but for the Chinese market. It is easy to understand why someone would be willing to share user device data, photos, audio, video, and other content with WeChat's parent company, Tencent, in exchange for such connection.

WeChat also offers crucial infrastructure for businesses operating in China and individuals with contacts there. Its connectiion to digital payment apps in China further complicates the position of US firms. In addition to WeChat's role in communications, it is the primary conduit of customer payments to US firms in China. Walmart, for example, depends on accepting payments via WeChat for its operations in China.[87] General Motors develops WeChat-based ad campaigns for the Chinese market, its largest global market.[88] Given that US companies rely on WeChat to do business in China,

WeChat does not have to depend solely on lobbying from social media trade groups. It can pressure firms across the US industrial spectrum to lobby on its behalf. WeChat's ability to leverage its corporate contacts highlights another way network effects enable data trafficking. This allows China to network sovereignty not just through the platform's users but also through corporations fearful of being denied access to WeChat.

Ultimately, the network effects of social media drive data trafficking. Resources like user advocacy and corporate lobbying empower Chinese tech firms operating in the United States. When users depend on these platforms, they advocate against restrictions on access. Corporations and the organizations that represent them have a financial incentive to ensure their continued place in the US corporate ecosystem. Continued market access generates data that forms the foundation for ever more targeted algorithms to increase the platform's user base.

Some Impacts of Social Data Trafficking

Advantage in Sino-US Artificial Intelligence Competition

The strategic data TikTok gathers embodies a key strength of the Chinese tech innovation ecosystem. AI, the computer science field that uses smart machines to perform tasks that typically require human intelligence, is at the core of the growth of the global economy. With control of TikTok and WeChat, plus access to Grindr's data, the Chinese government can achieve important gains in developing AI tools. The private sector's improved ability to create products is only part of the picture, though. As we know, Chinese firms face multiple types of pressure from the Chinese government to share both their data and products. Holes in the US regulatory system are worrisome because they allow firms like TikTok to accumulate massive amounts of data to create AI products.

Synthetic media, colloquially known as "deepfakes," are used by some governments, corporations, and individuals to mislead people on social media. The technology of this tool, which relies on large social data corpora, is still evolving. Broadly speaking, synthetic media is real-looking media that is artificially produced, modified, or manipulated by automated tools, and it becomes more sophisticated as it accesses more data.[89] Fake speech, for example, is more difficult to detect than fake writing, counterfeit images, or fake video.[90] Deepfakes have been used most prominently and successfully by Russian trolls, but they have also been employed by homegrown terrorist groups. Russian actors used them in the 2016 and 2020 US presidential elections to influence election outcomes.[91]

TikTok offers a rich repository of video, audio, and image files for generative adversarial networks (GANs), machine learning models that generate novel images, text, video, and audio by comparing new data with large sets of existing data. GANs are useful for, among other things, producing deepfakes. The website thesecatsdonotexist.com uses machine learning to generate images of cats that are not actual, real-life animals and offers a helpful way of understanding how GANs work. Using real photos, an algorithm trains a GAN to produce false images that look authentic. GANs improve as their databases acquire diverse images. The same process is used with video and voice.

TikTok's US collection practices—including user metadata, location, screen time, phone hardware, installed apps, and network and proxy server information—already face state and federal lawsuits.[92] The Federal Trade Commission fined TikTok a record US$5.7 million for illegally collecting the data of children.[93] In California, a lawsuit against the firm alleges that the company shared face data with servers in the PRC.[94]

WeChat data also contributes to the development of AI tools. However, whereas ByteDance is a relative newcomer to the Chinese tech scene, WeChat's parent company, Tencent, is, as we've seen, one of China's tech "national champions," responsible for developing tools such as AI-based court systems, health diagnostics, and smart cities.[95] Tencent's scale, scope, and close government ties make WeChat data an appealing target for exploitation across a range of national sectors, including smart cities, self-driving cars, medical research and development, finance, and retail.[96]

WeChat and TikTok play multiple important economic roles. I have noted how, as key communication platforms in the United States for both entertainment and business, they gather extensive user data that facilitates AI growth. As platforms for advertisers and the influencer industry, as well as a foundation of US-China business ties, their economic role in the United States complicates policymakers' efforts to constrain their data-exploitation practices. However, they also pose a significant threat to the security of critical communications infrastructure.

Building Profiles of Sensitive Groups

Trafficking one individual's data might not ultimately result in a direct attack on their personhood, as with revenge porn or identity theft, yet it facilitates the development of technologies used to carry out such attacks. Moreover, someone based in the United States would find it difficult to trace whether their personal information contributes to technologies that foreign governments create to attack others. Combining data from significant hacks with that acquired via data trafficking creates a treasure trove for actors engaged in intelligence gathering, the cultivation of counterintelligence assets, and community modeling.

US public-sector employees face disproportionate risks from Chinese-owned social platforms because of their positions of public trust.[97] In response to this threat, the US military restricted the use of TikTok on military phones in December 2019, but this policy failed to fully achieve its aim because of the established pervasiveness of platform surveillance.[98] The app can monitor military members' households, gathering device information, location data, and user profiles, plus what the app describes in its privacy policy as simply "information about you from other publicly available sources."[99] Further, military personnel and their family members can use TikTok on personal phones—a loophole that introduces risk because rich profiles of users can still be built without work data. Personal accounts can be just as revealing as work accounts, or even more so. Data trafficking is so powerful because it can extend beyond one's commercial transactions and into the intimacy of family and home life.

Grindr's acquisition presented similar challenges in profile building, particularly because of the platform's focus on dating and sexuality. Following the 2015 Office of Personnel Management hack, the Chinese government allegedly acquired data stored by the agency about individuals with security clearances. No great mental leap is needed to imagine the national security risks that arise when the Chinese government gains access to US government employees' intimate exchanges, images, and videos, particularly when combined with security clearance information. Until 2011, the US armed forces subjected US service members to "don't ask, don't tell," a policy requiring that they conceal their sexual orientation at work or lose their job. On April 12, 2019, the Trump administration reinstated a ban on service by transgender soldiers, later revoked by the Biden administration on January 25, 2021.[100] Due to concerns about discrimination and professional consequences, some nonmilitary US government employees also avoid disclosing their sexual orientation.[101]

But the Grindr issue points to a larger concern: that any policies or practices in the US government that create a discriminatory environment for employees offer an opening for Chinese government intelligence. Historian and Biden National Security Council director for China Julian Gewirtz and communications scholar Moira Weigel note that the risks presented by LGBTQ+ government workers' confidential data underscore the risk that all US government employees generate on social platforms.[102] The mosaic of useful intelligence that security clearance data can create when combined with dating app data is a particularly potent example.

Silicon Valley's illiberal bent enables poor encryption practices to thrive in the United States. As the only reliable communications infrastructure between the United States and China, WeChat holds a communication monopoly over people with ties to China who wish to maintain contact with friends, families, research groups, and business partners. WeChat users with China-based phones (even if the individuals are located outside of China) must agree to the app's terms of service, which stipulate that any communication through the app is subject to content surveillance.[103] The network effects of the WeChat US-China communication monopoly thereby extend the reach of the Chinese terms of service, making foreign users subject to WeChat's data trafficking.

Such extraterritorial oversight presents a security risk for anyone who installs it on their phone. The University of Toronto's Citizen Lab found that communications between WeChat accounts not registered to phones in China also faced extensive surveillance for content deemed politically sensitive in China.[104] Potential implications are far-reaching—from Chinese government surveillance to censorship of content about Hong Kong, Tibet, and Xinjiang to bespoke mis- and disinformation campaigns targeted at overseas Chinese users. In short, WeChat's policies combine with Chinese government regulations to enable the surveillance of users of the platform outside of China.[105]

The network effects of TikTok, Grindr, and WeChat drive the prevalence of the platforms' use and cement their role as critical communications infrastructure. Their centrality as tools for communication among family members, friends, and sexual partners results in useful insights for profile building, particularly with respect to sensitive groups.

Censorship and Misinformation on Critical
Communications Infrastructure

One way a state can exercise its sovereign reach is to single out and classify individual posts as aberrant. TikTok and WeChat have already removed posts sensitive to Chinese sovereign-interest issues, such as Taiwan, Tiananmen Square, and the Hong Kong democracy movement.[106] Although we can think of such deletion as censorship, as social media platforms become more influential in areas from election security to public health, control of social content also becomes a form of critical infrastructure security.

TikTok removed Feroza Aziz, a makeup influencer, after she posted an inflammatory video decrying Chinese government detention of Uyghur Muslims in Xinjiang.[107] The video begins with Aziz instructing viewers on how to use an eyelash curler, but transforms into Aziz asking fans to research Uyghur Muslim detentions. She ends the video by completing her eyelash curling tutorial. To justify her removal, TikTok claimed that Aziz violated the terms of service with an earlier video satirically referencing Osama bin Laden, which she posted but later deleted. The timing of Aziz's ban from the platform following her Uyghur advocacy eyelash tutorial, however, underscores the platform's questionable rationale for censoring her.[108]

TikTok eventually reinstated Aziz, but the incident highlights how platforms can leverage community standards to limit speech. It also underscores the challenges regulators face in determining why, how, and whether social media platforms censor users. Without understanding how companies make these decisions, regulators cannot assess harm or attempt to remediate it with legislation.

Indeed, shortly after Aziz's ban, the *MIT Technology Review* analyzed leaked TikTok moderation materials that categorized content from Hong Kong, Tibet, Tiananmen, and Northern Ireland as causing "real-world harm."[109] The platform instructed moderators to mark the material "not for feed."[110] It also deleted videos of a lesbian Hindu-Muslim couple dancing for being "in violation of community guidelines" in December 2019.[111] In its second 2020 Transparency Report, TikTok acknowledged the removal of nearly 12 million videos in the United States.[112]

According to a whistleblower who spoke with the German website NetzPolitik, moderation on TikTok breaks down into four categories: "deleted," "visible to self," "not recommended," and "not for feed."[113] Other users cannot see "deleted" or content "visible to self." "Not "Not for feed" posts are more difficult to find via the search function.[114] "Not recommended" videos are also more difficult to find via the search function.[115] The leaked moderation guidelines also instruct that political content during election periods be categorized as "not recommended" and suggest a systemic effort to shape the type of political content that appears on the platform.[116]

TikTok asserts that it promotes only apolitical content, but such a claim is a political statement in itself. Putting aside the paradox of an "apolitical social media platform," this policy determination can chill speech. In November 2019, several former TikTok employees alleged that the firm encouraged them to censor content that involved vaping, heavy kissing, and "social or political topics."[117] Opaque content moderation on US-based social media platforms underscores how platforms constrain speech because of corporate interests. However, while US-based social media companies censor content as a corporate practice, reflecting the illiberalism of the US tech sector, Chinese firms, in addition to their own profit motivation, face continuous content-related pressure from regulators. And the Chinese Party-state's definition of "unsafe content" is far broader than the definitions used in liberal democracies. As a result, TikTok's links to the PRC place it at high risk of political pressure. Indeed, the company has limited critiques of the Chinese government by banning individual users. As tech expert Shanthi Kalathil observes, the type of information lost to public view fundamentally changes the information landscape.[118]

Ultimately, like any social media platform operating in the United States, TikTok can set its own community standards, as long as they do not violate US law. It is not responsible for content posted on the platform, under Section 230 of the Communications Decency Act, which treats platforms not as editors or curators of news but as information infrastructure.[119] The TikTok case, then, reveals how US laws make users vulnerable from external pressure for data trafficking.

WeChat plays a complicated role in the censorship apparatus for users in the United States. As discussed earlier in this chapter, Judge Beeler stayed the Trump executive order banning financial transactions with WeChat on the First Amendment grounds that it prevented speech and expression.[120] The Biden administration officially dropped both bans in June 2021.[121]

These actions demonstrated the complexity of WeChat's role in the US information environment. Preventing the use of the communications platform limits speech, but using the platform subjects users to censorship. Users with friends, family, and business associates in China suffer from WeChat bans, but users with WeChat accounts registered in China—even if they are communicating from North America—also face extraterritorial surveillance.[122] WeChat illustrates the gridlock of US-China tech competition. The same platform that enables communication between families, friends, and businesses, also censors and surveils those same users. Consumers, businesses, and policymakers face the challenge of accessing the social and economic benefits of Chinese-based platforms while mitigating their ability to extend the extraterritorial reach of Chinese laws.

As with TikTok, government attempts to constrain WeChat in the United States foundered. However, the story does not end with reports of isolated incidents. As the network effects of social platforms make them ever more instrumental in critical communications infrastructure, their power increases. Users may come for the make-up tutorials, but the algorithms generated by their data become national security assets.

Conclusion

This chapter has traced the dynamics by which social media platforms expand the reach of Chinese firms and the Chinese government. First, social platforms rely on network effects to generate a wealth of insights, which support algorithms that gather even more user data. Chinese firms' access to the US market then supports data mining of US-based consumers and algorithm development that draws on user engagement. It also gives them a competitive advantage in leading-edge, data-driven products—with as yet unknown implications for future political power and industries. Ultimately, data-rich algorithms draw people onto social media platforms, but the platforms' allure does more than just increase traffic; it expands China's power in the international system. An entire generation of users depends so heavily on TikTok for news, socializing, and entertainment that they advocated strongly for it when the US government tried to shut it down for national security reasons in fall 2020.[123] While Grindr serves as a public square for the LGBTQ+ community, and WeChat is the lone reliable communication artery between the United States and China, US firms offering similar types of services and data gathering in China face bans. US tech companies can only dream of inspiring the same passionate outcry for access to service in China that TikTok received in the United States. This asymmetry of data gathering drives one-sided data trafficking rather than data trade.

The Trump administration's TikTok and WeChat ban attempts demonstrate how blocking firms from operating in the US market fails to address the importance of network effects in US communities and businesses. Without national privacy legislation protecting US-based users, US firms will contend with perpetual challenges from firms that operate in the United States and China and can gather data in both. Allowing Chinese tech companies to operate in the United States magnifies their power over critical communications infrastructure. An important first step in stabilizing the US innovation ecosystem in an era of increased Sino-US tensions is to develop comprehensive data privacy regulations that offer predictable enforcement and guidelines. Such an approach can involve stakeholder engagement from Chinese and US firms.[124] However, it must also mitigate the competitive advantage Chinese firms gain from asymmetrical market access.

India offers an instructive comparison. The country banned fifty-nine Chinese apps on June 29, 2020, including TikTok and WeChat, arguing that they undermine India's sovereignty, integrity, and national security.[125] India's Ministry of Electronics and Information Technology proclaimed that TikTok and the other banned apps were "stealing and surreptitiously transmitting users' data in an unauthorised manner to servers which have locations outside India," and said that the ban would safeguard "Indian mobile and internet users."[126] It highlighted the national security risks TikTok and the other apps pose, emphasizing that "the compilation of these data, its mining and profiling by elements hostile to national security and defence of India, which ultimately impinges upon the sovereignty and integrity of India, is a matter of deep and immediate concern which requires emergency measures."[127] India's government articulated the issues of data mining and user profiling that arise for Chinese corporations under Chinese government oversight. And in many ways, the Indian government's response highlights how digital sovereignty shapes national border debates. The ban coincided with border skirmishes between China and India over Kashmir, which led India to reevaluate its assertion of not only territorial but also digital sovereignty.[128]

Similarly, although many US critics contend that the General Data Protection Regulation is too unwieldy, platforms operating in Europe have responded by changing their terms of service. US consumers, by contrast, lack such affirmative protections and are thus subject to Chinese corporate data-gathering. The challenge that current and formerly Chinese-owned social media platforms pose emerges from the US system of innovation. US users and corporations rely on social platforms due to their network effects both within and beyond the United States. As this book demonstrates, platforms entering the US market offer opportunities to generate new jobs and markets, but due to the extractive nature of the US system, also enable data trafficking.

The US government regularly discusses limiting the power of tech monopolies, but long-term systemic change remains aspirational. The Trump administration's executive orders, Grindr's forced divestment, and the Biden administration CFIUS review represent case-by-case oversight of social media platforms that traffic data, albeit in a way curtailed by the power of corporations in the United States. Yet as these one-off efforts attempt to move forward, those same social media platforms grow and become more critical to the US information order. And as social platforms face scrutiny, the immersive world of online gaming—the subject of Chapter 6—experiences widespread Chinese corporate investment.

6

Gaming

The Porous Boundaries of Virtual Worlds

When COVID-19 shuttered live music venues around the world, American rapper Travis Scott performed live for more than 12 million people.[1] Rather than crowding into the Rose Bowl or Madison Square Garden, Scott's fans came together on Fortnite, a free-to-play online video game first released in 2017 that has since amassed more than 350 million users worldwide. For fifteen minutes in April 2020, Fortnite provided a precious communal concert experience to fans social distancing under stay-at-home orders.[2]

Scott and his fans were not the only ones to move their social lives onto Fortnite. People around the world, particularly school-age kids and young adults, were also making this shift. For example, over 60 percent of the demographic for Fortnite is in the eighteen-to-twenty-four age group.[3] The remainder skews younger.[4] Socializing online accelerated during the COVID-19 pandemic.[5] Children who were out of school used the platform to interact with friends.[6] One *Washington Post* story quoted a parent as saying their kids were playing Fortnite "like their lives depended on it."[7] Yet while such gaming platforms provide distanced social nourishment, they map social behaviors in an unprecedented way.

On Fortnite, avatars obscure users' nationality; they interact in a space that seems to float above real-world political conflicts. This fluidity, though, is precisely what challenges boundaries of digital sovereignty and seeds conflict in the US-China relationship. In the gaming sector, data trafficking from the United States to China faces no checks at the border. The two countries are much more closely entwined in the gaming industry than they are in other sectors, with the Chinese gaming behemoth Tencent holding sizeable financial stakes across the industry.

Corporations lack an incentive to publicly disclose how they gather, use, or share their data. The US system, in particular, protects private gaming companies, which benefit from the shroud of secrecy afforded to firms without a stock market listing. Public firms face pressure from shareholders to raise capital and grow their market, both of which benefit from access to the Chinese market. As a result, gaming platforms offer tantalizing data-trafficking sites for the Chinese government.

Trafficking Gaming Data

Data generated from gaming platforms has a multitude of uses, but in the context of data trafficking from the United States to China, three key areas of concern rise to prominence. First, gaming platforms offer a form of social life. The data (and all activity) on the platform allows for extraterritorial understanding of a country's interactions and its people. Second, financial transactions on the platforms reveal both money usage and money problems. For example, using financial transaction data on one such platform, researchers were able to determine the likelihood that an individual would engage in impulsive spending and even identified behaviors consistent with gambling disorders.[8] Finally, gaming platforms map social interactions and networks.

Corporations already gather personal data about users on gaming platforms. Beyond the direct political considerations of the extraterritorial control over data trafficking that gaming facilitates, Chinese firms' expansion into the US gaming industry provides them with an unmatchable competitive advantage in the US market. Chinese firms collect data about users that feeds into algorithms and operations; these, in turn, advance the competitiveness of the Chinese gaming industry.

Online gaming, like social media platforms, harvests data about individuals and communities alike. People live active social lives on gaming platforms. Friends interact. Fans "attend" concerts. Individuals adorn and alter their online personas, expressing their artistic and creative preferences. Identity formation becomes visible: users choose their avatar's gender, and they select the avatar's tools, movements, and style.

When participants conduct financial transactions on gaming platforms, the platforms gather insights into the ways people use money. Gambling addictions are laid bare. Credit card numbers link individuals and their resources, identities, and preferences. The fluidity of users' identities on gaming platforms facilitates not only legal data trafficking but also money laundering through virtual currencies. Underdeveloped US government oversight of Chinese-owned gaming platforms, paired with Chinese government scrutiny of China's tech sector, has transformed games into a prime location for data trafficking.

Because platforms can observe and track how individuals spend their time on them, years of playtime have produced years of interactive user data. The data corpora that gaming platforms generate are among the richest produced by any form of social media. Yet protections for user data privacy cannot keep up with the rapid pace of game development.

Distinctive Features of Gaming Data

Like social platforms, games map community behaviors. But games differ from social platforms in the practices of user engagement they encourage and, by extension, the type of data they gather. Digital design researcher Torill Mortensen explains that personal influence, social interaction, and development in relation to other players and the game enhance a user's enjoyment of the gaming environment.[9] Communities emerge as the gamers interact regularly in a game, often developing sets of norms or forms of interaction and producing a distinctive type of community data.[10]

The system of gaming avatars, or virtual identities, further distinguishes social platform data from gaming data. While on social platforms, users can try out new identities, on gaming platforms, users can adopt what Mark J. P. Wolf refers to as "player-characters," or characters that users control, with missions and motivations decided by the story.[11] These include personal avatars, actors seen in the third person, and first-person role-playing characters whose name, appearance, and abilities users create.[12] The procedural rhetoric, community construction, and distinctive identity formation within gaming enrich the user data the platforms generate. Communications scholar Alexander Galloway further argues that gaming platforms train players to see the informational systems around them.[13] However, while the gaming systems enable users to develop a more nuanced understanding of the algorithms that shape the world of the game, they obscure where the data for the algorithm is located and how it functions in a geopolitical context.

Gaming is one of the largest entertainment markets in the world. The size of the 2020 and 2021 Chinese gaming market was an estimated nearly US$50 billion.[14] The size of the gaming market in the United States in 2021 was US$85.86 billion.[15] Though the US market exceeds the Chinese gaming market in total size, Chinese tech firm Tencent is not only a leader in both the global gaming industry, but also takes on a prominent role in releasing or financing many top titles in the US market.

Tencent rose to prominence with its communication platform QQ in 1999. It later developed WeChat, which transformed into the multiuse app at the core of China's ubiquitous mobile payments system.[16] Yet Tencent is more than a gaming company; it is a data company, gathering massive amounts of data via video games and storing it.[17] Like all firms domiciled in China, Tencent is required to follow local laws, and must share its data on request by the Chinese government under the national security frameworks.[18]

To diversify their gaming investments, Chinese tech firms have purchased stakes in several large US gaming platforms. Since 2011, Tencent has engaged in an extensive campaign to acquire whole or partial stakes in US gaming companies, including Activision Blizzard (acquired by Microsoft in 2022), Riot Games, and Epic Games, among others.[19] Firms with at least partial Chinese ownership produced blockbuster titles such as Fortnite, League of Legends, and World of Warcraft through the beginning of 2022, when League of Legends and World of Warcraft began operating with Microsoft as their parent company. Fortnite alone brought in over US$5 billion in revenue in 2020 and nearly US$6 billion in 2021.[20] In this chapter, I use case studies from Activision Blizzard, Riot Games, and Epic Games to trace how Tencent gathers network, financial, and user data within the US market that, once incorporated into China's data corpus, can be used by China to conduct mis- and disinformation campaigns, gain strategic industrial advantages, and control important infrastructure in the United States.

Tencent's international growth relies on the Chinese government's support of prominent national tech firms. China promotes the success of domestic products first. Communications scholars Qiaolei Jiang and Anthony Y. H. Fung contend that the rise of nationalism connected to Chinese technology products' growing market dominance alienates and concerns neighboring countries because of anxiety about the Chinese Communist Party's global ambitions.[21] In parallel, nationalism in media production means that domestic tech products are tailored to local tastes, making them more appealing to Chinese users.[22]

The Chinese government seeks to use artificial intelligence military operations, including autonomous weapons systems, among other AI technologies. All of these technologies require extensive corporate data gathering.[23,24] The focus on "smart" or "intelligent" warfare emerged in 2015 in China's military-strategic guidelines.[25] Tencent is one of several AI tech national champions tasked with enhancing the use of tech in warfare. China's Ministry of Science and Technology specifically commissioned Tencent, along with tech firms Alibaba, Baidu, and iFLYTEK, to lead China's AI advancement efforts. As part of its mandate, the company must also develop global AI industry partnerships and prominence.

Building on success in the Chinese domestic market, Tencent increased its global market share and, by extension, its capacity for data gathering. The firm's data collection in gaming, like its data collection in social media, promotes not only corporate growth but also national gains in AI and other strategic sectors. As part of the above-mentioned 2015 strategic restructuring focused on innovation and new frontiers of military power, China established the People's Liberation Army's Strategic Support Force, integrating cyber, electronic, psychological, and other capabilities.[26] In 2017, the Chinese military released an off-cycle update, two years (rather than the usual interval of six) after its 2015 report.[27] It highlighted new military strategies with an increasing role for AI in military power.[28] Tencent is well-positioned to contribute Chinese AI tools for military use because of the vast scale of its data-gathering practices, which enhance its AI expertise.

Tencent's connections to the Chinese government extend beyond the military and into the civilian world with a wide range of public administration efforts. As one of China's major smart-city technology suppliers, it also operates several platforms that inform China's social credit system. Throughout this book, I examine how WeChat, the firm's marquee social media product, also contributes to the monitoring of individual and population-level health, finances, social connections, and beyond.

With the support of such robust corporate data-gathering, other Chinese laws, such as the 2017 Cybersecurity Law, facilitate Tencent's data transfer to the Chinese government. Because China's 2017 Cybersecurity Law requires firms to store all data generated in China on Chinese-government-owned servers,[29] if Tencent moves any user data from the United States to China, it transfers that data directly into the control of the Chinese government.

Ultimately, the massive data sets available to Tencent, thanks to its large-scale investments in gaming platforms, reveal the behavior and preferences of people outside of China. While this benefits Tencent financially and the Chinese government strategically, such data gathering also centers power in the private sector. Tencent faces no clear limits on amassing such data through commercial means in the United States, despite the firm's close alignment with China's long-term national security interests. The limited protections for domestically generated data in the United States make data trafficking an attractive option for companies such as Tencent that have both commercial and political incentives to aggregate data in the Chinese market.

In light of Tencent's close relationship with the Chinese government and the company's data-gathering practices, the Trump administration, as discussed earlier, banned the use of Tencent's WeChat platform in the United States via an August 6, 2020, executive order.[30] The ban, which the Biden administration later rescinded, jeopardized a critical line of communication between the United States and China.[31] At the same time, it failed to impose any restrictions on the largest avenue for data gathering available to Tencent in the United States: the gaming industry. Oddly, few users and regulators push back against Tencent's gaming-related data trafficking.[32] Corporate ownership structures, data gathering, and currency on gaming platforms work together to traffic data, one avatar at a time.

Corporate Data Structures: Ownership and Transparency

Corporate ownership structures are another characteristic of the tech sector that enables data trafficking. Tencent has owned 40 percent of the US company Epic Games since 2012.[33] Epic Games is best known as the maker of Fortnite, which was the most-played video game in the United States through 2020.[34] That same year, Fortnite became an official college eSport, with scholarships available.[35] Though the game's user numbers declined following a dispute with Apple's App Store, it remains a cultural institution in the gaming world. Tencent's dominant role in the global gaming industry across a wide range of countries and gaming platforms is illustrated in the following figure.

Private shareholders control Epic Games. Tim Sweeney, the company's founder and CEO, owns over 50 percent of the company, while Tencent, as mentioned above, owns 40 percent.[36] Epic Games' two major stakeholders are therefore a single individual and a foreign company with roughly US$73.5 billion in annual revenue.[37] As a major corporation and dominant figure in the gaming industry, Tencent has disproportionate leverage.

Because of this ownership structure, Epic's decision-making process is not public. Private companies are notorious for their lack of transparency, and they have much less stringent corporate reporting requirements than public companies do. The firms also have no accountability to public shareholders.

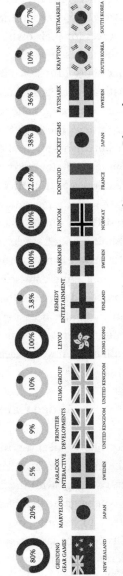

Tencent Games
Foreign Gaming Investment-Ownership Stakes (Grouped by Approximate Annual Revenue)

>$3B in Revenue (USD)

5%	40%	13.5%	17.7%	25.6%	5%	100%	84%
ACTIVISION BLIZZARD	EPIC GAMES	KAKAO	NETMARBLE	SEA LIMITED	UBISOFT	RIOT GAMES	SUPERCELL
UNITED STATES	UNITED STATES	SOUTH KOREA	SOUTH KOREA	SINGAPORE	FRANCE	UNITED STATES	FINLAND

$1B-$3B in Revenue (USD)

**Additional Investments
(Without Disclosed Stakes %)**

MAJORITY %	MINORITY%
MINICLIP (SWITZERLAND)	YAGER DEVELOPMENT (GERMANY)
KLEI ENTERTAINMENT (CANADA)	VOODOO (FRANCE)
10 CHAMBERS COLLECTIVE (SWEDEN)	BOHEMIA INTERACTIVE (CZECHIA)

<$1B in Revenue (USD)

80%	20%	5%	9%	10%	100%	3.8%	100%	100%	22.6%	38%	36%	10%	17.7%
GRINDING GEAR GAMES	MARVELOUS	PARADOX INTERACTIVE	FRONTIER DEVELOPMENTS	SUMO GROUP	LEYOU	REMEDY ENTERTAINMENT	SHARKMOB	FUNCOM	DONTNOD	POCKET GEMS	FATSHARK	KRAFTON	NETMARBLE
NEW ZEALAND	JAPAN	SWEDEN	UNITED KINGDOM	UNITED KINGDOM	HONG KONG	FINLAND	SWEDEN	NORWAY	FRANCE	JAPAN	SWEDEN	SOUTH KOREA	SOUTH KOREA

Figure 6.1 Tencent Games Ownership Prior to Microsoft Acquisition of Activision Blizzard

Though free from the legal financial reporting requirements of public firms, private companies still must balance the interests of different majority stakeholders. Unsurprisingly, investors in private firms with a small number of owners take an active role in management.[38] Privately held firms with high ownership concentration are likely to see one shareholder leverage their resources for their own private interests.[39] Smaller numbers of investors also produce less-reliable accounting information.[40] Unreliable accounting information is a further indicator that corporate ownership structure correlates with other risks, including ineffectual data governance.

By contrast, public companies in the United States must conduct rigorous reporting. The 2002 Sarbanes-Oxley Act stipulated increased transparency requirements for public corporations and financial institutions.[41] The development of new environmental, social, and governance indices by S&P Global requires reporting on issues beyond financial performance.[42] Similarly, new data security regulations in California, the European Union, Japan, Korea, and China create risk for firms by subjecting them to greater oversight. Publicly traded stocks incorporate that regulatory risk into their share value. But private firms such as Epic Games face no pressure to publicize their plans for managing data-security risks related to investments. Nor are investors compelled to reveal the company's data governance practices. Private firms do encounter occasional pushback from users. However, networked communities tend to retain most of their users, despite data privacy concerns, as we have seen with Facebook, Fortnite, and similar platforms.

Video Game Basics: Fortnite and Socialization

Fortnite is ideally positioned to serve as a platform for data trafficking. Understanding how Fortnite plays this role requires understanding how users engage with the game. Fortnite is a game in the "battle royale" genre, a type of game that blends survival, exploration, and scavenging as players strive to become the "last one standing."[43] Users take the Fortnite Battle Bus between lands to participate in combat with other users over extended periods of gameplay.[44] The game offers multiple virtual lands that users can build up or break down, and it tracks players' worldbuilding and destruction within the game.

Fortnite's users interact socially during gameplay. One of the central features of gameplay is bonding by playing on a team with friends.[45] An individual can play and interact as a solo player, as part of a duo, or with a "squad."[46] Companies, or governments, can then use data about these social interactions to map social networks.

Fortnite's immersive structure and extended gameplay link individual and group practices to payment data. Fortnite gathers extensive information about individuals' preferences via each user's avatar by tracking the in-game purchases that distinguish one player from another. By observing and recording solo, duo, and squad gameplay, the game also develops a rich understanding of how and with whom users interact online and offline.

In addition to tracking shifts in players' habits over time, the platform collects geographic time-series information about users as they construct and destroy their Fortnite lives. Each Fortnite land can accommodate no more than a hundred players at a time, grouped by regional server.[47] This server structure makes it possible to manage the heavy data use required by the platform. More importantly, it offers precise geolocation data for players both at specific moments and over time.

The data generated by the Fortnite community and by each player offers profiles of users and their finances, social lives, and actions, social lives, and actions. Epic Games possesses massive troves of community data that can be used to both aggregate and disaggregate the data corpora of users. Cultural critic Aisha Hassan argues that Fortnite has become a place to hang out, a digital "third place" akin to an offline skate park or Facebook in its aughties heyday.[48] Informatics scholar Constance Steinkuehler and communications scholar Dmitri Williams first introduced the idea of the third place to describe online spaces for interaction beyond the workplace and home, drawing on earlier literature about analog third places by scholars such as James S. Coleman and Robert Putnam.[49] For our purposes, what is most important about Fortnite as a third place is that it offers the platform's users a way to cultivate social capital. For instance, in a study of student-athletes, communication scholars Hank DeHay and Blair Browning, in conjunction with kinesiologist Jimmy Sanderson, revealed that through Fortnite, the subjects managed their social capital in relation to their role as athletes.[50] The platform connected student-athletes and their real-life fans to one another while concurrently gathering data on how everyone was affiliated.[51]

On Fortnite, socializing that might have once occurred offline happens online. On February 2, 2019, Marshmello, an electronic dance music (EDM) DJ, performed twice in a twelve-hour time span in Fortnite's "Pleasant Park" location.[52] During his performances, Marshmello appeared wearing his customary modified hazmat suit and headpiece with a smiley face and eyes that were X-ed out—a chilling image for anyone concerned about digital surveillance.[53] Users stopped their gameplay for the duration of the performances and watched the show(s) alone yet together, through their screens.

The Marshmello event offered users a new form of online socialization that rapidly caught on. Each concert lasted just ten minutes and nineteen seconds, but the performances' social impact was profound. Marshmello subsequently posted a recording of his show on YouTube, where by April 2022 it had garnered 62 million views.[54] In the four days following the concert, the DJ's Instagram following grew by 1 million people.[55] Marshmello's weekly YouTube views subsequently increased by more than 100 million.[56]

What at the time seemed like a revolution in online socialization has since become a commonplace form of group engagement. Marshmello's concert would have been considered quarantine-compliant in 2020. The COVID-19 pandemic has accelerated the availability of user data on platforms such as Fortnite that allow for online group gatherings.

Finances and Fortnite

In addition to tracking data about online collective socialization practices, Fortnite keeps records of users' financial transactions. Fortnite is a "freemium," or "free-to-play" game, meaning that it does not charge for access to use but requires payment for additional features or services. To embellish their chosen avatar, users can add a "skin," or costume.[57] Skins give users a way to express themselves and can even be used to change a player's perceived gender in the game. Another way users set themselves apart is by purchasing dances (called "emotes" in gameplay) that their avatars can perform.[58] In addition, players can use "harvesting tools," or pickaxes of various sorts, to mine or break up Fortnite lands.[59]

All these enhancements require a financial expenditure within the game. Players must convert their real-world local currency into V-Bucks, which can then be used to purchase skins or other items from "loot boxes," a form of treasure common in many video games.[60] Loot boxes contain performance- or aesthetic-altering tools. By tracking users' expenditures, Fortnite maps their financial resources (and, some say, their social class). According to the company, Fortnite is not a "pay-to-win" game.[61] However, it has a wide range of mechanisms for eliciting financial investment from its users.

Skins and other for-purchase enhancements distinguish players from one another. In a 2019 report from the Children's Commissioner for England, young players reported feeling socially pressured to buy skin enhancements in Fortnite.[62] As one child featured in the report said, "If you're a default skin, people think you're trash."[63] Payments made using real-world money on the platform fund the visual image that players project. As the Children's Commissioner report illustrates, those financial transactions are part of the process of self-definition.[64] Financial investment is thus closely entwined with the cultivation of identity in Fortnite.

Payment practices on Fortnite reveal more than just users' aesthetic or social preferences. While payments in a virtual world might seem abstract, Edward Castronova notes that trading real-world currency for virtual currency is "nothing more than an ordinary foreign exchange market."[65] As part of analyzing users' financial behavior, researchers tracked the number of payments each player made by method, the number of hours the player spent on the platform, and whether the player had a close friend who also played Fortnite.[66] Thus, the platforms not only track actual expenditures connected to users' real names, but also reveal user individuality—specifically, users' desire for uniqueness, aesthetics, status, and community identity.[67]

In addition to facilitating the tracking of individual users' spending habits, V-Bucks and loot boxes have played a role in criminal money-laundering practices that involve synthetic currency. In a January 13, 2019, report, the security firm Sixgill and *The Independent*'s Anthony Cuthbertson traced how criminals would use stolen credit cards to illegally purchase V-Bucks, then sell them to other players at a discounted rate, effectively "cleaning" the money involved.[68] Notably, the report found that Epic Games' laxness concerning the sale of discounted V-Bucks contributed to the growth of the secondary black market for virtual currency on the gaming platform.

Data Security: The Case of Epic Games

Epic Games has long faced questions from fans about the security of the data it gathers. In 2018, users balked at the launch of the Epic Games Store because it presented an inconvenient alternative to the ubiquitous distribution platform Steam, and also because of concerns about user data privacy.[69] The Epic Games Store, with its limited game download offerings, used Fortnite to lure users away from Steam's more robust selection of games and other content. To do so, the Epic Games Store copied Steam's model. It then took advantage of Fortnite's popularity to drive users to the Epic Games Store to make gaming purchases. In the Epic Games Store, users can download Fortnite software patches and purchase items with V-Bucks.

Founded in 2003, Steam is a US-based video game distribution platform that was once the industry incumbent. Its business model is inherently data-driven. The platform offers freemium games and patches,[70] and sells other games, including blockbusters such as those in the Counter-Strike and Grand Theft Auto series.[71] Users on the Steam platform can chat with friends and share information.[72] Through all this activity, the platform gathers data about its users and their preferences. In their criticism of the Epic Games Store, users noted that when they use the store, Epic Games makes copies of individuals' Steam files without their explicit permission.[73] Whenever an Epic Games Store user agreed to import their friends from the Steam platform, the store would make a copy of the Steam data stored on the individual's local server. Valve Corporation, which developed Steam, asserted that the information was "private user data, stored on the user's home machine," and was "not intended to be used by other programs or uploaded to any 3rd party service."[74] The Epic Games Store, like Steam, allows its users to meet and chat with friends, which enables the store to leverage their social networks to induce users to spend more time at the store. Epic Games is using its market power to build a store backed by Tencent.

When users complained that the move to distribute Fortnite via the Epic Games Store might have been the result of Tencent's influence, Steve Allison, the Epic Games Store's general manager, pushed back. In a Q&A session at the 2018 Game Developers Conference in San Francisco, Allison responded:

> Tencent has no, zero, input into our business. They do not talk to us about what we are doing. They don't suggest what we should be doing. They don't make any decisions for us. They are not in our building. Everything we do is with our team, and the final point of conversation when it goes up to the top is Tim [Sweeney, CEO]. And Tim does not take any orders from Tencent. Believe me.[75]

Despite Allison's assurances, users have no way of knowing what happens to their data and why, because Epic Games is a private company. The only information users receive comes via marketing communications from executives who profit from the platform's user base.

Based on a reading of the company's terms of service, the company assumes no liability for any form of data transfer, among other things:

> The Services and all information, content, materials, and products (including software), and other services are provided on an "as is" and "as available" basis. Epic makes no representations or warranties of any kind, express or implied, as to the operation of the Services, or the information, content, materials, products (including software), or other services included on or otherwise made available to you through the Services. You expressly agree that your use of the Services is at your sole risk.

The terms of service continue, underscoring Epic's protection from liability:

> To the full extent permissible by law, Epic will not be liable for any loss of profits or any indirect, incidental, punitive, special, or consequential damages arising out of or in connection with these Terms.

The company limits its financial liability to no more than the amount the consumer paid for any given game.[76] In the case of Fortnite, this liability is US$0 for the base version of the game.

Because of the combination of private ownership and a limited number of shareholders, Fortnite and Epic Games have stunningly little accountability for the data they collect and where it is stored. Claims that the data is not accessible through military-civil fusion, the Chinese government principle that all corporate resources must be available for military use, cannot be externally verified. Users must trust major shareholders who wish to retain them as customers. Gaming firms resist disclosing data storage and usage, and Tencent continues to collect data.

Epic Games has a history of data security violations. And because its users have no window into the company's corporate governance structure, they unwittingly share data with a firm that lacks data transparency requirements and has extensive connections to the Chinese military.

Links to China: Activision Blizzard and the Blitzchung Affair

Activision Blizzard is a prominent global leader in massively multiplayer on-line role-playing games (MMORPGs) and the international eSports circuit.[77] Tencent acquired 4.99 percent of Activision Blizzard in November 2016.[78] As noted above, Microsoft bought Tencent out of the firm in 2022, but Tencent's partial ownership of the firm transformed how users think of games as a site of political expression.

The case of Activision Blizzard is particularly fascinating because Microsoft's acquisition transferred ownership from a Chinese national champion to an American firm that proudly refers to itself on its corporate website as one of "the companies remaking the Chinese economy" along with Chinese concerns such as Alibaba, Baidu, and Tencent.[79] Clearly, there is a difference between a firm based in China that depends for its very exist-ence on the Chinese government and a firm based in the United States that depends on China for its continued market growth. Microsoft's most com-prehensive subsidiary firm, however, is in China, as is its largest research and development facility outside the United States. Therefore, both Tencent and Microsoft face pressure to share data with Chinese regulators, even if not to an equal degree. Furthermore, Tencent's period of involvement in Activision Blizzard changed perceptions, perhaps irrevocably, of the safety and security of the global gaming industry.

Among Activision Blizzard's most popular games are World of Warcraft (WoW), Hearthstone, and Overwatch, all major eSports platforms. WoW is a mythological MMORPG introduced in 2004 as part of the Activision Blizzard fantasy universe.[80] Overwatch is a team-based, multiplayer first-person shooter game.[81] It has a massive eSports following. Hearthstone is another powerful eSports platform, a free-to-play digital collectible card game built on WoW mythology. As in Fortnite, players can choose the world in which they want to play. In WoW, players can also decide how and with whom they want to socialize, thereby feeding information about their social connections into the game.

In addition to tracking its users' social connections, WoW follows their game-playing preferences. Researchers have demonstrated that users are highly skeptical of purchases that improve gameplay and believe they give players an unfair advantage. This skepticism about pay-to-win practices renders the data gathered from individual purchases even more valuable. It reveals individuals' social and aesthetic preferences about the role of money in the game. Sorting players in this way tells the platform who has the money to afford to play at the higher levels (and thus offer a more appealing target for advertisers). This information can also be valuable to sell to third parties as well. Microtransactions and the social markers they create, as explained above, also structure social status among players.[82]

Activision Blizzard's Hearthstone platform was at the center of a controversy that underscores the risks gaming companies face when they operate in both the US and Chinese markets and answer to both US and Chinese investors. In October 2019, Activision Blizzard shut down the player Ng Wai Chung (known as Blitzchung) in Hearthstone's eSports champions league because while on the platform he expressed support for the protests occurring at the time in Hong Kong.[83] The company also banned two broadcasters who were moderating the platform when Blitzchung spoke out. When pressed about the incident, J. Allen Brack, then president of Activision Blizzard, offered the following apology:

> Blizzard had the opportunity to bring the world together in a tough Hearthstone eSports moment about a month ago, and we did not. We moved too quickly in our decision making, and then, to make matters worse, we were too slow with talk to all of you. When I think about what I'm most unhappy about, it's really two things: The first is we didn't live up to the high standards that we really set for ourselves, and the second is we failed in our purpose, and for that, I am sorry, and I accept accountability.[84]

In his apology, Brack conspicuously failed to mention his company's censorship of speech on the platform. This overt act of pro-Chinese self-censorship on Activision Blizzard's part—despite Tencent's minimal ownership stake in the company—demonstrates the compromised position occupied by a US firm with a Chinese partnership and a large Chinese market. Even though Activision Blizzard eventually reinstated the player and the two broadcasters, its censorship raises important data-trafficking questions. Activision Blizzard enabled censorship on its platform consistent with Chinese government views. The Blitzchung affair negatively affected Activision Blizzard's revenue, yet the company responded only neutrally, and only after the financial damage had already occurred.[85] Activision Blizzard forced Brack to step down nearly two years later. But he was ousted due to a lawsuit alleging persistent sexual harassment and sexism under his leadership rather than as a direct result of his role in the Blitzchung affair.[86] It remains to be seen how the company's practices will shift under Microsoft's ownership. One thing is certain though: Censorship on Activision Blizzard's gaming platform transformed the global perception of gaming, heightening awareness of its role as a field of competition and geopolitical leverage in US-China relations.[87]

Acquisition Strategies and Data Use: Riot Games

To expand their global capacity, several Chinese firms have acquired stakes in major US gaming platforms. In addition to its partial ownership of Activision Blizzard and Epic Games, Tencent holds 100 percent ownership of Riot Games, a firm founded and headquartered in Los Angeles, California. Having initially acquired 93 percent of the firm in February 2011 for US$400 million, Tencent acquired the remaining 7 percent of Riot Games in December 2015 for an undisclosed amount.[88]

Riot Games is a dominant force in the gaming industry. The company's best-known product is League of Legends, a game with a peak of 8 million daily users, nearly four times daily peaks of the Steam gaming platform's top ten games.[89] Like Fortnite, League of Legends is rich with insights about players. The game can identify which champion a player chooses as their avatar and track how the player augments its characteristics over time, recording financial expenditures and aesthetic preferences in the process.

In 2021, League of Legends alone generated more than US$1.75 billion.[90] It is a multiplayer online battle arena game, and gameplay consists of groups of five "champions," or expert fighters, battling one another.[91] Players compete on different game "modes," or locations, within the game, and teams can include either user-controlled or computer-controlled players.[92] A team wins when its fighters successfully destroy the opposing team's base.

Like Fortnite, League of Legends is a freemium game supported by microtransactions. As with Fortnite, microtransactions allow players to change their aesthetic or purchase tools through in-game play. In addition to tracking these microtransactions, League of Legends logs the time each player spends on the platform.

Tencent's 100 percent ownership of Riot Games gives the firm complete control over the data gathered and stored not only on the League of Legends platform but also on other Riot Games platforms. By contrast, as a company traded on the NASDAQ stock exchange, Activision Blizzard must publicly report its financial information and any potential corporate risks, such as data breaches. And in its 40 percent partnership with Epic Games, Tencent must balance its interests against those of its fellow shareholder Tim Sweeney.

Riot Games' terms of service reflect Tencent's control. Its policy regarding user-generated content, stated below, holds that Riot Games has a right to use anything that its users upload to the platform in any way it sees fit:

> You should upload or transmit Your Content only if you agree that:
> 1. You grant us, from the time of uploading or transmission of Your Content, a worldwide, perpetual, irrevocable, sublicensable, non-exclusive, and royalty-free right and license to use, reproduce, distribute, adapt, modify, translate, create derivative works based upon, publicly perform, publicly display, digitally perform, make, have made, and import Your Content, including, all copyrights, publicity rights, trademarks, trade secrets, patents, industrial rights and all other intellectual and proprietary rights related to them, for the purpose of providing the Riot services without any compensation to you;
> 2. You waive any moral rights you may have in Your Content with respect to our use of Your Content to the maximum extent permitted by the laws of your jurisdiction. If local laws do not allow for waiver of moral rights, instead you grant Riot Games the right to use Your Content and all elements of Your Content with or without your name or pseudonym, as well as to freely edit Your Content.
> 3. You represent, warrant and agree that none of Your Content will be subject to any obligation, whether of confidentiality, attribution or otherwise, on the part of Riot Games and Riot Games won't be liable for any use or disclosure of Your Content.[93]

Riot Games' approach to managing user-generated content is relatively standard for the gaming industry. However, it is noteworthy when viewed against the backdrop of Tencent's role as a Chinese government tech national champion. In this context, we might wonder what happens to the data that Riot Games collects beyond its commercial use. How do Tencent and the third parties to which it transfers data from the platform use that data? Even if Tencent does not use the platform's data to advance the Chinese government's interests, Riot Games' users run the risk that the platform could begin doing so at any time.

Notably, Riot Games states what it *does not* share about its users in the context of what it *does* in fact transfer. Riot Games reserves the right to share its data due to legal requirements such as those outlined in China's Data Security Law and/or the Hong Kong National Security Law. The firm carefully delineates a version of privacy that is then undermined by the sharing practices it outlines in its privacy notice.[94]

> Summary: We don't share your contact info (such as your email or home address) with independent third parties without your knowledge except as described in this notice (like to enforce the Terms of Service, secure the Riot services, or if we're required to do so by law or respond to legal process). We do share non-contact info (like your Summoner Name, match history, game stats, and other aggregate or anonymous info), including publicly via the Riot Games API.
>
> If we ever stop providing Riot services or certain parts of them (like if we're bought out or invaded by Yordles), we may share your info with the buyer. Lastly, remember the stuff you share in social features (like chat and forums) is public—please be careful about how you use them![95]

The firm explains that it will share noncontact data about its users' behavior only in aggregate. However, aggregated user data is precisely the type of data that is most broadly applicable in AI platforms. Using the detailed information about community behavior, geolocation, and timestamping that firms collect, and with their potential access to device data, the firms can enhance their machine learning algorithms. In response to the US government's attempted forced sale of TikTok, the Chinese government has already deemed such algorithms to be of Chinese national security concern and therefore subject to national security review before sale to a foreign country.[96]

Arbitration: Riot Games

A particular weakness of US data security regulations is their reliance on legal arbitration, which notably favors corporations, for dispute resolution. In her article "Manufactured Consent: The Problem of Arbitration Clauses in Corporate Charters and Bylaws," legal scholar Ann M. Lipton argues that the Federal Arbitration Act favors corporate bylaws at the national level.[97] The practice is so extreme that state-level efforts to challenge corporate practices face an uphill battle. The dynamic becomes particularly important when state regulations offer greater user protections than those afforded by federal regulations, as in the case of user data collected from tech platforms.[98]

Lipton's analysis also evokes other work on corporations and consent. Sociologist Michael Burawoy, in his analysis of consent between corporations and their workers, suggests that corporations attempt to manufacture consent from their workers in anticipation of future struggles.[99] The terms of service of Riot Games and other gaming platforms depend on the same principles of manufactured consent that corporations use to control labor. After all, gaming companies' main product—data—is created in part by their users.

Notably, Riot Games uses different dispute resolution procedures in countries where data security regimes are more robust than that of the United States. Japan's Tokyo District Court has jurisdiction over Riot Games claims and the support of the country's 2017 Act on the Protection of Personal Information.[100] The Korean Civil Procedure Code is the arbiter of data security disputes in Korea, whose 2011 Personal Information Protection Act was one of the first and most stringent global digital information acts.[101] Residents of Europe can use the European Online Dispute Resolution platform, which works to protect the legal rights granted to citizens via the 2018 General Data Protection Regulation standards for data storage and security.[102] Although Riot Games does not explicitly state what it will do with the user data it collects, it is careful in communicating what it *can* do—comply with local laws. Users in countries without data protection regulations are therefore vulnerable to data trafficking at any time.[103]

Data-gathering practices render users vulnerable to data trafficking thanks to the long-standing erosion of consent and differing enforcement processes in the United States and elsewhere. The process of exporting data is much more difficult in those jurisdictions mentioned above—Japan, South Korea and the European Union—than it is in the United States due to local protections for individuals. Indeed, the systemic weaknesses of user consent are what ultimately do the most to endanger individuals and communities. Today, far from being a harmless escape from geopolitics, online play shapes the great game.

Conclusion

Whereas Chinese gaming companies can invest and gather data from US-based users, US gaming platforms face a harrowing competitive landscape in China. All games in China, both foreign and domestic, need a license to be distributed.[104] The licensing process assesses the game content.[105] It also gives regulators a tool to control whether a game can operate within the Chinese market. Few foreign games received licenses during a Chinese government-imposed licensing stoppage in 2018, and again from July 2021 to April 2022.[106] A new law introduced in April 2019 further reduced the pace of licensing.[107] The blocking of Korean gaming titles during a period of Sino-Korean tension underscores how vulnerable foreign licensing in this sector is to political dynamics. However, the licensing debate is only one small part of the asymmetry in trade between the United States and China in the gaming industry.

When Tencent owned part of Activision Blizzard, the platform chilled speech on its Hearthstone eSports platform. Riot Games' privacy policy allows data trafficking. Fortnite faces few disclosure requirements as the product of a private company. Together, these firms monitor US social life, while also facing the prospect of pressure from the Chinese government to share their data-generated insights.

Gaming platforms serve as important public sites where people from around the globe and all walks of life can participate in real-time social life. Games give people valuable ways of interacting, particularly at times when such opportunities might be limited, such as during the COVID-19 pandemic, in cases of physical disability, and even in efforts to reduce travel carbon footprints. Concerts by Travis Scott and Marshmello have generated online spaces for communal entertainment that users previously enjoyed by gathering in the same physical location. Yet, as this chapter has shown, this same rich online social life makes games a particularly appealing target for data trafficking.

Digital payments on gaming platforms not only play an important role in facilitating users' social lives, but also generate valuable data that ties gaming to economic and national security. When these fintech tools transcend the gaming industry, they bring with them the power to shape not just entertainment data but also national banking sectors. In Chapter 7, I explore how the fintech sector, while offering a potential tool for data trafficking, demonstrates a key challenge the Chinese government faces in expanding its data corpus—industry power grabs.

7

Money

The Risks of Data Trafficking for China

On a steamy summer day in Hangzhou, China, I stepped into the headquarters of e-commerce giant Alibaba. I was with congressional staffers on a tour of the company's campus as part of a delegation organized by the National Committee on US-China Relations. At the tour's end, we were met by Alibaba government relations manager Sydney Stone and her colleague Bill Anaya, head of international government relations for the Americas, who had flown in from Washington, DC. Stone and Anaya, both former congressional staffers, had traveled to Hangzhou for the day to speak with the US congressional staffers on their trip to China and shape their impression of Alibaba. In other words, the US system was supporting lobbying efforts not just in the United States but also in China. And Alibaba was willing to commit financial resources, human capital, and fossil fuels to the effort. The tour concluded with a visit to a grocery store and to a restaurant at Alibaba's corporate headquarters. We were assured we would not need paper currency for either destination. The campus's entire economy ran on Alipay, an Alibaba-affiliated mobile payment app and digital wallet.

Shortly after visiting Alibaba, our delegation met with officials at a local university. The university officials expressed surprise that we had been inside Alibaba headquarters. It was closed to them, though they were media and technology professionals from the same town. US lobbyists who had flown to China were able to meet with US regulators at the corporate headquarters, but media and technology researchers at the local elite, state-run university were excluded from the firm's private campus. This asymmetry of access underscores a fundamental tension in Chinese data-trafficking efforts. China's fintech sector, including Alipay and its major competitor WeChat Pay, offers the Chinese government a rich opportunity to network sovereignty through the dependence of other countries on Chinese digital payment solutions and other financial products. The sector also positions these private sector firms to challenge state dominance in Party strongholds.

Historically, financial information was the state's domain. State control of financial information extends from imperial personnel archives to Communist-era files, or *dangan*. Extensive gathering of financial information was characteristic of Chinese pre-modern governance systems.[1] Ledgers of merit and demerit identified individuals' moral strengths and failings.[2] Like China's premodern data-gathering practices, China's data corpus encompasses the data gathered and the way it structures local and international private sector interests. Before digital payments became widespread, state-owned UnionPay, the world's largest credit card brand, began operating with the approval of the People's Bank of China (PBOC), China's central bank.[3] Alipay and WeChat Pay connect to another framework for Chinese national data gathering: the social credit system, a data-driven governance experiment that links citizens' social and financial lives to government digital surveillance through a combination of private and public sector platforms. Despite the long history of financial data being entwined with Chinese government oversight, as fintech companies penetrate markets outside of China they also accrue influence rooted in corporate, rather than state, power.

In social media or gaming contexts, Chinese firms establish new industries that help construct Chinese national and international influence. In historically state-run sectors, where status in the state system confers access and connections, tech sector investment destabilizes existing power structures. The fintech sector offers an important view into not just how data trafficking works for China but also how it does not.

The problem that Chinese fintech firms pose for the Chinese government involves three competing aspirations. First, the Chinese government seeks to maintain control of the Chinese financial system. Second, China aspires to network sovereignty both nationally and internationally using tech firms. Third, Chinese tech firms aim to enrich their leaders and shareholders through international growth. These three goals are interconnected because strong government control over the fintech sector increases China's influence in the global financial sector. They also compete because strong Chinese government control over fintech draws concerns from international markets and constrains Chinese entrepreneurs.

Instability in the relationship between Chinese tech firms and the Chinese government has a ripple effect across the entire global data ecosystem. When the Chinese government pulled the DiDi rideshare app from the app store in China because of DiDi's decision to move forward with a US IPO without government approval, it tanked a major US stock offering. Retailers around the world on Chinese mobile payment apps for commercial transactions with Chinese consumers even outside China. Disagreement between the Chinese state sector and Chinese tech firms about how to interact in foreign markets destabilizes both the Chinese market and the markets that depend on money from China.

How China's Fintech Sector Enables Data Trafficking

Data trafficking occurs at the crossroads between the state sector and China's tech firms. Whatever interest tech firms may have in protecting the data of their users is caught amid the internal battle between the Chinese government and Chinese corporations. Alipay and WeChat depend on the Chinese state-run banking system for transactions in Chinese yuan. To open a WeChat Pay or Alipay account, one must typically have a Chinese bank account, which requires having a state-sponsored ID. To obtain such an ID, one needs a residence permit (*hukou)* or a long-term foreign residence permit, which allows a foreigner to live and work or study in China.[4] The bank account links to the state-owned banking system and to the holder's foreign or domestic residence permit number. Chinese fintech firms' reliance on the Chinese banking system inextricably links the state-run banking system to payment data. Alipay parent company Ant Group (formerly known as Ant Financial) and WeChat Pay parent company Tencent gather additional data about consumers around the world who use Chinese payment apps. Ultimately, the apps allow financial transactions made abroad to link to the Chinese yuan, the Chinese banking system, and domestic systems for tracking populations. Yet both Alipay and WeChat Pay extend the reach of the Chinese yuan by expanding the range of uses for the currency through digital payment apps that monitor users and share payment data. This is a form of data trafficking—the trafficking of global corporate transaction data into the Chinese banking system.

The Chinese government can access user data much more seamlessly than countries withless stringent government data storage requirements. Chinese government regulations expand the reach of Chinese social platforms by offering fintech services that increase their user base. For example, WeChat Pay is part of Tencent's WeChat, which links its financial data to everything from a user's vaccination status to their relationships.

To access WeChat Pay without a Chinese bank account, one needs a "red packet" gift from another user via WeChat, which allows the government to track social ties. Each packet is limited to 200 yuan (roughly US$30), but a person can send roughly 100 red packets per day.[5] This approach reinforces the power of the state banking system and maps user networks through shared financial transactions.

Alipay and WeChat Pay also enable transnational surveillance by the Chinese state. Both gather extensive data about users, going far beyond their financial transactions on the apps. They map how those transactions intersect with global geolocation data and other concurrent activities occurring on them. Payment apps, in short, support China's efforts to network sovereignty.

The firms also form a core of the social credit system.[6] In 2002, then-premier Zhu Rongji popularized the term *social credit system* to describe a narrow market reform initiative to pave the way for access to information about Chinese partners for foreign firms.[7] Reports from as early as 2007 suggest that credit records, tax payments, and contract performance could become part of one's social credit score.[8] The system evolved into a digital-reform project with the institution of 2014's Planning for the Construction of the Social Credit System, an effort to use social data to punish trust-breaking behaviors and reward trust-keeping ones. Payment data feeds directly into the system.[9]

Competing government-run and private-sector-run versions of the social credit system exist as trials to integrate national data. Alibaba and Tencent both have smart-city solutions that combine data gathered through city-wide surveillance systems, including digital payments.[10] The smart-city data merge with each firm's digital payments app.[11] Shanghai's Pudong New Area, one of the country's earliest commercial centers and the current financial center of mainland China, also has a state-run "city brain" designed to gather and integrate data about city functions. It surveils the area and can connect with both Alipay and WeChat Pay.[12]

China's fintech sector supports the government's efforts to enlarge the global digital footprint of the People's Republic of China. Alipay is the world's leading third-party mobile and online payment platform. In the United States, Ant Group operates Alipay, its most famous product. Chinese fintech companies also operate in South Africa, Norway, Kenya, Uganda, Tanzania,

Rwanda, and South Sudan with varying levels of local data collection. As in China, Alipay and WeChat Pay found success in these countries by filling gaps in available digital payment solutions. Even more significant than the adoption of Chinese fintech tools, though, is the way global data gathering through the apps extends the range of China's legal control.

China's 2021 Data Security Law requires that Chinese payment apps operating globally provide the Chinese government with access to payment data gathered around the world—not just data about individual users but also data about the vendors with whom they transact and the networks they pay. Through Hong Kong's 2020 national security law, the Chinese government has a mechanism for penalizing Chinese-based firms for any financial transactions deemed to endanger China's national security abroad. Digital payment apps broaden data gathering domestically and establish infrastructure for data trafficking internationally.

Although apps such as Alipay and WeChat Pay are helping to modernize China's financial sector and expand it internationally, they reveal a fundamental flaw in China's model. Leveraging private-sector investment for Party gains requires ceding power to the private sector. By gathering extensive financial profiles of individuals and facilitating payments in Chinese yuan, fintech firms are redrawing the path through which Chinese power has historically flowed—namely, the state-run banking sector. When this shift in power occurs in comparatively new industries like online gaming, the overall pie—the size of the market—increases. When it appears in a preexisting industry such as finance, public and private sector firms clash.

How Fintech Challenges Chinese State Control

In China, the fast-growing digital payments industry supplemented a slow-moving state banking system amid rapid economic liberalization. The rise of payment apps enabled the rapid liberalization of the financial sector.[13] Chinese "national champions" in fintech grew at the expense of legacy payment systems, marking an important moment of autonomy for China in its efforts to liberalize its economy.[14] By the same token, the rapid transition from a cash-based payment system to one so dominated by electronic payments that some merchants refuse to accept hard currency gave Chinese fintech companies a level of power in China that would be unimaginable in most countries. WeChat Pay and Alipay emerged to reduce China's dependence on Western financial tools such as credit cards. Although this strategy successfully rendered players such as Visa and Mastercard nonessential in the Chinese payment landscape, it also created the new internal challenge of powerful domestic fintech giants. The Chinese government must now contend with this power struggle.

On October 26, 2020, Ant Group made waves in the global investment circuit. The mainland-China-based firm, best known for its role in China's digital payments revolution, announced that it planned to raise an estimated US$34.5 billion in a world-record-setting initial public offering.[15] The IPO would be dually listed, raising capital on both the Hong Kong and Shanghai stock exchanges. Ant Group's founder, Jack Ma, also founded Alibaba, which holds the record for the biggest IPO in history. Like Alibaba, Ant Group (a firm in which Alibaba holds a one-third stake) operates in the United States. Unlike Ant Group, Alibaba held its IPO on the New York Stock Exchange. Ant Group was poised to be the biggest IPO in history—raising the profile of both exchanges—and would make Ma the eleventh-wealthiest person in the world.[16] Alibaba's power in the Chinese market draws on a wide range of investments across strategic sectors in China, offering Ma and the firm a comparatively high level of control for a private-sector entity in China's system. Figure 7.1 shows the relationship between the two firms.

Thus, when Ma condemned the Chinese state for its tech regulation efforts in a speech at Shanghai's Bund on October 24, 2020, speaking after China's vice president Wang Qishan, regulators took notice. Ma suggested that attempts to regulate the fintech industry were so backward that they were akin to regulating the airports as though they were railway stations.[17] On November 3, 2020, just days before Ant Group's planned IPO, Shanghai Stock Exchange officials halted it. Regulators thereby demonstrated their striking power over the Shanghai stock market and over Chinese financial and tech industries. Ma vanished from public life for three months shortly after his speech and was conspicuously missing from the final episode of his show, *Africa's Business Heroes*.[18] His absence raised concerns about his safety in a country where the unexplained disappearance of high-profile figures who challenge the Chinese government is not uncommon. He did not reappear until January 20, 2021, showing up in a fifty-second video that was part of a Chinese-government-sponsored literacy effort.[19] Ma's disappearance was only the beginning of a saga of intensifying regulations in the Chinese fintech sector, with laws introduced in 2021 that required more transparent data reporting by fintech companies.

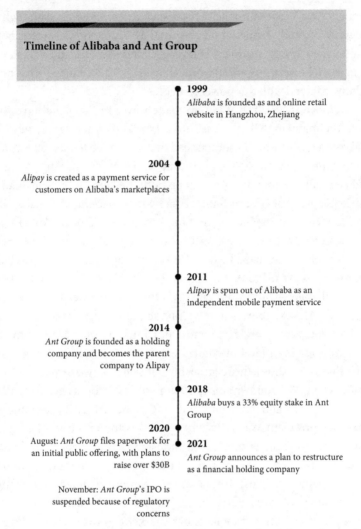

Timeline of Alibaba and Ant Group

1999
Alibaba is founded as and online retail website in Hangzhou, Zhejiang

2004
Alipay is created as a payment service for customers on Alibaba's marketplaces

2011
Alipay is spun out of Alibaba as an independent mobile payment service

2014
Ant Group is founded as a holding company and becomes the parent company to Alipay

2018
Alibaba buys a 33% equity stake in Ant Group

2020
August: *Ant Group* files paperwork for an initial public offering, with plans to raise over $30B

November: *Ant Group*'s IPO is suspended because of regulatory concerns

2021
Ant Group announces a plan to restructure as a financial holding company

Figure 7.1 Timeline of the Relationship between Alibaba and Ant Group from 1999 to 2021

After blocking Ant Group's IPO, regulators required the firm to restructure. On December 26, 2020, Pan Gongsheng, deputy governor of the PBOC, presented Ant Group with a massive set of restructuring requirements. The firm had to reorganize its credit, insurance, financial, and wealth management businesses, all of which competed with existing state sectors.[20] On January 15, 2021, the China Banking and Insurance Regulatory Commission banned sales of bank deposit products on third-party internet platforms.[21] Then, on January 27, following the China Banking and Insurance Regulatory Commission's annual meeting, the commission issued a statement outlining a plan to strengthen oversight of the financial activities of Internet platforms.[22] Alipay, JD.com, and DiDi subsequently removed interest-bearing products from their platforms.[23] Ant Group's announcement of its planned IPO marked a clear shift in the way the Chinese government regulates the fintech sector. Whereas previously fintech had enjoyed the lighter hand typically accorded to the private-sector-dominated tech industry, it would now clearly be subject to the heavy-handed finance regulations of the public sector. This flex of authority reestablished the hierarchy between private sector tech and the state banking sector. Private sector Chinese tech firms—and fintech firms in particular—accrue massive financial power, yet they operate in China at the pleasure of the Chinese government.

However, Chinese fintech firms such as Ant Group illustrate the long-term challenges the Chinese government faces. Ant Group and several other competitors, including Tencent and JD.com, began as mobile wallet services but evolved into offering interest-bearing financial products such as Alipay's Yu'ebao money market fund and its Huabei virtual credit card, as well as credit lines, loans, and deposit products. These products competed directly with those of Chinese state-run banks. This conflict is what led regulators to block such products from third-party platforms in January 2021.[24]

In 2020, Ant Group applied for and received a digital banking license in Singapore.[25] Singapore granted the license to a consortium of investors, including Greenland Financial Holdings Group, Linklogis, and Beijing Co-Operative Equity Investment Fund.[26] The move bolstered Ant Group's transition from digital payments into consumer finance.[27] Because the Chinese tech and consumer banking sectors have vastly different structures, Ant Group's shift from e-commerce to consumer finance was a shot across the bow for state-owned banks. The same firms that build out the data corpus have the potential to undermine Chinese state power. Chinese government efforts to control the growth of private-sector payment apps reflect anxiety about the gathering and use of data. Payment apps give tech firms power over the use of sovereign currency.

Chinese payment apps epitomize the tension between tech firms and China's financial sector. They gather data to support the Chinese state while simultaneously jeopardizing Chinese national interests by competing with the state sector. The Chinese government has therefore acted swiftly to control the industry. With the sector's increasing power, the Chinese banking system, a core element of Chinese state power, has retrenched control. On September 24, 2021, the PBOC declared all cryptocurrency transactions illegal, after forbidding Chinese banks from handling Bitcoin in 2013 and banning initial coin offerings in 2017.[28] The Chinese government has tools to control innovation in the financial sector. However, such moves also dampen innovation in high growth sectors.

How Transactional Communities Enable Data Trafficking

Increasingly, spending time in China requires access to digital payments apps. The political and economic restrictions placed payment apps by the banking system requires a financial connection to the state. Pilot programs of China's digital renminbi eCurrency advance the PRC government's power over the financial sector.

In contrast, the economic liberalization supported by Alipay and WeChat Pay drives consumer spending outside of China. The apps offer Chinese consumers a way to travel without cash and without having to exchange currency, an option that is of particular value because Chinese currency is not freely traded on the global foreign exchange market. WeChat Pay has operated in the United States since 2017 for Chinese tourists and students.[29] Alipay has also served the US market since 2017, in partnership with US payments processor First Data Corp.[30] Alipay has the most extensive payment network in the United States run by a Chinese platform. It began by operating as a payment platform at US sites popular with Chinese tourists. For example, New York City taxis began accepting Alipay in 2017.[31] People can also use Alipay at 99 Ranch Markets, a US-based chain of Asian markets, and at casinos in Las Vegas.[32] Airport vendors in Honolulu, New York, San Francisco, and Los Angeles accept Alipay mobile payments. According to a 2018 Nielsen report, 91 percent of Chinese travelers said they were more willing to spend money if Chinese mobile payments were accepted.[33] By reducing friction in the sales process, the apps broaden the ways Chinese consumers can spend. Thus, they present an opportunity to gather data that can be shared with the Chinese state and help US firms capitalize on the growth of China's economy.

Alipay's spread has been viral. Alipay's first systemic foray into payments in the United States was a contract to serve 7,000 Walgreens drugstores throughout the country in 2019. Walgreens had a preexisting agreement with Alibaba to sell goods to Chinese consumers through the Alibaba e-commerce site. The drugstore chain's decision to deploy Alipay is part of its efforts to secure a larger market for its products amid a dying US retail market and fierce competition from Amazon. The Alibaba e-commerce site is best known for its Singles Day sales event, the largest single day of online sales in the world. Alibaba's 2021 Singles Day event brought in over US$84.5 billion. Retailers such as 7-Eleven, Bloomingdale's, Saks Fifth Avenue, Neiman Marcus, and Macy's have since begun to accept the payment platform as well.[34] The firm's financial tools also provide a cudgel for the government—a tool it can use to control, or even stop, users' financial transactions.[35]

In her landmark book *New Money*, communications scholar Lana Swartz argues that paying and being paid are powerful components of what she terms a "transactional community."[36] In the modern nation-state, she argues, "cash pulls people together in a 'national community of shared fate'" that is not limited to members of a state.[37] Through the inclusion and exclusion of people in its payment apps, China circumscribes those who can join its transactional community as individuals who are willing to obey the laws of the Chinese state. Alipay and WeChat Pay have integrated the US consumer ecosystem into China's transactional community.

Alipay and WeChat Pay enable data trafficking by relying on the network effects of transactional communities. Payment apps gather two critical types of information. The first is data about sales, behavior, and products from US-based firms such as Walgreens and Bloomingdale's. The second type of data draws on social payment mechanisms that attract new users and map communities through personal relationships built by gifting and currency transactions.[38] As previously discussed, mosaic theory describes how public and nonpublic information is combined to create rich data sets, underscoring how the intersection of data conveys more information than standalone data points.[39] As with the other data-trafficking practices discussed in this book, the individual pieces of data are less important than the ability to compile that data across sectors and localities.

Business leaders want to preserve their access to capital provided by Chinese consumers and to payments for doing business in China, despite concerns about data trafficking. US regulators worry that Chinese mobile payment apps extend the utility of Chinese-government-issued currency and Chinese firms' ability to gather data in the United States.[40] Like other Chinese tech firms interested in gathering data in the United States, Chinese fintech firms have experienced murky and haphazard regulation enforcement by a competing range of government agencies. Like TikTok and WeChat, these firms face pressure from the Committee on Foreign Investment in the United States and presidential executive orders. In practice, however, such enforcement methods exercise only limited oversight of data-gathering practices. In January 2017, Ant Group signed an agreement to buy the American firm MoneyGram International, Inc., an agreement that CFIUS blocked in January 2018 due to security concerns.[41] Despite the blocked merger, reports suggest that Moneygram and Ant Group continued to work together.[42]

A January 5, 2021, Trump administration executive order banned financial transactions with WeChat Pay and Alipay, along with six other apps.[43] Notably, the ban drew authority from two laws designed to prevent national emergencies—the International Emergency Economic Powers Act (50 USC 1701 et seq.) and the National Emergencies Act (50 USC 1601 et seq.)—to block the apps.[44] Using the label "emergency" as a tool to prevent the apps from operating in the United States suggests that their presence is something more sinister than users' daily reality would imply. Given that the financial apps' transactions, rather than being emergencies, are integrated parts of the US consumer ecosystem, the ban faced immediate legal challenges and was ultimately repealed by the Biden administration.[45]

The threats that the Trump administration's executive order cited have existed for years. The executive order notes hacks of the Office of Personnel Management in 2014, the insurer Anthem in 2015, and Equifax in 2017.[46] In the end, hacking is beside the point if international users willingly share data with payment apps.

Conclusion

Payment apps create a framework for understanding how basic commercial practices gather and trade data across borders. They also empower fintech companies set standards and build networks that empower certain companies over others. Alipay and WeChat Pay gather longitudinal data that grows in scope and scale over time as the apps expand their coverage in the United States and other countries. That data is significant now, but it will increase in importance as machine learning and AI generate increasingly rich insights from large data sets.

In earlier chapters of this book, I have focused on the US system's challenges with consumer data gathering. Payment apps in China add another critical dimension to the picture. As Chinese fintech firms grow internationally, Chinese regulators persist in prioritizing domestic financial sector security. Fintech reveals the clashes between China's private and public sectors, which affect Chinese firms that deal in user financial data, and by extension their trade partners. Such efforts depend on relatively seamless cooperation between the government and the private sector. Maintaining stable growth in the Chinese tech industry and preserving the power of the state sector present an internal challenge to China's efforts to network sovereignty.

Not all strategic sectors have such a fraught relationship with the Chinese government. As I demonstrate in Chapter 8, other strategic sectors in China have thrived through government involvement. In the field of health tech, for one, Chinese firms work closely with the Chinese government to expand data gathering in sensitive areas ranging from blood samples to DNA, thereby trafficking data from bodies all over the world.

8

Health

Surveilling Borderless Biodata

As COVID-19 emerged in 2020, US government agencies clamored for access to testing kits to track the outbreak. In March, the Food and Drug Administration (FDA) approved a testing kit from BGI Americas.[1] The company is a subsidiary of the Chinese genome sequencing firm BGI Group (formerly the Beijing Genomics Institute), a partner of the Chinese National Human Genome Center.[2] The testing kit was the first Chinese diagnostic tool ever approved for the US market.[3] Three months later, Genetron Health, a Chinese firm that claims to use genetic data along with lifestyle and environmental insights to treat and prevent diseases, received approval to sell its COVID-19 testing kits.[4] Amid the desperation of the early period of the COVID-19 pandemic, these Chinese firms systematically gathered biodata in the United States. This desperation, paired with the lack of data oversight in the United States, is what enabled these firms to enter the US market. The compartmentalization of US agencies means limited protection for the consumers; the FDA is responsible for managing device safety, but it is not a cybersecurity agency.

The COVID-19 pandemic reveals the long-term risk presented by China's leading role in the global bioeconomy. While offering valuable humanitarian services, these firms also traffic in extremely sensitive data—health and genetic insights. Health data is at the center of the development of strategic biotechnology. Even before the COVID-19 pandemic, health information—such as the pattern of our heartbeats, our lung capacity, and our biological vulnerability to certain types of pathogens—had important national strategic implications. It reveals the health of a nation's citizens, as well as the vulnerability of its population to disease. Since the emergence of COVID-19, health surveillance has become even more intimately entwined with national security and economic stability. Communications scholar Gina Neff notes that in the West, health care resources lag behind systematic data gathering and integration, whereas in China, efforts such as the Chinese National Genome Project seek to advance the use of health data by bridging that gap.[5]

Regulatory decentralization in the health care sector demonstrates the dire consequences of data trafficking after it has already occurred. When users share health data, it can reveal information not just about them, but about their progeny. DNA, in particular, reveals our most private characteristics, with multigenerational consequences.

The central issue is that as data sources and data capabilities increase, only certain stakeholders—typically not consumers—gain greater power and agency over their data. Health-data gathering presents threats similar to those in the context of critical infrastructure. Extensive data gathering around human health offers the chance for a key competitive advantage in precision medicine, a new medical model that relies heavily on mass data gathering and tailors user health care recommendations by subgroups defined by genetic and other biological characteristics. Data-driven insights, derived from often insecure consumer health data infrastructure, undergird precision medicine. Insights into the DNA and physiology of individuals also enable a level of user manipulation that goes beyond gathering social or psychological insights.

In this chapter, I examine how disease testing, DNA sequencing, health tracking, blood testing, and other forms of health-data gathering operate with limited global mechanisms for oversight, despite the threat of generational damage to health sector competitiveness and national security. The pairing of a dysfunctional US health care system and Silicon Valley's exploitative data-gathering practices provides a foundation for China's rapid advancement in data-driven medicine and health care infrastructure. The US health care system is rooted in efforts to find financially profitable ways of managing human health, which has given rise to a wide range of tech investments designed to monetize human health data. In parallel, the Chinese government has identified health care, and specifically data-enabled health care, as a central feature of its strategic development goals. These two phenomena intersect to create fertile ground for health-data trafficking through the development of new health tech products that are not secured under US health care privacy laws and through the sale of health care products, services, and techniques to Chinese firms with close ties to the Chinese government.

Data trafficking in health tech violates individual health privacy, but more broadly, the movement of health data changes how corporations and governments can use the biodata of individuals. This applies both to the physical bodies of citizens and also to anyone whose biodata can be accessed or controlled by the state. To demonstrate how health-data trafficking expands the range of China's sovereignty, I first examine the benefits and risks of collecting health data. I then explore the political and economic tools the Chinese government deploys to acquire health data. By revealing the weaknesses in US health data protection, I explain how health-data trafficking occurs between the United States and China. Trafficking health-data offers access to—and potential control of—national biodata.

Risks and Benefits of Collecting Health Data

The emergent bioeconomy promises to shape the future of such sectors as medicine, health care delivery, and agriculture.[6] It relies on massive harvesting of biodata—DNA, health statistics, disease symptoms, and additional insights generated by our bodies. Analysts estimate that the market for the health IoT, including medical devices, systems, and software, will be at least US$300 billion by 2025.[7] Rather than gathering the details of our social or financial lives, these practices gather the building blocks of life.

Expanded remote sensing capabilities present an opportunity for physicians to gather reliable, long-term patient insights to develop more targeted treatment plans. Individuals can monitor themselves healthwise to log, for example, their blood pressure or blood sugar; cardiac and diabetic patients can thereby track their well-being. Though important before the COVID-19 pandemic, the ability to monitor and track patient health took on outsized importance as nonurgent health care rapidly moved online.

Population-scale data offers even richer potential insights. "Precision medicine" is a data-driven treatment approach that integrates patients' individual genetic data with their lifestyle and environmental data.[8] Computational analysis facilitates diagnoses relying on large data sets to make recommendations for individual patients.[9] Precision medicine also allows the analysis of less common diseases at the population level, presenting a window into treating rare, challenging illnesses.[10] In addition, precision medicine can monitor patients at scale to more quickly identify optimal treatment plans for specific subgroups.

Imagine being able to receive targeted treatment recommendations based on not just clinical trial data but also real-time reporting of the effects different drugs have on patients stratified by demographic groups. Clinicians hypothesize that genetic differences within and across patient populations yield different outcomes for different therapies. Thus, countries with large DNA databases benefit from their ability to track how precision treatments work for individuals with differing genetic backgrounds.[11]

Personalized health care delivers care to specific groups based on disease and patient characteristics drawn from large data sets.[12] "Smart health," health care driven by emerging devices and communication technologies, extends data utilization through mobile devices, smart cards, robots, sensors, and telehealth systems.[13] Health systems gather the same types of data that social, gaming, and payment platforms do, from location information to connections to payment. Because health data systems have a mandate to focus on monitoring human health, their data-gathering remit is much broader, including much more intimate biodata such as heart rate, blood sugar levels, and body temperature. But more significant than the data being gathered is the lack of limitations on smart health data systems. The only limitation on consumer-data gathering is consumer consent to services that are concurrently evolving in parallel with consumer usage. Current US health privacy regulations have failed to keep up as they focus on data gathered in health care settings, rather than through consumer technology.

Health apps present what security experts Ramesh Raskar and colleagues term the "utility-privacy trade-off."[14] During the COVID-19 pandemic, the increased utility of contact-tracing apps strengthened the argument in favor of trading privacy for utility. Such privacy trade-offs provide short- and medium-term social benefits. They also, however, present long-term security risks to users and nonusers alike by eroding data governance frameworks. The apps gather and aggregate data using unclear consent practices, which means they could share private information that might compromise users.[15] In aggregate, the problem is even more significant: biodata offers population-level insights that could lead both to the creation of devastating bioweapons and to monumental health care advances. Both have the potential to shift global power dynamics.

Personal health information is one of the few areas in the United States with national data protections. Still, the regulations lag far behind the technology. Consider the Health Insurance Portability and Accountability Act of 1996 (HIPAA), which gives individuals control over who sees and aggregates their health information.[16] HIPAA's design fails to consider the wide range of today's health-data-gathering tools.

To explain the challenges health data governance presents, bioethicists Effy Vayena and Alessandro Blasimme suggest breaking the health-data ecosystem down into three related parts: data sources, data capabilities, and data stakeholders. These three parts combine in services, including cloud computing, IoT devices, networking technologies, 3D printing, robotics, social networks, and AI.[17] anonymous data within these systems can be reidentified.[18] In the context of health information specifically, researchers Latanya Sweeney, Akua Abu, and Julia Winn have shown that relinking names and contact information to profiles in the Personal Genome Project is possible using publicly available information.[19] As the healthcare industry focuses more on precision medicine, the market for health data is increasing daily. Medical devices, software, systems, and services, including insurance, rely on extensive biodata gathering.

Digital health delivery methods amplify these challenges. Telehealth, for example, broadly refers to the use of information and communications technologies in health care settings. These practices rely on third-party providers, who charge a premium for services that comply with US health care regulations but also operate in a regulatory environment that fails to punish tech firms for massive data breaches.

Even simple data integration undermines the integrity of health care data. The use of data aggregated outside its original therapeutic context, such as in mental health apps, could provide population-level insights that can be exploited if such data is not protected under consumer privacy laws.[20] Equally concerning is the rise of commercial health trackers. Fitbit, Apple Health, Strava, and others offer opt-in self-monitoring for health and fitness purposes. Ancestry.com, 23andMe, and other such companies sequence DNA for eager customers, who are not protected under patient confidentiality laws. 23andMe fails to clearly inform customers how their data might be used for medical research.[21] Individuals subject not just their own DNA but also that of their relatives to ambiguous biodata-sharing consent agreements.[22] These wholly commercial entities conduct a wide range of activities using DNA, which once again presents serious privacy issues for users. DNA sequencing firms can trace consumers' risk for genetic mutations in parallel with their ancestry, crafting a mosaic of the genomic landscape not just of individuals but also of whole communities over generations.

Perhaps most profoundly, as one of the few categories of data protected in the United States, health data illustrates how the data of individuals provides a population-level benefit. In 2015, physician Sachin Jain and colleagues argued that an individual's "digital phenotype," which consists of their interactions on social media, in online communities, through wearable technologies, and on mobile devices, can be used to assess human health.[23] Since then, our digital footprints have expanded, as has the range of data available for integration into the overall picture of our health. When Jain and colleagues wrote their article, they noted the privacy limitations of health-data gathering and integration as a carve-out.[24] Five years later, biomedical ethicists Christophe Schneble, Bernice Elger, and David Shaw asserted that all our data will eventually become health data. By this, they meant that the range of inputs gathered from our bodies, devices, homes, and cities will feed into a picture of our overall health, making carve-outs for specific health data secondary at best, irrelevant at worst.[25] These practices have laid the foundation for a regime of biocitizenship defined by tracking and surveillance of biodata.

Building the Biometric State: Challenges and Opportunities for China

In China, accruing health data does not merely confer an abstract competitive advantage; it is central to the country's public policy goals.[26] In 2010, the Chinese government identified biotech as a "strategic emerging industry," prioritizing its development through national industrial policies such as Made in China 2025.[27] China's State Council has deemed health data a "fundamental, strategic resource."[28] The Chinese government has designated Tencent, in particular, as a leader in the integration of health and AI.[29] Since 2016, various policy moves by the Chinese government have urged the integration of health care with AI and robotics, in step with the national development of China's health care industry. This has supported the expansion of health care capacity and incentivized health care providers to leverage digital technologies for precision medicine and AI-enabled health products.[30] Consequently, China's 14th Five-Year Plan (2021–2025) emphasizes hierarchical diagnosis and treatment, which is a practice of rationally allocating medical resources. In parallel with efforts to improve China's health care industry, the Chinese government increased barriers for foreign health care firms seeking to operate in China.

China's interest in biotech as a national strategic resource evokes what historian Keith Breckenridge identifies as a biometric state, one that administers the lives of citizens based on human measurements such as fingerprints and DNA. Breckenridge highlights the expansive capabilities of a biometric state that "brings with it possibilities for storing and processing data, and for generating feedback about individuals that was simply unmanageable" in early models of statehood.[31]

Since the 2003 SARS epidemic, the Chinese government has deployed biodata surveillance, but the COVID-19 pandemic integrated existing biodata surveillance with China's social media and financial surveillance systems. During SARS, the government set up a nationwide mandatory reporting system, infectious disease surveillance databases, and thermal scanners at airports, hospital entrances, and railway stations. During the COVID-19 pandemic, the Chinese government has strengthened it is monitorying capabilities by issuing individual "health codes" for both surveillance and population segregation. Ant Group (which runs Alipay) and tech firm Tencent (WeChat's parent company) developed the health codes. The codes are a feature of both Alipay and WeChat that affect how people can access state services, depending on red, yellow, or green QR codes that indicate where the user can travel. Alipay and WeChat also offer electronic IDs that give users access to government services without having to show their state-issued ID card. How the platforms generate health codes is not fully transparent to users, but reports link it at least in part to apply for and submitting antibody tests. Some potential parameters include fever, clinic visit records, purchases of fever-reducing drugs, travel to high-risk regions, and COVID-19 case exposure or self-disclosed symptoms.[32] It is still unclear who owns the data and how the government will regulate health codes.[33] Health codes linked to social media and fintech apps are now a norm in China for citizens, noncitizen residents, and visitors alike. Biodata surveillance and monitoring synthesize transactional communities with biometric citizenship.[34] These interactions reveal how health tech structures state-citizen relations.

Imagining how such practices can act as a precondition of access to China and the Chinese market does not require a huge leap.[35] Foreign firms face barriers to the Chinese market, but health data's strategic position in China's public policy landscape further magnifies these challenges. China maintains comprehensive human genetic resources (HGR) regulations that prohibit foreign companies from independently acquiring or exporting human biospecimens from China.[36] China instituted stringent health care data requirements after its HGR regulations were updated in July 2019, becoming some of the world's strictest.[37] The HGR regulations also require shared patents for any "exploratory research," broadly defined, that is conducted by joint ventures in China.[38]

All foreign health care firms operating in China must have a Chinese ownership stake of at least 30 percent. And the Office of Human Genetic Resources Administration within the Ministry of Science and Technology must approve the ownership arrangement, which involves a difficult and uncertain bureaucratic process.[39] This requirement is a significant departure from the allowances for Chinese firms in the United States. Beyond national-level regulations, several provinces have restrictions on the gathering of sensitive data via biotech devices, effectively limiting their markets to domestic devices.[40]

China's long-term international strategy for health-data gathering already exists. Developing sophisticated DNA-based tools requires collecting DNA from diverse populations. China's population is estimated to be between 91 and 92 percent Han Chinese, so the local market is insufficient for generating internationally dominant precision medicine efforts.[41] Chinese corporations must collect data overseas to develop comprehensive genome-related tools, including therapeutics to facilitate more accurate and timely decision-making by clinicians. Such therapeutics offer a helpful form of diagnostics, enabling physicians to make more accurate decisions. In parallel, they enable another form of health surveillance. The first country to create widespread precision medicine tools for the international market will control access to the most sophisticated medical supply chain, gaining an advantage in the critical field of health security.

One key element is the Health Silk Road, an effort to share Chinese health expertise with trade partners. If the terminology sounds familiar, that is because it has the same framing as the country's Digital Silk Road. The similarity of the names reinforces how the two frameworks fit together in Chinese government regulators' worldview. Where the Health Silk Road goes, so does the Digital Silk Road. As with the Silk Road of yore, riches emerge from the diversity of the offerings available for trade.

Building on the success of the temporary field hospitals established in Wuhan in the early days of the COVID-19 pandemic, Chinese firm BGI Genomics set up field labs worldwide. BGI dubbed these "Fire Eye" labs (*huo yan*) in reference to the Chinese mythological Monkey King's ability to see hidden threats. They included multiple labs in Israel established in conjunction with different Israeli partners. The firm says that the COVID-19 tests processed by these labs do not give access to patient data, yet the company's gene-sequencing equipment, an add-on for companies seeking to expand their lab capacity, has raised concerns. In Israel, BGI founded a lab with local DNA-testing firm MyHeritage, which also operates a DNA database. It relied on Chinese talent and equipment to carry out its testing, including Chinese RNA extraction tools.[42]

MyHeritage asserted that it would be testing for viral RNA in individuals seeking COVID-19 tests, and not collecting patients' DNA.[43] However, Israeli health management organizations (HMOs) refused to participate in the program because of concerns about the security of their members' DNA data. The Ministry of Health temporarily blocked the collaboration, but with coronavirus testing in short supply, the Israeli Defense Ministry eventually intervened and allowed the deal to move forward, albeit with more robust privacy practices in place.[44] Israel has a sophisticated digital economy, the technical capacity to evaluate such deals, and the flexibility (enabled by wealth) to choose between different global providers. Yet the country still faltered in protecting its citizens' biodata during a global crisis.

Highlighting the diplomatic utility of COVID-19 testing capability during a time of need, BGI also collaborated with AID Genomics to build a lab in Gaza with the support of both Israeli and Palestinian authorities. Witnessing a firm with close ties to the Chinese state bring together Israeli and Palestinian allies reinforces the point that sophisticated health-data gathering can subtly shift global security alliances through the promise of superior products backed by extensive global data. It also shows how data trafficking can operate simultaneously as a product innovation, a security risk, and a soft-power win.

Beyond Israel, Chinese firm BGI has reported building Fire Eye laboratories in Australia, Sweden, Ethiopia, Serbia, and Saudi Arabia.[45] A laboratory investment in the Solomon Islands came with a US$300,000 capital investment from the Chinese government.[46] BGI donated genomics labs to Ethiopia and Serbia.[47] Fire Eye laboratories have not only processed COVID-19 tests around the world but also performed "personalized medicine," using individual DNA to achieve optimal clinical results for a range of medical concerns.[48] As of August 2020, BGI had established fifty-eight such labs in eighteen countries.[49] The COVID-19 pandemic has offered a rapid market-growth opportunity for legal, voluntary DNA collection on a massive scale. Simultaneously, BGI has become a global leader in COVID-19 testing, deploying more than 35 million tests in more than 180 countries from the beginning of the COVID-19 pandemic to August 2020.[50]

Although BGI presents a commercial image to the public, the firm also maintains close state ties. In conjunction with the China National GeneBank, BGI established the Global Initiative on Open-Source Genomics for SARS-CoV-2, which invites scientists to share virus information, including the ages, genders, and locations of patients.[51] Although companies must follow local laws regarding data sharing, most countries' local laws fail to adequately protect health data. In the United States, a robust legal market for genomic data exists, within which BGI can insert its complicated state-capital dynamic. Such genomic data offers valuable tools for developing a long-term advantage in precision medicine, or for injecting uncertainty into a country's health security plan by building dependence on other geopolitical actors with their own strategic interests for important national health services.

Market-Driven Health: Weaknesses of US Bioeconomy Oversight

Health care in the United States operates at the crux of Popper's "paradox of tolerance," the idea that open societies, when not protected against authoritarianism, can be destroyed precisely because of their tolerance.[52] Market-based competition, public-private partnerships in standards-setting, and regulatory decentralization create an easily accessible health tech ecosystem. As with other forms of data gathering, market pressure, open standardization practices, and regulatory decentralization shape the tension between the openness of the US market and health data oversight. Regulatory fragmentation limits the control of health data. Market pressures drive companies to gather and share data with corporate partners to achieve economies of scale in data gathering. Firms sell their data to third parties for additional income streams (as allowed by most terms of service) and partner with third-party providers for data storage (necessary to reduce costs). Open standardization processes, designed to increase access to the market, inadvertently also allow the transfer of data internationally without protections.

The US health care data-regulation system is a patchwork of state data-protection laws paired with federal regulations addressing a few specific sectors.[53] Safeguarding health data requires expertise in cybersecurity, bioengineering, health care delivery, and economics.[54] Few health care regulators anywhere have such a skill set.

The loss of contextual integrity in the health care setting presents even graver challenges when data travels internationally. In such cases, the data refracts through multiple national and international data governance standards. Nationally, professional associations develop standards based on their areas of interest. State boards of medicine regulate medical practice in their domain. Local health districts within states face constraints related to the tax base and infrastructure of individual communities.

HIPAA fails to protect aggregated health data that could be used to develop transformational new population-level treatments or bioweapons. Data collected by fitness trackers has no protection, and neither do genetic insights gathered on voluntary commercial ancestry platforms. HIPAA's protections also disappear when health data is used purely for research purposes; clinicians can aggregate individuals' data as part of their investigation, introducing a loophole for products developed using population-scale data. Compounding the issue, reliable HIPAA oversight does not reach beyond US borders.[55] The FBI and the US Department of Health and Human Services, which oversee HIPAA violations, have no jurisdiction overseas.

Regulatory decentralization allows firms operating in the United States to select their preferred regulatory environment for tech product development. This means that companies can carefully define their preferred sector to gather health data without facing restrictive HIPAA data regulations. For example, if health care delivery presents too many constraints, consumer tech firms offer a much more open data-gathering environment. When combined with health data, non-health-related data can be used to identify personal traits, predict certain diseases, and gather behavioral information.[56] Instagram photos could reveal potential depression.[57] Facebook likes could identify the use of addictive substances. Together, nonprotected health data generates a rich mosaic profile of population-level health. Such data not only offers a resource for improved health care, but also provides a window into strategic national health weaknesses.

Not only does data security differ between sectors, but standards also differ across states. The Texas and California markets, for example, require different levels of responsiveness to consumer-data security issues. The regulations range from minimal oversight in Texas to comparatively high levels in California.

National-level updates to the Committee on Foreign Investment in the United States process (through FIRRMA) increased oversight of genomic data.[58] CFIUS oversight, however, targets individual companies only. It requires that regulators remain vigilant about cutting-edge industry changes that could create data security risks. The deliberative pace of CFIUS oversight also means that by the time the committee decides, corporations have already moved vast amounts of data abroad. Furthermore, CFIUS review focuses on new acquisitions and mergers. Existing companies already operating in the market, while technically under the committee's purview, can escape the committee's attention in an increasingly crowded field. Companies can still leverage less-sensitive health data at a large scale to gain a competitive advantage. The inconsistency of data protection reveals a systemic weakness that requires censuring individual firms to limit their access to sensitive data.

Infrastructural Insecurity

No systematic regulations protect DNA in the United States, though agencies have power to react to specific concerns. In October 2020, CFIUS blocked the acquisition of a San Diego fertility clinic by a Chinese firm.[59] Dr. Samuel Wood, president of San Diego's Gen 5 Fertility, which has a Chinese investor, noted that he did not "see any [security] risk at all." This differences in how a commercial health care providers and the United States government perceive the security risk of such an acquisition illustrate one of the US system's fundamental challenges with respect to securing health care infrastructure.[60]

As with other types of data, from social platform insights to payments, rapidly emerging new technology often develops faster than regulatory oversight. Without national privacy legislation designed to protect user data within the United States, regulators need to play catch-up with new technologies as they emerge. This is a problem when the data involved is as sensitive as nude photos, but when it involves genetic information, the issue becomes a generational tragedy. The following cases demonstrate how the lack of comprehensive data regulation allows health data generated in the United States outside the context of a doctor's office or insurer—where protections are already narrow—to be gathered by Chinese firms. If regulations do manage to protect the data, it is protected only after it has been acquired and transferred. The acquisition of PatientsLikeMe, a US-based social platform for symptom management, by the Chinese firm iCarbonX demonstrates two trends that have emerged throughout this book: how seemingly nonsensitive data becomes sensitive based on changing context, and how regulating data trafficking after the fact causes irreparable harm. iCarbonX combines genomics insights with data about metabolites, microbiomes, and lifestyle choices, and has deep ties to the Chinese government's health-tech system. Jun Wang, BGI's former CEO, founded iCarbonX. National champion tech giant Tencent backed the company.

The data gathered by PatientsLikeMe offered access to crowd-sourced knowledge about rare and emerging diseases, a rich resource for advanced research in precision medicine. Studies produced with the firm's data revealed findings such as the financial hurdles multiple sclerosis patients face and the ineffectiveness of a soy supplement for amyotrophic lateral sclerosis.[61] The platform's rising popularity promised a growing wealth of insights as well as detailed information about patients with these specific diseases.[62]

What began as a space designed to support patients with serious, rare diseases in an online community became a treasure trove of strategic data that could be used for precision medicine. In acquiring PatientsLikeMe in 2017, iCarbonX's sought to to mine the platform for data-driven insights about rare diseases. The bargain users made to exchange their data for community support on PatientsLikeMe likely did not include allowing a firm with close Chinese government ties to mine their personal disease data for strategic precision-medicine insights.[63] Even if they acquiesced broadly to "third-party data access," the consent process did not make this part of the transaction obvious.[64]

CFIUS forced iCarbonX's divestiture of PatientsLikeMe, but sensitive data had already moved abroad.[65] Once the acquisition happened, the holding company had access to user data. Forcing divestiture reduced the likelihood of further data gathering but provided no guarantee (or even any enforcement mechanism) that iCarbonX would not retain access to earlier data.

The PatientsLikeMe acquisition echoes the national security challenges presented by the US-owned fitness app Strava, whose geolocation capabilities have revealed the shape of foreign military bases and force movements. Data uploaded by military personnel in countries where the app was infrequently used, such as Iraq, Djibouti, and Syria, have exposed the presence of US troops there.[66] Strava poses a national security challenge to US military bases because its publicly accessible data maps their locations.

Whereas PatientsLikeMe mapped the social landscape of users with rare illnesses, firms such as the Chinese electronics giant Xiaomi gather an even more comprehensive range of health data about individuals via health trackers. Health tracking is yet another industry in which Silicon Valley pioneered intensive data gathering with minimal data privacy. Xiaomi's health tracker Mi Band (similar to a Fitbit) collects information about users' movements and various health statistics. It introduces many of the same risks that Strava does. The popular Mi Fit health and fitness data platform garnered more than 50 million downloads from the Google Play store.[67] Like Strava, the Mi Band and its Mi Fit platform link biodata with GPS data. Unlike Strava, China-based Anhui Huami Information Technology Co. Ltd. gathers and stores the device's data, according to its Google Play store listing. This 100 percent Chinese-owned subsidiary of Huami Corporation has an exclusive contractual relationship with Beijing Shunyuan Kaihua Technology Co. Ltd., which is 100 percent owned by Huami HK Limited (Hong Kong) and the Huami Corporation, based in the Cayman Islands as a variable interest entity.[68] Conducting detailed research to understand how and where their data will be stored exceeds the capacity of most users.

Mi de Fit consumers consent to use the technology on an "as is" basis, "with all faults," "as available."[69] Xiaomi does not guarantee that one's use of Mi Fit will be timely, uninterrupted, secure, or error free, or that content loss will not occur. It also does not claim that Mi Fit will be free from corruption, attacks, viruses, interference, hacking, or other security intrusions, and it disclaims any liability related to such security intrusion. In addition, the company repudiates any loss users experience that is caused by third parties, including communication line breakdown, technical problems, network and computer breakdown, and other forces majeures.

The insecurity of data on the Mi Fit and other such products is not limited to broad consent agreements. It also involves specific data storage locations. In a study of the security risks of four Chinese fitness trackers—the iHealth, H Band, Mi Fit, and Yoho Sports fitness trackers—all except the H Band stored data on Chinese servers, a requirement in order to grant the government access to the data.[70] All except the Mi Fit use Chinese platforms specifically for location services.[71] The decision to store data on Chinese-government-run servers, moreover, is not exclusive to Chinese firms: iHealth is a European-based company.[72]

Economic Threats

Market-based competition for health care has long been an area of significant controversy because of the conflict between human health outcomes and profitability.[73] The United States has worse health care outcomes and higher costs than countries with comparable economic development.[74] At the same time, the market-based system has been the driving factor behind trans-formative health care innovations.[75] The US system permits extensive data gathering with little oversight, creating an obvious opening for competitors to amass data to surpass the United States in precision medicine.

In the United States, stakeholders hold radically different positions on data ownership, privacy, and access.[76] The discordant financial interests of private insurers, hospital systems, health care providers, and medical device manufacturers leave the country uniquely vulnerable to firms interested in maximizing their financial interests in health care. Unlike in countries with national health care systems, in the United States private insurers hold most longitudinal clinical health care data.[77] US insurers and commercial health care firms can aggregate and deploy that data for commercial purposes if it does not violate HIPAA.

The US mergers and acquisitions market offers a rich source of biodata accessible to companies willing to pay for it. One of the earliest Chinese acquisitions of a US-based biotech company was WuXi PharmaTech's pur-chase of the US-based AppTec, a medical device testing and toxicology firm with expertise in biopharma manufacturing, biologics safety testing, and cellular therapeutics. Organic chemists Ge Li and John J. Baldwin founded Pharmacopeia Inc. in 1993 as a pharmaceutical R&D outsourcing firm.[78] Between 2000 and 2001, Li, Baldwin, and three Chinese partners set up WuXi PharmaTech in Jiangsu Province with the support of Jiangsu Taihushui Group Company.[79] In 2007, WuXi PharmaTech listed on the New York Stock Exchange for US$14 per share.[80] From 2007 to 2015, the firm raised cap-ital on the NYSE before delisting there and relisting on the Hong Kong and Shanghai stock exchanges.

After its NYSE IPO and acquisition of AppTec, WuXi PharmaTech became WuXi AppTec.[81] The firm had leveraged the US IPO system to raise capital to purchase a firm with complementary biological manufacturing, testing, and therapeutic developments. Together with the AppTec investment, WuXi Healthcare Ventures, the investment arm of WuXi PharmaTech, invested US$115 million in the Series E round of financing for 23andMe.[82] The in-vestment inextricably tied WuXi PharmaTech to one of the leading US-based personal genetics companies.

In 2013, wholly owned BGI subsidiary Beta Acquisition Corporation obtained extensive DNA data and sophisticated sequencing capabilities when it acquired Silicon Valley–based Complete Genomics.[83] BGI, and Complete

Genomics, the leading provider of whole human genome sequencing, together offer a sophisticated DNA sequencing operation. The Complete Genomics acquisition gave BGI access to a robust DNA data set from a wide range of people that could be studied using the company's technology.[84]

BGI acquired Complete Genomics through a cash-tender offer for all the company's outstanding stock shares. It did so legally and transparently. No US regulatory barriers to the acquisition were in place at the time. BGI's acquisition of Complete Genomics' sophisticated genomic sequencing capacity gave the firm a significant competitive advantage that it had paid for— a move possible in the US system. Both companies gained rich genomic data through legal commercial transactions, and both have built out a rich database of US genomic data and developed significant capacity for analyzing it. US firms, by contrast, are locked out of the Chinese market for genomic material.

Data Theft

Open standardization processes in which global industrial practices are public and interoperable, paired with minimal data security protections, allow strategic competitors such as Chinese firms to gather data directly from the US market. For example, global COVID-19 testing protocols promote the expansion of the market for and access to necessary testing kits. They also facilitate the movement of DNA across borders. Without robust protections for such data, efforts to resolve the health care crisis actually create a national security problem.

Another challenge presented by the US-market-based data system is the transparency of the standardization and certification system. Clear standards allow competition on the basis of price and quality, which provides clear market benefits. However, they also present significant weaknesses when certifications fail to consider a firm's reporting requirements to other governments. Companies that meet US government certification criteria can pass into sectors that accrue sensitive data.

The case of the WuXi PharmaTech spin-off WuXi NextCODE demonstrates how the US system of open standards-setting facilitates biodata trafficking from the United States to China. In 2015, WuXi AppTec acquired NextCODE Health, which Amgen spun out of deCODE Genetics, using US$15 million of venture capital funding. That same year, WuXi merged

NextCODE Health with WuXi's genome center to create WuXi NextCODE Genomics, headquartered in Shanghai and with bases in Cambridge, Massachusetts, and Reykjavik, Iceland. The following figure offers a timeline of WuXi AppTec's involvement with the global health sector.

In June 2019, WuXi NextCODE drew concern from US senators Marco Rubio and Chuck Grassley. Senators Grassley and Rubio wrote to Joanne M. Chiedi, then acting inspector general of the Department of Health and Human Services, regarding a report from the agency urging action on data security risks from Chinese firms in general, and WuXi NextCODE and BGI specifically.[85] In its response to Grassley and Rubio's letter and the Health

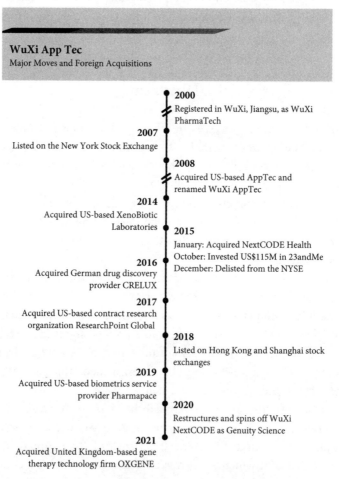

WuXi App Tec
Major Moves and Foreign Acquisitions

2000
Registered in WuXi, Jiangsu, as WuXi PharmaTech

2007
Listed on the New York Stock Exchange

2008
Acquired US-based AppTec and renamed WuXi AppTec

2014
Acquired US-based XenoBiotic Laboratories

2015
January: Acquired NextCODE Health
October: Invested US$115M in 23andMe
December: Delisted from the NYSE

2016
Acquired German drug discovery provider CRELUX

2017
Acquired US-based contract research organization ResearchPoint Global

2018
Listed on Hong Kong and Shanghai stock exchanges

2019
Acquired US-based biometrics service provider Pharmapace

2020
Restructures and spins off WuXi NextCODE as Genuity Science

2021
Acquired United Kingdom-based gene therapy technology firm OXGENE

Figure 8.1 WuXi AppTec's Major Corporate Developments and Acquisitions

and Human Services Report, WuXi NextCODE noted two key points. First, it is an international company with headquarters in the United States, rather than a for-profit company from China with ties to the Chinese government.

> We note that the Letter named the Company as a for-profit company from China with ties to the Chinese government. In fact, we are an international company with our global headquarter[s] in Cambridge, MA in the United States.[86]

This claim suggests that firms headquartered in the United States with large China operations do not face pressure from the Chinese government. Apple's massive transfer of iCloud data to Chinese-government-run servers in response to China's 2017 Cybersecurity Law debunks this claim. Indeed, in a December 30, 2016, *Washington Post* article, Ylan Q. Mui reported that WuXi NextCODE chief operating officer Hannes Smarason claimed a different strategy: "We're a U.S. company in the U.S., but we're a Chinese company in China."[87]

Second, WuXi NextCODE noted the separation of genomic data storage for its US and Chinese businesses: it uses a US cloud provider for its US businesses and a Chinese provider for its Chinese businesses.[88] This claim is misleading. As demonstrated by the TikTok case, where data storage and engineering locations differed, data storage locations can be separate from data processing locations and R&D facilities. WuXi NextCODE's statement evades any mention of data processing facilities. Despite increased US government inquiries into the firm's data security practices, the WuXi NextCODE case also demonstrates the Chinese government's proportionally powerful impact on the firm's operations: updates to China's HGR regulations in July 2019 forced it to restructure its data processing.[89]

The firm's evasive language concerning genomic data storage becomes even more intriguing when the company overtly states that it does not use Huawei's data storage or processing facilities:

> With respect to the concern of genomic data storage in the Letter, we would like to emphasize that we always separate the genomic data storage for our business in the US and our business in China. For our US business, we currently use a leading US cloud service provider; and for China-based business, we currently use a leading Chinese cloud service provider (which is not Huawei).[90]

The first claim is notably similar to claims made by TikTok made immediately before the Chinese government limited the export of its algorithm for national security reasons. In May 2019, WuXi NextCODE and WuXi AppTec worked with Huawei on the Chinese government's Precision Medicine Initiative to use genetic information to diagnose and treat diseases.[91] Three years earlier, in 2016, the Chinese government committed to an investment in precision medicine of US$9 billion over fifteen years.[92] The initiative dwarfs a similar US effort launched in 2016 with a budget of US$215 million. WuXi NextCODE's collaboration with the national champion data storage provider Huawei was already a sophisticated endeavor. And this is to say nothing of the lack of clarity surrounding which other Chinese cloud provider was involved. After all, China's two other leading cloud providers, Alibaba and Tencent, are tech national champions.[93]

In the wake of US concerns about WuXi NextCODE's China business, the firm spun off its US and European businesses into Genuity Science in June 2020.[94] This move, however, came only after four years of precision medicine development in conjunction with Huawei and WuXi AppTec. In a 2017 discussion of WuXi NextCODE, US analysts estimated that the company could have up to 2 million genomes available for processing.[95] Analysts conducted this assessment prior to the company's acquisition of Genomics Medicine Ireland, a firm focused on enrolling 10 percent of the Irish population in genome analysis.[96]

WuXi NextCODE is just one prominent case of a Chinese company leveraging US standards to expand its market for gathering genomic material. A report for the US-China Economic and Security Review Commission in 2019 identified twenty-three China-associated firms certified to perform US-based genetic testing.[97] The WuXi NextCODE case raises the question of how a Chinese firm working on China's national genetics medicine initiative could have been allowed to enter into contracts with the US Department of Defense. The reverse would never happen.

The WuXi NextCODE example demonstrates a third weakness in the US system that facilitates data trafficking: regulatory decentralization, which complicates efforts to oversee genetic testing. WuXi NextCODE leveraged this decentralization to allow trafficking of US genetic material to China as part of market-based solutions for health testing in the United States.

In February 2016, the College of American Pathologists accredited WuXi NextCODE's sequencing lab in China.[98] The state of California also licensed the lab for genetic testing, and the lab received the Clinical Laboratory

Improvement Amendments (CLIA) certification from the US Centers for Medicare and Medicaid (CMS). For data storage purposes, the firm used its partner DNAnexus, which offers HIPAA-compliant security.[99] However, these certifications are all meaningless in a transnational context because US agencies cannot enforce privacy laws in China. The CMS and CLIA certifications speak to the laboratory operations' professionalism, not their data security relationship with the Chinese government. Even following the spin-off of WuXi NextCODE from Genuity Science, it is not clear that the WuXi NextCODE labs would lose their certifications. In a for-profit US medical system, this is a meaningful area of concern.

US-based firms benefit from regulatory frameworks that enable biodata gathering. However, the additional layer of Chinese government pressure on Chinese firms for data gathering turn data-security practices into a national security issue. The lack of comprehensive data oversight in the United States, paired with strategic data gathering by the Chinese government, has positioned China to dominate the future of the bioeconomy. As Chinese health care devices, vaccines, testing, and platforms gain a competitive edge, China's biodata advantage will pose increasing health, national security, and economic risks to the United States and other countries around the world.[100] Whereas Chinese firms have gathered extensive data in the United States, foreign firms have no such access in China. This asymmetry of data gathering follows other industries' patterns, from social media to payments. But access to DNA data forms the foundation of research programs in such areas as therapeutics, AI, machine learning, and bioweapons. The stakes are much higher because of the intimacy of the data and the seriousness of the products it can generate. Whoever generates the largest and most diverse data set will have the power to define what constitutes national control over a population via health data.

Conclusion

Data trafficking has more potentially serious, long-term impacts in the health care context than it does in other contexts. The specs and blueprints of life move from the United States to China through a combination of open regulatory architecture, corporate investment, and market efficiencies. Health data ranges from the highly sensitive (DNA sequences) to the less sensitive (fitness routines). Some health data longitudinally models individuals' health circumstances. Other health data, such as DNA and blood samples, establishes generational control over users, holding the building blocks of life not just for the people who share their data but also for everyone who shares those individuals' genes. As life moves online, the scale of commercial health data increases. Mass data integration also has the potential to transform non-health-related data into sensitive personal insights.[101] Moreover, large troves of less-sensitive data can combine to build out sophisticated models of individuals and populations. Such models can support health promotion, disease prevention, and bioweapon development.

The United States and China would, we hope, share these discoveries for the benefit of humanity. Health tech companies and the Chinese state regard biodata as "assets." In this framing, people are also national assets, and their health data enhances their value. Both markets and states derive value from assets they own or rent and thereby control. How and when human life is a national asset is what is at stake here. If the COVID-19 vaccine race was any indication, the United States and China will continue to compete in health advances that have national security implications.

The US system is ill-prepared to manage health data in a world of data trafficking. The proliferation of commercially held genomic databases creates a scenario in which US citizens' biodata goes to the highest bidder. Insurance and medical records companies oppose even modest efforts to nationalize patient records. And attempts to limit foreign acquisitions of biodata have come years after initial investments in population DNA. While data trafficking is a problem in the case of firms such as TikTok, where gathering information about an individual or community for use years later might be possible, it could have appalling consequences in biodata, because DNA offers insights into not just present populations but also future generations.

The data that has made its way to China is available for massive experiments in personalized medicine and developments for the bioeconomy. China's bid to build global digital sovereignty by purchasing genetic material is continuing in Latin America, Africa, Europe, and North America, albeit with some new constraints in the European and North American contexts. By contrast, Chinese biodata faces such strict regulations that firms are spinning off Chinese headquarters out of fear Chinese regulators will accuse them of trafficking data. Health-data trafficking carries the potential for biohacking, bioterrorism, and competition in strategic health resources, which, as COVID-19 has shown us, are central to national security. Top-of-the-line care reliant on individual genetic material can be offered in a more efficient way when that genetic data is deployed at a national level. Efficient care is critical for stability, given that many parts of the world are dealing with aging populations. Health care data also creates meaningful opportunities for job growth in the knowledge economy and offers an advantage in developing the foundational technology of the future used in advanced biomanufacturing, drug delivery, AI, and augmented reality. The flip side of precision care, however, is precision destruction. Countries with robust global health databases can not only develop powerful tools to heal but also deny those tools to others—or, worse, develop strategic weapons of bioterrorism.

Biodata trafficking lies at the foundation of our humanity: our genetic code. In the context of health data, "consent" means something different. Users are agreeing to a new regime of health monitoring and surveillance that states and companies will use in ways that are difficult to understand and that might not even currently exist. When sharing DNA, they consent not just for themselves, but for their relatives and descendants. Biodata harvesting consolidates national power by revealing the building blocks of life for generations. Together, the US economy's market for health care services and technology and China's national data oversight laws have put users in a precarious position. In Chapter 9, I explore a different form of invasive data gathering shaped by the same dynamics, moving from our bodies to our homes.

9

Home

Data Through the Back Door

The common advertising adage "sex sells" needs to be updated for the data-trafficking era. While I was working on this book, consumer data gathering by Chinese firms became so prevalent that I started playing my own version of "six degrees of separation," asking people which devices they use and linking those devices to firms that collect data in the United States and store their data in China. Examples kept popping up. While helping my sister shop for a baby monitor, I found a well-reviewed product from LeFun Smart, a Chinese company that has a back end run by a Chinese-government-affiliated data-mining firm. When I was shopping for an automatic vacuum, Amazon recommended the bestselling, connected Eufy RoboVac, produced by a company that is wholly owned by the Chinese tech firm Anker Innovations. Like most apps, Eufy retains the ability to share data with third-party business affiliates and states that it will comply with local laws. What I was *not* expecting to find as I scoured Apple's App Store was a wide-ranging collection of connected vibrators that gather everything from temperature data to audio. Sex data sells, too.

Connected "sex tech" is only one small part of the rapid emergence of the Internet of Things (IoT), what communications scholar Laura DeNardis refers to as "the internet in everything."[1] The devices gather data about your home life. And the US tech landscape, where Chinese firms are enmeshed in the IoT fabric, allows that data to be trafficked. Communications scholar Philip N. Howard puts it best when he notes in his landmark book *Pax Technica*, "The Internet of Things is being weaponized."[2]

Many of these devices are great products—who doesn't love an efficient, well-priced robotic vacuum? But the lack of systemic US consumer data protection gives firms a free pass to amass consumer data as part of an opaque, exploitative, and rapidly changing agreement they make with their users. Even with educated consumption decisions, digital resignation—that feeling of hopelessness in the face of pervasive corporate data exploitation—diminishes consumers' willingness to question the increasing number of devices that gather their data.[3] How can someone who needs an automated device to vacuum their house find the time to repeatedly refresh the security terms on their home appliance app?

The rapid proliferation of connected devices draws not just on the US tech sector's exploitative data security practices but also on the freewheeling regulatory environment of the US consumer goods market. In Europe, consumers enjoy a wide range of different protections, most notably the General Data Protection Regulation for user data. In the United States, laws protect only certain categories of data or data generated by individuals in specific states. Similar differences exist in consumer products regulations. In the European Union, consumer products must meet statutory safety requirements before being introduced to the market.[4] By contrast, the US consumer products industry relies heavily on industry-driven voluntary consensus standards and recalls after the fact for products deemed unsafe by the US Consumer Product Safety Commission.[5]

The US tech and consumer products regulatory systems leave consumers and their most intimate data vulnerable to exploitation not just by US firms but also by Chinese firms and, by extension, the Chinese government. Fragmented government oversight fails to systematically protect consumer data. US companies fail to communicate to users how they use and store consumer device data. However, unlike social platforms and video games, consumer products emerge from a legacy of exploitative corporate behavior driven by low profit margins.

In this chapter, I use the gathering and movement of data in the home security, home appliance, child care, sex tech, and drone industries to show that data exploitation by the consumer goods industry is not strictly a tech issue; it is also fundamentally a US consumer goods issue. In the following sections, I examine how China's market dominance operates in the field of consumer devices. These devices involve data sharing that consumers are less immediately aware of, compared with the sharing that occurs on social media platforms. When using social media, consumers actively consent to participating, whereas using devices *forces* consumers to share their data via implied consent. The cases I present underscore how exploitative behaviors in the US consumer ecosystem enable data exploitation in the IoT. I argue that the limitations of the US consumer products regulatory system, paired with illiberal tech-sector tendencies and fragmented oversight of US-China data gathering, open the door to "data accidents," or failures of data security that emerge from the tightly interconnected home IoT environment.

"Data Accidents" and How Consumer Tech
Leads to Data Trafficking

As the supply chain disruptions of the COVID-19 era have demonstrated, the global consumer products industry relies on low-margin production and what sociologist Charles Perrow terms "interactively complex and tightly coupled" systems for production and distribution.[6] Tightly coupled systems operate rapidly and sequentially, in ways that are difficult to stop.[7] Interactive complexity refers to systems with outcomes that are unexpected—such as the results of an ancestry DNA test feeding into a precision medicine database. Such systems face cascading effects when something goes wrong (such as a supply chain disruption or an increase in oil prices). Interaction between complexly interactive and tightly coupled systems—such as consumer technologies—leads to what Perrow calls a "normal accident," wherein "multiple and unexpected interactions of failures are inevitable."[8]

Perrow's work focuses on acute catastrophic failures in systems such as nuclear power plants. However, communications scholar Joshua Braun builds on Perrow's argument in his analysis of data gathering in the online advertising sector, noting that in the digital world, rather than a single catastrophe, there "are millions of tiny, fleeting, sometimes comical occurrences, that get ignored or laughed off . . . destroying our privacy in the process."[9] Business professors Daniel Nunan and Maria Laura Di Domenico further expand Perrow's framing of "normal accidents" to include "data accidents," which are normal accidents perpetuated by highly connected data systems.[10]

Like normal accidents, data accidents are the product of complex interactivity, tightly coupled systems, and unanticipated, yet retrospectively inevitable, accidents. But data accidents differ from normal accidents in three ways. First, data systems become tightly coupled because of connected data storage infrastructure and widespread monopolies.[11] Second, in the case of a data accident, the "accident" results from a failure in the system's structure rather than its operations. Finally, data accidents are difficult to trace at the time they occur. Perrow offers a nuclear accident as an example of a normal accident to reflect the urgency of the systemic failures present in normal accidents. By contrast, Nunan and Di Domenico note that a data accident "only makes its presence felt by the subsequent (mis)use of data."[12] A data accident involves a data breach that occurs because of a confluence of factors related to the inherent fragility of the data security environment in which it exists.

Quite unexpectedly, this chapter itself exposed a data accident. I am a MacBook user and sent an early copy of this chapter to a colleague to review. When attempting to open the file, she repeatedly received virus notifications that prevented her from doing so. Some diligent sleuthing by the University of Virginia's information technology department revealed that the URL for the Eufy camera privacy policy that was included in the bibliography for this chapter linked to known malware and triggered the PC user's antivirus software. Eufy's dominance in the market is what brought the device to my attention in the first place. I incorporated its website into my bibliography not because of anything Eufy required me to do but because of the bibliographic requirements of writing a book. The data accident only became evident when I sent the file to a colleague whose PC antivirus software would not allow her to open it.

Data accidents are all around us, but they are not geographically bounded because data can easily be transferred, legally or otherwise. And such movement limits the extent of possible legal enforcement and remediation when data accidents occur. While the physical effects of a nuclear accident make such tragedies difficult to cover up for long, data accidents can remain undetected for years, only to be discovered incidentally.[13] All three features of data accidents underscore the risk of a data-trafficking "accident" in the consumer products industry, where tightly wound global supply chains enable the widespread distribution of products that gather data with limited oversight.[14]

Data accidents facilitate data trafficking by providing an additional pathway for moving and exploiting user data. As I discuss in earlier chapters of this book, consumer data gathering relies on complex systems of data regulation, corporate incentives, and consumer behaviors. Both the US consumer goods industry and the US tech industry create vulnerabilities because of how they are structured. In the context of the IoT, however, the interaction between the two sectors in the complicated US-China data-gathering landscape means that "data accidents" are to be expected.

Data collection in the consumer goods space evolves differently than it did in the tech sector. IoT data security risk grows incrementally as new product features are added, rather than dramatically, as when users migrate to a new social media platform. In vacuum cleaners, baby monitors, home security systems, and the like, "smartness" has evolved more slowly. As a result, consumer goods companies have escaped some of the public scrutiny that flashier social media platforms have endured.

The thin financial margins in the consumer products industry incentivize corporations to add data-driven systems to their products, even when consumers do not request them. Users thereby become part of a firm's product because their data provides valuable new revenue streams, especially for consumer goods companies with stagnant profit margins.[15] For example, on September 24, 2019, at the NIST "Human Factors in Smart Home Technologies" workshop in Gaithersburg, Maryland, Jason Mathew, the head of global IoT at Whirlpool Corporation, presented a video about how connected Whirlpool mixers help users make brownies.[16] Even to novice brownie bakers such as myself, it is hard to imagine a consumer need for a connected mixer. What *is* easy to imagine, though, are the benefits Whirlpool can gain from gathering data about how consumers use its device, particularly following the company's 2017 acquisition of the personalized recipe search and grocery delivery app Yummly.[17]

Consumer goods companies such as Whirlpool advance the market for connected devices for business purposes. Companies also have a clear incentive to move connected devices quickly to market. In a competitive tech marketplace, the first-mover advantage often makes the difference between failure and success.[18] The pervasive culture of misleading user consent guidelines—usually dressed up in language such as "transferring data to a third party for business purposes or to comply with local laws"—conceals data abuses. Users encounter a consumer goods system wherein firms with less robust cybersecurity teams create data vulnerabilities in users' homes. More connected devices, paired with low-margin businesses that have limited cybersecurity capacity, result in more-complex but less-secure consumer tech.

In contrast, just as Chinese government support for national champions in sectors other than tech supported the growth of such firms as Alibaba and Tencent, Chinese consumer goods firms benefit from local market subsidies and preferential market access.[19] Despite the complex relationship between Chinese tech entrepreneurs and the Chinese government, in most cases the Chinese government supports Chinese firms as they seek to enter the US market. Chinese IoT products in the United States leverage the governmental subsidies to create well-priced and often high-quality products that attract users and then gather their data. Chinese corporations pursue US market share amid lax US data protection practices and robust consumer demand for inexpensive products. The US market also serves as an escape hatch for Chinese corporations that face political uncertainty in China, where private-sector entrepreneurs must contend with intense government scrutiny, even beyond existing Chinese government data security regulations.[20]

Home Appliances

Most people are not in the habit of monitoring whether they are consenting to data gathering when they eat, but some connected home devices even know when you open your refrigerator door. Beyond posing a conundrum for avid snackers, this kind of monitoring can also provide such data points as how many people might be at home at a given time, when mealtimes are, and which foods people eat. This issue of consumer data gathering on devices has particularly interesting data trafficking implications when companies change hands.

In August 2018, I served as the scholar liaison for a group of congressional staffers traveling to China on a delegation through the National Committee on US-China Relations. While we were in Qingdao, our hosts from the Qingdao Municipal Committee of the Chinese Communist Party invited our group to visit the consumer products company Haier, a firm best known in the United States for making inexpensive mini refrigerators.

Haier emerged from the state-run Qingdao Refrigerator General Factory as part of the first wave of liberalization in the 1980s.[21] Haier's chairman and CEO, Zhang Ruimin, who took over Haier's leadership in 1984, has articulated clear plans for building a data platform and leveraging the IoT as part of a turnaround strategy for the electronics firm.[22] Haier had its initial public offering in 1993, listing Class A shares—shares for retail investors—on the Shanghai Stock Exchange. In 2018, the firm listed Class D shares on Germany's China Europe International Exchange, or CEINEX, a joint venture of Chinese and German stock exchanges.[23]

Zhang's role underscores Haier's position as a key player in the CCP's long-term strategic planning. In addition to being the company chairman and CEO, he was a delegate to the 19th National Congress of the CCP and an alternate delegate as far back as the 16th National Congress in 2002.[24] Zhang's long-standing role in CCP leadership, paired with Haier's origins in the state-run sector, highlights the difference between this firm and other global appliance firms, such as Samsung, Electrolux, and Whirlpool.

Jet-lagged and exhausted, our group visited the Haier headquarters to learn about refrigerator manufacturing. We quickly recognized that Haier had transcended its refrigerator company origins. Instead of mini refrigerators, we saw connected home appliances with sensors to surveil users' daily lives. As we toured kitchen mock-ups studded with stainless steel devices, our hosts told us that Haier was now a tech company. The firm's executives went on to note that not only was Haier's brand growing in the United States, but the company had also acquired a US legacy brand, GE Appliances, one of the oldest and most trusted consumer brands in the United States.

In June 2016, Haier purchased GE Appliances for US$5.4 billion.[25] Together, Haier and GE Appliances comprise the world's largest consumer appliance company.[26] The acquisition specifically targeted growth through the IoT.[27] Since purchasing GE Appliances, Haier has made good on this goal by delivering an entire line of connected consumer electronics called GE Smart Appliances.[28] Data is gathered via the appliances and stored on apps developed by Haier US Appliance Solutions, Inc. But what is perhaps more significant to investors is that Haier has foregrounded the development of its new proprietary platform for its IoT, the U+ Connect platform, which collects data through all connected GE Appliances and Haier products.[29] This move makes Haier as much a data company as a consumer products company.

The Haier U+ Connect platform leverages another Chinese firm that is likewise subject to the data localization requirements of China's 2017 Cybersecurity Law. Haier's partner for its home platform is the Chinese national champion search engine Baidu (known colloquially in the Western press as "China's Google").[30] Haier uses Baidu's TianGong smart IoT platform to connect equipment, manage devices, and store data for the U+ Connect platform that GE Appliances uses, thereby integrating GE Appliances into China's nationalized data storage system.[31] Even the name of the product evokes central government oversight. TianGong means "heavenly palace" in Mandarin. These characters evoke Tiananmen Square, the geographic center of China's past and current leadership, the site of both the Forbidden City and Great Hall of the People.

The transition to connected products has long been a concern among those who care about data security. Data security incurs new costs and expertise demands for low-margin consumer products companies. Time to market takes precedence over product security. Haier faces these challenges much as its competitors Whirlpool, Samsung, and Electrolux do. But Haier's use of Baidu back ends for GE-branded appliances further complicates existing cybersecurity concerns. The GE brand conceals Baidu's role in consumer data aggregation on smart appliances and its political and economic dependence on the cyber sovereignty regulations of the People's Republic of China.

While data at scale enhances corporate revenue streams, corporations conceal this motivation from consumers. When I called the GE Appliances help desk on July 1, 2019, to get information about where the company stores data from the appliances' apps, I received little assistance. The help desk assistant first replied, "All of your data is stored on your phone in the app." When I asked where the company stored data from the app, the call center worker responded, "I have no idea, not the slightest clue how to answer that. I have never been asked that question." After I requested more detail, the customer service agent forwarded me to the Consumer Relations department that handles faulty goods, but I obtained no additional information. Immediate consumer access to information about where consumer data is stored is limited, at best. The outsourcing of data further obscures the kind of data-labor bargain consumers make with firms by preventing access to individuals who have detailed knowledge about what users consent to.

Ultimately, Haier's networked devices operate on a Chinese consumer platform that reports back to data centers in China. This arrangement underscores the larger strategic framework of Chinese data-governance practices. Data generated domestically must stay in-country. Data generated outside China must still conform to China's regulatory framework.

China's approach to data ownership takes on even more significance with respect to its connection to the military. Through military-civil fusion, Haier's U+ Connect platform must acquiesce to Chinese military demands for access to corporate secrets. This requirement presents several challenges. First, the data gathered via Haier's U+ Connect system can enhance China's artificial intelligence capabilities, as articulated in the Made in China 2025 plan. Second, the platform creates an opportunity for the extension of Chinese surveillance into homes outside China. From a strategic standpoint, the expanded reach of the U+ Connect platform also allows for Chinese military control over digital platforms operating in US homes. This risk goes beyond the preexisting risks involved in the weaker security systems operating in most connected home appliances.

Market dominance offers several key advantages for Haier, but also for the Chinese government. Building popular household brands is a key element in developing soft power, enhancing China's attractiveness to citizens around the world.[32] And the Chinese government has identified soft power as a deficit in its comprehensive national power.

Haier influences US domestic politics through the US political system. The corporation Haier America Trading LLC (now known as Haier) started as a joint venture between US investor Michael Jemal and the Haier Group. Haier entered the US market through a partnership with a US firm, and it manufactures products in the United States. It has the legislative support of the congresspeople in the districts in which it invests. Unlike LeFun Smart, which operates in the United States under its Chinese brand name, Haier operates under the GE Appliances brand, one that is emblematic of US soft power.

Intimate Technologies: Baby Monitors and Sex Tech

Haier exemplifies the kind of data gathering that users might remain unaware of because of product integrations in long-standing consumer goods. Another key area of data gathering relates to even more personal areas and constitutes a form of intimate surveillance. Legal scholar Karen E. C. Levy, in her analysis of intimate surveillance in love, sex, and romantic relationships, identifies intimate surveillance as a form of interpersonal data gathering, a way for users to gather knowledge about "one's *own* intimate relations and activities."[33] Internet studies scholar Tama Leaver extends the idea of intimate surveillance to include "close and seemingly invasive monitoring by parents."[34] Technologies of intimate surveillance—such as baby monitors and connected sex toys—evolve in the same compromised Sino-US data-security landscape as low-margin consumer products that already perpetrate social abuses.

Baby monitors facilitate a particularly insecure form of intimate surveillance. The data they gather, about the home lives of children and their caretakers, is intensely personal. However, to keep the price of the commodity down, firms use general-purpose components, firmware, and software also used in other IoT devices.[35] LeFun Smart, a dominant brand in home surveillance (baby monitors, pet monitors, home security, etc.), manages the data collected via its products, but a different company, MINE Technology (formerly known as Shenzhen Mine Technology Co., Ltd), runs the app that controls the products. Nowhere in the materials for its baby monitors does the firm mention using a third party to handle its data. The company extracts data about intimate family moments behind consumers' bedroom doors.

Baby monitors also allow access to the ad hoc home office environments that emerged during the COVID-19 pandemic. As with many low-margin products, corporations producing them minimize their investment to maximize the products' low profitability.[36] The way the devices are distributed makes patching their security difficult.[37] Yet the monitors' persistent presence in users' homes makes them an appealing vehicle through which to exploit the integrated home technology environment and the increasing prevalence of at-home work. Such surveillance devices offer a platform for distributed denial-of-service attacks at residential sites that are now an extension of corporate workplaces.[38] Despite their pervasiveness, such devices are rarely included in organizational security testing.[39]

Although some firms have begun to offer monitors that use localized frequency-hopping spread-spectrum (FHSS) transmission to improve security, app-based monitoring appeals to many users. Baby monitors constitute just one category of intimate surveillance that increases data trafficking risks. Sex tech is another.

"Staying in touch" took on a completely new meaning during the COVID-19 pandemic. Connected sex toys offered long-distance partners a way of sharing intimate moments using remote-controlled devices. Also known as teledildonics, or digitally mediated intimacy, such devices contribute to the growing field of online sex work, in which individuals either give over or take control of a device to engage in sexual activity remotely.[40] Sadly, in addition to presenting novel opportunities for pleasure in a highly distributed society, connected sex toys present new opportunities for data trafficking.

Since 2016, the market share of connected sex toy companies has increased. Like many new technologies, teledildonics present an emergent area of concern in data security.[41] Sex tech products, like baby monitors, are insecure connected devices used in people's homes and risk introducing vulnerabilities into the home tech environment. In 2016 at DEF CON, a popular hacking conference, security researchers found that the We-Vibe 4 Plus, a couples vibrator manufactured by Canadian adult toy producer Standard Innovation, detected and sent real-time temperature and intensity data back to the manufacturer.[42] Sex crimes, such as remote rape via identity fraud, emerged in parallel with data trafficking as a form of data accident. Such phenomena can occur when users engage in sexual activity with someone other than their intended partner, whether through phishing, hacking, or catfishing.[43] But as with any new mediated technology, in addition to the potential for abuse among users, there is the risk of data breaches by third parties and of data exploitation by corporations.

Small vibrator companies also demonstrate one of the US regulatory model's fundamental weaknesses: its tendency to focus primarily on prominent firms. Small companies that offer cheap connected products have little incentive and few resources to invest in data security. They are unlikely targets for inquiry by the CFIUS or Congress, yet they gather intimate details from and about their users. Indeed, research suggests that big firms with more institutional ownership perform more careful risk audits.[44]

For example, the Magic Motion Flamingo vibrator, from Shanghai Maylian Industrial Co. Ltd., collects user content and identifiers linked to the user.[45] It also collects user insights, usage data, and diagnostics decoupled from the individual user.[46] In its English-language privacy policy, the firm notes that it transfers data gathered via the app—including voice chats, video, text, and usage data—to an Alibaba cloud server in Shanghai.[47] The app's privacy policy further notes that it shares user data according to local Chinese government regulations.[48]

One should note that Magic Motion is one of the more transparent vibrator companies. This information is readily available to users on its blog. Many of the firm's competitors supply no information that users could use to evaluate its products before downloading the apps linked to their devices from places such as the Apple App Store. The highly dispersed nature of the teledildonics industry presents a challenge to regulators. As a result, even though the data that companies such as Magic Motion can collect is arguably even more intimate than what Grindr might gather, industry oversight has lagged far behind security concerns.

The sex tech landscape provides an important reminder of the structural inequalities within the tech sector that are magnified by the unequal control of data. Journalist Emily Chang describes the unequal gender balance across the tech industry in Silicon Valley that affects how products are developed and what safety features they include.[49] Similarly, women in China's tech sector, too, face exclusion and harassment when they attempt to make their voices heard—even about devices designed for female pleasure.[50]

Sex data hacks pose a serious risk with respect to backdoor data gathering. It underscores how data trafficking magnifies the systemic vulnerabilities created by the US consumer goods industry. The people who are already the most disenfranchised by the US tech sector and most likely to be victims of exploitation—children, women, transgender individuals, queer people, economically disadvantaged people—also face disproportionate risks from data trafficking via intimate technologies.

Drones

While intimate surveillance creates opportunities for data accidents in the home, drones expand the risk of data accidents in consumer technologies that surveil our airspace. In the connected, unmanned consumer aircraft space, Chinese firms shape data-circulation policies on both the corporate and governmental levels in the United States. SZ DJI Technology Co. Ltd., commonly known as DJI, is a global leader in unmanned aircraft systems, or drone technology.[51] Drones serve a range of purposes, including shipping and delivery, aerial photography, building safety inspections, precision crop monitoring, storm tracking, thermal tracking for search and rescue operations, and entertainment. DJI drones are priced lower than those of the company's nearest competitors for similar products, and the Shenzhen-based firm dominates its market. According to the congressional testimony of Harry Wingo, a professor at the National Defense University, DJI could acquire up to 80 percent of the US drone market and up to 70 percent of the global market.[52]

DJI's products are central to the strategy outlined by China's industrial policies. By extension, the firm is a Chinese national champion and subject to military-civil fusion policies. DJI drones can send data to China, according to the DJI policy on "International Transfers of Personal Data." In particular, the DJI drone app gathers a wide range of material from the user's phone. The policy is as follows:

> DJI Products and Services connect to servers hosted in the United States, China, and Hong Kong. If you choose to use DJI Products and Services from the European Union or other regions of the world, then please note that you may be transferring your information outside of those regions for storage and processing. Also, we may transfer your data from the U.S., China, and Hong Kong to other countries or regions in connection with storage and processing of data, fulfilling your requests, and providing the services associated with DJI Products and Services.[53]

In this case, the consumer applications of the drones are shifting norms for data storage by reserving the right to move data from an individual's phone to servers in China.[54] DJI's privacy policy underscores the ways in which firms dominating data collection can influence data standards by making subtle shifts in storage practices that consumers fail to perceive.

This privacy policy first took effect the day before Europe's GDPR went into effect. The language related to European data transfers and the timing of DJI's policy statement suggest that the company released the statement in direct response to the GDPR—and underscores the importance of national policies in protecting consumer data. Without national policies, the onus is on consumers to read about and understand arcane data storage practices and their relationship to both individual and national security. To put it plainly, users must balance wanting to use a cool new toy with plodding through terms of service. Requiring technical homework in exchange for fun is hardly a recipe for careful digital hygiene.

Drones also complicate the idea of consent. Simply using the product denotes consent on the part of the consumer. The lack of transparency of DJI's data transfer agreement stands in stark contrast to the data localization requirements for any data that is generated in China. When we examine the DJI case, China's Cybersecurity Law looks less like an effort to protect cyber sovereignty than an effort to center data gathering in China.

Magnifying the asymmetry between US and Chinese commercial drone data gathering, DJI influences industrial practices in the United States concerning data storage and security. DJI's dominant position in the US market empowers the firm to establish the standards by which consumers measure other drones.[55] Stakeholders from DJI sit on the Federal Aviation Administration (FAA) board for drone safety to shape official drone standards for all products.

The DJI approach is in no way new. The irony of the situation is that as part of US efforts to dominate China's civil aviation industry, the United States was involved in establishing China's aerospace standards. Indeed, one can argue that the Chinese government is just following the same playbook for industrial dominance that the United States leveraged in China in the 1980s, 1990s, and early 2000s.

US regulators have sought to mitigate DJI's influence, but their attempts have repeatedly fallen victim to piecemeal US government regulatory efforts. In January 2020, the US Department of the Interior grounded its drone fleet, a portion of which is made up of DJI drones, because of cybersecurity concerns, including risks to users' phone data.[56] In October 2020, the US Department of Justice banned the use of agency funds to purchase foreign-made drones.[57] On December 18, 2020, the US Department of Commerce officially added DJI to its Entity List because of the firm's participation in high-tech surveillance and human rights abuses in China and other parts of the world.[58] The ban complicates US companies' efforts to provide DJI with parts or components for its drones, and it could also complicate the direct sale of US companies' products to DJI.[59] However, it has no impact on the DJI drones that are already on the US market. DJI held roughly 80 percent of the US drone market in 2021.[60] With nearly 2 million DJI drones circulating in the United States, drone data accidents are an inevitability.

Home Security

Home security systems are meant to protect users from threats that arise in their surroundings, but this effort fails when the very system offering that protection then exposes users to international security risks. EufyCam security systems, involving equipment that gathers data just outside users' doors, offer a good way of understanding this dynamic.

Eufy is the smart-home division of the Chinese electronics firm Anker Innovations, based in Shenzhen, China. If you buy an aftermarket mobile device charger, it is most likely from Anker. The firm offers smart robotic vacuums, video doorbells, baby monitors, the EufyLife health data tracker, and other such devices—including the aforementioned EufyCam security systems.

The EufyCam 2C is one of the company's bestselling products and uses artificial intelligence to distinguish humans who should be near a given property from those who should not. To do this, the EufyCam collects extensive biometric data, including the likenesses of people detected by the camera, in addition to the time, frequency, and duration of activities monitored by the service.[61] What is worth noting is that many individuals caught on camera by these systems have not consented to Eufy's access to or use of their data. Users can choose to store the information the system collects either locally or in the cloud.[62] Storing locally allows users to control who has access to the data. Storing on the cloud provides more reliable backup capabilities but increases the number of people who can access the data. Like many other products and services, the EufyCam collects data about the phone or other device via its app, including model number, device specifications, hardware and software version, signal intensity, and IP addresses, as well as time, frequency, and duration of use.[63] Users must understand and elect to change the settings for any default data-gathering services, to prevent efforts to collect their voice, biometric, and image information.[64] Requests to access, rectify, restrict, or object to the processing of user data must conform to the laws that govern the relationship between the user and the platform.[65] Users own the product (though bystanders do not), but the firm only agrees to provide full product functionality if they fully consent to data gathering.[66] Such a statement underscores how the bargain users enter into with the product operates on the company's terms.

The EufyCam also collects additional user information, including one's name, username, birth date, picture, and other unspecified profile details, from third-party sources, including Meta, Google, and Amazon.[67] As a result, the rampant data collection of Meta, Google, and Amazon all serve to enhance Eufy's data gathering. Also, Eufy refuses to commit to comply with Do Not Track signals in its users' browsers—that is, unless it is legally required to do so, as under the California Consumer Privacy Act. The persistent lack of legal data protections that would prevent PRC firms such as Eufy from rampant data abuses is another way the permissive US data security environment supports the firm's data gathering.

EufyCam's privacy policy allows the transfer of data to China. It notes:

> We process and back up personal information through its [our] global operations and control facilities. We currently operate[] data centers in the United States, China and Germany. For the purposes described in this Privacy Policy, your information may be transferred to these data centers in accordance with applicable law.
>
> Personal information collected and generated in connection with our operations in North America and Australia is processed and stored in data centers in the United States, except for cross-border transfers [that] are permitted under applicable law.[68]

In its statements about personal information transfer for China and the European Economic Area, the firm explicitly denotes the country where it will store the data—in China and Germany, respectively.[69] By contrast, the statements related to North America and Australia include the important caveat of allowing data transfers based on legal loopholes in these areas.[70] The policy underscores that local laws can protect users from data trafficking.

Conclusion

Device data gathering highlights the weaknesses of the US tech and consumer products regulatory systems. Both US and Chinese firms rely on US consumers' addiction to cheap consumer goods to build massive data-gathering infrastructure in the most intimate spaces of the home. The US consumer goods market has consistently failed to internalize externalities for the price of goods. This failure has historically meant that manufacturers could avoid considering issues such as environmental or social abuses committed during the production of consumer goods.

The lack of robust consumer-data standards reflects not only the US tech sector's illiberal control of consumer information but also a more broadly exploitative consumer products industry. Such products offer access not just to data about the home lives of users, but to the technical infrastructure that supplies that data. Consumer data-privacy legislation is just one way to address the challenges of consumer data gathering, as it is entwined in the entire US consumer products ecosystem. Reforming both the tech and consumer products sectors is necessary to prevent the intimate mapping of the nation, from dryer usage habits to travel patterns to sexual behavior.

In this chapter, I examined the intersection of data and the physical world, urging the reconsideration of practices of consent in the context of the proliferation of the IoT. Improved data-security practices force consumer goods manufacturers to take greater responsibility for the repercussions of their behavior in the global commons. In Chapter 10, I offer a framework for supporting continued US industrial development while mitigating exploitative practices that are bad for both consumers and national security.

10

Toward Data Stabilization

Historian Keith Breckenridge argues that technology has a long history of shaping how nations record and categorize their populations.[1] As tech platforms monitor more and more of our lives, the data that constitutes the nation expands in tandem. By taking advantage of people's dependence on tech platforms, data trafficking transfers power between nations, as when a social media platform such as TikTok depends on Chinese government approvals for its continued existence, or when Chinese firms in the United States send data from US-based home security platforms to China.

Companies like Zoom are already taking voluntary steps to manage consumer data security by issuing transparency reports that tell part of the story of how they gather and share consumer data. Other firms, like Apple, are introducing consent practices that allow users to protect their data from third-party apps. However, firms across a range of sectors resist disclosure of their data sharing practices with entities in China, failing to prove themselves as reliable stewards of consumer data.

The challenge presented by data trafficking is less about one data set, one person, or one product than about the social mosaic that Chinese regulators can develop from different pieces of data because of gaps in data governance. Individuals' concerns about the movement of their data, while valid, are only a small part of the problem. A broader concern is that weak data privacy practices that affect individuals yield masses of data that map the behaviors of entire societies. When combined, that data offers the Chinese government tools for setting long-term pathways for such goals as establishing global AI standards, surveilling DNA, and controlling critical infrastructure. Perhaps even more concerning are incipient possibilities in other areas yet to be imagined because we do not yet have the capability to process all of the data we are currently generating. But such practices do not exist in a vacuum. This book has laid out multiple ways in which the market for user data in the United States enables data trafficking. It has also enumerated the intertwined obstacles to solving this problem, including the lack of corporate accountability to investors and consumers regarding data safety;

the lack of an informed, empowered, or proactive consumer population; and an overburdened government apparatus for regulating the large and fast-moving tech sector. Finally, one result of globalization coming home to roost is that companies operating in the US with multinational ownership must balance diverse national loyalties and accountabilities. Restructuring the data gathering and use practices advanced by the US tech sector is not just important for protecting consumers in the US economy. It is an essential buffer against the Chinese government's model for managing data and content.

Monitoring Silicon Valley's attempts to curry favor in the Chinese market presents difficulties for the US government, which depends on media and technology firms to be economic growth engines. The relationships between Chinese and US tech companies are subject to ever more complex trade pressures. Companies that seek to maximize their global profits—from Disney and the NBA to WeChat and ByteDance—are having an increasingly difficult time escaping China's content-control infrastructure. And assessing the relationships between Chinese firms and their US counterparts is becoming ever more complicated. These internecine complications within the tech field are only a part of what constitutes the gridlock to progress on the issue of data security.

The US government's political priorities with regard to China compete with the financial interests of US capital markets. China's government has attempted to control digital content and internet platforms through the systemic leveraging of economies of scale, relying on a combination of fragmented US policymaking and US corporate exploitation. Threading the needle between careful data policymaking in response to Chinese government pressure and the toxic brew of anti-Asian sentiment in the United States makes these efforts even more challenging.

The flexible US tech regulatory landscape facilitates data extraction by Chinese firms. But what is perhaps most challenging is that this regulatory system drives the United States' economic growth. The United States must reevaluate how to balance the power generated by the US tech regulatory system with the persistent challenges presented by China's efforts to network sovereignty. A wholesale reassessment of the role of short-term economic gain from the tech sector relative to the long-term stability of national infrastructure is the only way to ensure that corporations do not extend the long arm of the Chinese state. Data use and gathering are path dependent. Companies that are able to exert global dominance on data storage and security practices now will have a clear advantage in future data-driven products and strategies for influence.

Managing data trafficking requires stabilizing multiple layers of the US innovation ecosystem. Because the global innovation landscape is enriched by data sharing, governments and corporations can only really mitigate, rather than end, data trafficking. The mitigation tactics include engaging with citizens, corporations, multistakeholder organizations, the media, and research communities to develop and execute a coordinated, nuanced response. Clearer consent frameworks for individual users, more robust liability requirements, and national data-privacy guidance can protect users, national security, and US businesses' long-term competitiveness while mitigating the risk of nontransparent, large-scale data transfers from the United States to China.

In previous chapters I have explained how data trafficking occurs and why safeguarding consumer and industrial data is essential. In this chapter, I offer a framework for managing data trafficking, drawing on literature related to another complex global security issue tethered to economic growth: climate change. As with climate change, it is difficult to educate the public on the seemingly low-level changes to the stability and security of their environment as chronic problems needing to be addressed. Such educational challenges are compounded by the difficulty of encouraging even minor lifestyle adjustments that would help improve the stability and security of their environment.

As with climate change, the worst effects of data trafficking will not be visible in the immediate term. Rather, they will be the result of an accumulation over time of intelligence resources, industrial advantages, social insights, financial data, and biomedical data over time. Radical change would stem the tide of data trafficking. But incremental change would at least avoid some of the worst impacts—namely, China's dominance of the twenty-first century data economy and control over areas as diverse as biodata and critical communication infrastructure. As with climate action, progress requires not one specific change but a constellation of often inconvenient, economically consequential actions that require shifts in behavior, trade, and communications.

It is unsatisfying to acknowledge that the United States is structurally ill-equipped to address issues of climate change as they intersect with individual behavior and corporate incentives, despite the importance of immediate action. The challenge of transforming the US data economy is similar. Despite needing transformative structural change, it can only reliably handle incremental solutions, if that. There are critics who argue that transforming the US tech economy would only make the United States like China by increasing oversight to a degree that undermines the US market economy. While I do not think such an approach is desirable, I also find it a remarkable feat of optimism to assume that the US government in its current form could enact such sweeping changes to the tech economy. Instead, I argue that the most feasible response to data trafficking is not data localization—storing data locally in individual nations—but rather data stabilization. This would establish clear pathways for redefining control of critical infrastructure, tracking user data movement across borders, and for transparent user access to such information.

As I demonstrate in this book, data trafficking grows from the network effects of consumer markets. For example, spotty oversight of sensitive data generated from large user bases, such as those used for human health insights, enables trafficking. Low-cost manufacturing systems have razor-thin margins that create the type of "data accidents" discussed in Chapter 9, where complex processes with few extra resources to devote to security allow data exploitation to become a likely, if inadvertent, outcome. Ultimately, rapid expansion of user bases, regulatory limitations, and cost constraints generate conflict between governments and corporations over the use of data. As a result, users have little say in what happens to the digital material of their lives. At the same time, economies around the world increasingly rely on user data to power new systems and tools. China's size and state-run economy allow it to strive toward a self-contained national data ecosystem that incorporates data from around the world. Such a self-contained approach is difficult to conceive of in the United States, however, as the user base is smaller and the tech sector relies on the autonomy of companies to trade and operate across borders. In the following section, I propose a model for stabilizing data flows to develop an incremental but unified approach to managing data trafficking.

Data Stabilization Wedges

From the realms of outer space to the intimacy of our bedrooms, data gathering has expanded in both scope and scale in mind-boggling ways. Yet, as this book has underscored, related protections for consumers and industries have not kept up. This imbalance introduces concerns for users and also for managing user data, from the most utilitarian to the most intimate. In this section I offer some suggestions for how to map a safe data policy.

Data security has much in common with climate change in that what benefits consumers and corporations in the short term ultimately works against their long-term best interests. Corporations and policymakers use similar arguments to justify inaction in both areas—the potential for economic damage, the extreme complexity of the problem, the need for better research/expertise than is currently available, claims that the issue is for future generations to address, and so on. These excuses provide a balm to concerned groups and individuals but fail to address legitimate problems that are worsening by the day.

Nevertheless, calls for massive systemic change, which would demand significant cost and inconvenience, are difficult to implement. Dealing with data trafficking, as with climate issues, requires a nuanced, multipronged approach that acknowledges political, corporate, and even individual resistance to systemic change. I therefore suggest drawing from a proposed climate change mitigation strategy to address concerns about data trafficking. Ecology and evolutionary biology scholar Stephen Pacala and physicist Robert H. Socolow introduced the concept of "stabilization wedges" incremental solutions for managing climate change, arguing that when combined can help to tackle the climate crisis.[2] The following figure represents how different tools can be deployed to manage data flows.

Stabilization is an apt term because it acknowledges that such strategies are not a way out of a crisis but rather a mechanism for managing an overwhelming challenge. The stabilization idea works particularly well in the context of data trafficking because it offers a clear alternative to unfettered data movement by corporations as well as to localization or data nationalism, wherein all a country's data remains within that country, thereby limiting international exchange. If we imagine our data as water, current regulations in the United States allow torrential flow like Niagara Falls. In China, the control of data flow is rigid, akin to the massive technical infrastructure of the Three Gorges Dam. A middle path, one that is being pioneered—but has not been perfected—by the European Union, Japan, Australia, and others, is careful oversight and controlled release. Data stabilization represents a middle path between unbridled capitalism and the highly restricted national control of data. Using stabilization wedges allows data movement to become predictable and manageable. Openness with guardrails could thereby stem data trafficking.

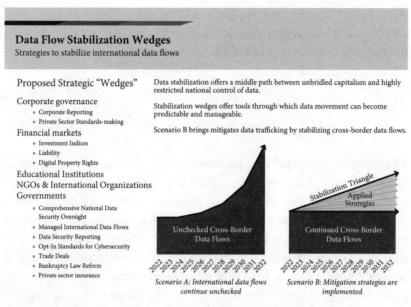

Data Flow Stabilization Wedges
Strategies to stabilize international data flows

Proposed Strategic "Wedges"

Corporate governance
  ○ Corporate Reporting
  ○ Private Sector Standards-making
Financial markets
  ○ Investment Indices
  ○ Liability
  ○ Digital Property Rights
Educational Institutions
NGOs & International Organizations
Governments
  ○ Comprehensive National Data
    Security Oversight
  ○ Managed International Data Flows
  ○ Data Security Reporting
  ○ Opt-In Standards for Cybersecurity
  ○ Trade Deals
  ○ Bankruptcy Law Reform
  ○ Private sector insurance

Data stabilization offers a middle path between unbridled capitalism and highly restricted national control of data.

Stabilization wedges offer tools through which data movement can become predictable and manageable.

Scenario B brings mitigates data trafficking by stabilizing cross-border data flows.

Stabilization Triangle
Applied Strategies

Unchecked Cross-Border Data Flows

Continued Cross-Border Data Flows

2022 2023 2024 2025 2026 2027 2028 2029 2030 2031 2032

2022 2023 2024 2025 2026 2027 2028 2029 2030 2031 2032

Scenario A: International data flows continue unchecked

Scenario B: Mitigation strategies are implemented

Figure 10.1 Policy Wedges as a Tool to Stabilize Data Flows

In the following sections, I offer suggestions to employ stabilization wedges as tools to reduce opportunities for data trafficking. Each wedge aligns with a different type of institution that can and should participate in the stabilization of data flows. The solutions are part of a larger planned data stabilization system that can be added to or subtracted from as needed. I propose a comprehensive approach that draws on a range of established strategies to regulate, rather than stop, international data flows. However, as is true for climate stabilization wedges, the system must be updated continually to factor in new tools as they become available. It is also essential to coordinate the support of industries and governments. I propose shifts in corporate governance, financial sector reform, improved government oversight, enhanced consumer education, and international management of data flows as strategies that will stem the tide of data trafficking.

Corporate Governance

Because the corporate management of data shapes the US consumer data landscape, corporate governance needs to be one—though not the only—feature of a pragmatic approach to data stabilization. Part of the stabilization process requires genuine action by firms to mitigate data trafficking. The economic importance of US-China trade means corporate governance practices are essential to managing user data gathering.

Corporate Reporting

A key step in preventing data trafficking is requiring firms to share more detailed information about where their data goes, who processes it, and who has access to it. Data storage practices need to be transparently disseminated—not deeply buried in terms of service or a transparency report for regulators, but clearly and openly available to users. Data is an asset that can secure financing for corporations. Investors must therefore be fully informed about how this valuable resource is stored and used. Whether and how investors can be encouraged to respond accordingly to information about firms' data processes and privacy is another important topic addressed further below.

What this means in practice is that transparency reporting needs to be more widely standardized across a wider range of industries. Transparency reporting needs to occur not just by companies in industries with known consumer data risks like social media and communications, but across all types of industries that gather and use consumer data, from health monitors to sex toys to washing machines.

Existing data reporting must be made more reliable. The California Consumer Privacy Act, a landmark regulation intended to enhance consumer data privacy in the largest market in the United States, demonstrates the difficulty of independently administering effective regulatory solutions. Following the act's implementation on January 1, 2020, users reported noncompliance, partial compliance, unclear compliance practices, and contested claims that undermined the law's efficacy.[3] Noncompliant firms made no effort to equip individuals to access or delete their data. Partially compliant firms offered to delete some data, though not all, or provided no means by which users could do so themselves. What the Californa Consumer Privacy Act demonstrates is that even with enhanced government regulations and corporate reporting requirements, bringing corporations more fully into the regulatory process is necessary to have any hope for accountability.

Private Sector Standards-Setting

To protect their consumers, their intellectual property, and their products, some corporations have developed proprietary data storage and security standards. Greater industry coordination around these standards is needed to ensure greater transparency, identify best practices, and ensure an effective response to violations of norms as determined jointly by corporations, regulators, and citizens.

Shared standards among firms in competitive fields are not impossible; precedents can be found in other industries. For instance, the energy industry has implemented comprehensive, industrywide safety standards through organizations such as the American Gas Association, the Independent Petroleum Association of America, and the Sport and Social Industry Association. This approach, though controversial among environmental groups, has allowed industries to self-regulate on key safety issues. Granted, it is a flawed system that failed to prevent ecological tragedies such as the Deepwater Horizon oil spill, where the eponymous oil rig exploded and sank, causing the largest marine oil spill in history. But the precedent and foundation of corporate standard-sharing on some issues can lay the groundwork for broader cooperation on other issues such as those impacting national security. Self-regulation in the tech industry within the framework of a nationwide data security plan would improve upon current oversight, which permits a freelance approach to industry-driven policymaking.

The Cyberspace Solarium Commission, a bipartisan, bicameral group tasked with developing consensus-based cybersecurity strategy for the United States, argues that enhanced standards-setting renders US data security practices more resilient and forms the foundation of cyber deterrence, or the prevention of offensive cyber operations by state and nonstate actors.[4] National and international data security standards offer the chance to anticipate and solve problems before they arise. More aggressive, coordinated involvement in data security standards between the US government and US corporations would provide an important hedge against the Chinese government's efforts to standardize global data flows.

Financial Markets

Financial appraisals of corporate market value must also incorporate assessments of consumer-data security in order to provide a market-based, external check on internal corporate practices and to reduce the risk of data exploitation. Requiring companies to internalize externalities (such as the impact of data breaches, or the national security impact of eroded national sovereignty) attributable to their weak data security regimes would incentivize data stewardship. In addition, several strategies already exist in the financial and insurance markets that could be used to address data exploitation.

Financial Reporting

Chinese rideshare company DiDi faced backlash from the Chinese government in part because of data sharing that would be required by its planned initial public offering on the NYSE and subsequent SEC reporting requirements. The SEC could examine ways to shift annual or quarterly reporting requirements to include more information about data use and security. Such a practice would require firms to submit, as part of their financial reporting, more detailed information about where they store data and how they prevent massive data breaches. Investors could then more efficiently assess the financial and security risks posed by that company's data security. Such an approach would also encourage the adoption of best practices for corporate data storage and security for financial reasons. After all, we manage what we measure. The transparency of security measures for critical infrastructure would also increase, which is essential for the long-term protection of US data infrastructure from a national security perspective.

Investment Indices

Enhanced reporting would support another mechanism for rewarding companies that have robust data security. Investment firms and ratings agencies are already developing environmental, social, and corporate governance investment indices that combine the stocks of companies with similar strengths in the areas of environmental protection, social responsibility, or accountable governance. They then aggregate investment options for corporate and individual investors who prioritize such issues.

Data security is included in some governance indices but increasingly offers a potential investment indexing opportunity.[5] Individual consumers are becoming more aware of the issues surrounding data security, and investors are progressively viewing corporate data security practices as a core business value. The advantage of Environmental, Social, and Governance (ESG) indices is that they internalize the externalities of data breaches by assigning financial value to corporate data governance. They also offer firms a vehicle through which to raise the capital necessary to fund data protection measures. However, at present, limited transparency in corporate data governance paired with opaque Chinese government regulations complicates efforts to incorporate this metric into indices.

Furthermore, enhancing investment outcomes on ESG indices gives investors a financial incentive to support national data security regulation. Researchers have found both a positive correlative and causative relationship between participation in ESG indices and strong stock market performance.[67] ESG indices also empower users to support companies that protect their data. On a larger scale, ESG outcomes have the potential to pressure companies to be on par with their peers on data governance issues. By no means are they a panacea, but they can expand the data stabilization toolbox. Enhanced reporting on data security issues then offers both an improved pathway to profitability and a tool to stem data trafficking.

Liability

If ESG indices are a carrot for improving corporate data governance, legal liability is a stick. Data breach insurance liability can shift companies' priorities by making firms financially responsible for any liabilities they generate through data losses. After the Equifax hack in the United States, in which the US government charged Chinese military officers for breaking into the nation's largest credit reporting bureau, consumers around the US received notices about a fund to provide affected consumers with credit monitoring services.[8] But the hackers did not act without assistance. Equifax's negligence in updating a critical security vulnerability allowed hackers to exploit the company's data.[9] The Equifax example underscores the importance of increasing liabilities for corporations that are negligent with consumer data.

Cybersecurity expert Robert K. Knake has long advocated for a strong cyber insurance market that mimics the energy industry's insurance requirements.[10] Rather than needing to go through the Federal Trade Commission, insurance markets would allow for a private sector alternative to penalize poor corporate data security practices that result in hacks or data trafficking. Knake proposes that firms operating within the United States should be fully insured against any loss that might result from private data-gathering activities. Such an approach would also ensure that insurance companies assess corporate data security risk in the underwriting process. If private sector firms were required to adhere to a basic standard of care in their cybersecurity operations, they could likely benefit from insurance against cyber attacks, or data trafficking.

Segments of the US government have already recommended this strategy to protect US critical infrastructure.[11] Still, the government has not implemented it. Liability for data breaches complements other cybersecurity reporting requirements by imposing a financial penalty on firms that lose data because of ineffective data-storage practices. The current indemnities for data loss are insufficient to influence individual firms to make the necessary changes. Requiring companies to take financial responsibility for what will likely be ever more significant data vulnerabilities is one way to incentivize them to protect their data on the front end.

Digital Property Rights

Digital property rights refers to the ownership or control of user data and of any related products or property. Although these rights present significant regulatory challenges, they offer users a framework for valuing and reclaiming data generated about them. When users control the rights to their digital lives, they have the option to monetize that data. Data is an asset that consumers create every day. One way to push back against digital resignation is to provide consumers with a way to turn that asset into money. When an iconic meme of a toddler giving side-eye to the camera sold for $74,000 as a nonfungible token, it underscored the value of user data to consumers. With the rise of digital property thanks to the markets for cryptocurrency and nonfungible tokens, data is increasingly being seen as a form of property to be controlled and managed. These products present significant challenges— including the climate-related impacts of energy-intensive blockchain-based properties, rampant scams, and the destabilization of markets—but they may spur public awareness of how corporations monetize data. Digital property rights for users could further establish publicly traded markets for data products that had previously been solely under the purview of tech executives who understand data's role as a business asset.

The Role of Governments

Market-based solutions alone, however, will not stem data trafficking, or overcome the fact that data-driven businesses lack sufficient privacy protections. Corporations whose data has been breached have faced penalties, both social and financial, yet those penalties have been small compared to the social damage caused. In addition to market-based protections, we need action from governments, which have many tools at their disposal to stem the tide of data trafficking. In this section, I identify two solutions. First, there is the option of tactical solutions, narrow actions meant to solve a specific problem. These take the form of legal changes, shifts in rules, and new practices. The second type of solution is a wholesale reimagining of the role of international data flows.

As I demonstrate in this book, data gathered from unexpected sources provides important insights into issues of health, national security, infrastructure, food supply, product development, and more. To prevent data trafficking, data security oversight must account for the ways data gathering impacts citizens' everyday lives. That is, any data stabilization policy must meet users where they are. What often gets overlooked in data security debates is the role that subnational governments play in regulating user data. Cities, counties, states, and other subnational entities manage the data of their citizens.

Although state and local governments are often the first points of contact for citizens in their interactions with government, they are chronically underfunded. An important first step to stabilizing data oversight is providing improved resources to state and local governments, particularly in underresourced areas. The case of Huawei's investment in telecommunications infrastructure in rural Nebraska underscores the long-term value of such an approach. While providing resources for subnational data stabilization is important, it must be part of larger tactical strategies at the national level. Here I outline a select number of national data stabilization tactics.

Opt-In Standards for Cybersecurity

Government agencies are essential to enforcing data security standards. In 2016, the Obama administration's Cybersecurity National Action Plan introduced several potential solutions to data trafficking based on existing government regulatory practices.[12] One plan suggested introducing a rating system similar to the Energy Star system that classifies the energy efficiency of appliances.[13] It would offer additional insights into the security of consumer products as well as into individual firms' data storage practices, which could be beneficial from a national security standpoint. Industry and government leaders could come together voluntarily to determine basic industry leadership standards. The proposed rating system also introduces an opportunity to educate in plain language all consumers over thirteen, the age of consent for data sharing in the United States, about the risks related to the accessibility and use of their data. This should be plain and simple like the warnings on cigarette packages: "Use of this product may cause the sale and loss of your private, personal information." However, the hypothetical rating system would face some of the same challenges as the Energy Star system: namely, third-party testing required to determine the ratings would increase the potential cost to market and, by extension, the cost to the consumer. As a result, consumers with sufficient financial resources would be able to choose more secure products, but price-sensitive consumers might not. One key consideration for government regulators is the degree to which it might be necessary to subsidize the tech sector to ensure equal access to privacy in data-driven products. Nevertheless, despite its limitations, this approach represents a valuable tool that could be used in conjunction with other data-stabilization measures.

Anti-Corruption Laws

Certain legal mechanisms can restrict the expansion of Chinese content control infrastructure into the United States. US corporations must follow US corporate law under the auspices of the Foreign Corrupt Practices Act (FCPA), which forbids companies from providing "anything of value" to a foreign official to gain or retain business. The US Department of Justice has interpreted this phrase widely with respect to China.[14] Under an expansive rubric, offering a foreign party control over information in exchange for the ability to operate in that foreign market could be construed as such an offer of value. The US government has not yet elected to prosecute this type of exchange under the FCPA, but the act offers a promising way of regulating Silicon Valley firms, which are financially motivated by the prospect of Chinese market access to participate in and thereby support China's expansion of its digital control infrastructure.

Bankruptcy Law Reform

Think about the most cringe-inducing content you have posted on social media. Now think about what could happen if that firm goes bankrupt and needs to sell all of their digital holdings. In the United States, when corporations leverage user data to secure their business, creditors can sell those assets in the event of a default.[15] With murky consumer data ownership and the rise in digital properties like nonfungible tokens, your awkward moment could become a digital asset available to sell off in the case of a corporate financial crisis. In practice, this means that when consumers agree to a corporation's terms of service, they must trust in that corporation's solvency or at least in its creditors' willingness to make ethical choices when the terms of bankruptcy require the sale of data.[16] Restructuring how data assets can be used to secure financing—and how creditors can sell data—would make valuable inroads into preserving consumer data security, while also preventing data trafficking via secondary markets.

The Chinese government sets at least one standard in data governance that the world should look to, namely that, long-term data management must be central to any forward-looking strategy to regulate across sectors. The Biden executive order that revoked the TikTok ban also set out a valuable framework for data threat assessment across sectors.[17] But such a framework depends on bipartisan buy-in for continuity, lest it be rescinded by a future administration. Data trafficking spans partisan divides. Policy responses should too.

The European Union and Japan have jointly established standards of *data adequacy*, a practice of ensuring sufficient, agreed-upon security standards for personal data transferred across borders.[18] Such properly overseen data flows stand as foils to the data-trafficking process. Datawise, what is occurring between Europe and Japan is the equivalent of legal employment immigration across borders. We can refer to data movement between the European Union and Japan as *data migration*, which involves the conscious, deliberate, procedure-driven process of selecting, preparing, extracting, and transferring data from one storage system to another in an information technology context. In data migration, data moves between systems that share standards for data adequacy and ensure equitable digital trade. Countries around the world, from Brazil and Singapore to India and Australia, are developing their own tools for managing their national data flows. While these practices are in conversation with, and often caught between, the United States and China, they also offer ways to stabilize global data flows. Without such national policies, data flows between China and the United States will benefit the country with the more restrictive policies and the bigger market.

Consumer Education

In liberal democracies, government data protection needs public buy-in to work. As with climate change, pressure from citizens helps give policymakers the courage to make decisions that may be unpopular with companies or inconvenient for consumers. Widespread public awareness of data trafficking will challenge digital resignation, or the public reluctance to challenge corporate data-gathering practices. The public needs to recognize that requiring consent to the movement of data affects not just individuals but also long-term economic and national stability.

Of course, similar issues exist in data security and climate change education. Media organizations specialize in covering acute events, such as fires, tsunamis, and major commercial hacks, and generic data security issues fail to deliver the level of excitement that today's twenty-four-hour news cycle demands. News organizations therefore need to nurture consumers' appetite for such media coverage through education.

Educational institutions can assist in combatting data trafficking by helping people understand how corporations collect and exploit user data. Learning about data security at the primary, secondary, and postsecondary levels is important. Digital hygiene, or the management of personal data disclosure and the protection of one's devices, should become an integral feature of curricula at every academic level as a tool to protect both users and institutions. Educational institutions often lack the time, expertise, and budget to cover these issues, especially in the face of pressure to make sure students meet basic standards. Such constraints are yet another reason it is so important to prioritize educational curricula that explain digital hygiene.

Even if users are fully aware of the types of data companies tend to share and aggregate and of the strategic and personal implications of this sharing, significant obstacles remain. Many of the tools firms use to gather data are convenient. They are fun. They seem harmless. In fact, they *are* largely harmless—until they are not. As with climate change, once the aggregate impacts of data trafficking shape new standards and norms, it becomes very difficult to restructure global data flows.

In truth, because we are so networked both on our devices and across our communities, educating one person has only a limited effect. In writing this book, I hope to help others better understand what their data vulnerabilities mean. The data of one person on their own may not be meaningful, but when combined across groups, as I hope this book has demonstrated, it provides rich insights that provide a map for contemporary life and future technologies. A comprehensive map allows for greater control of the world's digital resources, and thus agency over our own lives and nations, both now and in the future.

Managed International Data Flows

If educating consumers is the foundation of data stabilization, managing international data flows is the zenith. Establishing clearer boundaries between consumer data, government data, and commercial data protects national data corpora from international trafficking. Combatting data trafficking requires a carefully governed system of data flows.

Consumer education is only one small step, and, as with climate change, relying only on individual users to solve a collective problem lays the foundation for failure. Large-scale institutional interventions are necessary to stabilize global data flows. Multistakeholder and professional organizations also play important roles in establishing more robust international standards. However, to advance multistakeholder-driven data security standards, the US government must increase its representation at a wide range of standards-setting events. More support is also needed from civil society groups that advocate for users, independent of government and industry concerns.

Such an approach mirrors consumer standards established by governmental and industry groups in areas like organic food or energy efficiency. Professional organizations represent another nongovernmental venue for standards-setting. While such organizational standards overlap with standards set by industry organizations, they differ in that the membership consists of concerned individuals working in these fields, rather than strictly corporate representatives. For instance, the Institute of Electrical and Electronics Engineers guides its members through its code of conduct, focusing on practices to protect confidential information and intellectual property. Similarly, the US-based International Association for Computing Machinery has a code of ethics for its members that emphasizes honesty, confidentiality, and privacy.[19] Technical and research organizations' codes model similar frameworks for the general public. While these are voluntary codes without powerful enforcement mechanisms, they are important for laying out collective visions among members of these professions.

Both multistakeholder and professional organizations can also analyze individual products' data security standards and thereby offer security certifications for different types of standards for members. This approach empowers consumers to purchase equipment and apps with preapproved data security standards. Apple has moved in this direction by attempting to give consumers more in-depth information on the data security of offerings in its App Store. However, Apple's efforts affect only a relatively privileged group of users. They lack the heft and breadth of an industrywide standard. To bolster the work of multistakeholder and professional organizations, government intervention is essential.

Trade deals offer also an important way for countries to unite for the purpose of creating international data standards to stabilize data migration. The Comprehensive and Progressive Agreement for Trans-Pacific Partnership, comprising eleven Asia-Pacific countries, sets data storage and security standards for member nations.[20] Although the United States was initially one of the nations negotiating the agreement—originally called the Trans-Pacific Partnership—the Trump administration withdrew in 2017.

Multilateral organizations like the United Nations International Telecommunication Union offer a site to establish international norms for managing global data flows. Such multilateral organizations have also been fraught with tension between different models of data governance. Countries caught between the United States and China have faced pressure to choose between different models for data governance advocated by each country. One key example of this phenomenon is the United Nations Group of Governmental Experts on Developments in the Field of Information and Telecommunications in the Context of International Security (GGE).[21] The body, which was formed in the early 2000s, evolved from a place to discuss and establish cyber norms to a site of conflict over the global data order.[22] Liberal democratic countries remained affiliated with the GGE. Countries with a focus on extensive government control of the internet, led by Russia, called for the creation of the parallel Open-Ended Working Group (OEWG), an organization focused on cyber norms that have been adopted in Russia and China.[23] The GGE and OEWG have found some ways to work together, but the fracture between the organizations underscores the importance of a multilayered approach that does not rely on stable multilateral relationships.

From Trafficking to Stabilization

Data stabilization requires not just a rethinking of the data governance practices of individual countries, organizations, or users but a comprehensive framework for stable global data migration. Yet at the same time, comprehensive data stabilization ensures openness with guardrails, supporting individual users, equitable trade, and national security. By operating on multiple levels, data stabilization offers a path by which to find solutions for the technical impacts of data trafficking—with an eye toward managing international data flows on a large scale.

As with the climate, individual stabilization wedges are not a cure-all. Most countries around the world are already entwined with tech products from the United States, China, or both and are caught in the wake of the US-China tech competition. Even with data stabilization, Chinese government efforts to network sovereignty will likely persist. US and Chinese tech corporations will continue to face pressure to grow from financial markets, from their employees, and even from users. The US tech sector is likely to continue its reliance on extractive data practices to remain an engine of US economic might, and as a result, it will remain difficult to regulate. Efforts to stabilize data with technical solutions are important, but for such solutions to work, they must be accompanied by a larger reevaluation of consumer data gathering.

One of the major critiques of Pacala and Socolow's original stabilization wedges piece was that while it offered technical solutions available in the current system, it failed to acknowledge perhaps the most important option—systematically reducing consumption. Increasingly datafied lives are not an edict from on high. They are the product of inertia, pressure, and convenience. The most radical solution to data trafficking is for governments, corporations, and consumers to reevaluate the role that technology plays in mediating human life. User data is only becoming more intimate, pervasive, and important. With the advent of AI and machine learning, where autonomous systems use our data to make decisions for us, the window of opportunity to build secure, equitable data flows is rapidly closing. Rather than rushing to network life, we must instead discern why we invite tech firms into our lives, and what role they play in the societies where we live. Then, instead of being stuck in traffic, we might find a clear, predictable, and safer road ahead.

Epilogue

Data trafficking is only in its infancy. The promises of 5G, such as lightning-fast connection, enhanced service delivery, and more immersive digital environments, are still forthcoming. Companies are already preparing for 6G to enhance digital integration in areas ranging from health, transportation, medicine, agriculture, logistics, and beyond. Each of these areas bring new forms of data exploitation and vulnerability not just within nations, but between them. Nowhere are the stakes higher than in the US-China relationship.

Trafficking Data offers a framework for understanding the opportunities that China's extraterritorial data governance practices present to strengthen democracies. The first consideration is learning how to navigate the relationship between the Chinese government and tech companies in democracies that are trying to preserve a global tech sector. The second opportunity is contending with the difficulty of enforcing laws that run up against proprietary corporate resources and decision-making. The third opportunity is reconciling data standards between allied nations to create a more robust global network of data protection. My hope is that as users become more aware of their power, they can advocate for a more stable, transparent future – one where they have greater control of the data they generate not just on social platforms or in games but across all areas that form foundation of our digital world.

As I prepare to submit this book for production, there is some hope on the horizon. Governments in Japan, Korea, and the European Union are regularly enacting new data privacy legislation and coming together over common standards. California and other large states have implemented their own versions of data security legislation designed to protect consumers. The proliferation of state-level protections has increased pressure for national legislation. On June 3, 2022, the Senate and House of the United States Congress released draft legislation entitled the American Data Privacy and Protection Act (ADPPA), an effort to unify fragmented state and sector-specific laws at the national level. The Act attempts to minimize corporate data gathering, offer a national standard to protect states that lack robust enforcement capacity, and even extend the data privacy rights of minors to age 18.

However, like efforts that came before it, passage of national data privacy legislation is uncertain due to conflicts between competing interests in both the US government and the private sector. Even with Democratic majorities in the House and Senate and a Democratic President, disagreements about the 2022 bill exist within the Party over issues such as enforcement mechanisms, among others. When I asked a Congressional staffer familiar with the issue how I might respond in this book to the proposed legislation, he responded that I should write an additional chapter entitled "The Stalemate Continues . . . "

Competing industry and government interests have led to repeated standoffs in the implementation of national data privacy laws. Even if passed, the ADPPA would have a four-year moratorium on lawsuits to protect corporate interests in this transition. The competition between American corporate and national security interests in policymaking persists in complicating oversight. Such legislation may eventually stem the tide of data trafficking but would still delay meaningful enforcement for years.

Even though it has been passed into law, the California Consumer Privacy Act has been riddled with enforcement challenges, largely because of the difficulty of bringing lawsuits under it. Lawsuits as a form of enforcement require resources and time that are often difficult for individual users to bring forth. They also put the burden of enforcement on outside entities, something that is particularly difficult to assess due to proprietary corporate data-gathering practices.

Enforcement via lawsuit is a time-honored approach in US policymaking, but it also underscores the challenges of data stabilization. Not only does managing data flows typically require knowledge of proprietary technical systems, it also requires enforcement to occur after users have identified a problem. As I discuss throughout this book, economic and national security damage cannot be reversed once user data moves. Delaying enforcement until after users or prosecutors identify a problem means that even successful suits are ultimately failures on some level.

Waiting for data security breaches to happen before a law is enforced also means facing the resource constraints that already exist in the US system. From places like the Federal Trade Commission to the Committee on Foreign Investment in the United States, agencies lack sufficient resources to assess the legality of the vastly expanding scope of consumer data gathering.

Other governments have been much more responsive. Europe's General Data Protection Regulation passed in May 2016 and was implemented in May 2018. Tech-focused amendments to Japan's 2003 Act on the Protection of Personal Information have come into effect in the order of months.

Even with robust data privacy laws in place, data trafficking persists. In Japan, a country that has had robust privacy laws on the books for years, the lack of transparency in data storage practices has led to data trafficking. Journalists at Japan's Asahi Shimbun reported in 2021 that Line, a social media platform that is ubiquitous in the country, allowed data to be accessed by a subcontractor in China. The move made the data of Japanese Line users subject to Chinese government oversight without the knowledge of Line's CEO or its users.

Japan has been a leader in the protection of consumer data, particularly as it relates to China. The country amended its Act on the Protection of Personal Information directly in response to China's 2017 Cybersecurity Law, which required that corporate data be stored on Chinese government-run servers. Yet even with such protections in place for years prior, users and even Line's CEO did not know where their data was being stored or the laws to which it was subject. Only robust investigative reporting revealed the breach.

I do not present a rosy vision of the impact of China's expansive data governance frameworks here. But it remains important to track these developments and respond to the degree possible. In many ways, China's proactive approach to managing consumer data offers lessons for other countries around the world. Chinese laws treat data generated by companies and by users as valuable resources and rightly consider data as central to the future of economic growth, national security, and long-term autonomy.

Trafficking Data demonstrates the importance of finding common ground on data security both within and between countries around the world to stave off extraterritorial Chinese government data oversight. This is not easy, and it is mired in disagreements both within and between even developed democracies. However, it remains an essential task to preserving national digital sovereignty. By tracing how China and the US have shaped the global movement of data, I hope this book empowers citizens around the world to navigate the complex terrain created by Silicon Valley, Washington, and Beijing.

English-Pinyin-Chinese Glossary

11th Five-Year Plan	*Shiyi Wu Guihua*	十一五规划
12th Five-Year Plan	*Shier Wu Guihua*	十二五规划
13th Five-Year Plan	*Shisan Wu Guihua*	十三五规划
14th Five-Year Plan	*Shisi Wu Guihua*	十四五规划
Agreement Among the Governments of the SCO Member States on Cooperation in the Field of Ensuring International Information Security	*Shang He Zuzhi Chengyuan Guo Baozhang Guoji Xinxi Anquan Zhengfu Jian Hezuo Xieding*	《上合组织成员国保障国际信息安全政府间合作协定》
Alibaba	*Alibaba*	阿里巴巴
Alipay	*Zhifubao*	支付宝
Anbang Insurance Group Co., Ltd.	*Anbang Baoxian Jituan*	安邦保险集团
Anker Innovations	*Anke Chuangxin*	安克创新
Ant Group	*Mayi Jituan*	蚂蚁集团
Baidu	*Baidu*	百度
BeiDou Navigation Satellite System	*Beidou Weixing Daohang Xitong*	北斗卫星导航系统
Beijing Co-operative Equity Investment Fund Management Co., Ltd.	*Beijing Guquan Touzi Fazhan Guanli Youxian Gongsi*	北京股权投资发展管理有限公司
Beijing Kunlun Tech Co., Ltd.	*Beijing Kunlun Wan Wei Keji Gufen Youxian Gongsi*	北京昆仑万维科技股份有限公司
Beijing Shunyuan Kaihua Technology Co., Ltd.	*Beijing Shun Yuan Kai Hua Keji Youxian Gongsi*	北京顺源开花科技有限公司
Beijing Tiexue Technology Co., Ltd.	*Beijing Tie Xue Keji Gufen Gongsi*	北京铁血科技股份公司
Beijing Tourism Group	*Beijing Shoulü Jituan*	北京首旅集团
Beijing Yidian Wangju Technology Co., Ltd.	*Beijing Yidian Wang Ju Keji Youxian Gongsi*	北京一点网聚科技有限公司

Belt and Road Initiative	*Yidai Yilu*	一带一路
BGI Group	*Hua Da Jiyin*	华大基因
body	*tishen*	体身
ByteDance	*Zi Jie Tiaodong*	字节跳动
Central Military Commission	*Zhonghua Renmin Gongheguo Zhongyang Junshi Weiyuanhui*	中华人民共和国中央军事委员会
ChemChina	*Zhongguo Huagong Jituan*	中国化工集团
Chengxin Pan	*Pan Chengxin*	潘成鑫
China Aerospace and Satellite Technology Corporation	*Zhongguo Hangtian Keji Jituan*	中国航天科技集团
China Banking and Insurance Regulatory Commission	*Zhongguo Yinhang Baoxian Jiandu Guanli Weiyuanhui*	中国银行保险监督管理委员会
China Civil Aviation Authority	*Zhongguo Minyong Hangkongju*	中国民用航空局
China National Electronics Import & Export Corporation	*Zhongguo Dianzi Jin Chukou Zong Gongsi*	中国电子进出口总公司
China National GeneBank	*Guojia Jiyinku*	国家基因库
China National Human Genome Center	*Guojia Renlei Jiyinzu Beifang Yanjiu Zhongxin*	国家人类基因组北方研究中心
China National Offshore Oil Corporation	*Zhongguo Haiyang Shiyou Zong Gongsi*	中国海洋石油总公司
China Satellite Communications Co., Ltd.	*Zhongguo Weitong Jituan Gufen Youxian Gongsi*	中国卫通集团股份有限公司
Chinese Cybersecurity Law	*Zhonghua Renmin Gongheguo Wangluo Anquan Fa*	中华人民共和国网络安全法
city brain	*chengshi danao*	城市大脑
community of common destiny	*renlei mingyun gongtongti*	人类命运共同体
core socialist values	*shehui zhuyi hexin jiazhiguan*	社会主义核心价值观
Cryptography Law of the PRC	*Zhonghua Renmin Gongheguo Mima Fa*	中华人民共和国密码法
cyber sovereignty	*wangluo zhuquan*	网络主权
cyberpower	*wangluo qiangguo*	网络强国
Cybersecurity Review Measures	*Wangluo Anquan Shencha Banfa*	网络安全审查办法
Cybersecurity White Paper	*Zhongguo Wangluo Anquan Chanye Baipishu*	《中国网络安全产业白皮书》
Cyberspace Administration of China	*Zhonghua Renmin Gongheguo Guojia Hulianwang Xinxi Bangongshi*	中华人民共和国国家互联网信息办公室

Data Security Law	*Shuju Anquan Fa*	数据安全法
data sovereignty	*shuju zhuquan*	数据主权
Didi	*Didi*	滴滴
digital civilization	*shuzi wenming*	数字文明
Digital Silk Road	*Shuzi Sichou zhi Lu*	数字丝绸之路
DJI Technology Co., Ltd.	*Dajiang Chuangxin Keji Youxian Gongsi*	大疆创新科技有限公司
Douyin	*Douyin*	抖音
personal file	*geren dangan*	个人档案
Fire Eye laboratory	*Huo Yan shiyanshi*	火眼实验室
Ge Li	*Li Ge*	李革
Golden Shield Project	*Jindun Gongcheng*	金盾工程
Great Firewall	*Fanghuo Changcheng*	防火长城
Greenland Holdings Corp., Ltd.	*Lüdi Konggu Jituan Youxian Gongsi*	绿地控股集团有限公司
Haier Group Corporation	*Haier Jituan*	海尔集团
health code	*jiankang ma*	健康码
Health Silk Road	*Jiankang Sichou zhi Lu*	健康丝绸之路
Healthy China 2030	*Jiankang Zhongguo 2030*	健康中国2030
Hong Kong national security law	*Xianggang guojia anquan fa*	香港国家安全法
Houlin Zhao	*Zhao Houlin*	赵厚麟
Hu Gang	*Hu Gang*	胡刚
Huabei	*Huabei*	花呗
Huawei Technologies Co., Ltd.	*Huawei Jishu Youxian Gongsi*	华为技术有限公司
hukou	*hukou*	户口
information sovereignty	*xinxi zhuquan*	信息主权
intellectualization	*zhineng hua*	智能化
interconnection	*hulian hutong*	互联互通
Internet Plus Healthcare	*Hulianwang Jia Yiliao Jiankang*	互联网＋医疗健康
Jack Ma	*Ma Yun*	马云
James Lu	*Lu Fubin*	陆复斌
JD.com	*Jingdong*	京东
Jiang Zemin	*Jiang Zemin*	江泽民
Jiangsu Taihushui Group Company	*Jiangsu Taihushui Jituan Youxian Gongsi*	江苏太湖水集团有限公司
Linklogis	*Lian Yi Rong Keji Jituan*	联易融科技集团
Lizhi Liu	*Liu Lizhi*	刘立之

Lu Wei	*Lu Wei*	鲁炜
Made in China 2025	*Zhongguo Zhizao 2025*	中国制造2025
Meng Wanzhou	*Meng Wanzhou*	孟晚舟
military strategic guidelines	*junshi zhanlüe fangzhen*	军事战略方针
Min Jiang	*Jiang Min*	蒋敏
Monkey King	*Sun Wukong*	孙悟空
Nathan Law	*Luo Guancong*	罗冠聪
National People's Congress	*Zhonghua Renmin Gongheguo*	中华人民共和国
	Quanguo Renmin Daibiao Dahui	全国人民代表大会
Ng Wai Chung	*Wu Weicong*	吴伟聪
nine-dash line	*jiu duan xian*	九段线
Pak Nung Wong	*Huang Bonong*	黄伯农
Pan Gongsheng	*Pan Gongsheng*	潘功胜
Party-State	*Yi Dang Zhi*	一党制
People's Bank of China	*Zhongguo Renmin Yinhang*	中国人民银行
People's Liberation Army	*Zhongguo Renmin Jiefangjun*	中国人民解放军
Strategic Support Force	*Zhanlüe Zhiyuan Budui*	战略支援部队
Planning Outline for the Construction of a Social Credit System	*Shehui Xinyong Tixi Jianshe Guihua Gangyao*	《社会信用体系建设规划纲要》
property management	*wuye*	物业
Provisions on the Governance of the Online Information Content Ecosystem	*Wangluo Xinxi Neirong Shengtai Zhili Guiding*	《网络信息内容生态治理规定》
Qiaolei Jiang	*Jiang Qiaolei*	蒋俏蕾
Qingdao Refrigerator General Factory	*Qingdao Dianbingxiang Zong Chang*	青岛电冰箱总厂
Qingming Huang	*Huang Qingming*	黄庆明
red packet	*hongbao*	红包
Ren Zhengfei	*Ren Zhengfei*	任正非
residence permit	*hukou*	户口
resident certificate	*juliu zheng*	居留证
Shanghai Cooperation Organization	*Shanghai Hezuo Zuzhi*	上海合作组织
Sina Weibo	*Xinlang Weibo*	新浪微博
socialism with Chinese characteristics	*zhongguo tese shehui zhuyi*	中国特色社会主义

space dream	*taikong meng*	太空梦
Standardization Administration of China	*Guojia Biaozhunhua Guanli Weiyuanhui*	国家标准化管理委员会
State Council of the People's Republic of China	*Zhonghua Renmin Gongheguo Guowuyuan*	中华人民共和国国务院
substitute body	*tishen*	替身
Syaru Shirley Lin	*Lin Xiaru*	林夏如
Tencent	*Tengxun*	腾讯
Tencent QQ	*Tengxun QQ*	腾讯QQ
Third Plenary Session of the 18th Central Committee of the Communist Party of China	*Zhongguo Gongchandang Di Shiba Jie Zhongyang Weiyuanhui Di San Ci Quanti Huiyi*	中国共产党第十八届中央委员会第三次全体会议
Three Represents Campaign	*San ge Daibiao Zhongyao Sixiang*	「三个代表」重要思想
Tiananmen Mothers	*Tiananmen Muqin*	天安门母亲
Tiangong	*Tiangong*	天宫
Tsingtao beer	*Qingdao pijiu*	青岛啤酒
Wang Jun	*Wang Jun*	王俊
Wang Qishan	*Wang Qishan*	王岐山
Wanning Sun	*Sun Wanning*	孙皖宁
We shall drink to our heart's content to celebrate our success, but if we should fail let's fight to our utmost until we all die.	*Ren sheng de yi xu jin huan, ju gong jin cui, si er hou yi.*	人生得意需尽欢，鞠躬尽瘁，死而后已.
WeChat	*Weixin*	微信
Weibo Corporation	*Beijing Weimeng Chuangke Wangluo Jishu Youxian Gongsi*	北京微梦创科网络技术有限公司
Wentong Zheng	*Zheng Wentong*	郑文通
White Paper on the Internet in China	*Zhongguo Hulianwang Zhuangkuang Baipishu*	《中国互联网状况》白皮书
World Internet Conference	*Shijie Hulianwang Dahui*	世界互联网大会
WuXi AppTec	*Yao Ming Kangde*	药明康德
Xi Jinping	*Xi Jinping*	习近平
Xiaomi	*Xiaomi*	小米
Yellow Peril	*Huang Huo*	黄祸
Yuebao	*Yue bao*	余额宝
Yuen Yuen Ang	*Hong Yuanyuan*	洪源远
Yunshang Guizhou	*Yunshang Guizhou*	云上贵州

Zepp Health	*Huami Keji*	华米科技
Zhang Ruimin	*Zhang Ruimin*	张瑞敏
Zhejiang Dahua Technology Co., Ltd.	*Zhejiang Dahua Jishu Gufen Youxian Gongsi*	浙江大华技术股份有限公司
Zhima Credit	*Zhima Xinyong*	芝麻信用
Zhu Rongji	*Zhu Rongji*	朱镕基

Notes

Chapter 1

1. United States Department of Justice, "China-Based Executive."
2. Hawley, "Senator Hawley's Letter"; Goh, "U.S. Lawmakers Ask Zoom."
3. Bylund, "Zoom Stock Surged 425%"; Zoom Video Communications, "Zoom Video Communications Reports Fourth Quarter."
4. Marczak and Scott-Railton, *Move Fast*; Zoom Video Communications, "Zoom 10-K."
5. Herlo et al., *Practicing Sovereignty*; Floridi, "Fight for Digital Sovereignty"; Couture and Toupin, "What Does the Notion of 'Sovereignty' Mean"; Mueller, *Will the Internet Fragment*; DeNardis, *Global War for Internet Governance.*
6. Mueller, *Will the Internet Fragment*; Mueller and Badiei, "Governing Internet Territory."
7. Roberts et al., "Safeguarding European Values"; Mann and Daly, "Geopolitics, Jurisdiction and Surveillance"; DeNardis, *Global War for Internet Governance.*
8. Zuboff, *Age of Surveillance Capitalism.*
9. Information Office of the State Council of the People's Republic of China, "White Paper."
10. Cyberspace Administration of China, "Wangluo anquan shencha banfa."
11. Cyberspace Administration of China, "Wangluo anquan shencha banfa."
12. Stone and Wood, "China's Military-Civil Fusion Strategy"; Nie, "Space Privatization"; U.S.-China Economic and Security Review Commission, "Technology, Trade, and Military-Civil Fusion"; Laskai, "Civil-Military Fusion"; Kania and Vorndick, "Weaponizing Biotech"; Segal, "Seizing Core Technologies."
13. National People's Congress, "Zhonghua renmin gongheguo."
14. Lipsitz, *Possessive Investment*; Mallapragada, "Asian Americans as Racial Contagion"; Man, "Anti-Asian Violence"; Lew-Williams, *Chinese Must Go*; Lee, "'Yellow Peril' and Asian Exclusion." Such discrimination follows a history of anti-Chinese immigration policies in the 1800s and 1900s, the internment of Japanese Americans during World War II, and post–World War II "yellow peril" characterizations of Asian communities.
15. Zakaria, "New China Scare."
16. Yan, "Rise of China in Chinese Eyes."
17. Pan, "The 'China Threat.'"
18. Zhang, "#StopAsianHate."
19. Leibold, "Surveillance in China's Xinjiang"; Hargreaves, "Online Monitoring of 'Localists.'"
20. Mahdavi, *Gridlock.*
21. 32 C.F.1. § 701.31 (2005). See Pozen, "Mosaic Theory."

22. Duhigg, "How Companies Learn."
23. Doctorow, "Barlow's Legacy."
24. Hamilton, "California Student."
25. Norris, *Chinese Economic Statecraft.*
26. Wong, *Techno-Geopolitics.*
27. Gagliardone, *Politics of Technology,* 15.
28. Mahdavi, *Gridlock*; Mahdavi, *From Trafficking to Terror.*
29. Nolin, "Data as Oil."
30. Palmer, "Data Is the New Oil."
31. Organisation for Economic Co-Operation and Development, *Data-Driven Innovation.*
32. Khatri and Brown, "Designing Data Governance."
33. Gitelman and Jackson, "Introduction," 2.
34. Lindtner, Anderson, and Dourish, "Cultural Appropriation."
35. Draper and Turow, "Corporate Cultivation of Digital Resignation," 1824.
36. Elliott, *Role of Consent in Human Trafficking.*
37. Elliott, *Role of Consent in Human Trafficking.*
38. United Nations Office on Drugs and Crime, "Guidance Note."
39. Amaya, *Trafficking.*
40. Shamir, "Labor Paradigm for Human Trafficking."
41. Araujo et al., "From Purchasing Exposure to Fostering Engagement"; Bilro and Loureiro, "Consumer Engagement Systematic Review."
42. Cate and Mayer-Schönberger, "Notice and Consent."
43. Laurent et al., "Authenticated and Privacy-Preserving Consent Management."
44. Hamilton, "ByteDance's Head of Security"; Hale, "Chinese Tech Giant ByteDance."
45. Shamir, "Labor Paradigm for Human Trafficking."
46. Smythe, "Communications."
47. Kücklich, "Precarious Playbour"; Scholz, *Digital Labor.* Communications scholar Jack Linchuan Qiu argues that tech firms produce two types of iSlaves: the "manufacturing iSlave," factory workers involved in electronics production, often based in China and often working for little or no pay under deeply exploitative conditions, and what we will focus on in greater detail here, the "manufactured" or consumer iSlave, who supplies attention labor on digital platforms through exploitative labor bargains. Qiu's framing brings to the fore the cycles of labor debt and exploitation that migrant workers in China face, and which are often excluded from conversations about trafficking, from the tech sector to manufacturing to construction. Exploitative labor conditions enable labor brokers to delay payment to workers for years, or abscond with worker pay completely. Qiu's contributions to the analysis of the exploitative dynamic of the Chinese tech sector underscore the foundations of data trafficking. Qiu, *Goodbye iSlave.*
48. Andrejevic, "Work of Being Watched."
49. Swartz, *New Money.*

50. Gray, Buyukozturk, and Hill, "Blurring the Boundaries"; Henry and Powell, "Technology-Facilitated Sexual Violence"; Lawson, "Platform Vulnerabilities"; Sobieraj, "Bitch, Slut, Skank, Cunt"; Richard and Gray, "Gendered Play"; Gray, "Intersecting Oppressions"; Abreu and Kenny, "Cyberbullying and LGBTQ Youth"; Saunders, *Ethnopolitics in Cyberspace*; Lauckner et al., " 'Catfishing,' Cyberbullying, and Coercion"; Powell, Scott, and Henry, "Digital Harassment"; Backe, Lilleston, and McCleary-Sills, "Networked Individuals"; Hoffmann and Jonas, "Recasting Justice," 15; McInroy, "Pitfalls, Potentials, and Ethics."

51. Luo, Zhang, and Duan, "Social Media."

52. Luo, Zhang, and Duan, "Social Media."

53. Zuboff, *Age of Surveillance Capitalism*.

54. Kleiner and Appelbaum, *Resisting the Surveillance State*.

55. Harley, "Maps, Knowledge, and Power."

56. Giddens, "Nation-State and Violence."

57. Morris, *Practical Data Migration*.

58. European Commission, "European Commission Adopts."

59. Nakashima, "Hacks of OPM Databases."

60. Department of Justice Office of Public Affairs, "Member of Sophisticated Hacking Group Indicted."

61. Benner, "U.S. Charges Chinese Military."

62. Sanger et al., "Marriott Data Breach"; Giles, "US Suspects Chinese State Hackers."

63. Federal Aviation Administration, "Airspace."

64. Liedholm Johnson, "Mineral Rights."

65. Collins, *Space Race*.

66. Woods, "Litigating Data Sovereignty."

67. Couldry and Mejías, *Costs of Connection*; Couldry and Mejias, "Data Colonialism."

68. Couldry and Mejias, "Data Colonialism."

69. Office of the U.S. Trade Representative, "People's Republic of China."

70. Calzati, "Decolonising 'Data Colonialism,' " 6.

71. Grossman et al., *Chinese Views*.

72. Taplin, *Move Fast and Break Things*.

73. Khan, " 'Zoombombing' Houses of Worship"; Marks, "Privacy Risks of Your Baby Monitor"; Morrison, "Case Against Smart Baby Tech."

74. Benthall and Viljoen, "Data Market Discipline."

75. Agreda, "Ethics of Autonomous Weapons Systems."

76. Grossman et al., *Chinese Views*.

77. Stallings, "Handling of Personal Information."

78. Vaidhyanathan, *Googlization of Everything*; Zuboff, *Age of Surveillance Capitalism*.

79. Vaidhyanathan, *Antisocial Media*; Zuboff, *Age of Surveillance Capitalism*; West, *Buy Now*.

80. Liu, Zhang, and Chhachhar, "Comparative Study."

81. DeNardis, *Global War for Internet Governance*; DeNardis and Raymond, "Multistakeholderism"; Mueller, *Will the Internet Fragment*; Mueller, *Networks and States*.

82. Douglas, "Preventing Genocide"; Persily and Tucker, *Social Media and Democracy*.

83. Brayne, "Big Data Surveillance"; Fojas, *Border Optics*.

84. Lin, *Taiwan's China Dilemma*.

85. Schneier, "We're Back to Feudalism."

86. Zakaria, "Rise of Illiberal Democracy."

87. Desch, "America's Liberal Illiberalism"; Yan, "Chinese Values vs. Liberalism."

88. Krishnan, "Foreign Intelligence Surveillance Court"; Hinds, Williams, and Joinson, "'It Wouldn't Happen to Me.'"

89. Seppänen, "Interrogating Illiberalism," 268.

90. Maghrabi, "Threats of Data Security"; Wang and Ali, "Data Security and Threat Modeling."

91. Sukharev, "Economic Crisis"; Karan, "Responding to Global Public Health Crises."

92. Hardin, "Tragedy of the Commons."

93. Licoppe and Smoreda, "Are Social Networks Technologically Embedded?"

94. Rice, *Church of Facebook*; Kietzmann et al., "Social Media?"

95. Harris, "How Amazon Became a Pandemic Giant"; Stateler and Kinder, "Amazon and Walmart"; West, *Buy Now*.

96. McKune and Ahmed, "Contestation and Shaping," 3835.

97. Jiang, "Authoritarian Informationalism"; Creemers, "China's Conception of Cyber Sovereignty."

98. Seppänen, "Interrogating Illiberalism."

99. Odell, *Chinese Regime Insecurity*, 124.

100. Greitens, "Surveillance, Security, and Liberal Democracy."

101. Huang, "Pandemic and the Transformation," 1.

102. Lee, "Forced Technology Transfer."

103. Lee, "Forced Technology Transfer"; Milhaupt, "The State as Owner"; García-Herrero and Tan, *Deglobalisation*.

104. Lindtner, *Prototype Nation*; Yang, "China's 'Fake' Apple Store."

105. Schubert and Heberer, "State-Business Relations."

106. Lieberthal, "Introduction"; Mertha, "'Fragmented Authoritarianism 2.0.'"

107. Kokas, "China's 2021 Data Security Law."

108. Carothers, "Rejuvenating Democracy Promotion," 122.

109. Liu, "Rise of Data Politics," 56.

110. Personal Information Protection Commission, "Personal Information Protection Act"; Personal Information Protection Commission, "Act on the Protection of Personal Information"; Kittane et al., "Privacy and Data Protection"; Government of Australia, "Privacy Act 1988."

111. European Union, "General Data Protection Regulation."

112. Stanger, "Consumers vs. Citizens," 29.

113. European Union, "General Data Protection Regulation"; Umeda, "Online Privacy Law"; Office of the Privacy Commissioner of Canada, "Summary of Privacy Laws in Canada."

Chapter 2

1. Shaban, "Apple Stars."
2. Zuboff, *Age of Surveillance Capitalism*, v; Laidler, "Undermining Democracy."
3. Chen, "Big Data, Big Dream."
4. Lee, *AI Superpowers*; Selby, "Data Localization Laws."
5. 960 F. Supp. 456 (D. Mass. 1997).
6. Mueller, *Will the Internet Fragment?*
7. Miller, "Intelligence Coup of the Century."
8. Popper, *Open Society and Its Enemies.*
9. Popper, *Open Society and Its Enemies.*
10. Brenner, "Protecting America's Critical Infrastructure"; Government Accountability Office, "Critical Infrastructure Protection"; Stouffer et al., *Guide to Industrial Control Systems Security.*
11. MacKenzie, *ICAO*; International Civil Aviation Organization, "Convention on International Civil Aviation"; Darwin, "Outer Space Treaty Note"; Dembling and Arons, "Evolution of the Outer Space Treaty."
12. Turner, *From Counterculture to Cyberculture*; Borsook, "Cyberselfish."
13. Defense Advanced Research Projects Agency, "Breakthrough Technologies"; Defense Advanced Research Projects Agency, "60 Years."
14. Hughes, "Facing the Global Competitiveness Challenge."
15. United States Department of Defense, "Department of Defense Cyber Strategy 2018."
16. Nakashima, "Hacks of OPM Databases."
17. White House, "Executive Order on Protecting Americans' Sensitive Data."
18. Ford, "Executive Order 11858."
19. Ford, "Executive Order 11858."
20. Homeland Security Act of 2002, https://www.dhs.gov/sites/default/files/publications/hr_5005_enr.pdf.
21. The White House, "Statement by President"; Garamone, "President Signs."
22. House Financial Services Committee, "H. Rept. 115-784—Foreign Investment Risk Review Modernization Act of 2018," https://www.congress.gov/congressional-report/115th-congress/house-report/784/1.
23. Reuters, "U.S. Opens National Security Investigation Into TikTok."
24. *Reno v. ACLU*, 521 US 844 (1997).
25. Office for Civil Rights, "Summary of the HIPAA Privacy Rule."
26. Federal Trade Commission, "Children's Online Privacy Protection Rule ('COPPA')."
27. Federal Trade Commission, "Children's Online Privacy Protection Rule ('COPPA')."
28. Federal Trade Commission, "Children's Online Privacy Protection Rule ('COPPA')."
29. Federal Trade Commission, "Children's Online Privacy Protection Rule ('COPPA')."
30. Smith, "Alexa, Who Owns My Pillow Talk?"; Haber, "Internet of Children"; Lutz and Newlands, "Privacy and Smart Speakers."
31. Federal Trade Commission, "FTC Imposes $5 Billion Penalty."
32. *Employees' Retirement System of Rhode Island et al. v. Mark Zuckerberg et al.*, Delaware Court of Chancery, Case No. 2021-0617-JRS.

33. *Employees' Retirement System of Rhode Island et al. v. Mark Zuckerberg et al.*, Delaware Court of Chancery, Case No. 2021-0617-JRS.

34. *Employees' Retirement System of Rhode Island et al. v. Mark Zuckerberg et al.*, Delaware Court of Chancery, Case No. 2021-0617-JRS.

35. Federal Trade Commission, "FTC Authorizes Investigations"; Federal Trade Commission, "FTC Streamlines."

36. DiGrazia, "Cyber Insurance, Data Security."

37. Vullo, "Cybersecurity Requirements."

38. Vullo, "Cybersecurity Requirements."

39. California Consumer Privacy Act, AB-375, 2018, https://leginfo.legislature.ca.gov/faces/billTextClient.xhtml?bill_id=201720180AB375.

40. Marsden, "Virginia Consumer Data Protection."

41. Ratcliffe, "Partisans Are Coming"; Lewis, "Will Texas Soon Join."

42. Turner and Security.org Team, "47 States Have Weak."

43. White House, "National Cyber Strategy."

44. White House, "National Cyber Strategy."

45. Sarah D. Lande U.S. China Friendship Education Fund, *"Old Friends."*

46. Congressional Research Service, "US-China Cyber Agreement."

47. Congressional Research Service, "US-China Cyber Agreement."

48. Pelley and Krebs, "Fired Director"; Sanger and Perlroth, "Trump Fires a Cybersecurity Official."

49. Inserra, "Top Four Four Homeland Security Priorities."

50. United States Department of State, "The Clean Network."

51. Siripurapu, Chatzky, and McBride, "What Is the Trans-Pacific Partnership."

52. Eleftheriou-Smith, "China's President 'Turned Down.' "

53. DeNardis and Raymond, "Multistakeholderism," 573.

54. DeNardis and Raymond, "Multistakeholderism."

55. Ding, "Balancing Standards"; National Research Council, *Standards, Conformity Assessment, and Trade.*

56. Liaropoulos, "Exploring the Complexity of Cyberspace Governance"; Rosenbach and Chong, *Governing Cyberspace.*

57. Ruggie, "Multilateralism."

58. Wen, "2020 Zhongguo hulianwang qiye baiqiang gongbu"; Elegant, "Ma Biggest IPO—Again."

59. PL 116-222, https://www.congress.gov/bill/116th-congress/senate-bill/945.

60. Klein, "Chinese Acquisitions."

61. Deutsche Welle, "US Passes Bill That Could Delist."

62. Kokas, *Building a Transparent Web*; Calhoun, "Why Do Chinese Companies List."

63. Zhang and King, "Decision to List Abroad."

64. Kokas, "Chilling Netflix."

65. Gao, " 'Double-Faced' Lu Wei Jailed."

66. Yang and Murgia, "Microsoft Worked with Chinese Military."

67. Gallagher, "How U.S. Tech Giants."

68. Arsène, "Global Internet Governance."

69. Liu, "Elon Musk: Tesla Won't Share Car Data."
70. Moss, "Tesla Opens Data Center in Shanghai, China."
71. O'Connor, "How Chinese Companies Facilitate Technology Transfer."
72. Standing Committee of the National People's Congress, "Zhonghua renmin gongheguo wangluo anquanfa."
73. Oster, "Chinese Gaming Billionaire Buys"; French, "Why M&A Due Diligence."
74. Lazarow, "Silicon Valley's Role."
75. Childs and Zegart, "Divide Between Silicon Valley"; Liu, Trubek, and Wilkins, "Mapping the Ecology."
76. Kokas, "Building a Transparent Web."
77. Gillespie, *Custodians of the Internet*; Vaidhyanathan, *Antisocial Media*.
78. Lu, "China Enhances Regulation"; Zhang, "Government Responses"; Guluzade, "Role of China's State-Owned Companies"; Wei, "China's Xi Ramps Up Control."

Chapter 3

1. Lyu, "Duo guojia hulianwang"; Sun, "Fawang huihui, 'DiDi' bulou"; Cybersecurity Administration of China, "Guanyu xiajia 'DiDi chuxing' app."
2. Google Finance, "DiDi Global Inc."
3. Reuters, "Beijing City Looks to Take DiDi Under State Control."
4. China Computer News, "Pinglun: Fuzhi yamaxun."
5. Moss, "Tesla to Store China Data Locally."
6. Securities Exchange Commission, "Elon Musk Settles SEC Fraud."
7. Lieberthal, "Introduction"; Mertha, "'Fragmented Authoritarianism 2.0'"; Zeng, "Artificial Intelligence."
8. Zeng, "Artificial Intelligence."
9. Theoretical Studies Center Group of the Cyberspace Administration of China, "Shenru guanche Xi Jinping."
10. Ang, "Autocracy with Chinese Characteristics."
11. Ang, "Autocracy with Chinese Characteristics."
12. Information Office of the State Council of the People's Republic of China, "White Paper on the Internet in China."
13. Xi, "Xi Jinping jiu gongtong."
14. China Daily, "Cyber Sovereignty."
15. China Daily, "Cyber Sovereignty."
16. For excellent, detailed dives into the idea of cyber sovereignty in China, see the works of Rogier Creemers, C. Thomas Goodnight, Yu Hong, Elsa Kania, Samm Sacks, Florian Schneider, Adam Segal, Hong Shen, Yi Shen, Johannes Thumfart, Anqi Wang, and Graham Webster.
17. Thumfart, "Norm Development of Digital Sovereignty."
18. Renmin Ribao, "Wangluo zhuquan."
19. Renmin Ribao, "Wangluo zhuquan."

20. Liu, "Rise of Data Politics."
21. Kokas, "China's 2021 Data Security Law."
22. White, "China's Tech Platforms."
23. Browne, "Digital Epidermalization."
24. Benjamin, "Informed Refusal."
25. Karsten and West, "China's Social Credit System."
26. Liang, "COVID-19 and Health Code."
27. Liu, "Multiple Social Credit Systems in China"; Creemers, "China's Social Credit System."
28. Karsten and West, "China's Social Credit System."
29. Lin, "China and the Global Economy."
30. Hancock, "China Nationalises Troubled Conglomerate."
31. Yuan, "Beijing Pushes for a Direct Hand."
32. State Council of China, "Zhonggong zhongyang guowuyuan"; State Administration of Press, "Xinwen chuban guangdian."
33. USC US-China Institute, "Decision of the Central Committee."
34. Central Committee of the Communist Party of China, "Decision of the Central Committee"; China Daily, "Cyber Sovereignty."
35. Aycock, "China Pressing for State Investments."
36. Aycock, "China Pressing for State Investments."
37. Frank, "Phoenix New Media."
38. Dreyer, *Chinese Defense and Foreign Policy*.
39. Perlmutter and LeoGrande, "Party in Uniform."
40. Walsh and Francis, "China's Defense Innovation System."
41. Snape and Wang, "Finding a Place for the Party."
42. Lieberthal, *Governing China*; Russo, "Politics in the Boardroom"; Livingston, "New Challenge."
43. Reuters Staff, "Alibaba's Jack Ma."
44. Lin and Milhaupt, "Party Building or Noisy Signaling?"
45. State Council of China, "Guanyu tiaozheng fabu."
46. Mozur, Zhong, and McCabe, "TikTok Deal Is Complicated."
47. Sanger, "TikTok Deal Exposes a Security Gap."
48. Weiss and Bonvillian, "Complex, Established 'Legacy' Sectors."
49. Kow, Gui, and Cheng, "Special Digital Monies."
50. DeLuna, "What Do Alipay and WeChat Pay."
51. Chorzempa, Triolo, and Sacks, "China's Social Credit System."
52. Reuters, "China Says Rejecting Physical Cash Is Illegal."
53. Chan, "When One App Rules Them All."
54. Chan, "When One App Rules Them All."
55. Bank of China, "Zhongguo yinhang gufen."
56. Cheng, "How Ant Financial Grew."
57. Leng and Goh, "Ant Financial Pauses."
58. Griffiths, "China Is Rolling Out Facial Recognition."

59. Griffiths, "China Is Rolling Out Facial Recognition."
60. Griffiths, "China Is Rolling Out Facial Recognition."
61. Creemers, "Privilege of Speech"; Schneider, *China's Digital Nationalism.*
62. MacKinnon, *Consent of the Networked*; Ng, *Blocked on Weibo.*
63. Wedeman, "China's Corruption Crackdown."
64. Swanson and Bradsher, "Chinese Companies to Face More Scrutiny"; Xinhua, "Chinese Investment in Australia Plummets"; Bhardwaj, "Chinese Investment in India"; Monitoring Report, "Chinese Investment in Pakistan."
65. Fannin, "How the US-China Trade War Has Starved."
66. Qian, "Deciphering the Prevalence of Neighborhood Enclosure."
67. Yang, "The Politics of the Dang'an."
68. Yang et al., "Services and Surveillance During the Pandemic Lockdown."
69. Fan, "Yiren quezhen quanxiaoqu."
70. Lü, "Privacy and Data Privacy Issues."
71. Chorzempa, Triolo, and Sacks, "China's Social Credit System."
72. Hoffman, "Engineering Global Consent."
73. Zhao, "China's Quest for 'Soft Power.'"
74. Qiu, "Reflections on Big Data."
75. Leibold, "Surveillance in China's Xinjiang"; Byler, *In The Camps.*
76. Fravel, *Strong Borders, Secure Nation*; Feigenbaum, *China's Techno-Warriors.*
77. Mitchell and Diamond, "China's Surveillance State"; Lin and Purnell, "World with a Billion Cameras."
78. Eko, Kumar, and Yao, "Google This."
79. Eko, Kumar, and Yao, "Google This."
80. State Administration of Press, "Xinwen chuban guangdian."
81. Gow, "Core Socialist Values."
82. Standing Committee of the National People's Congress, "Wangluo anquanfa."
83. Cyberspace Administration of China, "Wangluo xinxi neirong."
84. Standing Committee of the National People's Congress, "Wangluo anquanfa."
85. Kokas, "Platform Patrol."
86. Campbell, "Apple to Move Chinese iCloud Keys"; Xinhua, "Pingguo guonei yonhu"; Xinhua, "Pingguo neidi iCloud."
87. Kokas, "Platform Patrol"; Apple, "Learn More About iCloud in China Mainland."
88. Kokas, "China's 2021 Data Security Law."
89. Cyberspace Administration of China, "Wangluo anquan shencha banfa."
90. Standardization Administration for Market Regulation and Standardization Administration of China, "Guojia biaozhun geren."
91. Miles, "U.S. Asks China Not to Enforce Cyber Security Law"; Ryder, "China's Personal Information Specifications"; Standardization Administration for Market Regulation and Standardization Administration of China, "Guojia biaozhun geren."
92. Maranto, "Who Benefits from China's Cybersecurity Laws?"
93. Standardization Administration for Market Regulation and Standardization Administration of China, "Guojia biaozhun geren."

94. Sacks, Chen, and Webster, "Five Important Takeaways"; Cyberspace Administration of China, "Wangluo anquan shencha banfa"; National People's Congress, "Data Security Law."

95. National People's Congress, "Shouquan fabu zhonghua."

96. McBride and Chatzky, "Is 'Made in China 2025' a Threat?"

97. Xinhua, "Zhonggong zhongyang guanyu."

98. State Council of China, "Guowuyuan guanyu yinfa shisanwu."

99. State Council of China, "Guowuyuan guanyu yinfa shisanwu."

100. State Council of China, "Guowuyuan guanyu yinfa shisanwu."

101. Shanghai Municipal People's Government, " 'Smartest City' Title for Shanghai."

102. State Council of China, "Guowuyuan guanyu yinfa shisanwu."

103. National People's Congress and the Chinese People's Political Consultative Conference, "Zhonghua renmin gongheguo guomin jinji."

104. National People's Congress and the Chinese People's Political Consultative Conference, "Zhonghua renmin gongheguo guomin jinji."

105. State Council of China, "Guowuyuan guanyu yinfa zhongguo zhizao 2025 de tongzhi."

106. State Council of China, "Guowuyuan guanyu yinfa zhongguo zhizao 2025 de tongzhi."

107. State Council of China, "Zhonggong zhongyang guowuyuan guanyu zhichi hainan."

108. Schneider, *China's Digital Nationalism*; Creemers, "Cyber-Leninism."

109. Zaagman, "Cyber Sovereignty."

110. Hillman, "Competing with China's Digital Silk Road." Related iterations of the term "Digital Silk Road," like "Information Silk Road" (*xinxi sichouzhilu*) and "Silk Road online" (*wangshang sichouzhilu* or *hulian hutong zhi sichou*), predated the term that was eventually adopted by the CCP.

111. Xi, "Xi Jinping zai."

112. Xi, "Xi Jinping zai."

113. Greene and Triolo, "Will China Control the Global Internet."

114. Fung, "How China's Huawei Took the Lead."

115. Zaagman, "Cyber Sovereignty."

116. DeLuna, "What Do Alipay and WeChat Pay."

117. Mastro, "Stealth Superpower."

118. Yuan, "China's Role in Establishing and Building"

119. Shanghai Cooperation Organization, "Agreement Between the Governments of the Member States"; NATO Cooperative Cyber Defence Centre of Excellence, "Shanghai Cooperation Organization."

120. NATO Cooperative Cyber Defence Centre of Excellence, "Shanghai Cooperation Organization."

121. Permanent Representative of China et al., "Letter Dated to 12 September 2011"; NATO Cooperative Cyber Defence Centre of Excellence, "Updated Draft."

122. Permanent Representative of China et al., "Letter Dated to 12 September 2011."

123. Permanent Representative of China et al., "Letter Dated to 12 September 2011."

124. Permanent Representative of China et al., "International Code of Conduct for Information Security."

125. International Telecommunication Union, "Houlin Zhao."

126. International Telecommunication Union, "Houlin Zhao."

127. International Telecommunication Union, "Houlin Zhao."

128. International Telecommunication Union, "Biographies."

129. Miles, "Huawei Allegations Driven by Politics."

130. International Telecommunications, "Biographies."

131. Shields and Sebenius, "Huawei's Clout."

132. U.S.-China Economic and Security Review Commission, "High-Tech Development."

133. Wedeman, "China's Corruption Crackdown"; Kokas, "Cloud Control."

134. Lee, "Hacking into China's Cybersecurity Law."

135. Erie and Streinz, "Beijing Effect."

136. Weber, "Understanding the Global Ramifications."

137. Sirimanna, "Chinese Here for Cyber Censorship."

138. Sherman, "Vietnam's Internet Control."

139. Smolaks, "Tanzanian Minister Attempts."

140. Mallett-Outtrim, "30,000 More Security Cameras"; Mai, "Ecuador Is Fighting Crime."

141. Dahir, "China 'Gifted' the African Union."

142. Roussi, "Resisting the Rise of Facial Recognition."

143. Whitten-Woodring et al., "Poison If You Don't Know How to Use It"; Qiu, "Goodbye iSlave."

144. Greitens, "Dealing with Demand."

145. Greitens, "Dealing with Demand."

Chapter 4

1. Wong, "National Security Law."

2. Xinhua, "English Translation of the Law."

3. Government of the Hong Kong Special Administrative Region, "Implementation Rules for Article 43," 4.

4. Collier and Lackoff, "Vulnerability of Vital Systems."

5. Aradau, "Security That Matters."

6. Fujimoto et al., "Dynamic Data Driven Application Systems"; Zhou, Fu, and Yang, "Big Data Driven Smart Energy Management"; Das and Yamana, "Securing Big Data"; Tokody and Schuster, "Driving Forces Behind Smart City Implementations"; Das, Kant, and Zhang, *Handbook on Securing Cyber-Physical Critical Infrastructure*.

7. Thumfart, "Norm Development of Digital Sovereignty."

8. Slaughter, "Sovereignty and Power."

9. Duarte, *Network Sovereignty*.

10. Duarte, *Network Sovereignty*.

11. Toal, "Geopolitical Structures and Cultures," 80.
12. Swartz, *New Money*, 152.
13. Xinhua, "Xi Sends Congratulatory Letter."
14. Xinhua, "Xi Sends Congratulatory Letter."
15. Mastro, "Stealth Superpower."
16. Mastro, "Stealth Superpower."
17. National People's Congress, "Zhonghua renmin gongheguo shuju anquanfa"; [This title above needs more words than just the name of PRC, even when the full source title is provided in references.] Rafaelof et al., "Translation: China's 'Data Security Law (Draft).'"
18. Greitens, *Dictators and Their Secret Police*.
19. Carlson, *Unifying China*; Roche, Leibold, and Hillman, "Urbanizing Tibet."
20. Micheli et al., "Emerging Models of Data Governance"; Paik et al., "Analysis of Data Management."
21. Alecci, "How China Targets Uighurs."
22. Harrus and Wyndham, "Artificial Intelligence and COVID-19"; Choudary, *China's Country-as-Platform Strategy*.
23. Milhaupt and Zheng, "Beyond Ownership"; The Economist, "Party Is Eager to Expand"; Russo, "Politics in the Boardroom."
24. Milhaupt and Zheng, "Beyond Ownership."
25. Allen-Ebrahimian and Palmer, "China Threatens U.S. Airlines."
26. Wee, "Giving In to China."
27. Haas, "Marriott Apologises to China."
28. Villegas, "'Fast and Furious' Star"; "John Cena Apologises" [in Mandarin], posted by @RealWWEJohnCena, May 24, 2021, https://weibo.com/3477696732/Kh0DJb h7C?from=page_1006053477696732_profile&wvr=6&mod=weibotime&type= comment.
29. Knockel et al., "We Chat, They Watch."
30. Wong, *Techno-Geopolitics*, 114.
31. Wong, *Techno-Geopolitics*, 114.
32. Draper, *Identity Trade*; Napoli, *Social Media and the Public Interest*.
33. Kaska, Minárik, and Beckvard, "Huawei, 5G and China"; Campion, "From CNOOC to Huawei."
34. Cartwright, "Internationalising State Power."
35. Huawei, "China Mobile, Huawei."
36. Haveman and Vochteloo, "Huawei"; Kaska, Minárik, and Beckvard, "Huawei, 5G and China."
37. Campion, "From CNOOC to Huawei."
38. Kaska, Minárik, and Beckvard, "Huawei, 5G and China," 7.
39. Wu, Hoon, and Zhang, "Dos and Don'ts for Chinese Companies."
40. De Cremer and Tao, "Huawei's Culture."
41. Wei, "China's New Power Play"; National People's Congress, "Zhonghua renmin gongheguo shuju anquanfa" [See note above for same source.]; Milhaupt and Zheng, "Beyond Ownership."

42. Inkster, "Huawei Affair," 109.
43. Bowler, "Huawei"; Ruptly, "UK Parliament to Discuss."
44. Bundesministerium des Innern für Bau und Heimat, "Kabinett beschließt Entwurf"; Chazan, "Germany Sets High Hurdle"; Buchholz, "Which Countries Have Banned Huawei?"; Murphy and Parrock, "Huawei 5G"; Bicheno, "Romania Goes Ahead."
45. Tang, "Huawei Versus the United States," 4563.
46. Daily et al., "Geographic Distribution of Poverty"; Mastre, "New Concern."
47. Bureau of Industry and Security, "Addition of Entities."
48. Shattuck, "Stuck in the Middle," 107; Bureau of Industry and Security, "Addition of Entities."
49. Lide and Chun, "Overview of Broadband Funding Opportunities"; Lewis, "China and Technology"; Furchtgott-Roth, "Chinese Government Helps Huawei"; Segal, *Chinese Cyber Diplomacy.*
50. Brandom, "It Will Cost $1.8 Billion."
51. McPherson-Smith and Pociask, "Huawei Is Embedded"; Bartholomew, "China and 5G."
52. The White House, "Fact Sheet: The Bipartisan Infrastructure Deal"; [This needs a few more words in title, as Fact Sheet could be any number of pubs. Check if in refs] Infrastructure Investment and Jobs Act, HR 3684, 2021, https://www.congress.gov/bill/117th-congress/house-bill/3684/text.
53. The White House, "Fact Sheet: The Bipartisan Infrastructure Deal."
54. The White House, "Fact Sheet: The Bipartisan Infrastructure Deal."
55. Tang, "Huawei Versus United States."
56. Anzai and Suzuki, "Huawei Passes Apple."
57. Araújo, "Infrastructure Deployment"; Whalen, "Huawei Helped Bring Internet."
58. Campion, "From CNOOC to Huawei."
59. National Research Council, *Precision Agriculture.*
60. Ag Information Network, "AgriEdge Excelsior."
61. Syngenta Global, "Our Research Areas."
62. Chee, "EU Clears ChemChina's $43 Billion Takeover of Syngenta."
63. M&A Critique, "ChemChina Buys Out Syngenta."
64. Tully, "This Agriculture Giant"; McMahon, "Drones Provide a Bird's Eye View"; Ostrom, "New Pilot Program."
65. Syngenta US, "AgriEdge."
66. Hirsch, "Pickup Truck Sales Rise."
67. Federal Aviation Administration, "Satellite Navigation"; Brookes, "Weather Forecasting"; Chavez, Barrera, and Kanter, "Operational Satellite Concepts"; Zou, Lin, and Weng, "Absolute Calibration."
68. Chicago Council on Global Affairs, "Lieutenant General Armagno on the US Space Force."
69. Freeman, "An Uncommon Approach to the Global Commons."
70. Freeman, "An Uncommon Approach to the Global Commons."
71. Freeman, "An Uncommon Approach to the Global Commons"; U.S.-China Economic and Security Review Commission, *China's Views of Sovereignty.*

72. Parks, "Signals and Oil," 5.

73. Parks, *Cultures in Orbit*, 70.

74. Kharpal, "China Once Said"; Xinhua, "Xuexi jinxingshi Xi Jinping."

75. China Public Private Partnerships Center, "Guiding Opinions."

76. Waidelich, "China's Commercial Space Sector."

77. Wood, "China's Ground Segment"; Julienne, "China's Ambitions in Space."

78. Liu et al., "Evaluation of China's Commercial Space Sector."

79. Defense Intelligence Agency, "Challenges to Security in Space"; USC US-China Institute, "China's Commercial Space Industry"; Waidelich, "China's Commercial Space Sector."

80. Bryce Space and Technology, "China's Orbital Launch Activity."

81. China Satellite Space Communications Co. Ltd., "Company Profile."

82. Heginbotham et al., "The U.S.-China Military Scorecard."

83. Nie, "Space Privatization."

84. Nie, "Space Privatization."

85. Weeden and He, "U.S.-China Strategic Relations in Space."

86. Global Times, "Tesla 'Brakes' in China."

87. Emont, "Amazon's Heavy Recruitment of Chinese Sellers."

88. Emont, "Amazon's Heavy Recruitment of Chinese Sellers."

89. Mosco, *Smart City in a Digital World*; Mosco, *Pushbutton Fantasies*; He, Wang, and Zhang, "Standardizing Smart City's Cloud Service."

90. Mosco, *Smart City in a Digital World*; Greitens, "Dealing with Demand"; Byler, *Terror Capitalism.*

91. Bacchi, " 'I Know Your Favourite Drink.' "

92. Whittaker, "Security Lapse Exposed."

93. Tanzania Daily News, "Tanzania"; Alibaba Cloud, "Alibaba Cloud Continues to Invest in Malaysia"; Dun & Bradstreet, "Tencent Cloud Europe."

94. Aglionby, Feng, and Yang, "African Union Accuses China."

95. Atha et al., "China's Smart Cities Development."

96. Atha et al., "China's Smart Cities Development."

97. Hellström, "Critical Infrastructure and Systemic Vulnerability"; Li and Li-Zhen, "Vulnerability and Interdependency"; Tokody and Schuster, "Driving Forces Behind Smart City."

98. Yan, "Rise of China in Chinese Eyes."

99. Pan, "The 'China Threat.' "

100. Ali, *Farm Fresh Broadband.*

101. Stauss, "Status of Proposed CCPA-Like State Privacy Legislation"; Sargent, "GDPR One Year Later"; Dipshan, "GDPR's Global Impact"; Boyne, "Data Protection in the United States"; Turner and Security.org Team, "47 States."

102. Lenzerini, "Data Integration."

103. Cattell, Chilukuri, and Levy, "How Big Data Can Revolutionize Pharmaceutical R&D." [This needs a few more words in the shortened title.]

104. Uniform Commercial Code, "Rights After Default"; I.D. Systems Inc., "Form 8-K."

105. Woolley and Howard, "Computational Propaganda."

106. Woolley and Guilbeault, "Computational Propaganda."

Chapter 5

1. *U.S. WeChat Users All. v. Trump*, Case No. 20-cv-05910-LB (N.D. Cal. Sep. 10, 2020).
2. Chao, "How Social Cash Made WeChat the App for Everything."
3. Plantin and Seta, "WeChat as Infrastructure."
4. *U.S. WeChat Users All. v. Trump*, Case No. 20-cv-05910-LB (N.D. Cal. Sep. 10, 2020).
5. White House, "Executive Order on Protecting Americans' Sensitive Data."
6. Katz and Shapiro, "Systems Competition."
7. Marks, "Emergent Medical Data"; Yin, "Emergent Algorithmic Culture"; Ebrahim, "Algorithms in Business."
8. Prokop, "Cambridge Analytica Shutting Down"; Isaak and Hanna, "User Data Privacy"; Ahmed, "Cambridge Analytica Psychologist"; Burki, "Vaccine Misinformation."
9. Finn, *Documenting Aftermath*.
10. Ellcessor, *In Case of Emergency*; Ellcessor, "Care and Feeding"; Ellcessor, "Technologies, Bureaucracy, and Disaster."
11. NetChoice, "About Us."
12. Ferraro, Chipman, and Preston, "Identifying the Legal and Business Risks."
13. Franks and Waldman, "Sex, Lies, and Videotape"; Brown, "Deepfakes"; Chesney and Citron, "Deep Fakes."
14. Colbaugh and Glass, "Estimating Sentiment Orientation"; Zeng et al., "Social Media Analytics"; He et al., "Gaining Competitive Intelligence."
15. TechCrunch, "China Blocks Access."
16. O'Brien, "China's Global Reach"; Reuters, "American Lawyer Arrested."
17. Grindr, "About Us."
18. Rai, "White House Briefs TikTok Creators on Ukraine."
19. Plantin et al., "Infrastructure Studies," 296; Hughes, *Networks of Power*; Bijker, Hughes, and Pinch, *Social Construction*; Mayntz and Hughes, *Development of Large Technical Systems*; Bowker and Star, *Sorting Things Out*; Edwards, "Infrastructure and Modernity."
20. Driscoll, *Modem World*, 2.
21. Doyle, "TikTok Statistics"; Statista, "Number of Monthly Active Users."
22. Zhang, Wu, and Liu, "Exploring Short-Form Video Application Addiction."
23. SensorTower, "TikTok Becomes."
24. Zhang, "Infrastructuralization of TikTok"; Mittmann et al., " 'TikTok Is My Life.' "
25. "Memorandum in Support of Plaintiffs' Motion for Preliminary Injunction," Case No. 20-cv-02658 (CJN), filed September 23, 2020, i. https://www.docketalarm.com/cases/District_Of_Columbia_District_Court/1--20-cv-02658/TIKTOK_INC._et_al_v._TRUMP_et_al/43/1/.
26. "Memorandum in Support," 19.
27. Harwell and Romm, "Inside TikTok"; TikTok, "Terms of Service"; Keller et al., "How Ranking and Recommendation Algorithms"; Chandlee, "Understanding Our Policies."
28. Lyons, "K-Pop Fans"; Lorenz, Frenkel, and Browning, "TikTok Teens Tank."

29. Grindr, "About Us." Beijing Kunlun Tech Co. Ltd. acquired 60 percent of the firm in 2016 and the rest in 2018.

30. Miles, "Still Getting It on Online."

31. Shield, "Grindr Culture," 151.

32. Shield, "Grindr Culture."

33. Plantin and Seta, "WeChat as Infrastructure," 258.

34. Statista Research Department, "Most Used Social Media 2021"; Knockel et al., "We Chat, They Watch."

35. Sun and Yu, "WeChat and the Chinese Diaspora."

36. Tencent, "Tencent Announces 2020 Third Quarter Results."

37. Plantin and Seta, "WeChat as Infrastructure."

38. Bureau of Economic and Business Affairs, "Investment Affairs"; Feddo, "Protecting America's Open Investment Policy."

39. Whittaker, "Everything You Need to Know"; Kovach, "Facebook-Apple Skirmish."

40. Poon, "Corporate Capitalism"; Tan and Zhan, "Improving New Product Development"; Davenport and Dyché, "Big Data."

41. Isaak and Hanna, "User Data Privacy."

42. Bossetta, "Weaponization of Social Media"; Vishwanath, "Habitual Facebook Use"

43. Wong, "How China Uses LinkedIn."

44. Halpin and Nownes, *New Entrepreneurial Advocacy*; Cooper, Gulen, and Ovtchinnikov, "Corporate Political Contributions."

45. Vaidhyanathan, *Antisocial Media*.

46. TikTok, "Privacy Policy."

47. Transparency Register, "TikTok Information Technologies"; California Consumer Privacy Act, AB-375, 2018, https://leginfo.legislature.ca.gov/faces/billTextClient.xhtml?bill_id=201720180AB375.

48. Lee, "In Re: TikTok."

49. DeGrippo, "Understanding the Information TikTok Gathers."

50. TikTok, "Statement on TikTok's Content Moderation."

51. Cloutier, "Our Approach to Security."

52. TikTok, "Privacy Policy."

53. TikTok, "Privacy Policy."

54. Roumeliotis et al., "Exclusive."

55. Fung, "Chinese-Owned Social Site"; Romm, "Apple, TikTok Decline."

56. TikTok, "Law Enforcement."

57. Singh, "India Retains Ban"; Kastrenakes, "Pakistan Lifts TikTok Ban"; Mehran, "PTA Blocks TikTok"; Hussain, "Fourth Time's the Charm?"

58. Ryan, "Australia's Defence Department"; Bogle, "Australia's Defence Devices"; Liao, "After India and US."

59. Wells and Tilley, "Oracle Wins Bid."

60. White House, "Executive Order on Protecting Americans' Sensitive Data."

61. Chew, "Letter to Senators."

62. Wang, "China's Kunlun Tech Agrees"; Sanger, "Grindr Is Owned."

63. Grindr, "About Us"; Grindr, "Community Guidelines."

64. Sanger, "Grindr Is Owned."
65. Mac, "Grindr Had Dreams"; O'Donnell and Wang, "Behind Grindr's Doomed Hookup."
66. Markey and Blumenthal, "Senators Markey, Blumenthal to Grindr"; Jackson, "Committee on Foreign Investment."
67. Wang and Oguh, "Grindr's Chinese Owner"; Wang, "China's Kunlun Tech Agrees."
68. Karlsson, "Understanding of Bold Social Media Content."
69. Tziallas, "Gamified Eroticism."
70. Grindr, "Privacy Policy."
71. Ghorayshi and Ray, "Grindr Is Sharing"; Warner et al., "Privacy Unraveling"; Sanger, "Grindr Is Owned."
72. Grindr, "Privacy and Cookie Policy"; Grindr, "Privacy Policy."
73. Grindr, "Privacy Policy."
74. Grindr, "Privacy Policy."
75. Grindr, "Privacy Policy."
76. Jackson, "Committee on Foreign Investment."
77. Lyons, "TikTok Says It Will Stop"; Wille, "Redditor Who Reverse-Engineered."
78. Ministry of Foreign Trade and Economic Cooperation and Ministry of Science and Technology, "Guanyu tiaozheng fabu."
79. Lee, "Popular Musical.ly App."
80. CB Insights, "Complete List of Unicorn Companies"; CB Insights, "How TikTok's Owner Became the World's Most Valuable Unicorn."
81. U.S. Senate Committee on Commerce, Science, and Transportation, "Protecting Kids Online."
82. Shih, "Chinese Firm Harvests Social Media Posts."
83. Osawa and Oster, "Beijing Tightens Grip on ByteDance."
84. Wilde, "TikTok Time Bomb."
85. NetChoice, "About Us."
86. Kim and Telman, "Internet Giants as Quasi-Governmental Actors."
87. Li, "U.S. Businesses in China Face Uncertainty"; Chan, *Walmart in China*.
88. Wagner, "General Motors"; Moss, "Tiny GM Car Zips."
89. Chesney and Citron, "Deep Fakes."
90. Grumbling and Johnson, "Implications of Artificial Intelligence."
91. Kim, "New Evidence Shows"; National Intelligence Council, "Foreign Threats."
92. TikTok, "Privacy Policy"; Wille, "Redditor Who Reverse-Engineered."
93. Federal Trade Commission, "Video Social Networking App."
94. Allyn, "Class-Action Lawsuit."
95. Jia et al., Chinese Digital Platform Giants; Jing and Dai, "AI National Team"; Tencent, "Bridging Gaps"; Atha et al., China's Smart Cities Development.
96. Jia et al., "Application of Artificial Intelligence."
97. Liu, "Chinese-Owned Apps Pose Counterintelligence Threat"; Mazarr et al., *Hostile Social Manipulation*; Schmidt, Sanger, and Perlroth, "Chinese Hackers Pursue."
98. Cox, "Army Follows Pentagon Guidance."
99. TikTok, "Privacy Policy."

234 NOTES

100. Cooper and Shear, "Biden Overturns"; Norquist, "Military Service"; Don't Ask, Don't Tell Repeal Act of 2010, HR 6520, https://www.congress.gov/bill/111th-congress/house-bill/6520/text.
101. Sabharwal et al., "Inclusive Work Practices."
102. Gewirtz and Weigel, "Grindr and the 'New Cold War.'"
103. Shenzhen Tencent Computer Systems Company Limited, "Agreement on Software License and Service."
104. Knockel et al., "We Chat, They Watch."
105. Sun, "Is There a Problem with WeChat?"
106. Walker, Kalathil, and Ludwig, "Cutting Edge of Sharp Power."
107. Dickson, "Teen Hides Protest Video."
108. Lee, "TikTok Apologises."
109. Chen, "Leaked Excerpt of TikTok Moderation Rules."
110. Chen, "Leaked Excerpt of TikTok Moderation Rules"; Netzpolitik, "Auszug aus den Moderationskriterien von TikTok."
111. India Today Web Desk, "Viral Hindu-Muslim Lesbian Couple."
112. TikTok, "TikTok Transparency Report."
113. Chen, "Leaked Excerpt of TikTok Moderation Rules."
114. Chen, "Leaked Excerpt of TikTok Moderation Rules."
115. Chen, "Leaked Excerpt of TikTok Moderation Rules."
116. Chen, "Leaked Excerpt of TikTok Moderation Rules."
117. Harwell and Romm, "Inside TikTok"; Biddle, Ribeiro, and Dias, "TikTok Told Moderators"; Hern, "Revealed"; Shead, "TikTok Invites."
118. Kalathil, "Evolution of Authoritarian Digital Influence."
119. "Protection for Private Blocking and Screening of Offensive Material," 47 USC § 230, https://www.law.cornell.edu/uscode/text/47/.
120. Swanson and McCabe, "U.S. Judge Temporarily Halts"; *U.S. WeChat Users All. v. Trump*, Case No. 20-cv-05910-LB (N.D. Cal. Sep. 10, 2020).
121. White House, "Protecting Americans' Sensitive Data."
122. Knockel et al., "We Chat, They Watch."
123. White House, "Executive Order on Addressing the Threat Posed by WeChat."
124. Yu, "Risk Mitigation."
125. PIB Delhi, "Government Bans 59 Mobile Apps"; PTI, "India Bans TikTok."
126. PIB Delhi, "Government Bans 59 Mobile Apps"; Ministry of Electronics and Information Technology, "Government Blocks 118 Mobile Apps."
127. PIB Delhi, "Government Bans 59 Mobile Apps"; PTI, "India Bans TikTok."
128. Goldman, "India-China Border Dispute"; Anbarasan, "China-India Clashes."

Chapter 6

1. Webster, "More than 12 Million"; Keith Stuart, "More than 12M Players."
2. Centers for Disease Control, "Covid-19 and Your Health"; Shear, "Trump Extends Social Distancing."

3. Zaidi, "Chart of the Week."
4. Richtel, "Children's Screen Time."
5. Sherr, "Coronavirus."
6. Brandom, "It Will Cost $8 Billion."
7. Michelle Hainer, "Fortnite Has Been."
8. Cai, Wohn, and Freeman, "Who Purchases and Why?."
9. Mortensen, "Flow, Seduction, and Mutual Pleasures."
10. Egenfeldt-Nielsen, Heide Smith, and Pajares Tosca, *Understanding Video Games.*
11. Wolf, *Medium of the Video Game*, 98.
12. Carless, "GDCTV."
13. Galloway, *Gaming.*
14. Thomala, "Market Size."; Jiangcheng, "2021 Chinese Gaming Industry."
15. Thomala, "Market Size."
16. Yuan and Long, "Multi-Platform Strategy."
17. Perez and Deng, "Peek at the Company."
18. Rafaelof et al., "Translation: China's 'Data Security Law (Draft)."
19. Webster, "Chinese Internet Giant Tencent."
20. Iqbal, "Fortnite Usage and Revenue Statistics."
21. Bandow, "Xi Jinping Doubles Down"; Capri, "Techno-Nationalism"; Schoff and Mori, "US-Japan Alliance."
22. Jiang and Fung, "Games with a Continuum."
23. Kania, "Chinese Military Innovation"; Pang, "Zhinenghua junshi geming."
24. Kania, "Chinese Military Innovation"; Linghu, "Rengong zhineng wujia."
25. Xinhua, "China's Military Strategy"; State Council Information Office of the People's Republic of China, "Zhongguo de junshi zhanlüe"; Kania, "Chinese Military Innovation."
26. Kania and Costello, "Strategic Support Force"; Costello and McReynolds, *China's Strategic Support Force.*
27. Kania, "PLA's Latest Strategic Thinking"; Kania and Vorndick, "Weaponizing Biotech."
28. Kania, "Minds at War"; People's Daily, "Zhuanjia zhinenghua juebu"; China Military Online, "Dashang junshi zhinenghua."
29. Standing Committee of the National People's Congress, "Zhonghua renmin gongheguo."
30. White House, "Executive Order on Addressing the Threat Posed by WeChat."
31. Executive Order 10306, 2021.
32. Sun, "Tencent's Gaming Business."
33. Smith, "Fortnite Owner Epic Games."
34. Spangler, "'Fortnite' Revenue Dropped 25% in 2019."
35. Mendoza, "'Fortnite' Now An Official College Sport."
36. Smith, "Fortnite Owner Epic Games."
37. Smith, "Fortnite Owner Epic Games"; Clement, "Annual Revenue of Tencent Holdings."
38. Feng et al., "Financial Reporting Quality."

39. Morck, Shleifer, and Vishny, "Management Ownership and Market Valuation."
40. Beuselinck and Manigart, "Financial Reporting Quality."
41. Kulzick, "Sarbanes-Oxley."
42. S&P Global Ratings, "Transparency Statement."
43. Hornshaw, "History of Battle Royale."
44. Wilson, Loveridge, and James, "How to Play Fortnite."
45. Roach, "What Is Fortnite?"
46. Fortnite Team, "5 Tips."
47. Roach, "What Is Fortnite?"
48. Hassan, "Fortnite Is a Social Space."
49. Steinkuehler and Williams, "Where Everybody Knows"; Coleman, *Social Capital*; Putnam, *Bowling Alone*.
50. Sanderson, Browning, and DeHay, "It's the Universal Language."
51. Sanderson, Browning, and DeHay, "It's the Universal Language."
52. Nazmeeva, "Constructing the Virtual."
53. Ingham, "Why Marshmello's Fortnite Show."
54. YouTikTok, "Renegade Dance."
55. Ingham, "Why Marshmello's Fortnite Show."
56. Ingham, "Why Marshmello's Fortnite Show."
57. Ansari, "Fortnite Skins."
58. Carr, "Top 5 Most Popular Emotes."
59. Valens, "Every Fortnite."
60. Ganti, "How Does Fortnite Make Money?"; Chris Carter, "Fortnite Loot Box."
61. Dey, "Is Fortnite Turning."
62. Children's Commissioner for England, "Gaming the System."
63. Children's Commissioner for England, "Gaming the System."
64. Cai, Wohn, and Freeman, "Who Purchases and Why?"
65. Castronova, "Virtual Worlds," 30.
66. Cai, Wohn, and Freeman, "Who Purchases and Why?"
67. Li, Freeman, and Wohn, "Power in Skin"; Cai, Wohn, and Freeman, "Who Purchases and Why?"
68. Cuthbertson, "How Children Playing Fortnite."
69. Yu, "Steam"; Hruska, "Tim Sweeney."
70. Yu, "Steam."
71. Yu, "Steam."
72. Radulovic, "Steam Rolls Out."
73. Hruska, "Tim Sweeney."
74. Gatlan "Epic Promises."
75. Wilde, "Tim Sweeney."
76. Epic Games, "Epic Games Terms of Service."
77. Tan, "How WoW Became."
78. Fintel.io, "Tencent Holdings."
79. Microsoft, "About Microsoft's Presence in China."
80. Tan, "How WoW Became."

81. Hern, "Overwatch."
82. Evers, van de Ven, and Weeda, "Hidden Cost of Microtransactions."
83. Serrels, "Blizzard Pulls Blitzchung."
84. IGN, "Blizzard President Addresses."
85. Smith, "Boycott Blizzard Movement."
86. Spangler, "Blizzard President."
87. Trithara, "Toward Geopolitical Gaming."
88. Russell, "Tencent Takes Full Control."
89. Bailey, "League of Legends Player."
90. Martinello, "League of Legends."
91. Macabasco, "Absolute Beginner's Guide."
92. Macabasco, "Absolute Beginner's Guide."
93. Riot Games, "Terms of Service."
94. Riot Games, "Terms of Service."
95. Riot Games, "Terms of Service."
96. Moyer, "China on TikTok Sale."
97. Lipton, "Manufactured Consent."
98. Lipton, "Manufactured Consent."
99. Burawoy, *Manufacturing Consent*, 180.
100. Takase, "GDPR Matchup."
101. Wall, "GDPR Matchup."
102. Human Rights Watch, "EU General Data Protection Regulation."
103. Riot Games, "Terms of Service."
104. Takahashi, "China Is Approving More Foreign Games"; Ministry of Culture of the People's Republic of China, "Hulianwang wenhua jingyin."
105. Takahashi, "China Is Approving More Foreign Games"; Ministry of Culture of the People's Republic of China, "Hulianwang wenhua jingyin."
106. Takahashi, "China Is Approving More Foreign Games"; Wang, "Youxi handong chixu." Ye, "China Ends Gaming Approval Freeze."
107. National Press and Publication Administration, "Wangluo chuban fuwu."

Chapter 7

1. Fan, Morck, and Yeung, "Capitalizing China"; Naughton, *Chinese Economy*.
2. Brokaw, *Ledgers of Merit*.
3. Jiang, "Brief Prehistory."
4. Zhongguo zhengfuwang, "Guide to Service."
5. Renmin Yinhang Wangzhan, "Measures for the Administration"; Editorial Staff, "How to Send Red Packet."
6. Creemers, "Planning Outline"; Chorzempa, Triolo, and Sacks, "China's Social Credit System"; Chong, "Cashless China"; Raphael and Xi, "Discipline and Punish"; Liang et al., "Constructing a Data-Driven Society"; Jiang, "Brief Prehistory."

7. Raphael and Xi, "Discipline and Punish."
8. Chorzempa, Triolo, and Sacks, "China's Social Credit System."
9. Creemers, "Planning Outline"; State Council of China, "Guowuyuan guanyu yinfa."
10. Tencent Research Institute, "Wecity Weilai Chengshi"; Leifengwang, "Fali zhihui chengshi."
11. Liao, "Race to Be China's Top Fintech Platform."
12. Jiemian News, "Shanghaishi zhengfuyu Alibaba"; The Paper, "Yong chengshi danao."
13. Li, Wu, and Xiao, "Impact of Digital Finance."
14. Jiang et al., "Nexus Between Digital Finance."
15. Zhong, "Ant Group Set."
16. Macauley, Mak, and Bloomberg, "Jack Ma Just Added Billions."
17. Sina Finance, "Mayun waitan jinrong."
18. McMorrow and Pilling, "Jack Ma Disappears."
19. Zhang and Xin, "Jack Ma Gives Video Speech."
20. Pan, "Zhongguo renmin yinhang."
21. Song, "Zhongguo yinbaojianhui zhongguo."
22. China Banking and Insurance Regulatory Commission, "Zhongguo yinbaojianhui bangongting."
23. Gkritsi, "Alipay, JD Digits, DiDi"; Caijingwang, "Jimayi zhihou weixin"; Xinhua, "Jingying feifa mayi."
24. Deepti, "Alipay, JD Digits, DiDi Finance Pull Out"; Kejilie, "Zhongguo renmin yinhang"; Sohu, "Cunkuan shichang."
25. Chen, "Jack Ma's Ant Financial."
26. Shiao, "Ant Group, Greenland."
27. Zhao, "Research on the Consumer Finance System."
28. People's Bank of China, "Guanyu jinyibu fangfan"; BBC News, "China Bans Banks"; BBC, "China Bans Initial Coin Offerings."
29. Parker, "Can WeChat Thrive."
30. Surane and Wang, "China's Alipay Grabs Slice."
31. Verifone, "Alipay Taxi Payments."
32. Parulis-Cook, "Essential Guide."
33. Nielsen, "Over 90% Chinese Tourists."
34. Shopping Kim, "List of Stores."
35. Chong, "Cashless China"; Liang et al., "Constructing a Data-Driven Society."
36. Swartz, *New Money.*
37. Swartz, *New Money.*
38. Tang et al., "Towards Understanding."
39. Kerr, "Mosaic Theory."
40. Mohsin, "Biden Team Eyes Potential Threat."
41. O'Keeffe and Rudegeair, "U.S. Bars Merger."
42. Long, "Ant Financial and Moneygram."
43. Executive Office of the President, "Executive Order on Addressing the Threat."
44. Executive Office of the President, "Executive Order on Addressing the Threat."

45. Ferek and Wells, "TikTok Files Another Lawsuit"; Whalen, "Federal Court Issues Preliminary Injunction."
46. Executive Office of the President, "Executive Order on Addressing the Threat."

Chapter 8

1. GenomeWeb, "BGI Americas Gets US Emergency Use Authorization."
2. GenomeWeb, "BGI Americas Gets US Emergency Use Authorization"; Needham, "Special Report"; Institute of Genetics and Development Biology, "Jinian renlei jiyinzu."
3. US-China Economic and Security Review Commission, "Annual Report."
4. Prem, "Genetron Covid-19 Test."
5. Neff, "Why Big Data"; Cavalli-Sforza, " Chinese Human Genome Diversity Project."
6. For more detail on how scholars think about the bioeconomy and biocapital, see the important contributions of Joseph Dumit and Kaushik Sunder Rajan.
7. CIO Tech Team, "HK Sees Internet of Things."
8. Johnson et al., "Precision Medicine."
9. Ting et al., "Digital Technology and Covid-19."
10. Johnson et al., "Precision Medicine."
11. Aronson and Rehm, "Building the Foundation."
12. Rogowski et al., "Concepts of 'Personalization.' "
13. Aceto, Persico, and Pescapé, "Role of Information and Communication Technologies"; Bamiah et al., "Study on Significance."
14. Raskar et al., "Apps Gone Rogue."
15. Raskar et al., "Apps Gone Rogue."
16. Health Insurance Portability and Accountability Act of 1996, PL 104-191, https://www.govinfo.gov/content/pkg/PLAW-104publ191/pdf/PLAW-104publ191.pdf.
17. Vayena and Blasimme, "Health Research with Big Data."
18. Crawford, "Hidden Biases."
19. Sweeney, Abu, and Winn, "Identifying Participants."
20. Aceto, Persico, and Pescapé, "Role of Information and Communication Technologies."
21. Ducharme, "Major Drug Company."
22. Ducharme, "Major Drug Company."
23. Jain et al., "Digital Phenotype."
24. Jain et al., "Digital Phenotype."
25. Schneble, Elger, and Shaw, "All Our Data."
26. Central Committee of the Chinese Communist Party, "Shisiwu guihua he"; Nassar et al., "Precision Medicine."
27. US-China Business Council, "China's Strategic Emerging Industries"; Central People's Government of the People's Republic of China, "Guowuyuan guanyu jiakuai"; Kazmierczak et al., "China's Biotechnology Development"; US-China Economic and Security Review Commission, "Annual Report"; State Council of China, "Guowuyuan guanyu yinfa."

28. State Council of the People's Republic of China, "Guowuyuan bangongting guanyu."

29. Linghu, "Rengong zhineng wujia."

30. State Council of the People's Republic of China, "Guowuyuan yinfa jiankang"; Xinhua, "Zhonggong zhongyang"; Tan, Liu, and Shao, "Healthy China 2030"; State Council of the People's Republic of China, "Guowuyuan bangongting."

31. Breckenridge, *Biometric State*, 16.

32. Liang, "Covid-19 and Health Code"; Tan, Chiu-Shee, and Duarte, "From SARS to COVID-19."

33. Liang, "Covid-19 and Health Code."

34. Liang, "Covid-19 and Health Code."

35. Liang, "Covid-19 and Health Code."

36. Balzano, "Written Testimony"; State Council of the People's Republic of China, "Zhonghua renmin gongheguo."

37. State Council of the People's Republic of China, "Zhonghua renmin gongheguo"; Cyranoski, "China's Crackdown on Genetics."

38. State Council of the People's Republic of China, "Zhonghua renmin gongheguo."

39. Zhang et al., "China Further Removes Foreign Investment Restrictions"; Ministry of Health and Ministry of Foreign Trade and Economic Cooperation, "Zhongwai hezi"; US-China Economic and Security Review Commission, "Annual Report."

40. Office of the U.S. Trade Representative, "2019 Report to Congress"; US-China Economic and Security Review Commission, "Annual Report."

41. Central Intelligence Agency, "World Factbook"; National Bureau of Statistics, 国家统计局, "Sixth Census Data"; Central Intelligence Agency, "The World Factbook"; National Bureau of Statistics, "Diliuci renkou rucha shuju."

42. Reuters, "MyHeritage."

43. Reuters, "MyHeritage."

44. Orbach, "Israel's Ministry of Health"; Jaffe-Hoffman, "Coronavirus Testing in Israel."

45. BGI Group, "BGI Group Helping"; Needham, "Special Report"; BGI Group, "BGI Supports Saudi Arabia"; MGI, "MGI Helped Angola"; BGI Group, "Close Friends Stand Together."

46. Needham, "Special Report"; Solomon Islands Government, "Minister Manele Acknowledge Support."

47. Needham, "Special Report"; BGI Group, "Close Friends Stand Together"; MGI, "MGI Helped Angola."

48. Needham, "Special Report."

49. Needham, "Special Report."

50. Needham, "Special Report"; BGI Group, "BGI Group Helping"; US-China Economic and Security Review Commission, "Annual Report."

51. Needham, "Special Report."

52. Popper, *Open Society*.

53. National Academies, *Safeguarding the Bioeconomy*; US-China Economic and Security Review Commission, "Annual Report."

54. Kalkman et al., "Responsible Data Sharing."

55. Fleming, "HIPAA-Cratic or HIPAA-Critical."

56. Kosinski, Stillwell, and Graepel, "Private Traits and Attributes"; Reece and Danforth, "Instagram Photos"; Saeb et al., "Mobile Phone Sensor"; Schneble, Elger, and Shaw, "All Our Data."

57. Reece and Danforth, "Instagram Photos."

58. Jackson and Cimino-Isaacs, "CFIUS Reform Under FIRRMA."

59. Javers, "U.S. Blocked Chinese Purchase."

60. Javers, "U.S. Blocked Chinese Purchase."

61. Bedlack et al., "Lunasin Does Not Slow ALS Progression."

62. Frost and Massagli, "Social Uses of Personal Health Information"; Frost and Massagli, "PatientsLikeMe."

63. Pai and Bader, "Patient Similarity Networks"; Vegter, "Towards Precision Medicine."

64. PatientsLikeMe, "PatientsLikeMe Privacy Policy."

65. Levy and Farr, "Trump Administration Is Forcing."

66. Pérez-Peña and Rosenberg, "Strava Fitness App."

67. Google Play, "Zepp Life."

68. Huami Corporation, "Huami Corporation Form 20-F."

69. Xiaomi, "Xiaomi User Agreement."

70. Gouda, Hejji, and Obaidat, "Privacy Assessment."

71. Gouda, Hejji, and Obaidat, "Privacy Assessment."

72. Gouda, Hejji, and Obaidat, "Privacy Assessment."

73. Brock and Buchanan, *Ethical Issues*.

74. Burke and Ryan, "Complex Relationship"; Papanicolas, Woskie, and Jha, "Health Care Spending."

75. Ehrbeck, Henke, and Kibasi, "Emerging Market"; Hamblin, "Healthcare, Meet Capitalism."

76. Winter and Davidson, "Big Data Governance"; Rosenbaum, "Data Governance and Stewardship."

77. Institute of Medicine Roundtable on Value and Science-Driven Health Care, *Clinical Data*; NHS Digital, "Data Sets."

78. Paulson Institute, "A Chinese Pharmaceutical Start-Up."

79. Paulson Institute, "A Chinese Pharmaceutical Start-Up."

80. Paulson Institute, "A Chinese Pharmaceutical Start-Up."

81. WuXi PharmaTech Inc, "WuXi PharmaTech Acquires NextCODE"; Leung, "WuXi Biologics Readies Hong Kong Relisting"; WuXi AppTec, "WuXi AppTec Announces Listing."

82. GenomeWeb, "23andMe Raises $115M."

83. GenomeWeb Staff Reporter, "Complete Genomics"; BGI-Shenzhen, "BGI-Shenzhen Completes Acquisition."

84. Complete Genomics, "69 Genomes Data"; WuXi NextCODE, "WuXi NextCODE Clarifications."

85. Charles E. Grassley and Marco Rubio to Joanne M. Chiedi, June 10, 2019, https://www.finance.senate.gov/imo/media/doc/2019-06-10%20CEG%20MR%20to%20HHS%20OIG%20(Threats%20to%20Genomic%20Data).pdf; Department of Health and Human Services Office of the Inspector General, "Opportunities Exist."

86. WuXi NextCODE, "WuXi NextCODE Clarifications."

87. Mui, "China's $9 Billion Effort."

88. WuXi NextCODE, "WuXi NextCODE Clarifications."

89. State Council of the People's Republic of China, "Zhonghua renmin gongheguo"; Genuity Science, "WuXi NextCODE Restructures"; Martz, "Why the WuXi NextCODE Split."

90. WuXi NextCODE, "WuXi NextCODE Clarifications."

91. Dr. Hempel Digital Health Network, "Huawei Precision Medicine Cloud."

92. Cyranoski, "China Embraces Precision Medicine."

93. Schenker, "China Leaps Ahead"; GenomeWeb Staff Reporter, "WuXi NextCode Restructures"; Cyranoski, "China Embraces Precision Medicine"; White House, "Fact Sheet: President Obama's Precision Medicine Initiative."

94. Genuity Science, "WuXi NextCODE Restructures."

95. Buhr, "WuXi NextCODE Aims."

96. Keenan, "WuXi NextCODE Acquires GMI."

97. Kazmierczak et al., "China's Biotechnology Development."

98. WuXi NextCODE, "WuXi NextCODE Gains CAP Accreditation."

99. Anderson, "DNAnexus Expands Its Global Network"; Thomas, "WuXi PharmaTech Invests $15M in DNAnexus."

100. You, "Safeguarding the Bioeconomy."

101. Schneble, Elger, and Shaw, "All Our Data."

Chapter 9

1. DeNardis, *Internet in Everything*.

2. Howard, *Pax Technica*, 112.

3. Draper and Turow, "Corporate Cultivation of Digital Resignation."

4. European Commission, "General Product Safety Directive."

5. Consumer Product Safety Act, PL 92-573 and updates.

6. Perrow, *Normal Accidents*, 5.

7. Perrow, *Normal Accidents*.

8. Perrow, *Normal Accidents*, 5.

9. Braun, "Normal Accidents in the Digital Age."

10. Nunan and Di Domenico, "Big Data," 481.

11. Nunan and Di Domenico, "Big Data," 485.

12. Nunan and Di Domenico, "Big Data," 487.

13. Nunan and Di Domenico, "Big Data."

14. Nunan and Di Domenico, "Big Data," 485.

15. Winig, "GE's Big Bet"; Krauskopf, "GE Says Data Business."

16. Haney and Furman, "Human Factors."

17. Crunchbase, "Whirlpool Acquires Yummly."

18. Varadarajan, Yadav, and Shankar, "First-Mover Advantage."

19. Backaler, "Haier"; Global Trade Alert, "China: Government Subsidy Changes"; PRNewswire, "China Home Appliances"; Ni, "Study on How to Promote"; Borak and Xue, "DJI's Success."
20. Chen and Dickson, *Allies of the State*.
21. Yeung and Dewoskin, "From Survival to Success."
22. Yeung and Dewoskin, "From Survival to Success."
23. Vantage Asia, "Haier D-Share IPO."
24. Yu, "Haier Has a Plan"; Fewsmith, "Sixteenth National Party Congress."
25. Yu, "Haier Has a Plan."
26. GE Appliances, "GE Appliances and Haier."
27. Yu, "Haier Has a Plan."
28. GE Appliances, "GE Appliances and Haier."
29. GE Appliances, "GE Appliances and Haier."
30. Tencent Tech, "Baidu, Haier Partner."
31. Tencent Tech, "Baidu, Haier Partner."
32. Wang, "Public Diplomacy"; Nye, "Soft Power."
33. Levy, "Intimate Surveillance," 680.
34. Leaver, "Intimate Surveillance."
35. Stanislav and Beardsley, "Hacking IoT."
36. Stanislav and Beardsley, "Hacking IoT."
37. Stanislav and Beardsley, "Hacking IoT."
38. Stanislav and Beardsley, "Hacking IoT."
39. Stanislav and Beardsley, "Hacking IoT."
40. HackersOnBoard, "DEF CON 27"; Farley, "Prostitution."
41. Mozilla Foundation, "*Privacy Not Included"; SEC Consult, "Internet of Dildos."
42. Goldfisk and Follower, "DEF CON 24."
43. Sparrow and Karas, "Teledildonics."
44. Pagach and Warr, "Characteristics of Firms."
45. Apple, "Magic Motion."
46. Apple, "Magic Motion."
47. MagicMotion, "Magic Motion App Privacy Notice."
48. MagicMotion, "Magic Motion App Privacy Notice."
49. Chang, *Brotopia*.
50. Lindtner, *Prototype Nation*.
51. Heraldkeepers, "Drones Market Analysis."
52. Wingo, "Prepared Statement."
53. DJI, "DJI Privacy Policy."
54. DJI, "DJI Privacy Policy."
55. Chon, "DJI Is a More Elusive U.S. Target."
56. Bernhardt, "Temporary Cessation"; Peters, "US Just Showed"; Mozur, Barnes, and Krolik, "Popular Chinese-Made Drone."
57. Sullivan, "Policy on Funding."
58. Bureau of Industry and Security, "Addition of Entities."
59. Gartenberg and Brandom, "US Government Adds DJI."

60. Chon, "DJI Is a More Elusive U.S. Target."
61. EufyCam, "Amazon Privacy Policy."
62. EufyCam, "Amazon Privacy Policy."
63. EufyCam, "Amazon Privacy Policy."
64. EufyCam, "Amazon Privacy Policy."
65. EufyCam, "Amazon Privacy Policy."
66. EufyCam, "Amazon Privacy Policy."
67. EufyCam, "Amazon Privacy Policy."
68. EufyCam, "EufyCam Privacy Policy."
69. EufyCam, "EufyCam Privacy Policy."
70. EufyCam, "EufyCam Privacy Policy."

Chapter 10

1. Breckenridge, *Biometric State*.
2. Pacala and Socolow, "Stabilization Wedges."
3. Bensinger, "So Far."
4. King and Gallagher, "Cyberspace Solarium Commission Report."
5. Baker, "Cybersecurity Becoming Big ESG Concern."
6. Deng and Cheng, "Can ESG Indices Improve."
7. Giese et al., "Foundations of ESG Investing."
8. Federal Trade Commission, "Children's Online Privacy Protection Rule ('COPPA')."
9. Fair, "$575 Million Equifax Settlement."
10. Knake, "Creating a Federally Sponsored"; Knake, "Expanding Disclosure Policy."
11. King and Gallagher, "Cyberspace Solarium Commission Report"; White House, "Critical Infrastructure Protection."
12. White House, "Fact Sheet: Cybersecurity National Action Plan."
13. Commission on Enhancing National Cybersecurity, "Report on Securing and Growing the Digital Economy."
14. Chow, "Three Major Risks."
15. Guillou, "Privacy Issues in Bankruptcy Sales."
16. Drennan, "Consumer Data Privacy in Bankruptcy."
17. White House, "Executive Order on Protecting Americans' Sensitive Data."
18. Hickman and Asayama, "EU-Japan Adequacy Decision."
19. Association for Computing Machinery, "ACM Code of Ethics."
20. Australian Government Department of Foreign Affairs and Trade, "CPTPP Outcomes."
21. Tiirmaa-Klaar, *Evolution*.
22. Tiirmaa-Klaar, *Evolution*.
23. Ruhl et al., "Cyberspace and Geopolitics."

References

Abreu, Roberto L., and Maureen C. Kenny. "Cyberbullying and LGBTQ Youth: A Systematic Literature Review and Recommendations for Prevention and Intervention." *Journal of Child and Adolescent Trauma* 11, no. 1 (2018): 81–97.

Aceto, Giuseppe, Valerio Persico, and Antonio Pescapé. "The Role of Information and Communication Technologies in Healthcare: Taxonomies, Perspectives, and Challenges." *Journal of Network and Computer Applications* 107 (April 2018): 125–54.

Ag Information Network. "AgriEdge Excelsior." Last updated January 20, 2015. https://www.aginfo.net/report/30086/Line-on-Agriculture/AgriEdge-Excelsior.

Aglionby, John, Emily Feng, and Yuan Yang. "African Union Accuses China of Hacking Headquarters." *Financial Times*, January 29, 2018. https://www.ft.com/content/c26a9214-04f2-11e8-9650-9c0ad2d7c5b5.

Agreda, Angel Gomez de. "Ethics of Autonomous Weapons Systems and Its Applicability to Any AI Systems." *Telecommunications Policy* 44, no. 6 (July 2020): 1–15. https://doi.org/10.1016/j.telpol.2020.101953.

Ahmed, Nafeez. "Cambridge Analytica Psychologist Advising Global COVID-19 Disinformation Network Linked to Nigel Farage and Conservative Party." *Byline Times*, February 2, 2021. https://bylinetimes.com/2021/02/02/cambridge-analytica-psychologist-advising-global-covid-19-disinformation-network-linked-to-nigel-farage-and-conservative-party/.

Alecci, Scilla. "How China Targets Uighurs 'One by One' for Using a Mobile App." International Consortium of Investigative Journalists, November 24, 2019. https://www.icij.org/investigations/china-cables/how-china-targets-uighurs-one-by-one-for-using-a-mobile-app/.

Ali, Christopher. *Farm Fresh Broadband: The Politics of Rural Connectivity.* Cambridge, MA: MIT Press, 2021.

Alibaba Cloud. "Alibaba Cloud Continues to Invest in Malaysia: Alibaba Cloud Supports Malaysia's Digital Transformation." 2021. https://www.alibabacloud.com/campaign/malaysia.

Allen-Ebrahimian, Bethany, and James Palmer. "China Threatens U.S. Airlines over Taiwan References." *Foreign Policy*, April 27, 2018. https://foreignpolicy.com/2018/04/27/china-threatens-u-s-airlines-over-taiwan-references-united-american-flight-beijing/.

Allyn, Bobby. "Class-Action Lawsuit Claims TikTok Steals Kids' Data and Sends It to China." NPR, August 4, 2020. https://www.npr.org/2020/08/04/898836158/class-action-lawsuit-claims-tiktok-steals-kids-data-and-sends-it-to-china.

Amaya, Hector. *Trafficking: Narcoculture in Mexico and the United States.* Durham, NC: Duke University Press, 2020.

Anbarasan, Ethirajan. "China-India Clashes: No Change a Year After Ladakh Stand-Off." BBC News, June 1, 2021. https://www.bbc.com/news/world-asia-57234024.

Anderson, Angela. "DNAnexus Expands Its Global Network for Genomic Medicine to China." *Inside DNAnexus* (blog), April 22, 2015. https://blog.dnanexus.com/tag/wuxi-nextcode-genomics/.

Andrejevic, Mark. "The Work of Being Watched: Interactive Media and the Exploitation of Self-Disclosure." *Critical Studies in Media Communication* 19, no. 2 (2002): 230–48.

Ang, Yuen Yuen. "Autocracy with Chinese Characteristics: Beijing's Behind-the-Scenes Reforms." *Foreign Affairs*, April 16, 2020.

Ansari, Danish. "Fortnite Skins: List of the Most Popular Outfits in the Battle Royale." Republic World, August 19, 2020. https://www.republicworld.com/technology-news/gaming/fortnite-skins-list-of-the-most-popular-outfits-in-the-battle-roy ale.html.

Anzai, Akihide, and Wataru Suzuki. "Huawei Passes Apple to Become Second-Largest Smartphone Maker." Nikkei Asia, August 1, 2018. https://asia.nikkei.com/Business/Companies/Huawei-passes-Apple-to-become-second-largest-smartph one-maker.

Apple. "Learn More About iCloud in China Mainland." 2020. https://support.apple.com/en-us/HT208351.

Apple. "Magic Motion." App Store, 2021. https://apps.apple.com/us/app/magic-motion/id679035540.

Aradau, Claudia. "Security That Matters: Critical Infrastructure and Objects of Protection." *Security Dialogue* 41, no. 5 (October 2010): 491–514.

Araújo, Marco. "Infrastructure Deployment in Unprofitable Areas." Stockholm University, 2020. https://su.diva-portal.org/smash/get/diva2:1460607/FULLTEXT01.pdf.

Araujo, Theo, Jonathan R. Copulsky, Jameson L. Hayes, Su Jung Kim, and Jaideep Srivastava. "From Purchasing Exposure to Fostering Engagement: Brand-Consumer Experiences in the Emerging Computational Advertising Landscape." *Journal of Advertising* 49, no. 4 (2020): 428–45.

Aronson, Samuel J., and Heidi L. Rehm. "Building the Foundation for Genomics in Precision Medicine." *Nature* 526, no. 7573 (October 2015): 336–42.

Arsène, Séverine. "Global Internet Governance in Chinese Academic Literature. Rebalancing a Hegemonic World Order?" *China Perspectives*, 2016, 25–35.

Association for Computing Machinery. "ACM Code of Ethics and Professional Conduct." June 22, 2018. https://www.acm.org/code-of-ethics.

Atha, Katherine, Jason Callahan, John Chen, Jessica Drun, Kieran Green, Brian Lafferty, Joe McReynolds, et al. "China's Smart Cities Development: Research Report Prepared on Behalf of the U.S.-China Economic and Security Review Commission." SOS International LLC and U.S.-China Economic and Security Review Commission, January 2020. https://www.uscc.gov/sites/default/files/2020-04/China_Smart_Cit ies_Development.pdf.

Australian Government Department of Foreign Affairs and Trade. "CPTPP Outcomes: Trade in the Digital Age." January 2019. https://www.dfat.gov.au/trade/agr eements/in-force/cptpp/outcomes-documents/Pages/cptpp-digital.

Aycock, Jason. "China Pressing for State Investments in Key Tech Firms." Seeking Alpha, October 11, 2017. https://seekingalpha.com/news/3300570-china-pressing-state-inve stments-key-tech-firms.

Bacchi, Umberto. "'I Know Your Favourite Drink': Chinese Smart City to Put AI in Charge." World Economic Forum, December 9, 2020. https://www.weforum.org/age nda/2020/12/china-ai-technology-city/.

Backaler, Joel. "Haier: A Chinese Company That Innovates." *Forbes*, June 17, 2010. https://www.forbes.com/sites/china/2010/06/17/haier-a-chinese-company-that-innovates/?sh=21e8d7745648.

Backe, Emma Louise, Pamela Lilleston, and Jennifer McCleary-Sills. "Networked Individuals, Gendered Violence: A Literature Review of Cyberviolençe." *Violence and Gender* 5, no. 3 (May 14, 2018): 135–46.

Bailey, Dustin. "League of Legends Player Count Reaches Eight Million Concurrent Users." PCGamesN, September 18, 2019. https://www.pcgamesn.com/league-of-legends/player-count.

Baker, Sophie. "Cybersecurity Becoming Big ESG Concern." *Pensions and Investments*, October 2, 2017. https://www.pionline.com/article/20171002/PRINT/171009985/cybersecurity-becoming-big-esg-concern.

Balzano, John. "Written Testimony for U.S.-China Economic and Security Review Commission." US-China Economic and Security Review Commission, Washington, DC, May 7, 2020. https://www.uscc.gov/hearings/chinas-evolving-healthcare-ecosystem-challenges-and-opportunities.

Bamiah, M., S. Brohi, S. Chuprat, and J. Ab Manan. "A Study on Significance of Adopting Cloud Computing Paradigm in Healthcare Sector." Paper presented at the International Conference on Cloud Computing Technologies, Applications and Management, Dubai, United Arab Emirates, December 8–10, 2012.

Bandow, Doug. "Xi Jinping Doubles Down on Korean War Propaganda." *Foreign Policy*, November 18, 2020. https://foreignpolicy.com/2020/11/18/xi-jinping-korean-war-propaganda-chinese-intervention-nationalism/.

Bank of China. "Zhongguo yinhang gufen youxian gongsi geren zhanghao kaihu ji zonghe fuwu shenqingbiao" [Application form for individual account opening and comprehensive service of Bank of China Limited]. Baidu Wenku, November 2011. https://wenku.baidu.com/view/c2d3025b312b3169a451a40c.html.

Bartholomew, Carolyn. "China and 5G." *Issues in Science and Technology* 36, no. 2 (Winter 2020): 50–57.

BBC News. "China Bans Banks from Handling Bitcoin Trade." BBC, December 5, 2013. https://www.bbc.com/news/technology-25233224.

BBC News. "China Bans Initial Coin Offerings Calling Them 'Illegal Fundraising.'" BBC, September 5, 2017. https://www.bbc.com/news/business-41157249.

Bedlack, R. S., Paul Wicks, Timothy Vaughan, Alicia Opie, Rebecca Blum, Amanda Dios, and Ghazaleh Sadri-Vakili. "Lunasin Does Not Slow ALS Progression: Results of an Open-Label, Single-Center, Hybrid-Virtual 12-Month Trial." *Amyotrophic Lateral Sclerosis and Frontotemporal Degeneration* 20, no. 3–4 (April 2019): 285–93.

Benjamin, Ruha. "Informed Refusal: Toward a Justice-Based Bioethics." *Science, Technology, and Human Values* 41, no. 6 (2016): 967–90.

Benner, Katie. "U.S. Charges Chinese Military Officers in 2017 Equifax Hacking." *New York Times*, February 10, 2020. https://www.nytimes.com/2020/02/10/us/politics/equifax-hack-china.html.

Bensinger, Greg. "So Far, Under California's New Privacy Law, Firms Are Disclosing Too Lttle Data—or Far Too Much." *Washington Post*, January 21, 2020. https://www.washingtonpost.com/technology/2020/01/21/ccpa-transparency/.

Benthall, Sebastian, and Salome Viljoen. "Data Market Discipline: From Financial Regulation to Data Governance." *Journal of International and Comparative Law* 8, no. 2 (December 2021): 459–86.

Bernhardt, David. "Temporary Cessation of Non-Emergency Unmanned Aircraft Systems Fleet Operations." US Department of the Interior, January 29, 2020. https://www.doi.gov/sites/doi.gov/files/elips/documents/signed-so-3379-uas-1.29.2020-508.pdf.

Beuselinck, Christof, and Sophie Manigart. "Financial Reporting Quality in Private Equity Backed Companies: The Impact of Ownership Concentration." *Small Business Economics* 29, no. 3 (2007): 261–74. https://doi.org/10.1007/s11187-006-9022-1.

BGI Global. "BGI Supports Saudi Arabia to Establish Six Huo-Yan Laboratories to Enable COVID-19 Testing for 30% of the Population in the Next 8 Months." Press release, April 27, 2020. https://www.prnewswire.com/news-releases/bgi-supports-saudi-ara bia-to-establish-six-huo-yan-laboratories-to-enable-covid-19-testing-for-30-of-the-population-in-the-next-8-months-301047527.html.

BGI Group. "BGI Group Helping over 80 Countries for Timely COVID-19 Detection and Intervention." Press release, April 20, 2020. https://www.prnewswire.com/news-relea ses/bgi-group-helping-over-80-countries-for-timely-covid-19-detection-and-inter vention-301043895.html.

BGI Group. "Close Friends Stand Together Through Thick and Thin: BGI to Assist Serbian Government to Build Two 'Huo-Yan' Laboratories to Help Fight Pandemic." Press release, April 13, 2020. https://www.bgi.com/global/company/news/close-frie nds-stand-together-through-thick-and-thin-bgi-to-assist-serbian-government-to-build-two-huo-yan-laboratories-to-help-fight-pandemic/.

BGI-Shenzhen. "BGI-Shenzhen Completes Acquisition of Complete Genomics." Press release, March 18, 2013. https://www.prnewswire.com/news-releases/bgi-shenzhen-completes-acquisition-of-complete-genomics-198820331.html.

Bhardwaj, Naina. "Chinese Investment in India: Impact of New FDI Restrictions by New Delhi." *India Briefing News*, March 5, 2021. https://www.india-briefing.com/news/india-rethinking-its-fdi-policy-stance-with-china-what-we-know-21824.html/.

Bicheno, Scott. "Romania Goes Ahead with Huawei 5G Ban." Telecoms.com, April 15, 2021. https://telecoms.com/509382/romania-goes-ahead-with-huawei-5g-ban/.

Biddle, Sam, Paulo Victor Ribeiro, and Tatiana Dias. "TikTok Told Moderators: Suppress Posts by the 'Ugly' and Poor." The Intercept, March 16, 2020. https://theintercept.com/2020/03/16/tiktok-app-moderators-users-discrimination/.

Bijker, Wiebe, Thomas Hughes, and Trevor Pinch. *The Social Construction of Technological Systems.* Cambridge, MA: MIT Press, 1987.

Bilro, Ricardo Godinho, and Sandra Maria Correia Loureiro. "A Consumer Engagement Systematic Review: Synthesis and Research Agenda." *Spanish Journal of Marketing—ESIC* 24, no. 3 (2020): 283–307.

Bogle, Ariel. "TikTok Not Approved for Use on Australia's Defence Devices." ABC, January 15, 2020. https://www.abc.net.au/news/science/2020-01-16/defence-ban-tik tok-china-security-fears/11869512.

Borak, Masha, and Yujie Xue. "DJI's Success Fuels Shenzhen's Rise as Centre of Global Drone Industry." *South China Morning Post*, April 4, 2021. https://www.scmp.com/tech/big-tech/article/3128004/how-shenzhen-hi-tech-hub-china-became-drone-capi tal-world.

Borsook, Paulina. "Cyberselfish: Ravers, Guilders, Cyberpunks, and Other Silicon Valley Life-Forms." *Yale Symposium on Law and Technology* 4 (2001).

Bossetta, Michael. "The Weaponization of Social Media: Spear Phishing and Cyberattacks on Democracy." *Journal of International Affairs* 71, no. 1.5 (2018): 97–106.

Bowker, Geoffrey C., and Susan Leigh Star. *Sorting Things Out: Classification and Its Consequences.* Cambridge, MA: MIT Press, 1999.

Bowler, Tim. "Huawei: Why Is It Being Banned from the UK's 5G Network?" BBC News, July 14, 2020. https://www.bbc.com/news/newsbeat-47041341.

Boyne, Shawn Marie. "Data Protection in the United States." *American Journal of Comparative Law* 66, supp. 1 (July 2018): 299–343.

Brandom, Russell. "It Will Cost $1.8 Billion to Pull Huawei and ZTE out of US Networks, FCC Says." The Verge, September 4, 2020. https://www.theverge.com/2020/9/4/21422 939/huawei-zte-us-phone-networks-fcc-congress-reimbursement-cost.

Brandom, Russell. "It's Okay to Let Kids Play Fortnite During a Global Pandemic." The Verge, January 18, 2021. https://www.theverge.com/2021/1/18/22237487/new-york-times-video-game-quarantine-dread.

Braun, Joshua A. "Normal Accidents in the Digital Age: How Programmatic Advertising Became a Disaster." In *The Routledge Companion to Advertising and Promotional Culture*, edited by Emily West and Matthew P. McAllister. New York: Routledge, 2023.

Brayne, Sarah. "Big Data Surveillance: The Case of Policing." *American Sociological Review* 82, no. 5 (October 2017): 977–1008.

Breckenridge, Keith. *Biometric State: The Global Politics of Identification and Surveillance in South Africa, 1850 to the Present.* Cambridge, UK: Cambridge University Press, 2014.

Brenner, Joel. "Protecting America's Critical Infrastructure from Cyber Attacks." Internet Policy Research Initiative at MIT, March 23, 2017. https://internetpolicy.mit.edu/spe ech-brenner-infragard-criticalinfra-2017/.

Brock, Dan W., and Allen Buchanan. *Ethical Issues in For-Profit Health Care.* Washington, DC: National Academies Press, 1986.

Brokaw, Cynthia Joanne. *The Ledgers of Merit and Demerit: Social Change and Moral Order in Late Imperial China.* Princeton, NJ: Princeton University Press, 1991.

Brookes, Tim. "Weather Forecasting, Meteorology, Weather Prediction, Weather Forecasts." *National Geographic*, October 9, 2009. https://www.nationalgeographic.com/environment/article/weather-forecasting.

Brown, Nina I. "Deepfakes and the Weaponization of Disinformation." *Virginia Journal of Law and Technology* 23, no. 1 (2020): 59.

Browne, Simone. "Digital Epidermalization: Race, Identity and Biometrics." *Critical Sociology* 36, no. 1 (2010): 131–50.

Bryce Space and Technology. "China's Orbital Launch Activity." December 31, 2019. https://brycetech.com/reports/report-documents/China_Orbital_Launch_Activity_2 020.pdf.

Buchholz, Katharina. "Which Countries Have Banned Huawei?" Statista, 2020. https://www.statista.com/chart/17528/countries-which-have-banned-huawei-products/.

Buhr, Sarah. "WuXi NextCODE Aims for the Genomics Database 'Gold Standard' with New $240 Million." TechCrunch, September 7, 2017. https://techcrunch.com/2017/09/07/wuxi-nextcode-aims-for-the-genomics-database-gold-standard-with-new-240-million/.

Bundesministerium des Innern für Bau und Heimat. "Kabinett beschließt Entwurf für It-Sicherheitsgesetz 2.0." News release, December 16, 2020. http://www.bmi.bund.de/SharedDocs/pressemitteilungen/DE/2020/12/it-sig-2-kabinett.html?nn= 9390260.

Burawoy, Michael. *Manufacturing Consent: Changes in the Labor Process Under Monopoly Capitalism.* Chicago: University of Chicago Press, 1982.

Bureau of Economic and Business Affairs. "Investment Affairs." US Department of State, Division for International Finance and Development, 2021. https://www.state.gov/inv estment-affairs/.

Bureau of Industry and Security. "Addition of Entities to the Entity List, Revision of Entry on the Entity List, and Removal of Entities from the Entity List." Department of Commerce, December 22, 2020. https://www.federalregister.gov/documents/2020/12/ 22/2020-28031/addition-of-entities-to-the-entity-list-revision-of-entry-on-the-ent ity-list-and-removal-of-entities.

Burke, Leah A., and Andrew M. Ryan. "The Complex Relationship Between Cost and Quality in US Health Care." *AMA Journal of Ethics* 16, no. 2 (February 2014): 124–30.

Burki, Talha. "Vaccine Misinformation and Social Media." *Lancet Digital Health* 1, no. 6 (October 2019): E258–59. https://www.thelancet.com/journals/landig/article/PIIS2 589-7500(19)30136-0/fulltext.

Byler, Darren. *In the Camps: China's High-Tech Penal Colony.* New York: Columbia University Press, 2021.

Byler, Darren. *Terror Capitalism: Uyghur Dispossession and Masculinity in a Chinese City.* Durham, NC: Duke University Press, 2021.

Bylund, Anders. "Zoom Stock Surged 425% in 2020: Is It a Buy for 2021?" NASDAQ, December 29, 2020. https://www.nasdaq.com/articles/zoom-stock-sur ged-425-in-2020%3A-is-it-a-buy-for-2021-2020-12-29.

Cai, Jie, Donghee Wohn, and Guo Freeman. "Who Purchases and Why? Explaining Motivations for in-Game Purchasing in the Online Survival Game Fortnite." Paper presented at CHI Play, Barcelona, Spain, October 17, 2019.

Caijingwang. "Jimayi zhihou weixin jingdong baidu didi xiajia cunkuan yewu" [Following Ant, WeChat, JD, Baidu, DiDi off the shelf deposit business]. December 21, 2020. http://m.caijing.com.cn/article/195798.

Calhoun, George. "Why Do Chinese Companies List Their Shares in New York?" *Forbes*, 2020. https://www.forbes.com/sites/georgecalhoun/2020/08/14/why-do-chinese-companies-list-their-shares-in-new-york/.

Calzati, Stefano. "Decolonising 'Data Colonialism': Propositions for Investigating the Realpolitik of Today's Networked Ecology." *Television and New Media*, 2020, 914–29.

Campbell, Mikey. "Apple to Move Chinese iCloud Keys to China Servers, Opens Door to Government Data Requests." Apple Insider, February 24, 2018. https://appleinsider. com/articles/18/02/24/apple-to-move-chinese-icloud-keys-to-china-servers-opens-door-to-government-data-requests.

Campion, Andrew Stephen. "From CNOOC to Huawei: Securitization, the China Threat, and Critical Infrastructure." *Asian Journal of Political Science* 28, no. 1 (January 2020): 47–66. https://doi.org/10.1080/02185377.2020.1741416.

Capri, Alex. "Techno-Nationalism: What Is It and How Will It Change Global Commerce?" *Forbes*, December 20, 2019. https://www.forbes.com/sites/alexcapri/2019/12/20/tec hno-nationalism-what-is-it-and-how-will-it-change-global-commerce/.

Carless, Simon. "GDCTV: The Near Future of Media Distribution." Game Developer, May 17, 2005. https://www.gamedeveloper.com/pc/features-gdctv-the-near-future-of-media-distribution-.

Carlson, Allen. *Unifying China, Integrating with the World: Securing Chinese Sovereignty in the Reform Era.* Singapore: NUS Press, 2008.

Carothers, Thomas. "Rejuvenating Democracy Promotion." *Journal of Democracy* 31, no. 1 (2020): 114–23. https://doi.org/10.1353/jod.2020.0009.

Carr, Joey. "Top 5 Most Popular Emotes in Fortnite Season 4." Sportskeeda, September 29, 2020. https://www.sportskeeda.com/esports/top-5-popular-emotes-fortnite-season-4.

Carter, Chris. "Fortnite Loot Box and Battle Pass Beginner's Guide." Polygon, March 26, 2018.   https://www.polygon.com/2018/3/26/17164364/fortnite-battle-royale-guide-loot-box-battle-pass-shop-save-the-world-mode-v-bucks-price-money.

Cartwright, Madison. "Internationalising State Power Through the Internet: Google, Huawei and Geopolitical Struggle." Internet Policy Review 9, no. 3 (September 16, 2020): 1–18.

Castronova, Edward. "Virtual Worlds: A First-Hand Account of Market and Society on the Cyberian Frontier." Social Science Research Network, December 2001. https://papers.ssrn.com/abstract=294828.

Cate, Fred H., and Viktor Mayer-Schönberger. "Notice and Consent in a World of Big Data." International Data Privacy Law 3, no. 2 (2013): 67–73.

Cattell, Jamie, Sastry Chilukuri, and Michael Levy. "How Big Data Can Revolutionize Pharmaceutical R&D." McKinsey, April 2013. https://www.mckinsey.com/industries/pharmaceuticals-and-medical-products/our-insights/how-big-data-can-revolutionize-pharmaceutical-r-and-d#.

Cavalli-Sforza, L. Luca. "The Chinese Human Genome Diversity Project." Proceedings of the National Academy of Sciences 95, no. 20 (September 29, 1998): 11501–3. https://www.pnas.org/doi/10.1073/pnas.95.20.11501.

CB Insights. "The Complete List of Unicorn Companies." 2021. https://www.cbinsights.com/research-unicorn-companies.

CB Insights. "How TikTok's Owner Became the World's Most Valuable Unicorn." 2020. https://www.cbinsights.com/research/report/bytedance-tiktok-unicorn/.

Centers for Disease Control. "COVID-19 and Your Health." November 17, 2020. https://www.cdc.gov/coronavirus/2019-ncov/prevent-getting-sick/social-distancing.html.

Central Committee of the Chinese Communist Party. "Shisiwu guihua he 2035 nian yuanjing mubiao jianyi quanwen" [Full text of 14th Five-Year Plan and 2035 Vision Goals proposal]. October 2020. http://www.ciac.cas.cn/djywh/xxyd/202011/P020201116609474294415.pdf.

Central Committee of the Communist Party of China. "Decision of the Central Committee of the Communist Party of China on Some Major Issues Concerning Comprehensively Deepening the Reform." January 16, 2014. http://www.china.org.cn/china/third_plenary_session/2014-01/16/content_31212602_11.htm.

Central Intelligence Agency. "China—the World Factbook." April 7, 2021. https://www.cia.gov/the-world-factbook/countries/china/.

Central People's Government of the People's Republic of China. "Guowuyuan guanyu jiakuai peiyu he fazhan zhanlüexing xinxing chanye de jueding" [Decision of the State Council on accelerating the cultivation and development of strategic emerging industries]. 2010. http://www.gov.cn/zwgk/2010-10/18/content_1724848.htm.

Chan, Anita. Walmart in China. Ithaca, NY: Cornell University Press, 2011.

Chan, Connie. "When One App Rules Them All: The Case of WeChat and Mobile in China." Andreessen Horowitz, August 6, 2015.

Chandlee, Blake. "Understanding Our Policies Around Paid Ads." TikTok news release, October 3, 2019. https://newsroom.tiktok.com/en-us/understanding-our-policies-around-paid-ads.

Chang, Emily. Brotopia: Breaking Up the Boys' Club of Silicon Valley. New York: Portfolio, 2018.

Chao, Eveline. "How Social Cash Made WeChat the App for Everything." Fast Company, January 2, 2017. https://web.archive.org/web/20170103135948/https://www.fastcomp any.com/3065255/china-wechat-tencent-red-envelopes-and-social-money.

Chavez, Thomas D., Mark J. Barrera, and Matthew H. Kanter. "Operational Satellite Concepts for ESPA Rideshare." Paper presented at the IEEE Aerospace Conference, Big Sky, MT, March 3–10, 2007.

Chazan, Guy. "Germany Sets High Hurdle for Huawei." *Financial Times*, December 16, 2020. https://www.ft.com/content/cadc6d26-97e1-4e63-b6ca-f24110c90379.

Chee, Foo Yun. "EU Clears ChemChina's $43 Billion Takeover of Syngenta with Conditions." Reuters, April 5, 2017. https://www.reuters.com/article/us-syngenta-ag-m-a-chemchina-eu-idUSKBN17714T.

Chen, Angela. "A Leaked Excerpt of TikTok Moderation Rules Shows How Political Content Gets Buried." *MIT Technology Review*, November 2019. https://www.techn ologyreview.com/f/614758/tiktok-content-moderation-politics-protest-netzpolitik/.

Chen, Jie, and Bruce J. Dickson. *Allies of the State: China's Private Entrepreneurs and Democratic Change*. Cambridge, MA: Harvard University Press, 2010.

Chen, Lulu Yilun. "Jack Ma's Ant Financial Joins Singapore Digital Banking Race." Bloomberg, January 2, 2020. https://www.bloomberg.com/news/articles/2020-01-02/ ant-financial-applies-for-singapore-digital-banking-licenses.

Chen, Ming Shin. "China's Data Collection on US Citizens: Implications, Risks, and Solutions." *Journal of Science Policy and Governance* 15, no. 1 (October 2019): 14.

Chen, Wenhong. "Big Data, Big Dream, and Big Brother: The Emergence and Growth of Chinese Big Data." Paper presented at the International Communication Association Preconference on Data and Publics, May 24, 2018.

Cheng, Evelyn. "How Ant Financial Grew Larger than Goldman Sachs." CNBC, June 8, 2018. https://www.cnbc.com/2018/06/08/how-ant-financial-grew-larger-than-gold man-sachs.html.

Chesney, Robert, and Danielle Keats Citron. "Deep Fakes: A Looming Challenge for Privacy, Democracy, and National Security." Social Science Research Network, July 2018. https://papers.ssrn.com/sol3/papers.cfm?abstract_id=3213954.

Chicago Council on Global Affairs. "Lieutenant General Armagno on the US Space Force." 2020.

Children's Commissioner for England. "Gaming the System." October 2019. https://www. childrenscommissioner.gov.uk/publication/gaming-the-system/.

Childs, Kevin, and Amy Zegart. "The Divide Between Silicon Valley and Washington Is a National-Security Threat." *The Atlantic*, December 13, 2018. https://www.theatlantic.com/ ideas/archive/2018/12/growing-gulf-between-silicon-valley-and-washington/577963/.

China Banking and Insurance Regulatory Commission. "Zhongguo yinbaojianhui bangongting zhongguo renmin yinhang bangongting fabu guanyu guifan shangye yinhang tongguo hulianwang kaizhan geren cunkuan yewu youguan shixiang de tongzhi" [The General Office of China Banking and Insurance Regulatory Commission (CBIRC), the General Office of People's Bank of China (PBC), issued the notice con-cerning the regulation of commercial banks' personal deposit business through the internet]. January 15, 2021. http://www.cbirc.gov.cn/cn/view/pages/ItemDetail. html?docId=959871&itemId=926.

China Computer News. "Pinglun: Fuzhi yamaxun pingguo moshi xu shenxing" [Opinion: Copying Amazon and Apple needs to be done with caution]. Sina, December 13, 2011. http://tech.sina.com.cn/it/2011-12-13/11156486934.shtml.

China Court. "Zhongguo yidong weifayuan leiji fangwenliang chao erdian qiyici" [China Mobile WeCourt has been visited more than 270 million times]. May 7, 2020. https://www.chinacourt.org/article/detail/2020/05/id/5182377.shtml.

China Daily. "Cyber Sovereignty." December 16, 2015. http://www.chinadaily.com.cn/opinion/2015-12/18/content_22738714.htm.

China Military Online. "Dashang junshi zhinenghua fazhan de kuaiche" [Hitch a ride on the express train of the development of military intelligence]. November 14, 2017. http://www.81.cn/jfjbmap/content/2017-11/14/content_191788.htm.

China Public Private Partnerships Center. "Guiding Opinions of the State Council on Innovating the Investment and Financing Mechanisms in Key Areas and Encouraging Social Investment." April 14, 2015. http://www.cpppc.org/en/zy/994006.jhtml.

China Satellite Space Communications Co. Ltd. "Company Profile." 2021. http://english.csat.spacechina.com/n931656/n931661/index.html.

Chon, Gina. "DJI Is a More Elusive U.S. Target than Huawei." Reuters, December 17, 2021. https://www.reuters.com/markets/asia/dji-is-more-elusive-us-target-than-huawei-2021-12-17/.

Chong, Gladys Pak Lei. "Cashless China: Securitization of Everyday Life Through Alipay's Social Credit System—Sesame Credit." *Chinese Journal of Communication* 12, no. 3 (July 2019): 290–307.

Chorzempa, Martin, Paul Triolo, and Samm Sacks. "China's Social Credit System: A Mark of Progress or a Threat to Privacy?" Peterson Institute for International Economics, Washington, DC, June 2018.

Choudary, Sangeet Paul. "China's Country-as-Platform Strategy for Global Influence." Brookings Institution, Washington, DC, November 19, 2020. https://www.brookings.edu/techstream/chinas-country-as-platform-strategy-for-global-influence/.

Chow, Daniel. "Three Major Risks Under the Foreign Corrupt Practices Act for U.S. Multinational Companies Doing Business in China." *Fordham International Law Journal* 37, no. 4 (2014): 1183–92.

CIO Tech Team. "HK Sees Internet of Things as the Core to the Development of Digital Economy." CIO Tech Asia, January 19, 2022. https://ciotechasia.com/hk-sees-internet-of-things-as-the-core-to-the-development-of-digital-economy/.

Clement, J. "Annual Revenue of Tencent Holdings from 2008 to 2020 (in Billion Yuan)." Statista, April 16, 2021. https://www.statista.com/statistics/223649/revenue-of-tencent-holdings-since-2007/.

Cloutier, Roland. "Our Approach to Security." *TikTok*, August 16, 2019. https://newsroom.tiktok.com/en-us/our-approach-to-security/.

Colbaugh, Richard, and Kristin Glass. "Estimating Sentiment Orientation in Social Media for Intelligence Monitoring and Analysis." Paper presented at the International Conference on Intelligence and Security Informatics, May 23–26, 2010. https://doi.org/10.1109/ISI.2010.5484760.

Coleman, James S. *Social Capital in the Development of Human Capital: The Ambiguous Position of Private Schools.* Columbus, OH: ERIC Clearinghouse, 1988.

Collier, Stephen J., and Andrew Lackoff. "The Vulnerability of Vital Systems: How 'Critical Infrastructure' Became a Security Problem." In *Securing "the Homeland,"* edited by Myriam Dunn Cavelty and Kristian Soby Kristensen, 16–39. New York: Routledge, 2008.

Collins, Martin J. *Space Race: The U.S.-U.S.S.R. Competition to Reach the Moon.* San Francisco: Pomegranate Communications, 1999.

Commission on Enhancing National Cybersecurity. "Report on Securing and Growing the Digital Economy." National Institute of Standards and Technology, Gaithersburg, MD, December 2016. https://www.nist.gov/system/files/documents/2016/12/02/cybersecurity-commission-report-final-post.pdf.

Complete Genomics. "69 Genomes Data." 2020. https://www.completegenomics.com/public-data/69-genomes/.

Congressional Research Service. "US-China Cyber Agreement." 2015. https://fas.org/sgp/crs/row/IN10376.pdf.

Cooper, Helene, and Michael D. Shear. "Biden Overturns Trump's Transgender Military Ban." *New York Times*, January 25, 2021. https://www.nytimes.com/2021/01/25/us/politics/biden-transgender-military.html.

Cooper, Michael J., Huseyin Gulen, and Alexei V. Ovtchinnikov. "Corporate Political Contributions and Stock Returns." *Journal of Finance* 65, no. 2 (March 2010): 687–724.

Costello, John, and Joe McReynolds. *China's Strategic Support Force: A Force for a New Era*. Washington, DC: National Defense University Press, 2018.

Couldry, Nick, and Ulises Mejías. *The Costs of Connection: How Data Is Colonizing Human Life and Appropriating It for Capitalism*. Stanford, CA: Stanford University Press, 2019.

Couldry, Nick, and Ulises Mejías. "Data Colonialism: Rethinking Big Data's Relation to the Contemporary Subject." *Television and New Media* 20, no. 4 (2019): 336–49.

Couture, Stephane, and Sophie Toupin. "What Does the Notion of 'Sovereignty' Mean When Referring to the Digital?" *New Media and Society* 21, no. 10 (2019): 2305–22. https://doi.org/10.1177/1461444819865984.

Cox, Matthew. "Army Follows Pentagon Guidance, Bans Chinese-Owned TikTok App." Military.com, December 30, 2019. https://www.military.com/daily-news/2019/12/30/army-follows-pentagon-guidance-bans-chinese-owned-tiktok-app.html.

Crawford, Kate. "The Hidden Biases in Big Data." *Harvard Business Review*, April 1, 2013. https://hbr.org/2013/04/the-hidden-biases-in-big-data.

Creemers, Rogier. "China's Conception of Cyber Sovereignty: Rhetoric and Realization." In *Governing Cyberspace: Behavior, Power and Diplomacy*, edited by Dennis Broeders and Bibi Van Den Berg, 107–44. Lanham, MD: Rowman & Littlefield, 2020.

Creemers, Rogier. "China's Social Credit System: An Evolving Practice of Control." Social Science Research Network, May 9, 2018. https://papers.ssrn.com/abstract=3175792.

Creemers, Rogier. "Cyber-Leninism: The Political Culture of the Chinese Internet." In *Speech and Society in Turbulent Times: Freedom of Expression in Comparative Perspective*, edited by Monroe Price and Nicole Stremlau, 255–73. Cambridge, UK: Cambridge University Press, 2017.

Creemers, Rogier. "Planning Outline for the Construction of a Social Credit System (2014–2020)." China Copyright and Media, June 14, 2014. https://chinacopyrightandmedia.wordpress.com/2014/06/14/planning-outline-for-the-construction-of-a-social-credit-system-2014-2020/.

Creemers, Rogier. "The Privilege of Speech and New Media: Conceptualizing China's Communications Law in the Internet Age." In *The Internet, Social Media, and a Changing China*, edited by Jacques deLisle, Avery Goldstein, and Guobin Yang, 86–105. Philadelphia: University of Pennsylvania Press, 2016.

Crunchbase. "Whirlpool Acquires Yummly." May 2, 2017. https://www.crunchbase.com/acquisition/whirlpool-acquires-yummly--e1a1bb5f.

Cuthbertson, Anthony. "How Children Playing Fortnite Are Helping to Fuel Organised Crime." *The Independent*, January 13, 2019. https://www.independent.co.uk/news/

fortnite-v-bucks-discount-price-money-dark-web-money-laundering-crime-a8717 941.html.

Cybersecurity Administration of China. "Guanyu xiajia 'DiDi chuxing' app de tongbao" [Notification regarding the DiDi app takedown]. July 4, 2021. http://www.cac.gov.cn/2021-07/04/c_1627016782176163.htm.

Cyberspace Administration of China. "Wangluo anquan shencha banfa" [Measures for cybersecurity review]. April 13, 2020. http://www.cac.gov.cn/2020-04/27/c_15895 35450769077.htm.

Cyberspace Administration of China. "Wangluo xinxi neirong shengtai zhili guiding" [Provisions on ecological management of network information content]. December 15, 2019. http://www.cac.gov.cn/2019-12/20/c_1578375159509309.htm.

Cyberspace Administration of China. "Xi Jinping jiu gongtong goujian wangluo kongjian mingyun gongtongti tichu wudian zhuzhang" [Xi put forward five proposals on jointly building a community with a shared future in cyberspace]. December 16, 2015. http://www.cac.gov.cn/2015-12/16/c_1117478213.htm.

Cyberspace Administration of China. "Xi Sends Congratulatory Letter to World Internet Conference." September 26, 2021. https://www.wuzhenwic.org/2021-09/26/c_663 873.htm.

Cyranoski, David. "China Embraces Precision Medicine on a Massive Scale." *Nature News* 529, no. 7584 (January 2016): 9.

Cyranoski, David. "China's Crackdown on Genetics Breaches Could Deter Data Sharing." *Nature* 563, no. 7731 (November 2018): 301–2.

Dahir, Abdi Latif. "China 'Gifted' the African Union a Headquarters Building and Then Allegedly Had It Bugged." *Quartz Africa*, January 30, 2018. https://qz.com/africa/1192 493/china-spied-on-african-union-headquarters-for-five-years/.

Daily, Grant, Rodrigo Cantarero, Maria Rosario de Guzman, Soo-Young Hong, and Sarah Taylor. "The Geographic Distribution of Poverty." University of Nebraska–Lincoln, 2017. https://digitalcommons.unl.edu/mapquallifene/1.

Darwin, H. G. "The Outer Space Treaty Note." *British Yearbook of International Law* 42 (1967): 278–90.

Das, Sajal K., Krishna Kant, and Nan Zhang. *Handbook on Securing Cyber-Physical Critical Infrastructure*. Waltham, MA: Morgan Kaufmann, 2012.

Das, Sajal K., and Hayato Yamana. "Securing Big Data and IoT Networks in Smart Cyber-Physical Environments." Paper presented at the International Conference on Smart Digital Environments, Rabat, Morocco, July 21–July 23, 2017.

Davenport, Thomas H., and Jill Dyché. "Big Data in Big Companies." International Institute for Analytics, May 2013.

De Cremer, David, and Tian Tao. "Huawei's Culture Is the Key to Its Success." *Harvard Business Review*, June 11, 2015. https://hbr.org/2015/06/huaweis-culture-is-the-key-to-its-success.

Deepti, Sri. "Alipay, JD Digits, DiDi Finance Pull out All Bank Deposit Products: Report." Tech in Asia, January 28, 2021. https://www.techinasia.com/alipay-jd-digits-didi-fina nce-pull-bank-deposit-products-report.

Defense Advanced Research Projects Agency. "60 Years Defense Advanced Research Project Agency." 2018. https://www.darpa.mil/attachments/DARAPA60_publication-no-ads.pdf.

Defense Advanced Research Projects Agency. "Breakthrough Technologies for National Security." March 2015. https://www.darpa.mil/attachments/DARPA2015.pdf.

Defense Intelligence Agency. "Challenges to Security in Space." January 2019. https://apps.dtic.mil/sti/pdfs/AD1082341.pdf.

DeGrippo, Sherrod. "Understanding the Information TikTok Gathers and Stores." Proofpoint, January 8, 2020. https://www.proofpoint.com/us/blog/threat-protection/understanding-information-tiktok-gathers-and-stores.

DeLuna, JoAnn. "What Do Alipay and WeChat Pay Mean for Corporate Payments?" Business Travel News, August 16, 2018. https://www.businesstravelnews.com/Global/What-Do-Alipay-WeChat-Pay-Mean-for-Corporate-Payments.

Dembling, Paul, and Daniel Arons. "The Evolution of the Outer Space Treaty." *Journal of Air Law and Commerce* 33 (1967): 419–56.

DeNardis, Laura. *The Global War for Internet Governance.* New Haven, CT: Yale University Press, 2014.

DeNardis, Laura. *The Internet in Everything: Freedom and Security in a World with No Off Switch.* New Haven, CT: Yale University Press, 2020.

DeNardis, Laura, and Mark Raymond. "Multistakeholderism: Anatomy of an Inchoate Global Institution." *International Theory* 7, no. 3 (May 2015): 572–616.

Deng, Xiang, and Xiang Cheng. "Can ESG Indices Improve the Enterprises' Stock Market Performance? An Empirical Study from China." *Sustainability* 11, no. 17 (January 2019): 4765.

Department of Health and Human Services, Office of the Inspector General. "Opportunities Exist for the National Institutes of Health to Strengthen Controls in Place to Permit and Monitor Access to Sensitive Data." February 2019. https://oig.hhs.gov/oas/reports/region18/181809350.pdf.

Department of Justice Office of Public Affairs. "Member of Sophisticated China-Based Hacking Group Indicted for Series of Computer Intrusions, Including 2015 Data Breach of Health Insurer Anthem Inc. Affecting over 78 Million People." May 2019. https://www.justice.gov/opa/pr/member-sophisticated-china-based-hacking-group-indicted-series-computer-intrusions-including.

Desch, Michael C. "America's Liberal Illiberalism: The Ideological Origins of Overreaction in U.S. Foreign Policy." *International Security* 32, no. 3 (2008): 7–43.

Deutsche Welle. "US Passes Bill That Could Delist Chinese Companies from Stock Markets." December 3, 2020. https://www.dw.com/en/us-passes-bill-that-could-delist-chinese-companies-from-stock-markets/a-55805624.

Dey, Dipanjan. "Is Fortnite Turning into a Pay to Win Game?" EssentiallySports, September 2, 2020. http://www.essentiallysports.com/is-fortnite-turning-into-a-pay-to-win-game-esports-news/.

Dickson, E. J. "Teen Hides Protest Video in a Makeup Tutorial on TikTok." *Rolling Stone,* November 26, 2019. https://www.rollingstone.com/culture/culture-features/china-tiktok-uyghur-protest-censorship-918757/.

DiGrazia, Kevin. "Cyber Insurance, Data Security, and Blockchain in the Wake of the Equifax Breach." *Journal of Business and Technology Law* 13, no. 2 (January 2018): 255–77.

Ding, Jeffrey. "Balancing Standards: U.S. and Chinese Strategies for Developing Technical Standards in AI." National Bureau of Asian Research, 2020. https://www.nbr.org/publication/balancing-standards-u-s-and-chinese-strategies-for-developing-technical-standards-in-ai/.

Dipshan, Rhys. "GDPR's Global Impact May Be More Limited than You Think." *Legaltech News* (blog), October 6, 2021. https://www.law.com/legaltechnews/2021/10/06/gdprs-global-impact-may-be-more-limited-than-you-think-397-51646/.

DJI. "DJI Privacy Policy." January 1, 2020. https://www.dji.com/policy.

Doctorow, Cory. "Barlow's Legacy." *Duke Law and Technology Review* 18, no. 1 (2019): 61–68. https://scholarship.law.duke.edu/dltr/vol18/iss1/5/.

Douglas, Sarah. "Preventing Genocide: Reigniting the Staying Power of the Convention." *Dalhousie Journal of Legal Studies* 29 (2020): 75–96.

Doyle, Brandon. "TikTok Statistics—Everything You Need to Know." Wallaroo Media, January 1, 2021. https://wallaroomedia.com/blog/social-media/tiktok-statistics/.

Dr. Hempel Digital Health Network. "Huawei Precision Medicine Cloud: A Revolutionary Step in the Field of Genomics." 2019. https://www.dr-hempel-network.com/digital-health-technolgy/huawei-precision-medicine-genomics/.

Draper, Nora A. *The Identity Trade: Selling Privacy and Reputation Online.* New York: NYU Press, 2019.

Draper, Nora, and Joseph Turow. "The Corporate Cultivation of Digital Resignation." *New Media and Society* 21, no. 8 (March 2019): 1824–39.

Drennan, John A. "Consumer Data Privacy in Bankruptcy." Baker Donelson, Washington, DC, 2016. https://www.bakerdonelson.com/webfiles/Consumer_Data_Privacy_in_Bankruptcy.pdf.

Dreyer, June Teufel, ed. *Chinese Defense and Foreign Policy.* New York: Professors World Peace Academy, 1989.

Driscoll, Kevin. *The Modem World: A Prehistory of Social Media.* New Haven, CT: Yale University Press, 2022.

Du, Guodong, and Meng Yu. "Big Data, AI and China's Justice: Here's What's Happening." China Justice Observer, December 1, 2019. https://www.chinajusticeobserver.com/a/big-data-ai-and-chinas-justice-heres-whats-happening.

Duarte, Marisa Elena. *Network Sovereignty: Building the Internet Across Indian Country.* Seattle: University of Washington Press, 2017.

Ducharme, Jamie. "A Major Drug Company Now Has Access to 23andMe's Genetic Data. Should You Be Concerned?" *Time,* July 26, 2018. https://time.com/5349896/23andme-glaxo-smith-kline/.

Duhigg, Charles. "How Companies Learn Your Secrets." New York Times, February 16, 2012. https://www.nytimes.com/2012/02/19/magazine/shopping-habits.html.

Dun & Bradstreet. "Tencent Cloud Europe (Germany) Gmbh." 2021. https://www.dnb.com/business-directory/company-profiles.tencent_cloud_europe_%28germany%29_gmbh.a361b3006d61d1804e603782b407f744.html.

Ebrahim, Tabrez Y. "Algorithms in Business, Merchant-Consumer Interactions, and Regulation." *West Virginia Law Review* 123, no. 3 (2020): 873–906. https://heinonline.org/HOL/P?h=hein.journals/wvb123&i=903.

The Economist. "The Party Is Eager to Expand Its Influence Within Business." June 23, 2021. https://www.economist.com/special-report/2021/06/23/the-party-is-eager-to-expand-its-influence-within-business.

Editorial Staff. "How to Send Red Packet in WeChat App?" WebNots, 2020. https://www.webnots.com/how-to-send-red-packet-in-wechat/.

Edwards, Paul. "Infrastructure and Modernity: Scales of Force, Time, and Social Organization in the History of Sociotechnical Systems." In *Modernity and Technology,* edited by Thomas J. Misa, Philip Brey and Andrew Feenberg, 185–225. Cambridge, MA: MIT Press, 2002.

Egenfeldt-Nielsen, Simon, Jonas Heide Smith, and Susana Pajares Tosca. *Understanding Video Games: The Essential Introduction.* New York: Routledge, 2019.

Ehrbeck, Tilman, Nicolaus Henke, and Thomas Kibasi. "The Emerging Market in Health Care Innovation." McKinsey, May 1, 2010. https://www.mckinsey.com/industries/hea lthcare-systems-and-services/our-insights/the-emerging-market-in-health-care-inn ovation#.

Eko, Lyombe, Anup Kumar, and Qingjiang Yao. "Google This: The Great Firewall of China, the It Wheel of India, Google Inc., and Internet Regulation." *Internet Journal of Law* 15, no. 3 (January 2011): 3–14.

Eleftheriou-Smith, Loulla-Mae. "China's President 'Turned Down Mark Zuckerberg's Request to Name His Unborn Child.'" *The Independent*, October 5, 2015. https://www. independent.co.uk/news/people/china-s-president-xi-jinping-turns-down-mark-zuc kerberg-s-request-to-name-his-unborn-child-at-white-house-dinner-a6679156.html.

Elegant, Naomi Xu. "A Jack Ma Company Is Poised to Break the Record for Biggest IPO— Again." *Fortune*, August 21, 2020. https://fortune.com/2020/08/21/jack-ma-alibaba-ant-ipo-biggest-ever/.

Ellcessor, Elizabeth. "The Care and Feeding of 9-1-1 Infrastructure: Dispatcher Culture as Media Work and Infrastructural Transformation." *Cultural Studies* 35, no. 4–5 (2021): 792–813. https://doi.org/10.1080/09502386.2021.1895249.

Ellcessor, Elizabeth. *In Case of Emergency: How Technologies Mediate Crisis and Normalize Inequality.* New York: NYU Press, 2022.

Ellcessor, Elizabeth. "Technologies, Bureaucracy, and Disaster." *New Media and Society* 22, no. 9 (2020): 1733–38. https://doi.org/10.1177/1461444820945934. https://doi.org/ 10.1177/1461444820945934.

Elliott, Jessica. *The Role of Consent in Human Trafficking.* New York: Routledge, 2014.

Emont, Jon. "Amazon's Heavy Recruitment of Chinese Sellers Puts Consumers at Risk." *Wall Street Journal*, November 11, 2019. https://www.wsj.com/articles/amazons-heavy-recruitment-of-chinese-sellers-puts-consumers-at-risk-11573489075.

Epic Games. "Epic Games Terms of Service." 2021. https://www.epicgames.com/site/en-US/tos.

Erie, Matthew S., and Thomas Streinz. "The Beijing Effect: China's 'Digital Silk Road' as Transnational Data Governance." *New York University Journal of Law and Politics*, March 22, 2021. https://ssrn.com/abstract=3810256.

EufyCam. "Amazon Privacy Policy." Amazon, August 10, 2020.

EufyCam. "Eufycam Privacy Policy." 2020. https://support.eufylife.com/s/article/Priv acy-Policy-1617358267480.

European Commission. "European Commission Adopts Adequacy Decision on Japan, Creating the World's Largest Area of Safe Data Flows." News release, January 23, 2019. https://ec.europa.eu/commission/presscorner/detail/en/IP_19_421.

European Commission. "General Product Safety Directive." 2021. https://ec.europa. eu/info/business-economy-euro/product-safety-and-requirements/product-safety/ consumer-product-safety_en.

European Union. "General Data Protection Regulation." 2018. https://gdpr-info.eu/.

Evers, Ellen, N. van de Ven, and D. Weeda. "The Hidden Cost of Microtransactions: Buying In-Game Advantages in Online Games Decreases a Player's Status." *International Journal of Internet Science* 10, no. 1 (2015): 16.

Executive Office of the President. "Addressing the Threat Posed by Applications and Other Software Developed or Controlled by Chinese Companies." January 8, 2021. https:// www.federalregister.gov/documents/2021/01/08/2021-00305/addressing-the-threat-posed-by-applications-and-other-software-developed-or-controlled-by-chinese.

Fair, Lesley. "$575 Million Equifax Settlement Illustrates Security Basics for Your Business." Federal Trade Commission, July 22, 2019. https://www.ftc.gov/news-eve nts/blogs/business-blog/2019/07/575-million-equifax-settlement-illustrates-security-basics.

Fan, Joseph, Randall Morck, and Bernard Yeung. "Capitalizing China." National Bureau of Economic Research, Washington, DC, December 2011. https://www.nber.org/pap ers/w17687.

Fan, Xingmeng. "Yiren quezhen quanxiaoqu dousuan miqie jiechuzhe ma yaodui xiedi xiaodu ma quanwei huiying" [Is everyone a close contact in the whole community as one person got diagnosed? Should I disinfect the soles? . . . Authority response!]. February 16, 2020. http://www.gov.cn/fuwu/2020-02/16/content_5479755.htm.

Fannin, Rebecca. "How the US-China Trade War Has Starved Some Silicon Valley Start-Ups." CNBC, January 18, 2020. https://www.cnbc.com/2020/01/31/chinese-venture-capitalists-draw-back-silicon-valley-investments.html.

Farley, Melissa. "Prostitution, the Sex Trade, and the COVID-19 Pandemic." *Logos* 19, no. 1 (2020): 34.

Feddo, Thomas P. "Protecting America's Open Investment Policy." *National Law Journal*, September 2019. https://www.law.com/nationallawjournal/2019/09/25/protecting-americas-open-investment-policy/.

Federal Aviation Administration. "Airspace." In *Pilot's Handbook of Aeronautical Knowledge*, 1–12. Washington, DC: Federal Aviation Administration, 2016.

Federal Aviation Administration. "Satellite Navigation—GPS—How It Works." Last updated August 12, 2021. https://www.faa.gov/about/office_org/headquarters_offices/ato/service_units/techops/navservices/gnss/gps/howitworks/.

Federal Trade Commission. "Children's Online Privacy Protection Rule ('COPPA')." January 17, 2013. https://www.ftc.gov/enforcement/rules/rulemaking-regulatory-ref orm-proceedings/childrens-online-privacy-protection-rule.

Federal Trade Commission. "FTC Authorizes Investigations into Key Enforcement Priorities." July 1, 2021. https://www.ftc.gov/news-events/press-releases/2021/07/ftc-authorizes-investigations-key-enforcement-priorities.

Federal Trade Commission. "FTC Imposes $5 Billion Penalty and Sweeping New Privacy Restrictions on Facebook." July 24, 2017. https://www.ftc.gov/news-eve nts/press-releases/2019/07/ftc-imposes-5-billion-penalty-sweeping-new-privacy-restrictions.

Federal Trade Commission. "FTC Streamlines Consumer Protection and Competition Investigations in Eight Key Enforcement Areas to Enable Higher Caseload." September 14, 2021. https://www.ftc.gov/news-events/press-releases/2021/09/ftc-streamlines-inv estigations-in-eight-enforcement-areas.

Federal Trade Commission. "Video Social Networking App Musical.ly Agrees to Settle FTC Allegations That It Violated Children's Privacy Law." News release, February 27, 2019. https://www.ftc.gov/news-events/press-releases/2019/02/video-social-network ing-app-musically-agrees-settle-ftc.

Feigenbaum, Evan A. *China's Techno-Warriors: National Security and Strategic Competition from the Nuclear to the Information Age.* Palo Alto, CA: Stanford University Press, 2003.

Feng, Chen, Hope Ole-Kristian, Li Qingyuan, and Wang Xin. "Financial Reporting Quality and Investment Efficiency of Private Firms in Emerging Markets." *Accounting Review* 86, no. 4 (July 2011): 1255–88. https://doi.org/10.2308/accr-10040.

Ferek, Katy Stech, and Georgia Wells. "TikTok Files Another Lawsuit to Block Ban on App." *Wall Street Journal*, September 20, 2020. https://www.wsj.com/articles/tiktok-files-another-lawsuit-to-block-ban-on-app-11600541730.

Ferraro, Matthew F., Jason C. Chipman, and Stephen W. Preston. "Identifying the Legal and Business Risks of Disinformation and Deepfakes: What Every Business Needs to Know." WilmerHale, March 2020. https://www.wilmerhale.com/en/insights/client-ale rts/20200312-identifying-the-legal-and-business-risks-of-disinformation-and-deepfa kes-what-every-business-needs-to-know.

Fewsmith, Joseph. "The Sixteenth National Party Congress: The Succession That Didn't Happen." *China Quarterly*, no. 173 (2003): 1–16.

Finn, Megan. *Documenting Aftermath: Information Infrastructures in the Wake of Disasters*. Cambridge, MA: MIT Press, 2018.

Fintel.io. "Tencent Holdings Ltd Discloses 4.99% Ownership in Atvi / Activision Blizzard, Inc.—13F, 13D, 13G Filings." November 23, 2016. https://fintel.io/so/us/atvi/tencent-holdings.

Firouzi, Farshad, Amir M. Rahmani, K. Mankodiya, M. Badaroglu, G. V. Merrett, P. Wong, and Bahar Farahani. "Internet-of-Things and Big Data for Smarter Healthcare: From Device to Architecture, Applications and Analytics." *Future Generation Computer Systems* 78, no. 2 (January 2018): 583–86. https://doi.org/10.1016/j.future.2017.09.016.

Fleming, Grace. "HIPAA-Cratic or HIPAA-Critical: U.S. Privacy Protections Should Be Guaranteed by Covered Entities Working Abroad." *Minnesota Law Review* 331 (2014): 2375–407.

Floridi, Luciano. "The Fight for Digital Sovereignty: What It Is, and Why It Matters, Especially for the EU." *Philosophy and Technology* 33, no. 3 (2020): 369–78. https://doi.org/10.1007/s13347-020-00423-6.

Fojas, Camilla. *Border Optics: Surveillance Cultures on the US-Mexico Border*. New York: New York University Press, 2021.

Ford, Genrald. "Executive Order 11858." 1975. https://www.treasury.gov/resource-cen ter/international/foreign-investment/documents/eo-11858-amended.pdf.

Fortnite Team. "5 Tips for How to Play Fortnite with Friends." Epic Games, July 30, 2020. https://www.epicgames.com/fortnite/en-US/news/5-tips-for-how-to-play-fortnite-with-friends.

Frank, Peter. "Phoenix New Media Reconfigures Series E Financing for Yidian." CapitalWatch, April 2018. https://www.capitalwatch.com/article-1923-1.html.

Franks, Mary Anne, and Ari Ezra Waldman. "Sex, Lies, and Videotape: Deep Fakes and Free Speech Delusions." *Maryland Law Review* 78, no. 4 (2019): 891–98.

Fravel, M. Taylor. *Strong Borders, Secure Nation: Cooperation and Conflict in China's Territorial Disputes*. Princeton, NJ: Princeton University Press, 2008.

Freeman, Carla P. "An Uncommon Approach to the Global Commons: Interpreting China's Divergent Positions on Maritime and Outer Space Governance." *China Quarterly* 241 (2020): 1–21. https://doi.org/10.1017/S0305741019000730.

French, Jordan. "Why M&A Due Diligence Is So Important: A Cautionary Tale." Startups.com, 2018. https://www.startups.com/library/expert-advice/importance-of-merger-acquisition-due-diligence.

Frost, Jeana H., and Michael P. Massagli. "PatientsLikeMe: The Case for a Data-Centered Patient Community and How ALS Patients Use the Community to Inform Treatment Decisions and Manage Pulmonary Health." *Chronic Respiratory Disease* 6, no. 4 (November 2009): 225–29.

Frost, Jeana H., and Michael P. Massagli. "Social Uses of Personal Health Information within Patientslikeme, an Online Patient Community: What Can Happen When Patients Have Access to One Another's Data." *Journal of Medical Internet Research* 10, no. 3 (2008): e15. https://doi.org/10.2196/jmir.1053.

Fujimoto, Richard M., Nurcin Celik, Haluk Damgacioglu, Michael Hunter, Dong Jin, Young-Jun Son, and Jie Xu. "Dynamic Data Driven Application Systems for Smart Cities and Urban Infrastructures." Paper presented at the Winter Simulation Conference, Washington, DC, December 14–16, 2016.

Fung, Brian. "Chinese-Owned Social Site TikTok Tangles with Congress." CNN, November 4, 2019. https://www.cnn.com/2019/11/04/politics/tiktok-congress-hearing-no-show/index.html.

Fung, Brian. "How China's Huawei Took the Lead over U.S. Companies in 5G Technology." *Washington Post*, April 10, 2019. https://www.washingtonpost.com/technology/2019/04/10/us-spat-with-huawei-explained/.

Furchtgott-Roth, Harold. "Chinese Government Helps Huawei with 5G." *Forbes*, May 8, 2017. https://www.forbes.com/sites/haroldfurchtgottroth/2017/05/08/chinese-government-helps-huawei-with-5g/.

Gagliardone, Iginio. *The Politics of Technology in Africa: Communication, Development, and Nation-Building in Ethiopia.* Cambridge, UK: Cambridge University Press, 2016.

Gallagher, Ryan. "How U.S. Tech Giants Are Helping to Build China's Surveillance State." The Intercept, July 11, 2019. https://theintercept.com/2019/07/11/china-surveillance-google-ibm-semptian/.

Galloway, Alexander R. *Gaming: Essays on Algorithmic Culture.* Minneapolis: University of Minnesota Press.

Ganti, Akhilesh. "How Does Fortnite Make Money?" Investopedia, October 17, 2020. https://www.investopedia.com/tech/how-does-fortnite-make-money/.

Gao, Charlotte. "'Double-Faced' Lu Wei Jailed for 14 Years for Bribery." *The Diplomat*, March 27, 2019. https://thediplomat.com/2019/03/double-faced-lu-wei-jailed-for-14-years-for-bribery/.

Garamone, Jim. "President Signs Fiscal 2019 Defense Authorization Act at Fort Drum Ceremony." US Department of Defense, August 13, 2018. https://www.defense.gov/Explore/News/Article/Article/1601016/president-signs-fiscal-2019-defense-authorization-act-at-fort-drum-ceremony/.

García-Herrero, Alicia, and Junyu Tan. *Deglobalisation in the Context of United States-China Decoupling.* Brussels: Bruegel, 2020.

Gartenberg, Chaim, and Russell Brandom. "US Government Adds DJI to Commerce Blacklist over Ties to Chinese Government." *The Verge*, December 18, 2020. https://www.theverge.com/2020/12/18/22188789/dji-ban-commerce-entity-list-drone-china-transaction-blocked.

Gatlan, Sergiu. "Epic Promises to Fix Game Launcher After Privacy Concerns." BleepingComputer, March 15, 2019. https://www.bleepingcomputer.com/news/security/epic-promises-to-fix-game-launcher-after-privacy-concerns/.

GE Appliances. "GE Appliances and Haier Deliver a 'Smarter Home, Better Life' with Transformative, Time-Saving Technologies." News release, January 7, 2019. https://pressroom.geappliances.com/news/ge-appliances-and-haier-deliver-a-smarter-home-better-life-with-transformative-time-saving-technologies.

GenomeWeb. "23andMe Raises $115M in Series E Financing Round." October 14, 2015. https://www.genomeweb.com/business-news/23andme-raises-115m-series-e-financing-round.

GenomeWeb. "BGI Americas Gets US Emergency Use Authorization for Coronavirus Test." March 27, 2020. https://www.genomeweb.com/pcr/bgi-americas-gets-us-emergency-use-authorization-coronavirus-test.

GenomeWeb. "Complete Genomics, BGI Agree to $117.6M Merger." GenomeWeb, September 17, 2012. https://www.genomeweb.com/clinical-sequencing/complete-genomics-bgi-agree-1176m-merger.

GenomeWeb. "WuXi NextCODE Restructures, Rebrands as Genuity Science." June 23, 2020. https://www.genomeweb.com/business-news/wuxi-nextcode-restructures-rebrands-genuity-science.

Genuity Science. "WuXi NextCODE Restructures and Becomes Genuity Science." News release, June 23, 2020. https://www.prnewswire.com/news-releases/wuxi-nextcode-restructures-and-becomes-genuity-science-301081462.html.

Gewirtz, Julian, and Moira Weigel. "Grindr and the 'New Cold War': Why US Concerns over the App Are Dangerous." *The Guardian*, May 18, 2019. https://www.theguardian.com/commentisfree/2019/may/18/grindr-us-security-china-new-cold-war.

Ghorayshi, Azeen, and Sri Ray. "Grindr Is Sharing the HIV Status of Its Users with Other Companies." BuzzFeed News, April 2, 2018. https://www.buzzfeednews.com/article/azeenghorayshi/grindr-hiv-status-privacy.

Giddens, Anthony. "The Nation-State and Violence." *Capital and Class* 10, no. 2 (1986): 216–20.

Giese, Guido, Linda-Eling Lee, Dimitris Melas, Zoltán Nagy, and Laura Nishikawa. "Foundations of ESG Investing: How ESG Affects Equity Valuation, Risk, and Performance." *Journal of Portfolio Management* 45, no. 5 (June 2019): 69–83.

Giles, Martin. "The US Suspects Chinese State Hackers Are Behind the Marriott Hotel Data Breach." *MIT Technology Review*, December 12, 2018. https://www.technologyreview.com/2018/12/12/138715/the-us-has-blamed-chinese-state-hackers-for-the-marriott-hotel-data-breach/.

Gillespie, Tarleton. *Custodians of the Internet: Platforms, Content Moderation, and the Hidden Decisions That Shape Social Media.* New Haven, CT: Yale University Press, 2018.

Gitelman, Lisa, and Virginia Jackson. "Introduction." In *Raw Data Is an Oxymoron*, edited by Lisa Gitelman, 1–14. Cambridge, MA: MIT Press, 2013.

Gkritsi, Eliza. "Alipay, JD Digits, DiDi Remove All Bank Deposit Products." Tech Node, January 28, 2021. https://technode.com/2021/01/28/alipay-jd-digits-didi-remove-all-bank-deposit-products-report/.

Global Times. "Tesla 'Brakes' in China over Image Crisis, Despite Record Q1 Earnings." *Global Times*, April 27, 2021. https://www.globaltimes.cn/page/202104/1222245.shtml.

Global Trade Alert. "China: Government Subsidy Changes for Listed Company Haier in Year 2018." https://www.globaltradealert.org/intervention/76683/financial-grant/china-government-subsidy-changes-for-listed-company-haier-in-year-2018.

Goh, Brenda. "U.S. Lawmakers Ask Zoom to Clarify China Ties After It Suspends Accounts." Reuters, June 11, 2020. https://www.reuters.com/article/us-zoom-video-commn-privacy-idUSKBN23I3GP.

Goldfisk and Follower. "DEF CON 24—What We Learned Reverse-Engineering Bluetooth- and Internet-Enabled Adult Toys." YouTube, posted January 20, 2017. https://youtu.be/9Z3PomQpHOs.

Goldman, Russell. "India-China Border Dispute: A Conflict Explained." *New York Times*, September 8, 2020. https://www.nytimes.com/2020/06/17/world/asia/india-china-bor der-clashes.html.

Google Finance. "DiDi Global Inc—ADR (DiDi) Stock Price & News." https://www.goo gle.com/finance/quote/DIDI:NYSE.

Google Play. "Zepp Life (Formerly Mi Fit)." March 17, 2022, https://play.google.com/ store/apps/details?id=com.xiaomi.hm.health&hl=en_US&gl=US.

Gouda, Omar M., Dina J. Hejji, and Mohamamd S. Obaidat. "Privacy Assessment of Fitness Tracker Devices." Paper presented at the 2020 International Conference on Computer, Information and Telecommunication Systems, Hangzhou, China, October 5–7, 2020.

Government Accountability Office. "Critical Infrastructure Protection: Progress Coordinating Government and Private Sector Efforts Varies by Sectors' Characteristics." 2006.

Government of Australia. "Privacy Act 1988." Federal Register of Legislation, Canberra. https://www.legislation.gov.au/Details/C2021C00139.

Government of the Hong Kong Special Administrative Region. "Implementation Rules for Article 43 of the Law of the People's Republic of China on Safeguarding National Security in the Hong Kong Special Administrative Region Gazetted." News release, July 6, 2020. https://www.info.gov.hk/gia/general/202007/06/P2020070600784.htm.

Gow, Michael. "The Core Socialist Values of the Chinese Dream: Towards a Chinese Integral State." *Critical Asian Studies* 49, no. 1 (2016): 92–116.

Grandview Research. "Internet of Things in Healthcare Market Size, Share and Trends Analysis Report by Component (Service, System and Software), by Connectivity Technology (Satellite, Cellular), by End Use (CRO, Hospital and Clinic), by Application, and Segment Forecasts, 2019–2025." March 2019. https://www.grandviewresearch. com/industry-analysis/internet-of-things-iot-healthcare-market.

Gray, Kishonna L. "Intersecting Oppressions and Online Communities." *Information, Communication and Society* 15, no. 3 (2012): 411–28.

Gray, Kishonna L., Bertan Buyukozturk, and Zachary G. Hill. "Blurring the Boundaries: Using Gamergate to Examine 'Real' and Symbolic Violence Against Women in Contemporary Gaming Culture." *Sociology Compass* 11, no. 3 (2017).

Greene, Robert, and Paul Triolo. "Will China Control the Global Internet Via Its Digital Silk Road?" Carnegie Endowment for International Peace, Washington, DC, May 2020. https://carnegieendowment.org/2020/05/08/will-china-control-global-internet-via-its-digital-silk-road-pub-81857.

Greitens, Sheena Chestnut. "Dealing with Demand for China's Global Surveillance Exports." Brookings Institution, Washington, DC, April 2020. https://www.brooki ngs.edu/wp-content/uploads/2020/04/FP_20200428_china_surveillance_greitens_ v3.pdf.

Greitens, Sheena Chestnut. *Dictators and Their Secret Police: Coercive Institutions and State Violence*. Cambridge, UK: Cambridge University Press, 2016.

Greitens, Sheena Chestnut. "Surveillance, Security, and Liberal Democracy in the Post-COVID World." *International Organization* 74, supp. (December 2020): E169–E90.

Griffiths, James. "China Is Rolling Out Facial Recognition for All New Mobile Phone Numbers." CNN Business, December 2, 2019. https://www.cnn.com/2019/12/02/tech/china-facial-recognition-mobile-intl-hnk-scli/index.html.

Grindr. "About Us." 2019. https://www.grindr.com/about/.

Grindr. "Community Guidelines." 2019. https://www.grindr.com/community-guidelines/.

Grindr. "Privacy and Cookie Policy." May 20, 2020. https://www.grindr.com/privacy-policy/#collect.

Grindr. "Privacy Policy." 2019. https://www.grindr.com/privacy-policy/#share_EN.

Grossman, Derek, Christian Curriden, Logan Ma, Lindsey Polley, J. D. Williams, and Cortez A. Cooper III. *Chinese Views of Big Data Analytics*. Santa Monica, CA: RAND, 2020. https://www.rand.org/pubs/research_reports/RRA176-1.html.

Grumbling, Emily, and Anne Johnson. "Implications of Artificial Intelligence for Cybersecurity: Proceedings of a Workshop." In *Deep Fakes*, edited by Engineering National Academies of Sciences, and Medicine, 54–60. Washington, DC: National Academies Press, 2019.

Gryphon Scientific and Rhodium Group LLC. "China's Biotechnology Development: The Role of US and Other Foreign Engagement." US-China Economic and Security Review Commission, February 2019. https://www.uscc.gov/sites/default/files/Research/US-China%20Biotech%20Report.pdf.

Guillou, Céline M. "Privacy Issues in Bankruptcy Sales." *The Privacy Hacker* (blog), May 15, 2020. https://www.lexology.com/library/detail.aspx?g=b540a911-a3be-44a4-a49e-87cf2ffdff01.

Guluzade, Amir. "The Role of China's State-Owned Companies Explained." World Economic Forum, May 7, 2019. https://www.weforum.org/agenda/2019/05/why-chinas-state-owned-companies-still-have-a-key-role-to-play/.

Haas, Benjamin. "Marriott Apologises to China over Tibet and Taiwan Error." *The Guardian*, January 12, 2018. https://www.theguardian.com/world/2018/jan/12/marriott-apologises-to-china-over-tibet-and-taiwan-error.

Haber, Eldar. "The Internet of Children: Protecting Children's Privacy in a Hyper-Connected World." *University of Illinois Law Review*, no. 4 (2020): 1209–48.

HackersOnBoard. "DEF CON 27—smea—Adventures in Smart Buttplug Penetration Testing." YouTube, posted December 5, 2019. https://youtu.be/RnxcPeemHSc.

Hainer, Michelle. "Fortnite Has Been a Balm and a Frustration During the Pandemic." *Washington Post*, September 15, 2020. https://www.washingtonpost.com/lifestyle/2020/09/15/fortnite-pandemic/.

Hale, James. "Chinese Tech Giant ByteDance Reportedly Working to Bring TikTok's Operations Stateside." Tubefilter, May 29, 2020. https://www.tubefilter.com/2020/05/29/bytedance-tiktok-operations-china-us/.

Halpin, Darren R., and Anthony J. Nownes. *The New Entrepreneurial Advocacy: Silicon Valley Elites in American Politics*. New York: Oxford University Press, 2021.

Hamblin, James. "Healthcare, Meet Capitalism." *The Atlantic*, July 2, 2014. https://www.theatlantic.com/health/archive/2014/07/a-case-against-donating-to-hospitals/373637/.

Hamilton, Isobel Asher. "ByteDance's Head of Security Says It's Impossible for China to Get Hold of TikTok User Data Because It's Stored in the US." Business Insider, August 28, 2020. https://www.businessinsider.com/bytedance-security-chief-tiktok-data-stored-us-safe-from-china-2020-8.

Hamilton, Isobel Asher. "A California Student Is Suing TikTok, Alleging That It Surreptitiously Hoovered up Her Data and Sent It to China." *Business Insider*, December 3, 2019. https://www.businessinsider.com/tiktok-class-action-lawsuit-sending-data-china-2019-12.

Hancock, Tom. "China Nationalises Troubled Conglomerate Anbang." *Financial Times*, June 2018. https://www.ft.com/content/279318d4-75fd-11e8-b326-75a27d27ea5f.

Hanemann, Thilo, Daniel H. Rosen, Cassie Gao, and Adam Lysenko. "Two-Way Street: 2020 Update US-China Investment Trends." US-China Investment Project, May 2020.

Haney, Julie M., and Susanne M. Furman. "Human Factors in Smart Home Technologies Workshop." National Institute of Standards and Technology, September 24, 2019. https://www.nist.gov/system/files/documents/2019/09/18/smart_home_workshop_agenda.pdf.

Hardin, Garrett. "The Tragedy of the Commons." *Science* 162, no. 3859 (December 1968): 1243–48.

Hargreaves, Stuart. "Online Monitoring of 'Localists' in Hong Kong: A Return to Political Policing?" *Surveillance and Society* 15, no. 3–4 (2017): 425–31. https://doi.org/10.24908/ss.v15i3/4.6619.

Harley, J. B. "Maps, Knowledge, and Power." In *The Iconography of Landscape: Essays on the Symbolic Representation, Design and Use of Past Environments*, edited by Denis Cosgrove and Stephen Daniels, 277–312. Cambridge, UK: Cambridge University Press, 1988.

Harris, John. "How Amazon Became a Pandemic Giant—and Why That Could Be a Threat to Us All." *The Guardian*, November 18, 2020. http://www.theguardian.com/technology/2020/nov/18/how-amazon-became-a-pandemic-giant-and-why-that-could-be-a-threat-to-us-all.

Harrus, Ilana, and Jessica Wyndham. "Artificial Intelligence and COVID-19: Applications and Impact Assessment." American Association for the Advancement of Science, Washington, DC, 2021. https://www.aaas.org/sites/default/files/2021-05/AIandCOVID19_2021_FINAL.pdf.

Harwell, Drew, and Tony Romm. "Inside TikTok: A Culture Clash Where U.S. Views About Censorship Often Were Overridden by the Chinese Bosses." *Washington Post*, November 5, 2019. https://www.washingtonpost.com/technology/2019/11/05/inside-tiktok-culture-clash-where-us-views-about-censorship-often-were-overridden-by-chinese-bosses/.

Hassan, Aisha. "Fortnite Is a Social Space the Way Skateparks and Facebook Used to Be." *Quartz*, December 2018. https://qz.com/quartzy/1493147/fortnite-a-social-space-like-facebook-and-skateparks-once-were/.

Haveman, Michelle, and Jeroen Vochteloo. "Huawei: A Case Study on a Telecom Giant on the Rise." In *Multinational Management: A Casebook on Asia's Global Market Leaders*, edited by Rien T. Segers, 75–94. New York: Springer International, 2016.

Hawley, Josh. "Senator Hawley's Letter to Zoom on Chinese Censorship." 2020. https://www.hawley.senate.gov/sites/default/files/2020-06/Letter-Zoom-China-Censorship.pdf.

He, Wu, Jiancheng Shen, Xin Tian, Yaohang Li, Vasudeva Akula, Gongjun Yan, and Ran Tao. "Gaining Competitive Intelligence from Social Media Data: Evidence from Two Largest Retail Chains in the World." *Industrial Management and Data Systems* 115, no. 9 (October 2015): 1622–36.

He, Xueying, Yawei Wang, and Lan Zhang. "Standardizing Smart City's Cloud Service: A Case Study of Shanghai." Paper presented at the 15th International Conference of the Society for Global Business and Economic Development (SGBED), Beijing, 2018.

Heginbotham, Eric, Michael Nixon, Forrest E. Morgan, Jacob L. Heim, Jeff Hagen, Sheng Tao Li, Jeffrey Engstrom, et al. "The U.S.-China Military Scorecard: Forces, Geography, and the Evolving Balance of Power, 1996–2017." RAND Corporation, Santa Monica, CA, September 2015. https://www.rand.org/pubs/research_reports/RR392.html.

Hellström, Tomas. "Critical Infrastructure and Systemic Vulnerability: Towards a Planning Framework." *Safety Science* 45, no. 3 (March 2007): 415–30. https://doi.org/10.1016/j.ssci.2006.07.007.

Henry, Nicola, and Anastasia Powell. "Technology-Facilitated Sexual Violence: A Literature Review of Empirical Research." *Trauma, Violence, and Abuse* 19, no. 2 (2018): 195–208.

Heraldkeepers. "Drones Market Analysis, Trends, Growth, Size, Share and Forecast 2020 to 2026." MarketWatch, January 20, 2021. https://www.marketwatch.com/press-release/drones-market-analysis-trends-growth-size-share-and-forecast-2020-to-2026-2021-01-20.

Herlo, Bianca, Daniel Irrgang, Gesche Joost, and Andreas Unteidig. *Practicing Sovereignty: Digital Involvement in Times of Crises.* London, UK: Transcript Verlag, 2021.

Hern, Alex. "Overwatch: How Blizzard Redefined the First-Person Shooter." *The Guardian*, May 26, 2016. http://www.theguardian.com/technology/2016/may/26/overwatch-how-blizzard-redefined-the-first-person-shooter.

Hern, Alex. "Revealed: How TikTok Censors Videos That Do Not Please Beijing." *The Guardian*, September 25, 2019. https://www.theguardian.com/technology/2019/sep/25/revealed-how-tiktok-censors-videos-that-do-not-please-beijing.

Hickman, Tim, and Shino Asayama. "EU-Japan Adequacy Decision Now in Force." White and Case LLP, January 30, 2019. https://www.whitecase.com/publications/alert/eu-japan-adequacy-decision-now-force.

Hillman, Jonathan. "Competing with China's Digital Silk Road." Center for Strategic and International Studies, Washington, DC, February 2021. https://www.csis.org/analysis/competing-chinas-digital-silk-road.

Hinds, Joanne, Emma J. Williams, and Adam N. Joinson. "'It Wouldn't Happen to Me': Privacy Concerns and Perspectives Following the Cambridge Analytica Scandal." *International Journal of Human-Computer Studies* 143 (2020). https://doi.org/https://doi.org/10.1016/j.ijhcs.2020.102498.

Hirsch, Jerry. "Pickup Truck Sales Rise, Ram Catches Chevrolet Silverado." Trucks.com, January 7, 2020. https://www.trucks.com/2020/01/07/ram-catches-chevrolet-silverado/.

Hoffman, Samantha. "Engineering Global Consent: The Chinese Communist Party's Data-Driven Power Expansion." APO, October 2019. https://apo.org.au/node/263211.

Hoffmann, Anna Lauren, and Anne Jonas. "Recasting Justice for Internet and Online Industry Research Ethics." In *Internet Research Ethics for the Social Age: New Cases and Challenges*, edited by Michael Zimmer and Katharina Kinder-Kuranda, 3–18. Bern, Switzerland: Peter Lang, 2017.

Hornshaw, Phil. "The History of Battle Royale: From Mod to Worldwide Phenomenon." Digital Trends, April 10, 2019. https://www.digitaltrends.com/gaming/history-of-battle-royale-games/.

Howard, Philip N. *Pax Technica: How the Internet of Things May Set Us Free or Lock Us Up.* New Haven, CT: Yale University Press, 2015.

Hruska, Joel. "Tim Sweeney: The Epic Game Store Doesn't Spy on People." March 18, 2019. https://www.extremetech.com/gaming/287815-tim-sweeney-the-epic-game-store-doesnt-spy-on-people.

Huami Corporation. "Huami Corporation Form 20-F." April 12, 2019. https://www.annualreports.com/HostedData/AnnualReportArchive/h/NYSE_HMI_2018.pdf.

Huang, Qingming. "The Pandemic and the Transformation of Liberal International Order." *Journal of Chinese Political Science* 26, no. 1 (2021): 1–26.

Huawei. "China Mobile, Huawei, and Other Partners Set up a 5G Vonr+ (New Calling) Working Group." News release, September 1, 2021. https://www.huawei.com/en/news/2021/9/china-mobile-huawei-5g-vonr-new-calling.

Hughes, Kent H. "Facing the Global Competitiveness Challenge." *Issues in Science and Technology* 21, no. 4 (2005): 72–78.

Hughes, Thomas Parke. *Networks of Power: Electrification in Western Society, 1880–1930.* Baltimore, MD: Johns Hopkins University Press, 1993.

Human Rights Watch. "The EU General Data Protection Regulation." June 6, 2018. https://www.hrw.org/news/2018/06/06/eu-general-data-protection-regulation.

Hussain, Javed. "Fourth Time's the Charm? PTA Lifts Ban on TikTok After Company Assures It Will 'Control Indecent Content.'" *Dawn Pakistan*, November 19, 2021. https://www.dawn.com/news/1659025.

I.D. Systems Inc. "Form 8-K." Securities and Exchange Commission, Washington, DC, December 18, 2015. https://sec.report/Document/0001415889-15-004167/.

IGN. "Blizzard President Addresses Hong Kong Controversy, Blizzcon 2019." YouTube, posted November 1, 2019. https://www.youtube.com/watch?v=_VdHcTB_J4Y.

India Today. "Viral Hindu-Muslim Lesbian Couple Blasts TikTok for Taking Down Video: Rumors About Homophobia Are True." *India Today*, December 2019. https://www.indiatoday.in/trending-news/story/viral-hindu-muslim-lesbian-couple-blasts-tiktok-for-taking-down-video-rumors-about-homophobia-are-true-1625933-2019-12-06.

Industry and Security Bureau. "Addition of Certain Entities to the Entity List; Revision of Existing Entries on the Entity List." July 22, 2020. https://www.federalregister.gov/documents/2020/07/22/2020-15827/addition-of-certain-entities-to-the-entity-list-revision-of-existing-entries-on-the-entity-list.

Information Office of the State Council of the People's Republic of China. "White Paper on the Internet in China." June 8, 2010. https://www.chinadaily.com.cn/china/2010-06/08/content_9950198.htm.

Ingham, Tim. "Why Marshmello's Fortnite Show Will Prove 'Revolutionary' for the Music Industry." *Rolling Stone*, February 22, 2019. https://www.rollingstone.com/music/music-features/marshmello-fortnite-show-will-prove-revolutionary-for-the-music-industry-797399/.

Inkster, Nigel. "The Huawei Affair and China's Technology Ambitions." *Survival* 61, no. 1 (January 2, 2019): 105–11.

Inserra, David. "Top Four Homeland Security Priorities for the Next Administration." Heritage Foundation, Washington, DC, March 2016. https://www.heritage.org/homeland-security/report/top-four-homeland-security-priorities-the-next-administration.

Institute of Genetics and Development Biology, Chinese Academy of Sciences. "Jinian renlei jiyinzu gongzuo caotu huizhi he 1% xiangmu wancheng zuotanhui shunli zhaokai" [The symposium was held to commemorate the completion of the sketching of the human genome and the 1% Project]. June 26, 2021. http://www.genetics.cas.cn/xwzx/zhxw/202107/t20210704_6126593.html.

Institute of Medicine Roundtable on Value and Science-Driven Health Care. *Clinical Data as the Basic Staple of Health Learning: Creating and Protecting a Public Good.* Washington, DC: National Academies Press, 2010. https://www.ncbi.nlm.nih.gov/books/NBK54290/.

International Civil Aviation Organization. "Convention on International Civil Aviation." December 7, 1944. https://www.icao.int/publications/documents/7300_orig.pdf.

International Telecommunication Union. "Biographies." 2019. https://www.itu.int/en/ITU-T/Workshops-and-Seminars/201905/Pages/bios.aspx.

International Telecommunication Union. "Biography—Houlin Zhao." 2018. https://www.itu.int:443/en/osg/Pages/biography-zhao.aspx.

International Telecommunication Union. "Houlin Zhao: ITU Secretary-General." 2018. https://www.itu.int:443/en/osg/Pages/default.aspx.

Iqbal, Mansoor. "Fortnite Usage and Revenue Statistics (2022)." Business of Apps, January 11, 2022. https://www.businessofapps.com/data/fortnite-statistics/.

Iqbal, Mansoor. "Fortnite Usage and Revenue Statistics (2022)." Business of Apps, June 30, 2022. https://www.businessofapps.com/data/fortnite-statistics/.

Isaak, J., and M. J. Hanna. "User Data Privacy: Facebook, Cambridge Analytica, and Privacy Protection." *Computer* 51, no. 8 (August 2018): 56–59.

Jackson, James K. "The Committee on Foreign Investment in the United States (CFIUS)." Congressional Research Service, Washington, DC, August 2019. https://fas.org/sgp/crs/natsec/RL33388.pdf.

Jackson, James K., and Cathleen D. Cimino-Isaacs. "CFIUS Reform Under FIRRMA." Congressional Research Service, February 21, 2020.

Jaffe-Hoffman, Maayan. "Coronavirus Testing in Israel to Increase Sunday with New MyHeritage Lab." *Jerusalem Post*, June 6, 2020. https://www.jpost.com/health-science/coronavirus-tests-in-israel-to-increase-by-sunday-with-new-myheritage-lab-630452.

Jain, Sachin H., Brian W. Powers, Jared B. Hawkins, and John S. Brownstein. "The Digital Phenotype." *Nature Biotechnology* 33, no. 5 (May 2015): 462–63.

Javers, Eamon. "U.S. Blocked Chinese Purchase of San Diego Fertility Clinic over Medical Data Security Concerns." CNBC, October 16, 2020. https://www.cnbc.com/2020/10/16/trump-administration-blocked-chinese-purchase-of-us-fertility-clinic.html.

Jia, Kai, Martin Kenney, Juri Mattila, and Timo Seppala. "The Application of Artificial Intelligence at Chinese Digital Platform Giants: Baidu, Alibaba and Tencent." ETLA Economic Research, Helsinki, Finland, February 26, 2018. https://www.ssrn.com/abstract=3154038.

Jiang, Min. "Authoritarian Informationalism: China's Approach to Internet Sovereignty." *SAIS Review of International Affairs* 30, no. 2 (2010): 71–89.

Jiang, Min. "A Brief Prehistory of China's Social Credit System." *Communication and the Public* 5, no. 3–4 (September 2020): 93–98.

Jiang, Qiaolei, and Anthony Y. H. Fung. "Games with a Continuum: Globalization, Regionalization, and the Nation-State in the Development of China's Online Game Industry." *Games and Culture* 14, no. 7–8 (2017): 801–24.

Jiang, Xiuxiu, Xia Wang, Jia Ren, and Zhimin Xie. "The Nexus Between Digital Finance and Economic Development: Evidence from China." *Sustainability* 13, no. 13 (June 29, 2021): 1–17.

Jiangcheng, Isabella. "2021 China Gaming Industry Report Is Out, Highlighting Worries That Growth Cannot Continue as It Has." Superpixel, December 18, 2021. https://www.superpixel.com/article/18537/2021-china-gaming-industry-report-out-highlighting-worries-that-growth-cannot-continue-it-has.

Jiemian News. "Shanghaishi zhengfuyu Alibaba qianding zhanlue hezuo: 'Zhihui chengshi' jijiang dansheng xinyangben" [The Shanghai government has signed a strategic partnership with Alibaba: "Smart city" is about to produce a new model]. August 16, 2018. www.sohu.com/a/247664826_313745.

Jing, Meng, and Sarah Dai. "China Recruits Baidu, Alibaba and Tencent to AI 'National Team.'" *South China Morning Post*, November 21, 2017. https://www.scmp.com/tech/china-tech/article/2120913/china-recruits-baidu-alibaba-and-tencent-ai-national-team.

Johnson, Kevin B., Wei-Qi Wei, Dilhan Weeraratne, Mark E. Frisse, Karl Misulis, Kyu Rhee, Juan Zhao, and Jane L. Snowdon. "Precision Medicine, AI, and the Future of Personalized Health Care." *Clinical and Translational Science* 14, no. 1 (January 2021): 86–93. https://doi.org/10.1111/cts.12884.

Julienne, Marc. "China's Ambitions in Space: The Sky's the Limit." French Institute of International Relations, January 20, 2021. https://www.ifri.org/en/publications/etudes-de-lifri/chinas-ambitions-space-skys-limit.

Kalathil, Shanthi. "The Evolution of Authoritarian Digital Influence: Grappling with the New Normal." *Prism* 9, no. 1 (October 2020). https://www.16af.af.mil/News/Article/2389118/the-evolution-of-authoritarian-digital-influence-grappling-with-the-new-normal/.

Kalkman, Shona, Menno Mostert, Christoph Gerlinger, Johannes J. M. van Delden, and Ghislaine J. M. W. van Thiel. "Responsible Data Sharing in International Health Research: A Systematic Review of Principles and Norms." *BMC Medical Ethics* 20, no. 1 (March 2019): 21.

Kania, Elsa. "Chinese Military Innovation in Artificial Intelligence." US-China Economic and Security Review Commission, Washington, DC, June 2019. https://www.uscc.gov/sites/default/files/June%207%20Hearing_Panel%201_Elsa%20Kania_Chinese%20Military%20Innovation%20in%20Artificial%20Intelligence_0.pdf.

Kania, Elsa. "Minds at War: China's Pursuit of Military Advantage Through Cognitive Science and Biotechnology." *Prism* 8, no. 3 (2019): 82–101.

Kania, Elsa. "The PLA's Latest Strategic Thinking on the Three Warfares." *China Brief* 16, no. 13 (2016): 1–19.

Kania, Elsa, and John K. Costello. "The Strategic Support Force and the Future of Chinese Information Operations." *Cyber Defense Review* 3, no. 1 (2018): 105–22.

Kania, Elsa, and Wilson Vorndick. "Weaponizing Biotech: How China's Military Is Preparing for a 'New Domain of Warfare.'" Defense One, August 14, 2019. https://www.defenseone.com/ideas/2019/08/chinas-military-pursuing-biotech/159167/.

Karan, Abraar. "Responding to Global Public Health Crises." *AMA Journal of Ethics* 22, no. 1 (January 2020): 3–4. https://journalofethics.ama-assn.org/article/responding-global-public-health-crises/2020-01.

Karlsson, Amanda. "Understanding of Bold Social Media Content: A Study of Dick-Pics as a Way to Communicate." Umeå University, 2018.

Karsten, Jack, and Darrell West. "China's Social Credit System Spreads to More Daily Transactions." Brookings Institution, Washington, DC, June 18, 2018. https://www.brookings.edu/blog/techtank/2018/06/18/chinas-social-credit-system-spreads-to-more-daily-transactions/.

Kaska, Kadri, Tomáš Minárik, and Henrik Beckvard. "Huawei, 5G and China as a Security Threat." NATO Cooperative Cyber Defence Centre of Excellence, 2019. https://ccdcoe.org/library/publications/huawei-5g-and-china-as-a-security-threat/.

Kastrenakes, Jacob. "Pakistan Lifts TikTok Ban After Just 10 Days." The Verge, October 19, 2020. https://www.theverge.com/2020/10/19/21523094/pakistan-tiktok-ban-lifted-after-10-days.

Katz, Michael L., and Carl Shapiro. "Systems Competition and Network Effects." *Journal of Economic Perspectives* 8, no. 2 (1994): 93–115. https://doi.org/10.1257/jep.8.2.93.

Kazmierczak, Mark, Ryan Ritterson, Danielle Gardner, and Rocco Casagrande. "China's Biotechnology Development: The Role of US and Other Foreign Engagement." US-China Economic and Security Review Commission and Gryphon Scientific and Rhodium Group LLC, February 2019. https://www.uscc.gov/sites/default/files/Research/US-China%20Biotech%20Report.pdf.

Keenan, Joseph. "WuXi NextCODE Acquires GMI as Part of $400M Genomics Research Push in Ireland." Fierce Biotech, November 29, 2018. https://www.fiercebiotech.com/cro/wuxinextcode-acquires-gmi-as-part-400m-genomics-research-push-ireland.

Kejilie. "Zhongguo renmin yinhang Pan Gongsheng buneng shi keji chengwei weifa weigui xingwei de baohuse" [Pan Gongsheng, People's Bank of China: Technology can't be used as a cover for illegal activities]. April 14, 2021. http://www.kejilie.com/startup-partner/article/VNV3Yz.html.

Keller, Daphne, Heather West, Spandi Singh, Lisa A. Hayes, and Lauren Sarkesian. "How Ranking and Recommendation Algorithms Influence How We See the World." New America, Washington, DC, July 14, 2020. http://newamerica.org/oti/events/how-ranking-and-recommendation-algorithms-influence-how-we-see-world/.

Kerr, Orin. "The Mosaic Theory of the Fourth Amendment." *Michigan Law Review* 111, no. 3 (December 2012): 311–54.

Khan, Aysha. "'Zoombombing' Comes for Houses of Worship." Religion News Service, March 30, 2020. https://religionnews.com/2020/03/30/zoombombing-epidemic-comes-for-houses-of-worship/.

Kharpal, Arjun. "China Once Said It Couldn't Put a Potato in Space. Now It's Eyeing Mars." CNBC, June 30, 2021. https://www.cnbc.com/2021/06/30/china-space-goals-ccp-100th-anniversary.html.

Khatri, Vijay, and Carol V. Brown. "Designing Data Governance." *Communications of the ACM* 53, no. 1 (January 2010): 148–52. https://doi.org/10.1145/1629175.1629210.

Kietzmann, Jan H., Kristopher Hermkens, Ian P. McCarthy, and Bruno S. Silvestre. "Social Media? Get Serious! Understanding the Functional Building Blocks of Social Media." *Business Horizons* 54, no. 3 (May 1, 2011): 241–51.

Kim, Nancy S., and D. A. Jeremy Telman. "Internet Giants as Quasi-Governmental Actors and the Limits of Contarctual Consent." *Missouri Law Review* 80, no. 3 (2015): 723–70.

Kim, Young Mie. "New Evidence Shows How Russia's Election Interference Has Gotten More Brazen." Brennan Center for Justice, 2020. https://www.brennancenter.org/our-work/analysis-opinion/new-evidence-shows-how-russias-election-interference-has-gotten-more.

King, Angus, and Mike Gallagher. "Cyberspace Solarium Commission Report." Cyberspace Solarium Commission, Washington, DC, March 2020. https://www.solarium.gov/report.

Kittane, Purushotham, Inika Serah Charles, Aaron Kamath, and Gowree Gokhale. "Privacy and Data Protection." *National Law Review* 12, no. 19 (2021). https://www. natlawreview.com/article/privacy-and-data-protection-india-wrap-2020.

Klein, Jodi Xu. "Chinese Acquisitions of US Companies Plunge 95 Per Cent in 2018." *South China Morning Post*, January 9, 2019. https://www.scmp.com/business/china-busin ess/article/2181096/chinese-acquisitions-us-companies-fell-drastic-95-cent-2018.

Kleiner, Dmytri, and Jacob Appelbaum. *Resisting the Surveillance State and Its Network Effects*. Berlin: Republica, 2012.

Knake, Robert K. "Creating a Federally Sponsored Cyber Insurance Program." Council on Foreign Relations, November 2016.

Knake, Robert K. "Expanding Disclosure Policy to Drive Better Cybersecurity." Council on Foreign Relations, October 16, 2019. https://www.cfr.org/report/disclosure-policy-cybersecurity.

Knockel, Jeffrey, Christopher Parsons, Lotus Ruan, Ruohan Xiong, Jedidiah Crandall, and Ron Deibert. "We Chat, They Watch: How International Users Unwittingly Build up WeChat's Chinese Censorship Apparatus." *The Citizen Lab*, University of Toronto, May 2020, https://citizenlab.ca/2020/05/we-chat-they-watch/.

Kokas, Aynne. "Building a Transparent Web in China." James A. Baker III Institute of Public Policy, Houston, TX, January 22, 2014. http://bakerinstitute.org/research/build ing-transparent-web-transnational-social-media-cybersecurity-and-sino-us-trade/.

Kokas, Aynne. "Chilling Netflix: Financialization, and the Influence of the Chinese Market on the American Entertainment Industry." *Information, Communication and Society* 23, no. 3 (August 30, 2018): 407–19.

Kokas, Aynne. "China's 2021 Data Security Law: Grand Data Strategy with Looming Implementation Challenges." *China Leadership Monitor* no. 70 (Winter 2020): 1–13.

Kokas, Aynne. "Cloud Control: China's 2017 Cybersecurity Law and Its Role in US Data Standardization." Paper presented at TPRC47: The 47th Research Conference on Communication, Information and Internet Policy, Washington, DC, July 2019.

Kokas, Aynne. "Platform Patrol: China, the United States, and the Global Battle for Data Security." *Journal of Asian Studies* 77, no. 4 (2018): 923–33.

Kosinski, Michal, David Stillwell, and Thore Graepel. "Private Traits and Attributes Are Predictable from Digital Records of Human Behavior." *Proceedings of the National Academy of Sciences* 110, no. 15 (April 2013): 5802–5.

Kovach, Steve. "Facebook-Apple Skirmish Is the Latest in a Fight That Stretches Back More than a Decade." CNBC, December 23, 2020. https://www.cnbc.com/2020/12/23/ facebook-vs-apple-ten-year-war-over-internet-business.html.

Kow, Yong Ming, Xinning Gui, and Waikuen Cheng. "Special Digital Monies: The Design of Alipay and WeChat Wallet for Mobile Payment Practices in China." Paper presented at the Human-Computer Interaction (INTERACT) conference, 2017.

Krauskopf, Lewis. "GE Says Data Business on Track for over $1 Billion in Sales." Reuters, October 9, 2014. https://www.reuters.com/article/us-general-electric-dataanalysis-idUSKCN0HY1L320141009.

Krishnan, Meenakshi. "The Foreign Intelligence Surveillance Court and the Petition Clause: Rethinking the First Amendment Right of Access." *Yale Law Journal Forum*, February 20, 2021, 723–43.

Kücklich, Julian. "Precarious Playbour: Modders and the Digital Games Industry." *Fibreculture Journal* 5 (2005).

Kulzick, Raymond S. "Sarbanes-Oxley: Effects on Financial Transparency." *S.A.M. Advanced Management Journal* 69, no. 1 (2004): 43–49.

Laidler, John. "Harvard Professor Says Surveillance Capitalism Is Undermining Democracy." *Harvard Gazette*, 2019. https://news.harvard.edu/gazette/story/2019/03/harvard-professor-says-surveillance-capitalism-is-undermining-democracy/.

Laskai, Lorand. "Civil-Military Fusion: The Missing Link Between China's Technological and Military Rise." Council on Foreign Relations, January 29, 2019. https://www.cfr.org/blog/civil-military-fusion-missing-link-between-chinas-technological-and-military-rise.

Lauckner, Carolyn, Natalia Truszczynski, Danielle Lambert, Varsha Kottamasu, Saher Meherally, Anne Marie Schipani-McLaughlin, Erica Taylor, and Nathan Hansen. "'Catfishing,' Cyberbullying, and Coercion: An Exploration of the Risks Associated with Dating App Use Among Rural Sexual Minority Males." *Journal of Gay and Lesbian Mental Health* 23, no. 3 (2019): 289–306.

Laurent, Maryline, Jean Leneutre, Sophie Chabridon, and Imane Laaouane. "Authenticated and Privacy-Preserving Consent Management in the Internet of Things." *Procedia Computer Science* 151 (2019): 256–63.

Lawson, Caitlin E. "Platform Vulnerabilities: Harassment and Misogynoir in the Digital Attack on Leslie Jones." *Information, Communication and Society* 21, no. 6 (June 2018): 818–33.

Lazarow, Alexandre. "Silicon Valley's Role in Foreign Policy and What Others Can Learn from It." Atlantic Council, November 2, 2020. https://www.atlanticcouncil.org/blogs/geotech-cues/silicon-valleys-role-in-foreign-policy-and-what-others-can-learn-from-it/.

Leaver, Tama. "Intimate Surveillance: Normalizing Parental Monitoring and Mediation of Infants Online." *Social Media + Society* 3, no. 2 (April 2017). https://doi.org/https://doi.org/10.1177/2056305117707192.

Lee, Dami. "The Popular Musical.ly App Has Been Rebranded as TikTok." The Verge, August 2, 2018. https://www.theverge.com/2018/8/2/17644260/musically-rebrand-tiktok-bytedance-douyin.

Lee, Dave. "TikTok Apologises and Reinstates Banned US Teen." BBC News, November 28, 2019. https://www.bbc.com/news/technology-50582101.

Lee, Erika. "The 'Yellow Peril' and Asian Exclusion in the Americas." *Pacific Historical Review* 76, no. 4 (2007): 537–62. https://doi.org/10.1525/phr.2007.76.4.537.

Lee, John Z. "In Re: TikTok, Inc., Consumer Privacy Litigation Case 5:20-Cv-03390-Lhk." September 3, 2020. https://www.govinfo.gov/content/pkg/USCOURTS-cand-5_20-cv-03390/pdf/USCOURTS-cand-5_20-cv-03390-0.pdf.

Lee, Jyh-An. "Forced Technology Transfer in the Case of China." *Boston University Journal of Science and Technology Law* 26, no. 2 (2020): 324–52.

Lee, Jyh-An. "Hacking into China's Cybersecurity Law." *Wake Forest Law Review* 53, no. 1 (2018): 57–104.

Lee, Kai-fu. *AI Superpowers: China, Silicon Valley, and the New World Order.* New York: Houghton Mifflin Harcourt, 2018.

Leibold, James. "Surveillance in China's Xinjiang Region: Ethnic Sorting, Coercion, and Inducement." *Journal of Contemporary China* 29, no. 121 (2020): 46–60. https://doi.org/10.1080/10670564.2019.1621529.

Leng, Cheng, and Brenda Goh. "Ant Financial Pauses Credit Rating Service Amid Coronavirus Outbreak." Reuters, February 7, 2020. https://www.reuters.com/article/us-china-health-credit-ratings-idUSKBN2010UW.

Lenzerini, Maurizio. "Data Integration: A Theoretical Perspective." Paper presented at the ACM SIGACT-SIGMOD-SIGART Symposium on Principles of Database Systems, Madison, WI, June 3–5, 2002.

Leung, Danny. "WuXi Biologics Readies Hong Kong Relisting." FinanceAsia, January 6, 2017. https://www.financeasia.com/article/wuxi-biologics-readies-hong-kong-relisting/432813.

Levy, Ari, and Christina Farr. "The Trump Administration Is Forcing This Health Start-up That Took Chinese Money into a Fire Sale." CNBC, April 4, 2019. https://www.cnbc.com/2019/04/04/cfius-forces-patientslikeme-into-fire-sale-booting-chinese-investor.html.

Levy, Karen E. C. "Intimate Surveillance." *Idaho Law Review* 51, no. 3 (2015): 679–94.

Lewis, Jackson. "Will Texas Soon Join the Ranks of States Enacting Privacy Legislation?" *National Law Review* 9, no. 129 (May 2019). https://www.natlawreview.com/article/will-texas-soon-join-ranks-states-enacting-privacy-legislation.

Lewis, James Andrew. "China and Technology: Tortoise and Hare Again." Center for Strategic and International Studies, Washington, DC, August 2, 2017. https://www.csis.org/analysis/china-and-technology-tortoise-and-hare-again.

Lew-Williams, Beth. *The Chinese Must Go: Violence, Exclusion, and the Making of the Alien in America*. Cambridge, MA: Harvard University Press, 2021.

Li, Jie, Yu Wu, and Jing Jian Xiao. "The Impact of Digital Finance on Household Consumption: Evidence from China." *Economic Modelling* 86 (March 1, 2020): 317–26. https://doi.org/10.1016/j.econmod.2019.09.027.

Li, Lingyuan, Guo Freeman, and Donghee Yvette Wohn. "Power in Skin: The Interplay of Self-Presentation, Tactical Play, and Spending in Fortnite." Paper presented at the CHI PLAY, Ottawa, Canada, Virtual, November 2, 2020.

Li, Pei. "U.S. Businesses in China Face Uncertainty as White House Bans WeChat." Reuters, August 7, 2020. https://www.reuters.com/article/us-usa-wechat-trump-china-idUSKCN25320Z.

Li, Xiao-Juan, and Huang Li-Zhen. "Vulnerability and Interdependency of Critical Infrastructure: A Review." Paper presented at the Next Generation Infrastructure Systems for Eco-cities, November 11–13, 2010.

Liang, Fan. "COVID-19 and Health Code: How Digital Platforms Tackle the Pandemic in China." *Social Media + Society* 6, no. 3 (July 2020): 1–4.

Liang, Fan, Vishnupriya Das, Nadiya Kostyuk, and Muzammil M. Hussain. "Constructing a Data-Driven Society: China's Social Credit System as a State Surveillance Infrastructure." *Policy and Internet* 10, no. 4 (2018): 415–53.

Liao, Rita. "After India and US, Japan Looks to Ban TikTok and Other Chinese Apps." TechCrunch, July 28, 2020. https://techcrunch.com/2020/07/28/japan-proposes-tiktok-ban/.

Liao, Rita. "The Race to Be China's Top Fintech Platform: Ant vs. Tencent." TechCrunch, November 9, 2020. https://techcrunch.com/2020/11/09/tencent-vs-alibaba-ant-fintech/.

Liaropoulos, A. "Exploring the Complexity of Cyberspace Governance: State Sovereignty, Multi-Stakeholderism, and Power Politics." *Journal of Information Warfare* 15, no. 4 (2016): 14–26. https://www.jstor.org/stable/26487548.

Licoppe, Christian, and Zbigniew Smoreda. "Are Social Networks Technologically Embedded? How Networks Are Changing Today with Changes in Communication Technology." *Social Networks* 27, no. 4 (October 2005): 317–35.

Lide, Casey, and Jason P. Chun. "Overview of Broadband Funding Opportunities in the COVID-19 Relief Act." *National Law Review* 11, no. 19 (January 2021). https://www.natlawreview.com/article/overview-broadband-funding-opportunities-covid-19-relief-act.

Lieberthal, Kenneth. "Introduction: The 'Fragmented Authoritarianism Model' and Its Limitations." In *Bureaucracy, Politics, and Decision Making in Post-Mao China*, edited by David M. Lampton and Kenneth G. Lieberthal, 1–32. Berkeley: University of California Press, 1992.

Lieberthal, Kenneth. *Governing China: From Revolution Through Reform*. New York: W. W. Norton, 2004.

Liedholm Johnson, Eva. "Mineral Rights: Legal Systems Governing Exploration and Exploitation." Civil Engineering, KTH Sweden, 2010.

Lin, Justin Yifu. "China and the Global Economy." *China Economic Journal* 4, no. 1 (October 2011): 1–14. https://www.tandfonline.com/doi/abs/10.1080/17538963.2011.609612.

Lin, Lauren Yu-Hsin, and Curtis J. Milhaupt. "Party Building or Noisy Signaling? The Contours of Political Conformity in Chinese Corporate Governance." *Journal of Legal Studies* 50, no. 1 (January 1, 2021): 187–217. https://doi.org/10.1086/713189.

Lin, Liza, and Newley Purnell. "A World with a Billion Cameras Watching You Is Just Around the Corner." *Wall Street Journal*, December 6, 2019. https://www.wsj.com/articles/a-billion-surveillance-cameras-forecast-to-be-watching-within-two-years-11575565402. www.wsj.com.

Lin, Syaru Shirley. *Taiwan's China Dilemma: Contested Identities and Multiple Interests in Taiwan's Cross-Strait Economic Policy*. Stanford, CA: Stanford University Press, 2016.

Lindtner, Silvia M. *Prototype Nation*. Princeton, NJ: Princeton University Press, 2020.

Lindtner, Silvia, Ken Anderson, and Paul Dourish. "Cultural Appropriation: Information Technologies as Sites of Transnational Imagination." Paper presented at the ACM annual meeting, Cambridge, MA, 2012.

Linghu, Xiaochong. "Rengong zhineng wujia guojia xinyidai rengong zhineng kaifang chuangxin pingtai" [Artificial intelligence—five new AI platforms]. Easy Tech China, 2018. https://easytechchina.com/index.php?m=&c=media&a=show&id=3380.

Lipsitz, George. *The Possessive Investment in Whiteness: How White People Profit from Identity Politics*. Revised ed. Philadelphia: Temple University Press, 2006.

Lipton, Ann M. "Manufactured Consent: The Problem of Arbitration Clauses in Corporate Charters and Bylaws." *Georgetown Law Journal* 104, no. 3 (2015): 583–642.

Liu, Chuncheng. "Multiple Social Credit Systems in China." Social Science Research Network, 2019. https://papers.ssrn.com/abstract=3423057.

Liu, Irina, Evan Linck, Bhavya Lal, Keith W. Crane, Xueying Han, and Thomas J. Colvin. "Evaluation of China's Commercial Space Sector." IDA Science and Technology Institute, Washington, DC, September 2019. https://www.ida.org/-/media/feature/publications/e/ev/evaluation-of-chinas-commercial-space-sector/d-10873.ashx.

Liu, Jennine. "Chinese-Owned Apps Pose Counterintelligence Threat to Users." WorldAware, December 6, 2019. https://www.worldaware.com/resources/blog/chinese-owned-apps-pose-counterintelligence-threat-users.

Liu, Jian, Chen Zhang, and Abdul Razaque Chhachhar. "A Comparative Study of the Global Internet Governance System Between China and the United States." *Indian Journal of Science and Technology* 13, no. 23 (2020): 2303–10.

Liu, Lizhi. "The Rise of Data Politics: Digital China and the World." *Studies in Comparative International Development* 56, no. 1 (2021): 45–67. https://doi.org/10.1007/s12116-021-09319-8.

Liu, Sida, David M. Trubek, and David B. Wilkins. "Mapping the Ecology of China's Corporate Legal Sector: Globalization and Its Impact on Lawyers and Society." *Asian Journal of Law and Society* 3, no. 2 (November 2016): 273–97.

Liu, Xun. "Elon Musk: Tesla Won't Share Car Data with U.S. Government." CGTN, March 21, 2021. https://news.cgtn.com/news/2021-03-20/Elon-Musk-Tesla-will-never-share-data-with-any-government-YN1w7ypo2I/index.html.

Livingston, Scott. "The New Challenge of Communist Corporate Governance." Center for Strategic and International Studies, Washington, DC, January 15, 2021. https://www.csis.org/analysis/new-challenge-communist-corporate-governance.

Long, Danielle. "Ant Financial and Moneygram Form Strategic Partnership After Proposed $1.2M Merger Deal Fails." *The Drum*, January 9, 2018.

Lorenz, Taylor, Sheera Frenkel, and Kellen Browning. "TikTok Teens Tank Trump Rally in Tulsa, They Say." *New York Times*, June 21, 2020. https://www.nytimes.com/2020/06/21/style/tiktok-trump-rally-tulsa.html.

Lu, Lewis. "China Enhances Regulation of Technology Sector." *International Tax Review*, November 17, 2020. https://www.internationaltaxreview.com/article/b1p9189ddm05tg/china-enhances-regulation-of-technology-sector.

Lü, Yao-Huai. "Privacy and Data Privacy Issues in Contemporary China." *Ethics and Information Technology* 7, no. 1 (March 2005): 7–15.

Luo, Xueming, Jie Zhang, and Wenjing Duan. "Social Media and Firm Equity Value." *Information Systems Research* 24, no. 1 (2012): 146–63.

Lutz, Christoph, and Gemma Newlands. "Privacy and Smart Speakers: A Multi-Dimensional Approach." *The Information Society* 37, no. 3 (May 2021): 147–62.

Lyons, Kim. "K-Pop Fans and TikTok Teens Say They Reserved Tickets for Trump's Tulsa Rally to Leave Seats Empty." The Verge, June 21, 2020. https://www.theverge.com/2020/6/21/21298169/kpop-fans-tiktok-tickets-trump-tulsa-rally-empty-seats.

Lyons, Kim. "TikTok Says It Will Stop Accessing Clipboard Content on Ios Devices." The Verge, June 26, 2020. https://www.theverge.com/2020/6/26/21304228/tiktok-security-ios-clipboard-access-ios14-beta-feature.

Lyu, Yiyi. "Duo guojia hulianwang qiye jieshou wangluo anquan shenbao yuanyin shi shenme?" [Why are multinational corporations subject to security audits?]. *Zhongguo Guoqing*, July 2021. http://guoqing.china.com.cn/2021-07/07/content_77610601.htm.

M&A Critique. "ChemChina Buys out Syngenta." M&A Critique, 2016. https://mnacritique.mergersindia.com/chemchina-buys-syngenta/.

Mac, Ryan. "Grindr Had Dreams of Making the World Better for Queer People. Then a Chinese Gaming Company Bought It." BuzzFeed News, July 18, 2019. https://www.buzzfeednews.com/article/ryanmac/grindr-chinese-owner-company-chaos.

Macabasco, Agilio. "Absolute Beginner's Guide to League of Legends." Mobalytics, July 5, 2019. https://mobalytics.gg/blog/absolute-beginners-guide-to-league-of-legends/.

Macauley, Richard, Pei Yi Mak, and Bloomberg. "Jack Ma Just Added Billions to His Fortune. Here's Where He Ranks Now." *Fortune*, October 26, 2020. https://fortune.com/2020/10/26/jack-ma-ant-ipo-net-worth/#:~:text=Jack%20Ma%2C%20the%20former%20English,in%20Hong%20Kong%20and%20Shanghai.

MacKenzie, David. *ICAO: A History of the International Civil Aviation Organization.* Toronto, ON: University of Toronto Press, 2010.

MacKinnon, Rebecca. *Consent of the Networked: The Worldwide Struggle for Internet Freedom.* New York: Basic Books, 2012.

Maghrabi, Louai A. "The Threats of Data Security over the Cloud as Perceived by Experts and University Students." Paper presented at the World Symposium on Computer Applications Research, Sousse, Tunisia, January 18–20, 2014.

MagicMotion. "Magic Motion App Privacy Notice." May 25, 2018. http://blog.magicmotion.cn/?page_id=236.

Mahdavi, Pardis. *From Trafficking to Terror: Constructing a Global Social Problem.* New York: Routledge, 2014.

Mahdavi, Pardis. *Gridlock: Labor, Migration, and Human Trafficking in Dubai.* Stanford, CA: Stanford University Press, 2011.

Mai, Jun. "Ecuador Is Fighting Crime Using Chinese Surveillance Technology." *South China Morning Post*, January 21, 2018. https://www.scmp.com/news/china/diplomacy-defence/article/2129912/ecuador-fighting-crime-using-chinese-surveillance.

Mallapragada, Madhavi. "Asian Americans as Racial Contagion." *Cultural Studies* 35, no. 2–3 (2021): 279–90. https://doi.org/10.1080/09502386.2021.1905678.

Mallett-Outtrim, Ryan. "30,000 More Security Cameras and 17,000 Less Guns on Venezuelan Streets." Venezuelanalysis.com, November 27, 2013. https://venezuelanalysis.com/news/10198.

Man, Simeon. "Anti-Asian Violence and US Imperialism." *Race and Class* 62, no. 2 (2020): 24–33. https://doi.org/10.1177/0306396820949779.

Mann, Monique, and Angela Daly. "Geopolitics, Jurisdiction and Surveillance." *Internet Policy Review* 9, no. 3 (2020). https://doi.org/10.14763/2020.3.1501.

Maranto, Lauren. "Who Benefits from China's Cybersecurity Laws?" Center for Strategic and International Studies, Washington, DC, June 25, 2020. https://www.csis.org/blogs/new-perspectives-asia/who-benefits-chinas-cybersecurity-laws.

Marczak, Bill, and John Scott-Railton. "Move Fast and Roll Your Own Crypto: A Quick Look at the Confidentiality of Zoom Meetings." Citizen Lab, University of Toronto, April 2020. https://citizenlab.ca/2020/04/move-fast-roll-your-own-crypto-a-quick-look-at-the-confidentiality-of-zoom-meetings/.

Markey, Ed, and Richard Blumenthal. "Senators Markey, Blumenthal to Grindr, Third Parties: How Do You Protect Users' Sensitive Information." April 3, 2018. https://www.markey.senate.gov/imo/media/doc/grindr%20letter.pdf.

Marks, Mason. "Emergent Medical Data: Health Information Inferred by Artificial Intelligence." *UC Irvine Law Review* 11, no. 995 (March 14, 2021). https://ssrn.com/abstract=3554118.

Marks, Tove. "The Privacy Risks of Your Baby Monitor." VPNoverview, December 16, 2019. https://vpnoverview.com/privacy/devices/privacy-risks-baby-monitor/.

Marsden, David W. "Virginia Consumer Data Protection Act." 2021. https://lis.virginia.gov/cgi-bin/legp604.exe?211+sum+SB1392S.

Marshmello. *Marshmello Holds First Ever Fortnite Concert Live at Pleasant Park*, 2019. February 3, 2019. Accessed July 8, 2022. https://www.youtube.com/watch?v=NBsCzN-jfvA.

Martinello, Eva. "League of Legends Generated $1.5 Billion Revenue in 2019." Dot eSports, January 3, 2020. https://dotesports.com/league-of-legends/news/league-of-legends-generated-1-5-billion-revenue-in-2019.

Martz, Lauren. "Why the WuXi NextCODE Split Makes Strategic Sense for the Multinational Genomics Company." BioCentury, 2020. https://www.biocentury.com/

article/305577/why-the-wuxi-nextcode-split-makes-strategic-sense-for-the-multin ational-genomics-company.

Mastre, Brian. "New Concern over Chinese Spy Capabilities in Western Nebraska Cell Tower Equipment." 6 News WOWT, February 12, 2020. https://www.wowt.com/cont ent/news/New-concern-over-Chinese-spy-capabilities-in-Western-Nebraska-cell-tower-equipment--567819721.html.

Mastro, Oriana Skylar. "The Stealth Superpower: How China Hid Its Global Ambitions Who Will Run the World." *Foreign Affairs* 98, no. 1 (2019): 31–39.

Mayntz, Renate, and Thomas Hughes. *The Development of Large Technical Systems.* Boulder, CO: Westview Press, 2019.

Mazarr, Michael J., Abigail Casey, Alyssa Demus, Scott W. Harold, Luke J. Matthews, Nathan Beauchamp-Mustafaga, and James Sladden. *Hostile Social Manipulation: Present Realities and Emerging Trends.* Santa Monica, CA: RAND Corporation, 2019. https:// www.rand.org/pubs/research_reports/RR2713.html.

McBride, James, and Andrew Chatzky. "Is 'Made in China 2025' a Threat to Global Trade?" Council on Foreign Relations, May 2019. https://www.cfr.org/backgrounder/ made-china-2025-threat-global-trade.

McInroy, Lauren B. "Pitfalls, Potentials, and Ethics of Online Survey Research: LGBTQ and Other Marginalized and Hard-to-Access Youths." *Social Work Research* 40, no. 2 (2016): 83–94.

McKune, Sarah, and Shazeda Ahmed. "The Contestation and Shaping of Cyber Norms Through China's Internet Sovereignty Agenda." *International Journal of Communication* 12 (January 2018): 3835–55.

McMahon, Karen. "Drones Provide a Bird's Eye View." *Syngenta Thrive* (blog), 2016. https://www.syngenta-us.com/thrive/production/drones-birdseye-view.html.

McMorrow, Ryan, and David Pilling. "Jack Ma Disappears from His Own Talent Show." *Financial Times*, January 1, 2021. https://www.ft.com/content/a91dfeae-da1e-4348-8212-bbfbe94d93bd.

McPherson-Smith, Oliver, and Steve Pociask. "Huawei Is Embedded in Our Infrastructure and the Federal Government Subsidized It." *The Hill*, August 21, 2019. https://thehill. com/blogs/congress-blog/technology/458260-huawei-is-embedded-in-our-infrast ructure-and-the-federal.

Mehran, Khurram Ali. "PTA Blocks TikTok in Pakistan." News release, October 9, 2020. https://www.pta.gov.pk/en/media-center/single-media/pta-blocks-tiktok-in-pakis tan-091020.

Mendoza, Ron. "'Fortnite' Now an Official College Sport, Esports Scholarships Also Offered." *International Business Times*, January 23, 2020. https://www.ibtimes.com/ fortnite-now-official-college-sport-esports-scholarships-also-offered-2907997.

Mertha, Andrew. "'Fragmented Authoritarianism 2.0': Political Pluralization in the Chinese Policy Process." *China Quarterly* 200 (2009): 995–1012.

MGI. "MGI Helped Angola Build 5 'Huo-Yan' Laboratories, Greatly Increasing the Efficiency of Large-Scale Testing." July 16, 2020. https://en.mgi-tech.com/ news/202/.

Mi Fit. "Mi Fit User Agreement." https://cdn.awsbj0.fds.api.mi-img.com/mifit/1480831 742.html.

Micheli, Marina, Marisa Ponti, Max Craglia, and Anna Berti Suman. "Emerging Models of Data Governance in the Age of Datafication." *Big Data and Society* 7, no. 2 (July 2020): 1–15. https://doi.org/10.1177/2053951720948087.

Microsoft. "About Microsoft's Presence in China." News release. https://news.microsoft.com/about-microsofts-presence-in-china/. Accessed February 25, 2022.

Miles, Sam. "Still Getting It on Online: Thirty Years of Queer Male Spaces Brokered Through Digital Technologies." *Geography Compass* 12, no. 11 (2018): 1–13.

Miles, Tom. "Huawei Allegations Driven by Politics Not Evidence: U.N. Telecoms Chief." *Reuters*, April 5, 2019. https://www.reuters.com/article/us-usa-china-huawei-tech-un/huawei-allegations-driven-by-politics-not-evidence-u-n-telecoms-chief-idUSKCN1RH1KN.

Miles, Tom. "U.S. Asks China Not to Enforce Cyber Security Law." *Reuters*, September 26, 2017. https://www.reuters.com/article/us-usa-china-cyber-trade-idUSKCN1C11D1.

Milhaupt, Curtis J. "The State as Owner—China's Experience." *Oxford Review of Economic Policy* 36, no. 2 (2020): 362–79. https://doi.org/10.1093/oxrep/graa001. https://doi.org/10.1093/oxrep/graa001.

Milhaupt, Curtis J., and Wentong Zheng. "Beyond Ownership: State Capitalism and the Chinese Firm." *Georgetown Law Journal* 103, no. 3 (March 2015): 665–722.

Miller, Greg. "The Intelligence Coup of the Century." *Washington Post*, February 11, 2020. https://www.washingtonpost.com/graphics/2020/world/national-security/cia-crypto-encryption-machines-espionage/.

Ministry of Culture of the People's Republic of China. "Hulianwang wenhua jingyin danwei shenqing banshi zhinan" [Interim provisions on the administration of internet culture]. April 2011. https://www.mct.gov.cn/zxbs/bszn/201909/t20190930_847110.htm.

Ministry of Electronics and Information Technology (India). "Government Blocks 118 Mobile Apps Which Are Prejudicial to Sovereignty and Integrity of India, Defence of India, Security of State and Public Order." September 2, 2020. https://pib.gov.in/PressReleasePage.aspx?PRID=1650669.

Ministry of Foreign Trade and Economic Cooperation and Ministry of Science and Technology. "Guanyu tiaozheng fabu zhongguo jinzhichukou xianzhichukou jishumulu degonggao" [Announcements on the readjustment and release of the list of China's prohibited and restricted technology export]. August 28, 2020. http://www.most.gov.cn/tztg/202008/t20200828_158545.htm.

Ministry of Health and Ministry of Foreign Trade and Economic Cooperation. "Zhongwai hezi, hezuo yiliao jigou guanli zanxing banfa" [Interim measures for administration of Chinese-foreign joint venture and cooperative medical institutions, May 15, 2000. http://www.gd.gov.cn/zwgk/wjk/zcfgk/content/post_2531679.html.

Mitchell, Anna, and Larry Diamond. "China's Surveillance State Should Scare Everyone." *The Atlantic*, February 2, 2018. https://www.theatlantic.com/international/archive/2018/02/china-surveillance/552203/.

Mittmann, Gloria, Kate Woodcock, Sylvia Dörfler, Ina Krammer, Isabella Pollak, and Beate Schrank. "'TikTok Is My Life and Snapchat Is My Ventricle': A Mixed-Methods Study on the Role of Online Communication Tools for Friendships in Early Adolescents." *Journal of Early Adolescence*, June 2, 2021. https://doi.org/10.1177/02724316211020368.

Mohsin, Saleha. "Biden Team Eyes Potential Threat from China's Digital Yuan." *Bloomberg*, April 11, 2021. https://www.bloomberg.com/news/articles/2021-04-11/biden-team-eyes-potential-threat-from-china-s-digital-yuan-plans.

Monitoring Report. "Chinese Investment in Pakistan Under Increasing Scrutiny." *Profit by Pakistan Today*, August 10, 2018. https://profit.pakistantoday.com.pk/2018/08/10/chinese-investment-in-pakistan-under-increasing-scrutiny/.

Morck, Randall, Andrei Shleifer, and Robert W. Vishny. "Management Ownership and Market Valuation: An Empirical Analysis." *Journal of Financial Economics* 20 (January 1988): 293–315.

Morris, Johny. *Practical Data Migration*. London: Chartered Institute for IT, 2020.

Morrison, Sara. "The Case Against Smart Baby Tech." *Vox*, February 2020. https://www.vox.com/recode/2020/2/26/21152920/ibaby-hacking-smart-baby-monitors-bitdefender.

Mortensen, Torrill. "Flow, Seduction, and Mutual Pleasures." Paper presented at the Other Players Conference, Copenhagen, Denmark, 2004.

Mosco, Vincent. *Pushbutton Fantasies: Critical Perspectives on Videotex and Information Technology*. Norwood, NJ: Ablex, 1982.

Mosco, Vincent. *The Smart City in a Digital World*. Bingley, UK: Emerald Publishing, 2019.

Moss, Sebastian. "Tesla Opens Data Center in Shanghai, China." *Data Center Dynamics*, October 25, 2021. https://www.datacenterdynamics.com/en/news/tesla-opens-a-data-center-in-shanghai-china/.

Moss, Trefor. "Tesla to Store China Data Locally in New Data Center." *Wall Street Journal*, May 23, 2021. https://www.wsj.com/articles/tesla-to-store-china-data-locally-in-new-data-center-11622015001.

Moss, Trefor. "Tiny GM Car Zips Past Tesla to Lead China's Electric Vehicle Market." *Wall Street Journal*, November 13, 2020. https://www.wsj.com/articles/tiny-gm-car-zips-past-tesla-to-lead-chinas-electric-vehicle-market-11605278148.

Moyer, Edward. "China on TikTok Sale: Not So Fast." CNET, August 29, 2020. https://www.cnet.com/news/china-on-tiktok-sale-not-so-fast/.

Mozilla Foundation. "*Privacy Not Included: A Buyer's Guide for Connected Products." 2020. https://foundation.mozilla.org/en/privacynotincluded/.

Mozur, Paul, Julian E. Barnes, and Aaron Krolik. "Popular Chinese-Made Drone Is Found to Have Security Weakness." *New York Times*, July 23, 2020. https://www.nytimes.com/2020/07/23/us/politics/dji-drones-security-vulnerability.html.

Mozur, Paul, Raymond Zhong, and David McCabe. "TikTok Deal Is Complicated by New Rules from China over Tech Exports." *New York Times*, August 29, 2020. https://www.nytimes.com/2020/08/29/technology/china-tiktok-export-controls.html.

Mueller, Milton. *Networks and States: The Global Politics of Internet Governance*. Information Revolution and Global Politics. Cambridge, MA: MIT Press, 2010.

Mueller, Milton. *Will the Internet Fragment? Sovereignty, Globalization and Cyberspace*. New York: John Wiley & Sons, 2017.

Mueller, Milton L., and Farzaneh Badiei. "Governing Internet Territory: ICANN, Sovereignty Claims, Property Rights and Country Code Top-Level Domains." *Columbia Science and Technology Law Review* 18, no. 2 (2016): 435–91.

Mui, Ylan Q. "China's $9 Billion Effort to Beat the U.S. in Genetic Testing." *Washington Post*, December 30, 2016. https://www.washingtonpost.com/news/wonk/wp/2016/12/30/chinas-9-billion-effort-to-beat-the-u-s-in-genetic-testing/.

Munroe, Tony. "China Extends Crackdown on Jack Ma's Empire with Enforced Revamp of Ant Group." Reuters, April 12, 2021. https://www.reuters.com/business/chinas-ant-group-become-financial-holding-company-central-bank-2021-04-12/.

Murphy, Annabel, and Jack Parrock. "Huawei 5G: European Countries Playing 'Politics' with Network Bans, Chinese Company Says." Euronews, July 28, 2021. https://www.euronews.com/next/2021/07/28/huawei-eyes-a-place-within-europe-s-digital-future-despite-5g-bans-in-some-countries.

Nakashima, Ellen. "Hacks of OPM Databases Compromised 22.1 Million People, Federal Authorities Say." *Washington Post*, July 9, 2015. https://www.washingtonpost.com/news/federal-eye/wp/2015/07/09/hack-of-security-clearance-system-affected-21-5-million-people-federal-authorities-say/.

Napoli, Philip M. *Social Media and the Public Interest: Media Regulation in the Disinformation Age.* New York: Columbia University Press, 2019.

Nassar, Samuel F., Khadir Raddassi, Baljit Ubhi, Joseph Doktorski, and Ahmad Abulaban. "Precision Medicine: Steps Along the Road to Combat Human Cancer." *Cells* 9, no. 9 (September 2020): 1–17. https://doi.org/10.3390/cells9092056.

National Academies of Sciences, Engineering, and Medicine. *Safeguarding the Bioeconomy.* Washington, DC: National Academies Press, 2020.

National Bureau of Statistics. "Diliuci renkou rucha shuju" [Sixth Census data]. In *Tabulation of the 2010 Population Census of the People's Republic of China*, 2010. http://www.stats.gov.cn/tjsj/pcsj/rkpc/6rp/indexch.htm.

National Intelligence Council. *Foreign Threats to the 2020 US Federal Elections.* March 2021. https://www.dni.gov/files/ODNI/documents/assessments/ICA-declass-16MAR21.pdf.

National People's Congress. "Shouquan fabu zhonghua renmin gongheguo zianggang tebie zingzhengqu weihu guojia anquanfa" [Authorized to promulgate law of the Hong Kong Special Administrative Region of the People's Republic of China on safeguarding state security]. June 2020. http://www.xinhuanet.com/2020-06/30/c_1126179649.htm.

National People's Congress. "Zhonggong zhongyang guanyu zhiding shisanwu guihua de jianyi" [The CPC Central Committee's proposal on formulating the 13th Five-Year Plan]. November 3, 2015. http://www.gov.cn/xinwen/2015-11/03/content_2959432.htm.

National People's Congress. "Zhonggong zhongyang guowuyuan guanyu shenhua guoyou qiye gaige de zhidao yijian" [Guiding opinions of the CPC Central Committee and the State Council on deepening the reform of state-owned enterprises]. August 2015. http://www.gov.cn/zhengce/2015-09/13/content_2930440.htm.

National People's Congress. "Zhonggong zhongyang guowuyuan guanyu zhichi Hainan quanmian shenhua gaige kaifang de zhidao yijian" [Guiding opinions of the CPC Central Committee and the State Council on supporting Hainan in comprehensively deepening reform and opening up]. April 14, 2018. http://www.gov.cn/zhengce/2018-04/14/content_5282456.htm.

National People's Congress. "Zhonghua renmin gongheguo shuju anquanfa" [Data security law of the People's Republic of China]. 2020. http://www.npc.gov.cn/npc/c30834/202106/7c9af12f51334a73b56d7938f99a788a.shtml.

National People's Congress and the Chinese People's Political Consultative Conference. "Zhonghua renmin gongheguo guomin jingji he shehui fazhan dishisige wunian guihua he 2035 nian yuanjing mubiao gangyao" [14th Five-Year Plan for the national economic and social development of the People's Republic of China and the outline of the long-range goals to 2035]. March 12, 2021. http://www.xinhuanet.com/2021-03/13/c_1127205564.htm.

National Press and Publication Administration. "Wangluo chuban fuwu shenpi shixiang-chuban guochan wangluo youxizuopin shenpi" [Approval items for online publishing service—approval for publishing domestic online games]. April 19, 2019. http://www.nppa.gov.cn/nppa/contents/329/46004.shtml.

National Research Council. *Precision Agriculture in the 21st Century: Geospatial and Information Technologies in Crop Management*. Washington, DC: National Academies Press, 1997. https://www.nap.edu/catalog/5491/precision-agriculture-in-the-21st-century-geospatial-and-information-technologies.

National Research Council. *Standards, Conformity Assessment, and Trade: Into the 21st Century*. Washington, DC: National Academies Press, 1995.

NATO Cooperative Cyber Defence Centre of Excellence. "Huawei, 5G and China as a Security Threat." 2019. https://ccdcoe.org/library/publications/huawei-5g-and-china-as-a-security-threat/.

NATO Cooperative Cyber Defence Centre of Excellence. "Shanghai Cooperation Organization." 2018. https://ccdcoe.org/organisations/sco/.

NATO Cooperative Cyber Defence Centre of Excellence. 2015. "An Updated Draft of the Code of Conduct Distributed in the United Nations: What's New?" https://ccdcoe.org/incyder-articles/an-updated-draft-of-the-code-of-conduct-distributed-in-the-united-nations-whats-new/.

Naughton, Barry. *The Chinese Economy: Transitions and Growth*. Cambridge, MA: MIT Press, 2007.

Nazmeeva, Alina. "Constructing the Virtual as a Social Form." Master's thesis, Massachusetts Institute of Technology, 2019. https://dspace.mit.edu/handle/1721.1/123596.

Needham, Kirsty. "Special Report: COVID Opens New Doors for China's Gene Giant." Reuters, August 5, 2020. https://www.reuters.com/article/us-health-coronavirus-bgi-specialreport-idUSKCN2511CE.

Neff, Gina. "The Political Economy of Digital Health." In *Society and the Internet: How Networks of Information and Communication Are Changing Our Lives*, edited by Mark Graham and William H. Dutton, 281–92. Oxford, UK: Oxford University Press, 2019.

Neff, Gina. "Why Big Data Won't Cure Us." *Big Data* 1, no. 3 (August 2013): 117–23. https://doi.org/https://doi.org/10.1089/big.2013.0029.

NetChoice. "About Us." 2021. https://netchoice.org/about/.

Netzpolitik. "Auszug aus den Moderationskriterien von TikTok." November 2019. https://cdn.netzpolitik.org/wp-upload/2019/11/tiktok-auszug-moderationsregeln-abschrift-1.pdf.

Ng, Jason Q. *Blocked on Weibo: What Gets Suppressed on China's Version of Twitter (and Why)*. New York: The New Press, 2013.

NHS Digital. "Data Sets." April 2021. National Health Service, UK. https://digital.nhs.uk/data-and-information/data-collections-and-data-sets/data-sets.

Ni, Wufan. "A Study on How to Promote the Business Environment Competitiveness of China's Household Appliance Export Enterprises—Take the Example of 'Haier.'" *Journal of Cambridge Studies* 4, no. 3 (2009): 10.

Nie, Mingyan. "Space Privatization in China's National Strategy of Military-Civilian Integration: An Appraisal of Critical Legal Challenges." *Space Policy* 52 (May 2020). https://doi.org/https://doi.org/10.1016/j.spacepol.2020.101372.

O'Donnell, Carl, and Echo Wang. "Behind Grindr's Doomed Hookup in China, a Data Misstep and Scramble to Make Up." Reuters, May 22, 2019. https://www.reuters.com/article/us-usa-china-grindr-exclusive-idUSKCN1SS10H.

O'Keeffe, Kate, and Peter Rudegeair. "U.S. Bars Merger of Moneygram, China's Ant Financial." *Wall Street Journal*, January 3, 2019. https://www.wsj.com/articles/moneygram-and-ant-financial-halt-merger-deal-1514931496.

Odell, Rachel Esplin. *Chinese Regime Insecurity, Domestic Authoritarianism, and Foreign Policy*. Maxwell AFB, AL: Air University Press, 2019.

Office for Civil Rights. "Summary of the HIPAA Privacy Rule." July 26, 2013. https://www.hhs.gov/hipaa/for-professionals/privacy/laws-regulations/index.html.

Office of the Privacy Commissioner of Canada. "Summary of Privacy Laws in Canada." May 15, 2014. https://www.priv.gc.ca/en/privacy-topics/privacy-laws-in-canada/02_05_d_15/.

Office of the United States Trade Representative. "2019 Report to Congress on China's Wto Compliance." March 2020. https://ustr.gov/sites/default/files/2019_Report_on_China%E2%80%99s_WTO_Compliance.pdf.

Office of the United States Trade Representative. "The People's Republic of China: U.S.-China Trade Facts." 2020. https://ustr.gov/countries-regions/china-mongolia-taiwan/peoples-republic-china.

Oldenburg, Ray. *The Great Good Place: Cafés, Coffee Shops, Community Centers, Beauty Parlors, General Stores, Bars, Hangouts, and How They Get You Through the Day*. St. Paul, Minnesota: Paragon House, 1989.

Orbach, Meir. "Israel's Ministry of Health Shelves Myheritage's COVID-19 Testing Lab." CTECH by Calcalist, last updated April 1, 2020. https://www.calcalistech.com/ctech/articles/0,7340,L-3805353,00.html.

Organisation for Economic Co-Operation and Development. *Data-Driven Innovation: Big Data for Growth and Well-Being*. Paris: OECD Publishing, 2015.

Osawa, Juro, and Shai Oster. "Beijing Tightens Grip on ByteDance by Quietly Taking Stake, China Board Seat." The Information, August 16, 2021. https://www.theinformation.com/articles/beijing-tightens-grip-on-bytedance-by-quietly-taking-stake-china-board-seat.

Oster, Shai. "Chinese Gaming Billionaire Buys U.S. Gay Dating App Grindr." Bloomberg, January 11, 2016. https://www.bloomberg.com/news/articles/2016-01-12/china-tech-billionaire-buys-control-of-us-gay-dating-app-grindr.

Ostrom, Karyn. "New Pilot Program Delivers Innovative Digital Technology." *Syngenta Thrive* (blog), 2019. https://www.syngenta-us.com/thrive/news/new-pilot-program-delivers-innovative-digital-technology.html.

Pacala, S., and R. Socolow. "Stabilization Wedges: Solving the Climate Problem for the Next 50 Years with Current Technologies." *Science* 305, no. 5686 (2004): 968–72.

Pagach, Donald, and Richard Warr. "The Characteristics of Firms That Hire Chief Risk Officers." *Journal of Risk and Insurance* 78, no. 1 (2011): 185–211.

Pai, Shraddha, and Gary D. Bader. "Patient Similarity Networks for Precision Medicine." *Journal of Molecular Biology* 430, no. 18, part A (September 2018): 2924–38.

Paik, Hye-Young, Xiwei Xu, H. M. N. Dilum Bandara, Sung Une Lee, and Sin Kuang Lo. "Analysis of Data Management in Blockchain-Based Systems: From Architecture to Governance." *IEEE Access* 7 (2019): 186091–107. https://doi.org/10.1109/ACCESS.2019.2961404.

Palmer, Michael. "Data Is the New Oil." ANA Marketing Maestros, 2006. https://ana.blogs.com/maestros/2006/11/data_is_the_new.html.

Pan, Chengxin. "The 'China Threat' in American Self-Imagination: The Discursive Construction of Other as Power Politics." *Alternatives* 29, no. 3 (June 2004): 305–31. https://doi.org/10.1177/030437540402900304.

Pan, Gongsheng. "Zhongguo renmin yinhang hangzhang pangongsheng jiujinrong guanli bumen yuetan mayi jituan youguan qingkuang dajizhewen" [Pan Gongsheng, deputy governor of the People's Bank of China, was asked by the press about the financial regulatory authority's interview with Ant Group]. China Securities Regulatory Commission, December 27, 2020. http://www.csrc.gov.cn/pub/newsite/zjhxwfb/xwdd/202012/t20201227_389518.html.

Pang, Hongliang. "Zhinenghua junshi geming shuguang chuxian" [The intelligentization military revolution starts to dawn]. *PLA Daily*, January 28, 2016. http://www.mod.gov.cn/wqzb/2016-01/28/content_4637961.htm.

Papanicolas, Irene, Liana R. Woskie, and Ashish K. Jha. "Health Care Spending in the United States and Other High-Income Countries." *JAMA* 319, no. 10 (March 2018): 1024–39.

The Paper. "Yidong weifayuan nihui yong ma" [China Mobile WeCourt, can you use it?]. April 22, 2020. https://www.thepaper.cn/newsDetail_forward_7086973.

The Paper. "Yong chengshi danao bangzhu jueceyu yunying, Shanghai yizai duoge jiezheng kaizhan shijian" [Using the "city brain" to help with decision-making and operations, Shanghai has implemented it in several street towns]. September 19, 2018. www.sohu.com/a/254714178_260616.

Parker, Emily. "Can WeChat Thrive in the United States?" *MIT Technology Review*, August 11, 2017. https://www.technologyreview.com/2017/08/11/149977/can-wechat-thrive-in-the-united-states/.

Parks, Lisa. *Cultures in Orbit: Satellites and the Televisual.* Durham, NC: Duke University Press, 2005.

Parks, Lisa. "Signals and Oil: Satellite Footprints and Post-Communist Territories in Central Asia." *European Journal of Cultural Studies* 12 (May 2009): 137–56.

Parulis-Cook, Sienna. "The Essential Guide to Chinese Mobile Payments Overseas." Dragon Trail Interactive, March 27, 2018, https://dragontrail.com/resources/blog/chinese-mobile-payments-overseas-guide.

PatientsLikeMe. "PatientsLikeMe Privacy Policy." Accessed September 2, 2020. https://www.patientslikeme.com/about/privacy_full.

Paulson Institute. "A Chinese Pharmaceutical Startup Acquires an American Firm to 'Go Global.'" June 2016. http://www.paulsoninstitute.org/wp-content/uploads/2017/01/PPI_Case-Study-Series_WuXi-Pharma_English_R.pdf.

Pelley, Scott, and Chris Krebs. "Fired Director of U.S. Cyber Agency Chris Krebs Explains Why President Trump's Claims of Election Interference Are False." CBS News, November 30, 2020. https://www.cbsnews.com/news/election-results-security-chris-krebs-60-minutes-2020-11-29/.

People's Daily. "Zhuanjia zhinenghua juebu jinjin shi rengong zhineng" [Expert: Military intelligentization is not just artificial intelligence]. December 6, 2017. http://military.people.com.cn/n1/2017/1206/c1011-29689750.html.

People's Bank of China. "Guanyu jinyibu fangfan he chuzhi xuni huobi wenyi chaozuo fengxian de tongzhi" [Notification regarding further prevention and management of virtual currency transactions that promote risk]. September 24, 2021. http://www.pbc.gov.cn/goutongjiaoliu/113456/113469/4348521/index.html.

Perez, Bien, and Iris Deng. "A Peek at the Company That Has 500 Million Chinese Gamers Hooked." *South China Morning Post*. March 24, 2018. https://www.scmp.com/tech/enterprises/article/2138636/peek-inside-games-publisher-has-200-million-chinese-youth-hooked.

Pérez-Peña, Richard, and Matthew Rosenberg. "Strava Fitness App Can Reveal Military Sites, Analysts Say." *New York Times*, Jahnuary 29, 2018. https://www.nytimes.com/2018/01/29/world/middleeast/strava-heat-map.html.

Perlmutter, Amos, and William M. LeoGrande. "The Party in Uniform: Toward a Theory of Civil-Military Relations in Communist Political Systems." *American Political Science Review* 76, no. 4 (December 1982): 778.

Permanent Representative of China, Permanent Representative of Kazakhstan, Permanent Representative of Kyrgyzstan, Permanent Representative of the Russian Federation, Permanent Representative of Tajikistan, and Permanent Representative of Uzbekistan. "International Code of Conduct for Information Security." Annex to the Letter Dated 9 January 2015 from the Permanent Representatives of China, Kazakhstan, Kyrgyzstan, the Russian Federation, Tajikistan and Uzbekistan to the United Nations Addressed to the Secretary-General. United Nations, New York, January 9, 2015.

Permanent Representative of China, Permanent Representative of the Russian Federation, Permanent Representative of Tajikistan, and Permanent Representative of Uzbekistan. "Letter Dated to 12 September 2011 from Permanent Representatives of China, the Russian Federation, Tajikistan and Uzbekistan to the United Nations Address to the Secretary-General." United Nations, New York, September 12, 2011.

Permanent Representative of China, Permanent Representative of the Russian Federation, Permanent Representative of Tajikistan, Permanent Representative of Uzbekistan, Permanent Representative of Kazakhstan, and Permanent Representative of Kyrgyzstan. "Letter Dated 9 January 2015 from the Permanent Representatives of China, Kazakhstan, Kyrgyzstan, the Russian Federation, Tajikistan and Uzbekistan to the United Nations Addressed to the Secretary-General." United Nations, New York, January 13, 2015.

Perrow, Charles. *Normal Accidents: Living with High Risk Technologies*. Princeton, NJ: Princeton University Press, 1999.

Persily, Nathaniel, and Joshua A. Tucker. *Social Media and Democracy: The State of the Field, Prospects for Reform*. Cambridge, UK: Cambridge University Press, 2020.

Personal Information Protection Commission. "Act on the Protection of Personal Information." 2022. https://www.ppc.go.jp/en/legal/.

Personal Information Protection Commission. "Personal Information Protection Act (General Law)." 2020. https://www.privacy.go.kr/eng/laws_view.do?nttId=8186&imgNo=3.

Peters, Jay. "The US Just Showed It Still Believes Chinese-Made Drones Are a Security Risk." The Verge, January 29, 2020. https://www.theverge.com/2020/1/29/21113533/us-interior-department-chinese-drone-ban-grounding-security-dji.

PIB Delhi. "Government Bans 59 Mobile Apps Which Are Prejudicial to Sovereignty and Integrity of India, Defence of India, Security of State and Public Order." News release, June 29, 2020. https://pib.gov.in/Pressreleaseshare.aspx?PRID=1635206.

Plantin, Jean-Christophe, and Gabriele de Seta. "WeChat as Infrastructure: The Techno-Nationalist Shaping of Chinese Digital Platforms." *Chinese Journal of Communication* 12, no. 3 (July 2019): 257–73.

Plantin, Jean-Christophe, Carl Lagoze, Paul N. Edwards, and Christian Sandvig. "Infrastructure Studies Meet Platform Studies in the Age of Google and Facebook." *New Media and Society* 20, no. 1 (January 2018): 293–310.

Poon, Martha. "Corporate Capitalism and the Growing Power of Big Data: Review Essay." *Science, Technology, and Human Values* 41, no. 6 (November 2016): 1088–108.

Popper, Karl R. *The Open Society and Its Enemies.* Princeton, NJ: Princeton University Press, 2020.

Powell, Anastasia, Adrian J. Scott, and Nicola Henry. "Digital Harassment and Abuse: Experiences of Sexuality and Gender Minority Adults." *European Journal of Criminology* 17, no. 2 (2020): 199–223.

Pozen, David E. "The Mosaic Theory, National Security, and the Freedom of Information Act." *Yale Law Journal* 115 (2005): 628–79.

Prem, Prejula. "Genetron COVID-19 Test Receives FDA Emergency-Use Authorization." Bloomberg, June 6, 2020. https://www.bloomberg.com/news/articles/2020-06-06/genetron-covid-19-test-receives-fda-emergency-use-authorization.

PRNewswire. "China Home Appliances Markets, 2020–2026: Subsidy by the Chinese Government, Initiatives of Chinese Companies, COVID-19 Impact." November 13, 2020. https://www.prnewswire.com/news-releases/china-home-appliances-markets-2020-2026-subsidy-by-the-chinese-government--initiatives-of-chinese-companies-covid-19-impact-301172898.html.

Prokop, Andrew. "Cambridge Analytica Shutting Down: The Firm's Many Scandals, Explained." *Vox*, May 2, 2018. https://www.vox.com/policy-and-politics/2018/3/21/17141428/cambridge-analytica-trump-russia-mueller.

PTI. "India Bans TikTok, 58 Other Chinese Apps, Terms Them 'Prejudicial' to National Security." *The Print*, June 29, 2020. https://theprint.in/tech/india-bans-tiktok-58-other-chinese-apps-terms-them-prejudicial-to-national-security/451253/.

Putnam, Robert. *Bowling Alone: The Collapse and Revival of American Community.* New York: Simon & Schuster, 2000.

Qian, Junxi. "Deciphering the Prevalence of Neighborhood Enclosure Amidst Post-1949 Chinese Cities: A Critical Synthesis." *Journal of Planning Literature* 29, no. 1 (February 2014): 3–19.

Qiu, Jack Linchuan. *Goodbye iSlave: A Manifesto for Digital Abolition.* Champaign: University of Illinois Press, 2017.

Qiu, Jack Linchuan. "Goodbye iSlave: Making Alternative Subjects Through Digital Objects." In *Digital Objects, Digital Subjects*, edited by David Chandler and Christian Fuchs, ch. 12. London: University of Westminster Press, 2019.

Qiu, Jack Linchuan. "Reflections on Big Data: 'Just Because It Is Accessible Does Not Make It Ethical.'" *Media, Culture and Society*, August 2015.

Radulovic, Petrana. "Steam Rolls Out New, Sleek Chat Update." Polygon, July 25, 2018. https://www.polygon.com/2018/7/25/17613706/steam-chat-update-features.

Rafaelof, Emma, Rogier Creemers, Samm Sacks, Katharin Tai, Graham Webster, and Kevin Neville. "Translation: China's 'Data Security Law (Draft).'" New America, 2020. http://newamerica.org/cybersecurity-initiative/digichina/blog/translation-chinas-data-security-law-draft/.

Rai, Sarakshi. "White House Briefs TikTok Creators on Ukraine." *The Hill*, March 11, 2022. https://thehill.com/policy/technology/technology/597922-white-house-briefs-tiktok-creators-on-ukraine.

Raphael, René, and Ling Xi. "Discipline and Punish: The Birth of China's Social-Credit System." *The Nation*, January 2019. https://www.thenation.com/article/archive/china-social-credit-system/.

Raskar, Ramesh, Isabel Schunemann, Rachel Barbar, Kristen Vilcans, Jim Gray, Praneeth Vepakomma, Suraj Kapa, et al. "Apps Gone Rogue: Maintaining Personal Privacy in an Epidemic." March 2020. https://arxiv.org/abs/2003.08567.

Ratcliffe, R. G. "The Partisans Are Coming for Your Cities and Schools." *Texas Monthly*, May 5, 2017. https://www.texasmonthly.com/burka-blog/partisans-coming-cities-schools/.

Reece, Andrew G., and Christopher M. Danforth. "Instagram Photos Reveal Predictive Markers of Depression." *EPJ Data Science* 6, no. 1 (December 2017): 1–12.

Renmin Ribao. "Wangluo zhuquan: Yige burong huibi de yiti" [Cyber sovereignty: An unavoidable topic of discussion]. June 23, 2014. http://www.cac.gov.cn/2014-06/23/c_1111262370.htm.

Renmin Yinhang Wangzhan. "Feiyinhang zhifu jigou wangluo zhifu yewu guanli banfa" [Measures for the administration of online payment business of non-bank payment institutions]. March 2016. http://www.gov.cn/zhengce/2016-03/18/content_5055171.htm.

Reuters. "Alibaba's Jack Ma Is a Communist Party Member, China State Paper Reveals." November 27, 2018. https://www.reuters.com/article/us-alibaba-jack-ma-idUSKCN1NW073.

Reuters. "American Lawyer Arrested by HK Police in National Security Crackdown." January 5, 2021. https://www.reuters.com/article/us-hongkong-security-usa-idUSKBN29B0DB.

Reuters. "Beijing City Looks to Take DiDi Under State Control, Bloomberg News Reports." September 3, 2021. https://www.reuters.com/technology/beijing-city-looking-take-didi-under-state-control-bloomberg-news-2021-09-03/.

Reuters. "China Says Rejecting Physical Cash Is Illegal Amid E-Payments Popularity." December 9, 2018. https://www.reuters.com/article/us-china-payment-idUSKBN1O902F.

Reuters. "German Intelligence Unmasks Alleged Covert Chinese Social Media Profiles." December 10, 2017. https://www.reuters.com/article/us-germany-security-china-idINKBN1E40CA.

Reuters. "MyHeritage, China's BGI to Launch Coronavirus Lab in Israel." March 30, 2020. https://www.reuters.com/article/us-health-coronavirus-israel-bgi-genomic-idUKKBN21H1K1.

Reuters. "U.S. Opens National Security Investigation into TikTok, Sources Say." NBC News, November 1, 2019. https://www.nbcnews.com/tech/tech-news/u-s-opens-national-security-investigation-tiktok-sources-say-n1075211.

Rice, Jesse. *The Church of Facebook: How the Hyperconnected Are Redefining Community.* Colorado Springs, CO: David C. Cook, 2009.

Richard, Gabriela T., and Kishonna L. Gray. "Gendered Play, Racialized Reality: Black Cyberfeminism, Inclusive Communities of Practice, and the Intersections of Learning, Socialization, and Resilience in Online Gaming." *Frontiers: A Journal of Women Studies* 39, no. 1 (2018): 112–48.

Richtel, Matt. "Children's Screen Time Has Soared in the Pandemic, Alarming Parents and Researchers." *New York Times*, January 17, 2021. https://www.nytimes.com/2021/01/16/health/covid-kids-tech-use.html.

Riot Games. "Terms of Service." Last updated January 15, 2020. https://www.riotgames.com/en/terms-of-service.

Roach, Jacob. "What Is Fortnite?" Digital Trends, September 6, 2020. https://www.digitaltrends.com/gaming/what-is-fortnite/.

Roberts, Huw, Josh Cowls, Federico Casolari, Jessica Morley, Mariarosaria Taddeo, and Luciano Floridi. "Safeguarding European Values with Digital Sovereignty: An Analysis of Statements and Policies." *Internet Policy Review* 10, no. 3 (2021). https://policyreview.info/articles/analysis/safeguarding-european-values-digital-sovereignty-analysis-statements-and-policies.

Roche, Gerald, James Leibold, and Ben Hillman. "Urbanizing Tibet: Differential Inclusion and Colonial Governance in the People's Republic of China." *Territory, Politics, Governance*, December 2020, 1–21. https://doi.org/10.1080/21622671.2020.1840427.

Rogowski, Wolf, Katherine Payne, Petra Schnell-Inderst, Andrea Manca, Ursula Rochau, Beate Jahn, Oguzhan Alagoz, Reiner Leidl, and Uwe Siebert. "Concepts of 'Personalization' in Personalized Medicine: Implications for Economic Evaluation." *PharmacoEconomics* 33, no. 1 (January 2015): 49–59.

Romm, Tony. "Apple, TikTok Decline to Testify at Second Congressional Hearing Probing Tech's Ties to China." *Washington Post*, February 24, 2020. https://www.washingtonpost.com/technology/2020/02/24/apple-tiktok-congress-hearing-china/.

Rosenbach, Eric, and Shu Min Chong. "Governing Cyberspace: State Control vs. the Multistakeholder Model." Belfer Center for Science and International Affairs, Harvard Kennedy School, Cambridge, MA, 2019. https://www.belfercenter.org/publication/governing-cyberspace-state-control-vs-multistakeholder-model.

Rosenbaum, Sara. "Data Governance and Stewardship: Designing Data Stewardship Entities and Advancing Data Access." *Health Services Research* 45, no. 5, part 2 (2010): 1442–55. https://doi.org/10.1111/j.1475-6773.2010.01140.x.

Roumeliotis, Greg, Yingzhi Yang, Echo Wang, and Alexandra Alper. "Exclusive: U.S. Opens National Security Investigation into TikTok—Sources." Reuters, November 1, 2019. https://www.reuters.com/article/us-tiktok-cfius-exclusive/exclusive-u-s-opens-national-security-investigation-into-tiktok-sources-idUSKBN1XB4IL.

Roussi, Antoaneta. "Resisting the Rise of Facial Recognition." *Nature* 587, no. 7834 (November 2020): 350–53. https://www.nature.com/articles/d41586-020-03188-2.

Rubin, Shira, and Steve Hendrix. "Israel Moves to Head of Vaccine Queue, Offering Pfizer Access to Country's Health-Care Database." *Washington Post*, January 28, 2021. https://www.washingtonpost.com/world/middle_east/israel-pfizer-coronavirus-vaccine-privacy/2021/01/27/b9773c80-5f4d-11eb-a177-7765f29a9524_story.html.

Ruggie, John Gerard. "Multilateralism: The Anatomy of an Institution." *International Organization* 46, no. 3 (1992): 561–98.

Ruhl, Christian, Duncan Hollis, Wyatt Hoffman, and Tim Maurer. "Cyberspace and Geopolitics: Assessing Global Cybersecurity Norm Processes at a Crossroads." Carnegie Endowment for International Peace, Washington, DC, 2020.

Ruptly. "UK Parliament to Discuss Huawei's 5G Role After Johnson Green Light." January 28, 2020. https://www.ruptly.tv/en/events/202001281230-LIVE2625-UK-Parliament-to-discuss-Huawei-s-5G-role-after-Johnson-green-light.

Russell, Jon. "Tencent Takes Full Control of 'League of Legends' Creator Riot Games." TechCrunch, December 17, 2015. https://techcrunch.com/2015/12/17/tencent-takes-full-control-of-league-of-legends-creator-riot-games/.

Russo, Federica. "Politics in the Boardroom: The Role of Chinese Communist Party Committees." The Diplomat, December 24, 2019. https://thediplomat.com/2019/12/politics-in-the-boardroom-the-role-of-chinese-communist-party-committees/.

Ryan, Fergus. "Australia's Defence Department Calls Time Out on TikTok." Australian Strategic Policy Institute, Canberra, January 2020. https://www.aspistrategist.org.au/australias-defence-department-calls-time-out-on-tiktok/.

S&P Global Ratings. "Transparency Statement." 2020. https://www.spglobal.com/ratings/en/about/transparency.

Sabharwal, Meghna, Helisse Levine, Maria D'Agostino, and Tiffany Nguyen. "Inclusive Work Practices: Turnover Intentions Among LGBT Employees of the U.S. Federal Government." American Review of Public Administration 49, no. 4 (May 2019): 482–94. https://doi.org/10.1177/0275074018817376.

Sacks, Samm, Qiheng Chen, and Graham Webster. "Five Important Takeaways from China's Draft Data Security Law." New America, Washington, DC, July 2020. http://newamerica.org/cybersecurity-initiative/digichina/blog/five-important-take-aways-chinas-draft-data-security-law/.

Saeb, Sohrab, Mi Zhang, Christopher J. Karr, Stephen M. Schueller, Marya E. Corden, Konrad P. Kording, and David C. Mohr. "Mobile Phone Sensor Correlates of Depressive Symptom Severity in Daily-Life Behavior: An Exploratory Study." Journal of Medical Internet Research 17, no. 7 (July 2015): e175.

Sanderson, Jimmy, Blair Browning, and Hank DeHay. "'It's the Universal Language': Investigating Student-Athletes' Use of and Motivations for Playing Fortnite." Journal of Issues in Intercollegiate Athletics 13 (February 2020): 22–44.

Sanger, David E. "Grindr Is Owned by a Chinese Firm, and the U.S. Is Trying to Force It to Sell." New York Times, March 28, 2019. https://www.nytimes.com/2019/03/28/us/politics/grindr-china-national-security.html.

Sanger, David E. "TikTok Deal Exposes a Security Gap, and a Missing China Strategy." New York Times, September 20, 2020. https://www.nytimes.com/2020/09/20/us/politics/tiktok-trump-national-security.html.

Sanger, David E., and Nicole Perlroth. "Trump Fires a Cybersecurity Official Who Called the Election 'the Most Secure in American History.'" New York Times, December 8, 2020. https://www.nytimes.com/2020/11/18/us/politics/trump-fires-a-cybersecurity-official-who-called-the-election-the-most-secure-in-american-history.html.

Sanger, David E., Nicole Perlroth, Glenn Thrush, and Alan Rappeport. "Marriott Data Breach Is Traced to Chinese Hackers as U.S. Readies Crackdown on Beijing." New York Times, December 11, 2018. https://www.nytimes.com/2018/12/11/us/politics/trump-china-trade.html.

Sarah D. Lande U.S.-China Friendship Education Fund. "Old Friends": The Xi Jinping-Iowa Story. Muscatine, IA: Sarah D. Lande U.S.-China Friendship Education Fund, 2020.

Sargent, Jenna. "GDPR One Year Later: Slow Compliance, Lax Enforcement." SD Times, May 23, 2019. https://sdtimes.com/data/gdpr-one-year-later-slow-compliance-lax-enforcement/.

Saunders, Robert A. Ethnopolitics in Cyberspace: The Internet, Minority Nationalism, and the Web of Identity. Lanham, MD: Lexington Books, 2011.

Schenker, Jennifer L. "China Leaps Ahead in Precision Medicine." The Innovator, August 27, 2019. https://innovator.news/china-leaps-ahead-in-precision-medicine-72cfc 469df3d.

Schmidt, Michael S., David E. Sanger, and Nicole Perlroth. "Chinese Hackers Pursue Key Data on U.S. Workers." New York Times, July 9, 2014. https://www.nytimes.com/2014/ 07/10/world/asia/chinese-hackers-pursue-key-data-on-us-workers.html.

Schneble, Christophe Olivier, Bernice Simone Elger, and David Martin Shaw. "All Our Data Will Be Health Data One Day: The Need for Universal Data Protection and Comprehensive Consent." Journal of Medical Internet Research 22, no. 5 (May 2020). https://doi.org/doi:10.2196/16879.

Schneider, Florian. China's Digital Nationalism. Oxford, UK: Oxford University Press, 2018.

Schneier, Bruce. "When It Comes to Security, We're Back to Feudalism." Wired, November 26, 2012, 2012. https://www.wired.com/2012/11/feudal-security/.

Schoff, James L., and Satoru Mori. "The US-Japan Alliance in an Age of Resurgent Techno-Nationalism." Sasakawa Peace Foundation, Washington, DC, March 2020. https:// www.spf.org/en/jpus/spf-asia-initiative/spf-asia-initiative004.html.

Scholz, Trebor. Digital Labor: The Internet as Playground and Factory. New York: Routledge, 2012.

Schubert, Gunter, and Thomas Heberer. "State-Business Relations Under Xi Jinping: Steering the Private Sector and Private Entrepreneurs." In Chinese Politics and Foreign Policy Under Xi Jinping, edited by Arthur S. Ding and Jagannath P. Panda, 105–30. New York: Routledge, 2020.

Seamons, Ryder. "China's Personal Information Specifications: Revised." Harris Bricken, July 15, 2020. http://harrisbricken.com/chinalawblog/chinas-personal-information-specifications-revised/.

SEC Consult. "Internet of Dildos: A Long Way to a Vibrant Future—from IoT to IoD." February 1, 2018. https://sec-consult.com/blog/detail/internet-of-dildos-a-long-way-to-a-vibrant-future/.

Securities and Exchange Commission. "Elon Musk Settles SEC Fraud Charges; Tesla Charged with and Resolves Securities Law Charge." News release, September 29, 2018. https://www.sec.gov/news/press-release/2018-226.

Segal, Adam. "Chinese Cyber Diplomacy in a New Era of Uncertainty." Hoover Institution, Stanford, CA, June 2017.

Segal, Adam. "Seizing Core Technologies: China Responds to U.S. Technology Competition." China Leadership Monitor, June 1, 2019. https://www.prcleader.org/ segal-clm-60.

Selby, John. "Data Localization Laws: Trade Barriers or Legitimate Responses to Cybersecurity Risks, or Both?" International Journal of Law and Information Technology 25, no. 3 (July 2017): 213–32.

SensorTower. "TikTok Becomes the First Non-Facebook Mobile App to Reach 3 Billion Downloads Globally." July 14, 2021. https://sensortower.com/blog/tiktok-downloads-3-billion.

Seppänen, Samuli. "Interrogating Illiberalism Through Chinese Communist Party Regulations." Cornell International Law Journal 52, no. 2 (Summer 2019): 267–311.

Serrels, Mark. "Blizzard Pulls Blitzchung from Hearthstone Esports Tournament over Support for Hong Kong Protests." CNET, October 8, 2019. https://www.cnet.com/

news/blizzard-pulls-blitzchung-from-hearthstone-esports-tournament-over-supp
ort-for-hong-kong-protests/.

Shaban, Hamza. "Apple Stars at Giant Tech Confab CES—Without Actually Being There." *Washington Post*, January 7, 2019. https://www.washingtonpost.com/technology/
2019/01/07/apple-burns-google-giant-billboard-touting-privacy-ces/.

Shamir, Hila. "A Labor Paradigm for Human Trafficking." *UCLA Law Review* 60, no. 1 (2012).

Shanghai Cooperation Organization. "Agreement Between the Governments of the Member States of the Shanghai Cooperation Organization on Cooperation in the Field of Information Security." NATO Cooperative Cyber Defence Centre of Excellence, Talinn, Estonia, 2008.

Shanghai Municipal People's Government. "'Smartest City' Title for Shanghai." November 20, 2020. http://www.shanghai.gov.cn/nw48081/20201120/6b2b10d2fdcf4538b0da8
8a193373c5e.html.

Shattuck, Thomas J. "Stuck in the Middle: Taiwan's Semiconductor Industry, the U.S.-China Tech Fight, and Cross-Strait Stability." *Orbis* 65, no. 1 (January 1, 2021): 101–17.

Shead, Sam. "TikTok Invites UK Lawmakers to Review Algorithm After Being Probed on China Censorship Concerns." CNBC, November 5, 2020. https://www.cnbc.com/2020/
11/05/tiktok-invites-uk-lawmakers-to-review-algorithm-after-china-probe.html.

Shear, Michael D. "Trump Extends Social Distancing Guidelines Through End of April." *New York Times*, April 1, 2020. https://www.nytimes.com/2020/03/29/us/politics/
trump-coronavirus-guidelines.html.

Shenzhen Tencent Computer Systems Company Limited. "Agreement on Software License and Service of Tencent Weixin." 2021. https://weixin.qq.com/cgi-bin/readt
emplate?lang=en_US&t=weixin_agreement&s=default&cc=CN.

Sherman, Justin. "Vietnam's Internet Control: Following in China's Footsteps?" *The Diplomat*, December 11, 2019. https://thediplomat.com/2019/12/vietnams-internet-
control-following-in-chinas-footsteps/.

Sherr, Ian. "Coronavirus Has a Lot of People Playing Fortnite and Watching Twitch." CNET, March 14, 2020. https://www.cnet.com/news/coronavirus-has-a-lot-of-peo
ple-playing-fortnite-and-watching-twitch/.

Shiao, Vivien. "Ant Group, Greenland-Linked Consortium Selected for Digital Wholesale Bank Licences." *Business Times*, December 4, 2020. https://www.businesstimes.com.
sg/banking-finance/ant-group-greenland-linked-consortium-selected-for-digital-
wholesale-bank-licences.

Shield, Andrew D. J. "Grindr Culture: Intersectional and Socio-Sexual." *Ephemera* 18, no. 1 (2018): 148–61.

Shields, Todd, and Alyza Sebenius. "Huawei's Clout Is So Strong It's Helping Shape Global 5G Rules." Bloomberg, February 1, 2019. https://www.bloomberg.com/news/articles/
2019-02-01/huawei-s-clout-is-so-strong-it-s-helping-shape-global-5g-rules.

Shou, Zi Chew. "Letter to Senators Blackburn, Wicker, Thune, Blunt, Cruz, Moran, Capito, Lummis, and Daines." *New York Times*, June 30, 2022. https://int.nyt.com/data/
documenttools/tik-tok-s-response-to-republican-senators/e5f56d3ef4886b33/full.pdf

Shih, Gerry. "Chinese Firm Harvests Social Media Posts, Data of Prominent Americans and Military." *Washington Post*, September 14, 2020. https://www.washingtonpost.
com/world/asia_pacific/chinese-firm-harvests-social-media-posts-data-of-promin
ent-americans-and-military/2020/09/14/b1f697ce-f311-11ea-8025-5d3489768ac8_st
ory.html.

Shopping Kim. "List of Stores That Accept Alipay for Payment." November 8, 2021. https://shoppingkim.com/list-of-stores-that-accept-alipay-for-payment/.

Singh, Manish. "India Retains Ban on TikTok and 58 Other Chinese Apps." TechCrunch, January 26, 2021. https://social.techcrunch.com/2021/01/26/india-retains-ban-on-tik tok-uc-browser-and-57-other-chinese-apps/.

Sina Finance. "Mayun waitan jinrong fenghui yanjiang quanwen: Zhongguo jinrongye haishi qingshaonian" [Full text of Jack Ma's speech at the Bund Summit]. October 24, 2020. https://finance.sina.com.cn/money/bank/bank_hydt/2020-10-24/doc-iiznezxr 7822563.shtml.January 26, 2021.

Sirimanna, Bandula. "Chinese Here for Cyber Censorship." *Sunday Times* (Colombo, Sri Lanka), February 14, 2010. http://www.sundaytimes.lk/100214/News/nws_02.html.

Siripurapu, Anshu, Andrew Chatzky, and James McBride. "What Is the Trans-Pacific Partnership (TPP)?" Council on Foreign Relations, 2020. https://www.cfr.org/backg rounder/what-trans-pacific-partnership-tpp.

Slaughter, Anne-Marie. "Sovereignty and Power in a Networked World Order." *Stanford Journal of International Law* 40, no. 2 (2004): 283–328.

Smith, Anne Logsdon. "Alexa, Who Owns My Pillow Talk? Contracting, Collaterizing, and Monetizing Consumer Privacy Through Voice-Captured Personal Data." *Catholic University Journal of Law and Technology* 27 (2018): 186–226.

Smith, Connor. "The Boycott Blizzard Movement Is Weighing on Activision Blizzard Stock." *Barron's*, October 14, 2019. https://www.barrons.com/articles/blizzard-boyc ott-activision-stock-51571070932.

Smith, Dylan. "Fortnite Owner Epic Games Is Now Valued at $17.3 Billion." Digital Music News, August 7, 2020. https://www.digitalmusicnews.com/2020/08/07/fortnite-epic-games-valuation/.

Smolaks, Max. "Tanzanian Minister Attempts to Speed up Local Data Center Launch." Data Center Dynamics, June 13, 2016. https://www.datacenterdynamics.com/en/news/tanzanian-minister-attempts-to-speed-up-local-data-center-launch/.

Smythe, Dallas W. "Communications: Blindspot of Western Marxism." *Canadian Journal of Political and Social Theory* 1, no. 3 (Fall 1977): 1–27.

Snape, Holly, and Weinan Wang. "Finding a Place for the Party: Debunking the 'Party-State' and Rethinking the State-Society Relationship in China's One-Party System." *Journal of Chinese Governance* 5, no. 4 (October 2020): 477–502.

Sobieraj, Sarah. "Bitch, Slut, Skank, Cunt: Patterned Resistance to Women's Visibility in Digital Publics." *Information, Communication and Society* 21, no. 11 (2018): 1700–14.

Sohu. "Cunkuan shichang biantian jianguan qiangshi dongdao gaoxi lanchu yinhang huosu zhenggai zhouqi fuxi chanpin liangliang" [Changes in the deposit market! Regulatory authorities supervised high interest. Bank rapidly rectified. Cycle interest-bearing products disillusion]. February 23, 2021. www.sohu.com/a/452243133_115865.

Solomon Islands Government. "Minister Manele Acknowledge Support from China." News release, April 20, 2020. http://www.mfaet.gov.sb/media-center/press-releases/foreign-affairs-news.html?catid=181&id=181:minister-manele-acknowledge-supp ort-from-china.

Song, Yan. "Zhongguo yinbaojianhui zhongguo renminyinhang fabu guanyu guifan shangye yinhang tongguo hulianwang fazhan geren cunkuan yewu youguan shixiangde tongzhi" [China Banking and Insurance Regulatory Commission (CBIRC) People's Bank of China (PBC) issued the notice concerning the regulation of commercial banks' personal deposit business through the internet]. China Government Network, January 15, 2021. http://www.gov.cn/xinwen/2021-01/15/content_5580273.htm.

Spangler, Todd. "Blizzard President J. Allen Brack Exits Amid Sex Harassment Lawsuit." *Variety*, August 3, 2021. https://variety.com/2021/digital/news/blizzard-j-allen-brack-exits-sexual-harassment-lawsuit-1235033387/.

Spangler, Todd. "'Fortnite' Revenue Dropped 25% in 2019 but Was Still the Year's Top-Earning Game with $1.8 Billion Haul." *Variety*, January 2, 2020. https://variety.com/2020/digital/news/fortnite-top-earning-game-2019-1203455069/#:~:text=%E2%80%9CFortnite%E2%80%9D%20remained%20the%20biggest%20game,according%20to%20research%20firm%20SuperData.

Spangler, Todd. "'Fortnite' Revenue Dropped 25% in 2019 but Was Still the Year's Top-Earning Game with $1.8 Billion Haul." *Variety*, January 2, 2020. https://variety.com/2020/digital/news/fortnite-top-earning-game-2019-1203455069/#:~:text=%E2%80%9CFortnite%E2%80%9D%20remained%20the%20biggest%20game,according%20to%20research%20firm%20SuperData.

Sparrow, Robert, and Lauren Karas. "Teledildonics and Rape by Deception." *Law, Innovation and Technology* 12, no. 1 (January 2020): 175–204.

Stallings, William. "Handling of Personal Information and Deidentified, Aggregated, and Pseudonymized Information Under the California Consumer Privacy Act." *IEEE Security and Privacy* 18, no. 1 (2020): 61–64.

Standardization Administration for Market Regulation and Standardization Administration of China. "Guojia biaozhun geren xinxi anquan guifan 2020 ban zhengshi fabu" [The 2020 version of the national standard "Personal Information Security Standards" was officially released]. GB/T 35273-2020. October 1, 2020. https://www.secrss.com/articles/17713.

Standing Committee of the National People's Congress. "Zhonghua renmin gongheguo wangluo anquanfa" [Cybersecurity law of the People's Republic of China]. 2016. http://www.npc.gov.cn/npc/c30834/201611/270b43e8b35e4f7ea98502b6f0e26f8a.shtml.

Stanger, Allison. "Consumers vs. Citizens in Democracy's Public Sphere." *Communications of the ACM* 63, no. 7 (2020): 29–31. https://doi.org/10.1145/3359553.

Stanislav, Mark, and Tod Beardsley. "Hacking IoT: A Case Study on Baby Monitor Exposures and Vulnerabilities." Rapid7, September 29, 2015. https://www.rapid7.com/globalassets/external/docs/Hacking-IoT-A-Case-Study-on-Baby-Monitor-Exposures-and-Vulnerabilities.pdf.

State Administration of Press, Publication, Radio, Film and Television. "Xinwen chuban guangdian zongju duiwai zhuanxiang chuban lingyu jiji tansuo shixing teshu guanligu zhidu" [The State Administration of Press, Publication, Radio, Film and Television has actively explored the implementation of a special management unit system in the field of foreign special publications]. June 2016. http://www.gov.cn/xinwen/2016-06/02/content_5079134.htm.

State Council Information Office of the People's Republic of China. "Zhongguo de junshi zhanlüe" [China's military strategy]. May 26, 2015. http://www.mod.gov.cn/affair/2015-05/26/content_4588132.htm.

State Council of China. "Guanyu tiaozheng fabu zhongguo jinzhi chukou xianzhi chukou jishu mulu de gonggao" [Announcements on the readjustment and release of the catalogue of China's technologies prohibited and restricted from export]. August 2020. http://www.gov.cn/zhengce/zhengceku/2020-08/29/content_5538299.htm.

State Council of China. "Guowuyuan guanyu yinfa shisanwu guojia xinxihua guihua de tongzhi" [Notice of the State Council on the issuance of the 13th Five-Year National Informatization Plan]. January 2016. http://www.gov.cn/zhengce/content/2016-12/27/content_5153411.htm.

State Council of China. "Guowuyuan guanyu yinfa zhongguo zhizao 2025 de tongzhi" [Notice of the State Council on the issuance of the Made in China 2025 Plan]. May 8, 2015. http://www.gov.cn/zhengce/content/2015-05/19/content_9784.htm.

State Council of the People's Republic of China. "Guowuyuan bangongting guanyu cujin he guifan jiankang yiliao dashuju yingyong fazhan de zhidao yijian" [Guiding opinions of the General Office of the State Council on promoting and regulating the application and development of big data in health and medical care]. June 21, 2016. http://www.gov.cn/zhengce/content/2016-06/24/content_5085091.htm.

State Council of the People's Republic of China. "Guowuyuan bangongting guanyu cujin hulianwang yiliao jiankang fazhan de yijian" [State Council opinions on advancing internet plus medical healthcare]. April 28, 2018. http://www.gov.cn/zhengce/content/2018-04/28/content_5286645.htm.

State Council of the People's Republic of China. "Guowuyuan yinfa jiankang zhongguo guihua gangyao" [State Council issued the outline of the Healthy China 2030 Plan]. October 25, 2016. http://www.gov.cn/zhengce/2016-10/25/content_5124174.htm.

State Council of the People's Republic of China. "Regulations on Management of Human Genetic Resources." News release, June 10, 2019. http://english.www.gov.cn/policies/latest_releases/2019/06/10/content_281476708945462.htm.

State Council of the People's Republic of China. "Zhonghua renmin gongheguo renlei yichuan ziyuan guanli tiaoli" [Regulations of the People's Republic of China on the management of human genetic resources]. May 28, 2019. http://www.gov.cn/zhengce/content/2019-06/10/content_5398829.htm.

Stateler, Laura, and Molly Kinder. "Amazon and Walmart Have Raked in Billions in Additional Profits During the Pandemic, and Shared Almost None of It with Their Workers." Brookings Institution, Washington, DC, 2020. https://www.brookings.edu/blog/the-avenue/2020/12/22/amazon-and-walmart-have-raked-in-billions-in-additional-profits-during-the-pandemic-and-shared-almost-none-of-it-with-their-workers/.

Statista. "Most Used Social Media 2021." Accessed November 22, 2021. https://www.statista.com/statistics/272014/global-social-networks-ranked-by-number-of-users/.

Statista. "Number of Monthly Active Users (MAU) of TikTok Worldwide from January 2018 to September 2021." September 2021. https://www.statista.com/statistics/1267892/tiktok-global-mau/.

Stauss, David. "Status of Proposed CCPA-Like State Privacy Legislation as of March 29, 2021." Byte Back, 2021. https://www.bytebacklaw.com/2021/03/status-of-proposed-ccpa-like-state-privacy-legislation-as-of-march-29-2021/.

Steinkuehler, Constance A., and Dmitri Williams. "Where Everybody Knows Your (Screen) Name: Online Games as 'Third Places.'" Journal of Computer-Mediated Communication 11, no. 4 (2017): 885–909.

Stone, Alex, and Peter Wood. "China's Military-Civil Fusion Strategy." Air University, June 15, 2020. https://www.airuniversity.af.edu/CASI/Display/Article/2217101/chinas-military-civil-fusion-strategy/.

Stouffer, Keith, Victoria Pillitteri, Suzanne Lightman, Marshall Abrams, and Adam Hahn. Guide to Industrial Control Systems Security. National Institute of Standards and

Technology Special Publication 800-82, Revision 2. June 2015. https://nvlpubs.nist.gov/nistpubs/SpecialPublications/NIST.SP.800-82r2.pdf.

Stuart, Keith. "More Than 12M Players Watch Travis Scott Concert in Fortnite." *The Guardian*, April 24, 2020. http://www.theguardian.com/games/2020/apr/24/travis-scott-concert-fortnite-more-than-12m-players-watch.

Sukharev, Oleg S. "Economic Crisis as a Consequence COVID-19 Virus Attack: Risk and Damage Assessment." *Quantitative Finance and Economics* 4, no. 2 (2020): 274–93.

Sullivan, Katharine T. "Policy on Funding Unmanned Aircraft Systems." Office of Justice Programs, US Department of Justice, October 5, 2020. https://www.ojp.gov/sites/g/files/xyckuh241/files/media/document/ojporderfundingdrones.pdf.

Sun, Kunming. "Fawang huihui, 'DiDi' bulou—weihe fumei shangshi de DiDi wangluo anquan shenbao nan guogan?" [The law is extensive, DiDi didn't escape—why did DiDi's US stock market listing not pass its data security review?]. Tianjin Law Society, July 2021. http://www.tjsfxh.com/2021/ssfx1_0711/18325.html.

Sun, Leo. "Tencent's Gaming Business Could Be Trump's Next Target." The Motley Fool, September 24, 2020. https://www.fool.com/investing/2020/09/24/tencent-gaming-business-may-be-trump-next-target/.

Sun, Wanning. "Is There a Problem with WeChat?" China Matters, April 2019. https://chinamatters.org.au/wp-content/uploads/2019/04/China-Matters-Explores-April-2019.pdf.

Sun, Wanning, and Haiqing Yu, Eds. *WeChat and the Chinese Diaspora: Digital Transnationalism in the Era of China's Rise*. New York: Routledge, 2022.

Surane, Jennifer, and Selina Wang. "China's Alipay Grabs Slice of U.S. Market with First Data." Bloomberg, May 9, 2017. https://www.bloomberg.com/news/articles/2017-05-08/china-s-alipay-grabs-slice-of-u-s-market-with-first-data-deal.

Swanson, Ana, and Keith Bradsher. "Chinese Companies to Face More Scrutiny as Bill Clears House." *New York Times*, December 2, 2020. https://www.nytimes.com/2020/12/02/business/economy/chinese-companies-to-face-more-scrutiny-as-bill-clears-house.html.

Swanson, Ana, and David McCabe. "U.S. Judge Temporarily Halts Trump's WeChat Ban." *New York Times*, September 20, 2020. https://www.nytimes.com/2020/09/20/business/economy/court-wechat-ban.html.

Swartz, Lana. *New Money: How Payment Became Social Media*. New Haven, CT: Yale University Press, 2020.

Sweeney, Latanya, Akua Abu, and Julia Winn. "Identifying Participants in the Personal Genome Project by Name." *SSRN Electronic Journal*, April 2013. http://www.ssrn.com/abstract=2257732.

Syngenta Global. "Our Research Areas: Helping Growers Produce Successful Crops Every Year." 2021. https://www.syngenta.com/en/innovation-agriculture/research-and-development/our-research-areas.

Syngenta US. "AgriEdge." Last updated 2020. https://www.syngenta-us.com/agriedge.

Takahashi, Dean. "China Is Approving More Foreign Games, but Not So Many American Ones." VentureBeat, February 18, 2020. https://venturebeat.com/2020/02/18/china-is-approving-more-foreign-games-but-not-so-many-american-ones/.

Takase, Kensaku. "GDPR Matchup: Japan's Act on the Protection of Personal Information." IAPP, August 29, 2017. https://iapp.org/news/a/gdpr-matchup-japans-act-on-the-protection-of-personal-information/.

Tan, Alden. "How WoW Became the Most Popular MMORPG in the World." *Word-of-Mouth and Referral Marketing Blog,* December 25, 2017. https://www.referralcandy.com/blog/world-of-warcraft-marketing-strategy/.

Tan, Kim Hua, and Yuanzhu Zhan. "Improving New Product Development Using Big Data: A Case Study of an Electronics Company." *R&D Management* 47, no. 4 (2017): 570–82.

Tan, Shin Bin, Colleen Chiu-Shee, and Fábio Duarte. "From SARS to COVID-19: Digital Infrastructures of Surveillance and Segregation in Exceptional Times." *Cities,* October 8, 2021. https://doi.org/10.1016/j.cities.2021.103486.

Tan, Xiaodong, Xiangxiang Liu, and Haiyan Shao. "Healthy China 2030: A Vision for Health Care." *Value in Health Regional Issues* 12C (2017): 112–14.

Tang, Min. "Huawei Versus the United States? The Geopolitics of Exterritorial Internet Infrastructure." *International Journal of Communication* 14 (August 24, 2020): 4556–77.

Tang, Shiliang, Ziming Wu, Xinyi Zhang, Gang Wang, Xiaojuan Ma, Haitao Zheng, and Ben Zhao. "Towards Understanding the Adoption and Social Experience of Digital Wallet Systems." Paper presented at the Hawaii International Conference on System Sciences, Honolulu, HI, January 8, 2019.

Tanzania Daily News. "Tanzania: China's Huawei Facilitates Industrialization Drive in Tanzania." AllAfrica.com, January 10, 2021. https://allafrica.com/stories/202101100 020.html.

Taplin, Jonathan. *Move Fast and Break Things: How Facebook, Google, and Amazon Have Cornered Culture and What It Means for All of Us.* New York: Hachette Book Group, 2017.

TechCrunch. "China Blocks Access to Twitter, Facebook After Riots." July 7, 2009. https://social.techcrunch.com/2009/07/07/china-blocks-access-to-twitter-facebook-after-riots/.

Tencent. "Bridging Gaps in Healthcare Industry with Technology." November 2019. https://www.tencent.com/en-us/articles/2200933.html.

Tencent. "Tencent Announces 2020 Third Quarter Results." News release, November 12, 2020.

Tencent Research Institute. "WeCity Weilai Chengshi 2.0 Baipishu" [WeCity Future City 2.0 white paper]. Zhongguo Shugu, September 15, 2020. http://www.cbdio.com/BigD ata/2020-09/21/content_6160291.htm.

Tencent Tech. "Baidu, Haier Partner on Smart Home Products and Platform Development." *Marbridge Daily* (blog), March 7, 2018. https://www.marbridgecon sulting.com/marbridgedaily/2018-03-07/article/108657/baidu_haier_partner_on_ smart_home_products_and_platform_development.

Thomala, Lai Lin. "Market Size of the Online Gaming Market in China from 2011 to 2019 with Forecasts Until 2023." Statista, February 17, 2022. https://www.statista.com/statist ics/284942/market-volume-of-online-gaming-market-in-china/.

Thomas, Uduak Grace. "WuXi PharmaTech Invests $15M in DNAnexus, Signs Cloud Infrastructure Agreement." GenomeWeb, April 22, 2015. https://www.genomeweb.com/informatics/wuxi-pharmatech-invests-15m-dnanexus-signs-cloud-infrastruct ure-agreement.

Thumfart, Johannes. "The Norm Development of Digital Sovereignty Between China, Russia, the EU, and the US: From the Late 1990s to the COVID Crisis 2020/2021 as a Catalytic Event." In *Data Protection and Privacy: Enforcing Rights in a Changing World,* edited by Dara Hallinan, Ronald Leenes, and Paul de Hert, 1–44. Oxford: Hart, 2021.

Tiirmaa-Klaar, Heli. "The Evolution of the UN Group of Governmental Experts on Cyber Issues." The Hague Center for Strategic Studies, 2021. https://hcss.nl/wp-content/uplo ads/2021/12/Cyberstability-Paper-Series.pdf#page=15.\

TikTok. "Law Enforcement." August 30, 2018. https://www.tiktok.com/legal/law-enfo rcement.

TikTok. "Privacy Policy." December 20, 2020. https://www.tiktok.com/legal/privacy-pol icy?lang=en.

TikTok. "Statement on TikTok's Content Moderation and Data Security Practices." October 24, 2019. https://newsroom.tiktok.com/en-us/statement-on-tiktoks-content-moderation-and-data-security-practices.

TikTok. "Terms of Service." February 2019. https://www.tiktok.com/legal/terms-of-use?lang=en.

TikTok. "TikTok Transparency Report 2020 H1." September 22, 2020. https://www.tik tok.com/safety/resources/transparency-report-2020-1?lang=en.

Ting, Daniel Shu Wei, Lawrence Carin, Victor Dzau, and Tien Y. Wong. "Digital Technology and COVID-19." *Nature Medicine* 26, no. 4 (March 2020): 459–61.

Toal, Gerald. "Geopolitical Structures and Cultures: Towards Conceptual Clarity in the Critical Study of Geopolitics." In *Geopolitics: Global Problems and Regional Concerns*, edited by Lasha Tchantouridze, 75–102. Winnipeg, MB: Center for Defence and Security Studies, 2004.

Tokody, Dániel, and György Schuster. "Driving Forces Behind Smart City Implementations—the Next Smart Revolution." *Journal of Emerging Research and Solutions in ICT* 1 (December 20, 2016): 1–16. https://doi.org/10.20544/ERS ICT.02.16.P01.

Transparency Register. "TikTok Information Technologies UK Limited." European Union, April 28, 2020. https://ec.europa.eu/transparencyregister/public/consultation/displaylobbyist.do?id=165202837974-32.

Trithara, Dakoda. "Toward Geopolitical Gaming: Exploring the Tension Between Blizzard Entertainment and Political Forces." *Journal of Information Technology and Politics* 19, no. 1 (2022): 65–82. https://doi.org/10.1080/19331681.2021.1922326. https://doi.org/10.1080/19331681.2021.1922326.

Tully, Shawn. "This Agriculture Giant Is Bringing in the Drones to Modernize Farming from Cornfields to Vineyards." *Fortune*, June 19, 2018. https://fortune.com/2018/06/19/syngenta-chemchina-drones-farming/.

Tucker, Hank. "Tim Sweeney's Fortune Jumps To $7.4 Billion As Epic Games Scores $28.7 Billion Valuation." Forbes. Accessed July 8, 2022. https://www.forbes.com/sites/han ktucker/2021/04/15/tim-sweeneys-fortune-jumps-to-74-billion-as-epic-games-sco res-287-billion-valuation/.

Turner, Fred. *From Counterculture to Cyberculture: Stewart Brand, the Whole Earth Network, and the Rise of Digital Utopianism.* Chicago: University of Chicago Press, 2010.

Turner, Gabe, and Security.org Team. "47 States Have Weak or Nonexistent Consumer Data Privacy Laws." Security.org, April 14, 2020. https://www.security.org/resources/digital-privacy-legislation-by-state/.

Tziallas, Evangelos. "Gamified Eroticism: Gay Male 'Social Networking' Applications and Self-Pornography." *Sexuality and Culture* 19, no. 4 (2015/12/01/ 2015): 759–75. https://doi.org/10.1007/s12119-015-9288-z.

Umeda, Sayuri. "Online Privacy Law: Japan." Library of Congress, June 2012. https://www.loc.gov/law/help/online-privacy-law/2012/japan.php.

United Nations Office on Drugs and Crime. "Guidance Note on 'Abuse of a Position of Vulnerability' as a Means of Trafficking in Persons in Article 3 of the Protocol to Prevent, Suppress and Punish Trafficking in Persons, Especially Women and Children, Supplementing the United Nations Convention Against Transnational Organized Crime." 2012. https://www.unodc.org/documents/human-trafficking/2012/UNODC_2012_Guidance_Note_-_Abuse_of_a_Position_of_Vulnerability_E.pdf.

United States Department of Commerce. "Executive Order on Addressing the Threat Posed by WeChat." August 20, 2020. https://www.whitehouse.gov/presidential-actions/executive-order-addressing-threat-posed-wechat/.

United States Department of Defense. "Department of Defense Cyber Strategy 2018." 2018. https://media.defense.gov/2018/Sep/18/2002041658/-1/-1/1/CYBER_STRATEGY_SUMMARY_FINAL.PDF.

United States Department of Justice. "China-Based Executive at U.S. Telecommunications Company Charged with Disrupting Video Meetings Commemorating Tiananmen Square Massacre." December 18, 2020. https://www.justice.gov/opa/pr/china-based-executive-us-telecommunications-company-charged-disrupting-video-meetings.

United States Department of State. "The Clean Network." 2020. https://2017-2021.state.gov/the-clean-network/index.html.

USC US-China Institute. "China's Commercial Space Industry." July 15, 2021. https://china.usc.edu/chinas-commercial-space-industry.

USC US-China Institute. "Decision of the Central Committee of the Communist Party of China on Some Major Issues Concerning Comprehensively Deepening the Reform." University of Southern California, Annenberg School, November 2013. https://china.usc.edu/decision-central-committee-communist-party-china-some-major-issues-concerning-comprehensively.

US-China Business Council. "China's Strategic Emerging Industries: Relevant Government Players." August 2012. https://www.uschina.org/sites/default/files/seis_by_sector_0.pdf.

U.S.-China Economic and Security Review Commission. "2020 Annual Report to Congress." December 2020. https://www.uscc.gov/sites/default/files/2020-12/2020_Annual_Report_to_Congress.pdf.

U.S.-China Economic and Security Review Commission. China's Views of Sovereignty and Methods of Access Control. Washington, DC: U.S.-China Economic and Security Review Commission, 2008.

U.S.-China Economic and Security Review Commission. "High-Tech Development." November 2018. https://www.uscc.gov/sites/default/files/2019-09/Chapter%204%20Section%201-%20Next%20Generation%20Connectivity_0.pdf.

U.S.-China Economic and Security Review Commission. "Technology, Trade, and Military-Civil Fusion: China's Pursuit of Artificial Intelligence, New Materials, and New Energy." June 7, 2019. https://www.uscc.gov/hearings/technology-trade-and-military-civil-fusion-chinas-pursuit-artificial-intelligence-new.

US-China Investment Project. "The US-China Investment Hub." 2020. https://www.us-china-investment.org/vc-data.

U.S. Senate Committee on Commerce, Science, and Transportation. "Protecting Kids Online: Snapchat, TikTok, and YouTube." October 26, 2021. https://www.commerce.senate.gov/2021/10/protecting-kids-online-snapchat-tiktok-and-youtube.

Vaidhyanathan, Siva. Antisocial Media: How Facebook Disconnects Us and Undermines Democracy. New York: Oxford University Press, 2018.

Vaidhyanathan, Siva. *The Googlization of Everything (and Why We Should Worry)*. Berkeley, CA: University of California Press, 2012.

Valens, Ana. "Every Fortnite: Battle Royale Harvesting Tool and Pickaxe." Dot eSports, July 30, 2018. https://dotesports.com/fortnite/news/fortnite-battle-royale-harvesting-tool-pickaxe-skin-guide-31050.

Vantage Asia. "Haier D-Share IPO Breaks New Ground." December 12, 2018. https://www.vantageasia.com/haier-d-share-ipo-breaks-new-ground/.

Varadarajan, Rajan, Manjit S. Yadav, and Venkatesh Shankar. "First-Mover Advantage in an Internet-Enabled Market Environment: Conceptual Framework and Propositions." *Journal of the Academy of Marketing Science* 36, no. 3 (November 2007): 293–308.

Vayena, Effy, and Alessandro Blasimme. "Health Research with Big Data: Time for Systemic Oversight." *Journal of Law, Medicine and Ethics* 46, no. 1 (2018): 119–29.

Vegter, M. W. "Towards Precision Medicine: A New Biomedical Cosmology." *Medicine, Health Care and Philosophy* 21, no. 4 (December 2018): 443–56. https://doi.org/https://doi.org/10.1007/s11019-018-9828-z.

Verifone. "Alipay Taxi Payments." October 2017. https://www.verifone.com/en/us/press-release/alipay-taxi-payments.

Villegas, Paulina. "'Fast and Furious' Star John Cena Apologizes to China for Calling Taiwan a Country." *Washington Post*, May 25, 2021. https://www.washingtonpost.com/nation/2021/05/25/john-cena-apology-to-china-about-taiwan-comment/.

Vishwanath, Arun. "Habitual Facebook Use and Its Impact on Getting Deceived on Social Media." *Journal of Computer-Mediated Communication* 20, no. 1 (January 2015): 83–98. https://doi.org/10.1111/jcc4.12100.

Vullo, Maria T. "Cybersecurity Requirements for Financial Services Companies." 23 New York Code, Rules and Regulations 500 (2017): 14.

Wagner, I. "General Motors Company's Vehicle Sales by Key Country in FY 2020." Statista, February 15, 2021. https://www.statista.com/statistics/304367/vehicle-sales-of-general-motors-by-country/.

Waidelich, Brian. "China's Commercial Space Sector Shoots for the Stars." East Asia Forum, March 13, 2021. https://www.eastasiaforum.org/2021/03/13/chinas-commercial-space-sector-shoots-for-the-stars/.

Walker, Christopher, Shanthi Kalathil, and Jessica Ludwig. "The Cutting Edge of Sharp Power." *Journal of Democracy* 31, no. 1 (2020): 124–37.

Wall, Alex. "GDPR Matchup: South Korea's Personal Information Protection Act." IAPP, January 8, 2018. https://iapp.org/news/a/gdpr-matchup-south-koreas-personal-information-protection-act/.

Walsh, Kathleen A., and Ed Francis. "China's Defense Innovation System: Making the Wheels Spin." University of California, San Diego, September 2011. https://escholarship.org/uc/item/3hx613nj.

Wang, Echo. "China's Kunlun Tech Agrees to U.S. Demand to Sell Grindr Gay Dating App." Reuters, May 13, 2019. https://www.reuters.com/article/us-grindr-m-a-beijingkunlun-idUSKCN1SJ28N.

Wang, Echo, and Chibuike Oguh. "Grindr's Chinese Owner Says to Sell Social Media App for $608 Mln." Reuters, March 6, 2020. https://www.reuters.com/article/us-grindr-m-a-investors-exclusive-idUSKBN20T0IR.

Wang, Honggui. "Youxi handong chixu manyan banhao fafang quanmian zanting" [Gaming winter continues, issue of edition is suspended]. 163 Money, September 19, 2018. https://money.163.com/18/0919/16/DS351P6H002580S6.html.

Wang, Paul, and Amjad Ali. "Data Security and Threat Modeling for Smart City Infrastructure." Paper presented at the International Conference on Cyber Security of Smart Cities, Industrial Control System and Communications (SSIC), August 2015.

Wang, Yiwei. "Public Diplomacy and the Rise of Chinese Soft Power." *Annals of the American Academy of Political and Social Science* 616, no. 1 (March 2008): 257–73.

Warner, Mark, Andreas Gutmann, M. Angela Sasse, and Ann Blandford. "Privacy Unraveling Around Explicit HIV Status Disclosure Fields in the Online Geosocial Hookup App Grindr." Paper presented at the Proceedings of the ACM Human-Computer Interaction, November 2018.

Weber, Valentin. "Understanding the Global Ramifications of China's Information-Control Model." In *AI, China, Russia, and the Global Order: Technological, Political, Global, and Creative Perspectives*, edited by Nicholas D. Wright, 72–77. Washington, DC: Department of Defense and Joint Chiefs of Staff, 2018.

Webster, Andrew. "Chinese Internet Giant Tencent Now Owns the Studio Behind League of Legends." The Verge, December 17, 2015. https://www.theverge.com/2015/12/17/10410952/riot-games-league-of-legends-acquired-tencent.

Webster, Andrew. "More than 12 Million People Attended Travis Scott's Fortnite Concert." The Verge, April 23, 2020. https://www.theverge.com/2020/4/23/21233946/travis-scott-fortnite-concert-astronomical-record-breaking-player-count.

Wedeman, Andrew. "China's Corruption Crackdown: War Without End?" *Current History* 116, no. 791 (September 2017): 210–16.

Wee, Sui-Lee. "Giving In to China, U.S. Airlines Drop Taiwan (in Name at Least)." *New York Times*, July 25, 2018. https://www.nytimes.com/2018/07/25/business/taiwan-american-airlines-china.html.

Weeden, Brian, and Xiao He. "U.S.-China Strategic Relations in Space." In *Avoiding the "Thucydides Trap,"* edited by Dong Wang and Travis Tanner, 81–103. New York: Routledge, 2020.

Wei, Lingling. "China's New Power Play: More Control of Tech Companies' Troves of Data." *Wall Street Journal*, June 12, 2021. https://www.wsj.com/articles/chinas-new-power-play-more-control-of-tech-companies-troves-of-data-11623470478.

Wei, Lingling. "China's Xi Ramps Up Control of Private Sector. 'We Have No Choice but to Follow the Party.'" *Wall Street Journal*, December 10, 2020. https://www.wsj.com/articles/china-xi-clampdown-private-sector-communist-party-11607612531.

Weiss, Charles, and William B. Bonvillian. "Complex, Established 'Legacy' Sectors: The Technology Revolutions That Do Not Happen." *Innovations: Technology, Governance, Globalization* 6, no. 2 (April 2011): 157–87.

Wells, Georgia, and Aaron Tilley. "Oracle Wins Bid for TikTok in U.S., Beating Microsoft." *New York Times*, September 14, 2020.

Wen, Shangfang. "2020 Zhongguo hulianwang qiye baiqiang gongbu: Ali duoguan ATM xinshidai" [China's top 100 internet companies 2020 announced: Alibaba winning, ATM new era]. *Kuaikeji*, October 30, 2020. https://news.mydrivers.com/1/721/721024.htm.

West, Emily. *Buy Now: How Amazon Branded Convenience and Normalized Monopoly.* Cambridge, MA: MIT Press, 2022.

Whalen, Jeanne. "Federal Court Issues Preliminary Injunction Halting Administration's Ban of Chinese App WeChat." *Washington Post*, September 21, 2020. https://www.washingtonpost.com/technology/2020/09/20/wechat-ban-blocked-trump/.

Whalen, Jeanne. "Huawei Helped Bring Internet to Small-Town America. Now Its Equipment Has to Go." *Washington Post*, October 10, 2019. https://www.washingtonp ost.com/business/2019/10/10/huawei-helped-bring-internet-small-town-america-now-its-equipment-has-go/.

White, Edward. "China's Tech Platforms Become Propaganda Tools in Putin's War." *Financial Times*, March 11, 2022. https://www.ft.com/content/d460c6f6-ffc7-4d61-9350-bef378fcc5c5.

The White House. "Critical Infrastructure Protection." May 22, 1998. https://fas.org/web siteimprovementform.html.

The White House. "Executive Order on Addressing the Threat Posed by WeChat." August 6, 2020. https://www.federalregister.gov/documents/2020/08/11/2020-17700/address ing-the-threat-posed-by-wechat-and-taking-additional-steps-to-address-the-natio nal-emergency.

The White House. "Executive Order on Protecting Americans' Sensitive Data from Foreign Adversaries." June 9, 2021. https://www.whitehouse.gov/briefing-room/presi dential-actions/2021/06/09/executive-order-on-protecting-americans-sensitive-data-from-foreign-adversaries/.

The White House. "Fact Sheet: Cybersecurity National Action Plan." February 9, 2016. https://obamawhitehouse.archives.gov/the-press-office/2016/02/09/fact-sheet-cybers ecurity-national-action-plan.

The White House. "Fact Sheet: President Obama's Precision Medicine Initiative." News release, January 30, 2015. https://obamawhitehouse.archives.gov/the-press-office/2015/ 01/30/fact-sheet-president-obama-s-precision-medicine-initiative.

The White House. "Fact Sheet: The American Jobs Plan." Last updated March 31, 2021. https://www.whitehouse.gov/briefing-room/statements-releases/2021/03/31/fact-sheet-the-american-jobs-plan/.

The White House. "National Cyber Strategy of the United States." September 2018. https://trumpwhitehouse.archives.gov/wp-content/uploads/2018/09/National-Cyber-Strategy.pdf.

The White House. "Statement by President Donald J. Trump on H.R. 5515." News *release*, August 13, 2018. https://www.whitehouse.gov/briefings-statements/statement-presid ent-donald-j-trump-h-r-5515/.

Theoretical Studies Center Group of the Cyberspace Administration of China. "Shenru guanche Xi Jinping zongshuji wangluo qiangguo zhanlüe sixiang zhashi tuijin wangluo anquan he xinxihua gongzuo" [Implementing Secretary Xi Jinping's strategic thinking on strengthening China through the internet to make solid progress in cybersecurity and IT application]. September 15, 2017. http://www.qstheory.cn/dukan/qs/2017-09/ 15/c_1121647633.htm.

Whittaker, Zack. "Everything You Need to Know About Facebook, Google's App Scandal." TechCrunch, February 1, 2019. https://social.techcrunch.com/2019/02/01/facebook-google-scandal/.

Whittaker, Zack. "Security Lapse Exposed a Chinese Smart City Surveillance System." TechCrunch, May 3, 2019. https://social.techcrunch.com/2019/05/03/china-smart-city-exposed/.

Whitten-Woodring, Jenifer, Mona S. Kleinberg, Ardeth Thawnghmung, and Myat The Thitsar. "Poison If You Don't Know How to Use It: Facebook, Democracy, and Human Rights in Myanmar." *International Journal of Press/Politics* 25, no. 3 (July 2020): 407–25. https://doi.org/10.1177/1940161220919666.

Wilde, Molly. "TikTok Time Bomb: App Poses Potential Security Threat." *The Gavel* (Boston College), January 26, 2020. http://www.bcgavel.com/2020/01/26/tiktok-time-bomb-app-poses-potential-security-threat/.

Wilde, Tyler. "Tim Sweeney 'Does Not Take Any Orders from Tencent,' Says Epic." PC Gamer, March 22, 2019. https://www.pcgamer.com/tim-sweeney-does-not-take-any-orders-from-tencent-says-epic/.

Wille, Matthew. "Redditor Who Reverse-Engineered the TikTok App Claims It's a Huge Data Collection Scheme." *Input*, July 2020. https://www.inputmag.com/tech/redditor-reverse-engineers-tiktok-app-claims-massive-data-collection-scheme.

Wilson, Iain, Sam Loveridge, and Ford James. "How to Play Fortnite Advice for Absolute Beginners." Games Radar, May 7, 2021. https://www.gamesradar.com/how-to-play-fortnite/.

Wingo, Harry. "Prepared Statement of Harry Wingo." U.S. Senate, June 18, 2019. https://www.commerce.senate.gov/services/files/12FD98A3-D857-40B8-8388-B983F91DFF70.

Winig, Laura. "GE's Big Bet on Data and Analytics." *MIT Sloan Management Review*, December 18, 2016. https://sloanreview.mit.edu/case-study/ge-big-bet-on-data-and-analytics/.

Winter, Jenifer Sunrise, and Elizabeth Davidson. "Big Data Governance of Personal Health Information and Challenges to Contextual Integrity." *The Information Society* 35, no. 1 (January 2019): 36–51. https://doi.org/10.1080/01972243.2018.1542648.

Wolf, Mark J. P. *The Medium of the Video Game.* Austin: University of Texas Press, 2001.

Wong, Edward. "How China Uses LinkedIn to Recruit Spies Abroad." *New York Times*, September 27, 2019. https://www.nytimes.com/2019/08/27/world/asia/china-linkedin-spies.html.

Wong, Natalie. "National Security Law: Hong Kong Activist Nathan Law Reveals He Has Left City." *South China Morning Post*, July 3, 2020. https://www.scmp.com/news/hong-kong/politics/article/3091619/national-security-law-hong-kong-activist-nathan-law-reveals.

Wong, Pak Nung. *Techno-Geopolitics: U.S.-China Tech War and the Practice of Digital Statecraft.* London: Routledge, 2021.

Wood, Peter. "China's Ground Segment." China Aerospace Studies Institute, March 1, 2021. https://www.bluepathlabs.com/uploads/1/1/9/0/119002711/2021-03-01_chinas_ground_segment.pdf.

Woods, Andrew Keane. "Litigating Data Sovereignty." *Yale Law Journal* 128, no. 2 (2018): 328–407.

Woolley, Samuel C., and Douglas R. Guilbeault. "Computational Propaganda in the United States of America: Manufacturing Consensus Online." Oxford Internet Institute, Oxford, UK, May 2017). http://blogs.oii.ox.ac.uk/politicalbots/wp-content/uploads/sites/89/2017/06/Comprop-USA.pdf.

Woolley, Samuel C., and Philip N. Howard. *Computational Propaganda: Political Parties, Politicians, and Political Manipulation on Social Media.* Oxford, UK: Oxford University Press, 2018.

Wu, Friedrich, Lim Siok Hoon, and Yuzhu Zhang. "Dos and Don'ts for Chinese Companies Investing in the United States: Lessons from Huawei and Haier." *Thunderbird International Business Review* 53, no. 4 (June 2011): 501–15.

WuXi AppTec. "WuXi Apptec Announces Listing of Initial Public Offering of Common Stock on Shanghai Stock Exchange." May 8, 2018. https://www.wuxiapptec.com/news/wuxi-news/1808.

WuXi NextCODE. "WuXi NextCODE Clarifications to Public Letter Sent to Department of Health and Human Services Acting Inspector General Joanne M. Chiedi." News release, June 11, 2019. https://www.prnewswire.com/news-releases/wuxi-nextcode-clarifications-to-public-letter-sent-to-department-of-health-and-human-services-acting-inspector-general-joanne-m-chiedi-300865510.html.

WuXi NextCODE. "WuXi NextCODE Gains CAP Accreditation." Contract Pharma, February 23, 2016. https://www.contractpharma.com/contents/view_breaking-news/2016-02-23/wuxi-nextcode-gains-cap-accreditation/.

WuXi PharmaTech Inc. "WuXi Pharmatech Acquires NextCODE Health to Create Global Leader in Genomic Medicine." January 9, 2015. https://www.prnewswire.com/news-releases/wuxi-pharmatech-acquires-nextcode-health-to-create-global-leader-in-genomic-medicine-300018311.html.

Xi, Jinping. "Xi Jinping zai 'Yi Dai Yi Lu' guoji hezuo gaofeng luntan kaimushishang de yanjiang" [Full Text of President Xi's Speech at Opening of Belt and Road Forum]. May 14, 2017. http://2017.beltandroadforum.org/n100/2017/0514/c24-407.html.

Xiaomi. "Xiaomi User Agreement." 2022. https://www.mi.com/global/about/agreement/.

Xinhua. "China's Military Strategy (Full Text)." May 27, 2015. http://english.www.gov.cn/archive/white_paper/2015/05/27/content_281475115610833.htm.

Xinhua. "Chinese Investment in Australia Plummets as Increasing Scrutiny Hurts Confidence." *People's Daily Online*, March 1, 2021. http://en.people.cn/n3/2021/0301/c90000-9823161.html.

Xinhua. "English Translation of the Law of the People's Republic of China on Safeguarding National Security in the Hong Kong Special Administrative Region." 2020. http://www.xinhuanet.com/english/2020-07/01/c_139178753.htm.

Xinhua. "Jingying feifa mayi baidu jingdong tengxun xiajia hulianwang cunkuan chanpin" [Business illegal! Ant, Baidu, JD.Com and Tencent pulled online deposit products from their shelves]. December 21, 2020. http://www.xinhuanet.com/legal/2020-12/21/c_1126884992.htm.

Xinhua. "Pingguo guonei yonhu icloud jiang qianhui Guizhou" [Apple domestic users iCloud to move back to Guizhou]. January 11, 2018. http://www.xinhuanet.com/tech/2018-01/11/c_1122241456.htm.

Xinhua. "Xi Sends Congratulatory Letter to World Internet Conference." *China Daily*, September 26, 2021." https://www.chinadaily.com.cn/a/202109/26/WS614fd003a310cdd39bc6b8a3.html.

Xinhua. "Xi Jingping xiang 2021 shijie hulianwang dahui Wuzhen fenghui zhi hexin" [Xi Jinping sent a congratulatory letter to the 2021 World Internet Conference Wuzhen summit]. September 26, 2021. http://www.news.cn/politics/leaders/2021-09/26/c_1127903074.htm.

Xinhua. "Xuexi jinxingshi Xi Jingping de hangtian qing" [Xi Jinping's love of space]. April 12, 2021. http://www.xinhuanet.com/politics/xxjxs/2021-04/12/c_1127322037.htm.

Yan, Xuetong. "Chinese Values vs. Liberalism: What Ideology Will Shape the International Normative Order?" *Chinese Journal of International Politics* 11, no. 1 (2018): 1–22. https://doi.org/10.1093/cjip/poy001.

Yan, Xuetong. "The Rise of China in Chinese Eyes." *Journal of Contemporary China* 10, no. 26 (February 2001): 33–39.

Yang, Fan. "China's 'Fake' Apple Store: Branded Space, Intellectual Property and the Global Culture Industry." *Theory, Culture and Society* 31, no. 4 (2014): 71–96. https://doi.org/10.1177/0263276413504971.

Yang, Jie. "The Politics of the Dang'an: Spectralization, Spatialization, and Neoliberal Governmentality in China." *Anthropological Quarterly* 84 (March 2011): 507–33. https://doi.org/10.1353/anq.2011.0023.

Yang, Yuan, and Madhumita Murgia. "Microsoft Worked with Chinese Military University on Artificial Intelligence." April 2019. https://www.ft.com/content/9378e 7ee-5ae6-11e9-9dde-7aedca0a081a.

Yang, Zhenjie, Guilan Zhu, Linda Chelan Li, and Yilong Sheng. "Services and Surveillance During the Pandemic Lockdown: Residents' Committees in Wuhan and Beijing." *China Information* 35, no. 3 (2021): 420–40.

Ye, Josh. "China Ends Gaming Approval Freeze, Grants First Licenses since July Last Year." *Reuters*, April 11, 2022, sec. Technology. https://www.reuters.com/technology/ china-grants-gaming-licence-xd-title-first-since-july-document-2022-04-11/

Yeung, Arthur, and Kenneth Dewoskin. "From Survival to Success: The Journey of Corporate Transformation at Haier." William Davidson Institute, Ann Arbor, MI, July 1998.

Yin, Yiyi. "An Emergent Algorithmic Culture: The Data-Ization of Online Fandom in China." *International Journal of Cultural Studies* 23, no. 4 (July 1, 2020): 475–92. https://doi.org/10.1177/1367877920908269.

You, Edward H. "Safeguarding the Bioeconomy: U.S. Opportunities and Challenges." U.S.-China Economic and Security Review Commission, Washington, DC, March 10, 2017. https://www.uscc.gov/sites/default/files/Ed_You_Testimony.pdf.

YouTikTok. "Renegade Dance—New Trend 2019 (Tik Tok Compilation)—YouTube." Posted *October* 21, 2019. https://www.youtube.com/watch?v=MXMx3oxiUPU.

Yu, Wenchi. "Risk Mitigation and Creating Social Impact: Chinese Technology Companies in the United States." Ash Center for Democratic Governance and Innovation, Harvard University, Cambridge, MA, April 2021. https://ash.harvard.edu/ files/ash/files/wenchi_yu_policy_brief.pdf?m=1618407028.

Yu, Xie. "Haier Has a Plan to Turn Around Its US$5.6 Billion GE Appliances Unit." *South China Morning Post*, October 23, 2017. https://www.scmp.com/business/ companies/article/2116486/chinas-haier-has-plan-help-continue-turnaround-ge-appliances.

Yu, Yun. "Steam—the Gaming Platform Before There Were Platforms." *Digital Innovation and Transformation* (blog), February 23, 2017. https://digital.hbs.edu/platform-digit/ submission/steam-the-gaming-platform-before-there-were-platforms/.

Yuan, Jing-Dong. "China's Role in Establishing and Building the Shanghai Cooperation Organization (SCO)." *Journal of Contemporary China* 19, no. 67 (November 2010): 855–69.

Yuan, Li. "Beijing Pushes for a Direct Hand in China's Big Tech Firms." *Wall Street Journal*, October 11, 2017. https://www.wsj.com/articles/beijing-pushes-for-a-direct-hand-in-chinas-big-tech-firms-1507758314.

Yuan, Rong, and Jiancheng Long. "Multi-Platform Strategy: Tencent Case Study." *International Journal of Science and Research* 6, no. 3 (2015): 6.

Zaagman, Elliott. "Cyber Sovereignty and the PRC's Vision for Global Internet Governance." Jamestown Foundation, Washington, DC, June 2018. https://jamest own.org/program/cyber-sovereignty-and-the-prcs-vision-for-global-internet-gov ernance/.

Zaidi, Amina. "Chart of the Week: A Deep Dive into Fortnite." Verto Analytics, May 23, 2018. https://vertoanalytics.com/chart-week-deep-dive-fortnite/.

Zakaria, Fareed. "The New China Scare: Why America Shouldn't Panic About Its Latest Challenger." *Foreign Affairs* 99 (2020): 52–69.

Zakaria, Fareed. "The Rise of Illiberal Democracy." *Foreign Affairs* 76, no. 6 (1997): 22–43.

Zeng, Daniel, Hsinchun Chen, Robert Lusch, and Shu-Hsing Li. "Social Media Analytics and Intelligence." *IEEE Intelligent Systems* 25, no. 6 (November 2010): 13–16. https://doi.org/10.1109/MIS.2010.151.

Zeng, Jinghan. "Artificial Intelligence and China's Authoritarian Governance." *International Affairs* 96, no. 6 (2020): 1441–59. https://doi.org/10.1093/ia/iiaa172.

Zhang, Albert. "#StopAsianHate: Chinese Diaspora Targeted by Ccp Disinformation Campaign." *The Strategist*, 2021. https://www.aspistrategist.org.au/stopasianhate-chin ese-diaspora-targeted-by-ccp-disinformation-campaign/.

Zhang, Cinder Xinde, and Tao-Hsien Dolly King. "The Decision to List Abroad: The Case of ADRs and Foreign IPOs by Chinese Companies." *Journal of Multinational Financial Management* 20, no. 1 (February 2010): 71–92.

Zhang, Jane, and Zhou Xin. "Jack Ma Gives Video Speech to Rural Teachers After Three Months of Silence." *South China Morning Post*, January 20, 2021. https://www.scmp.com/tech/big-tech/article/3118454/alibaba-founder-jack-ma-delivers-video-speech-chinas-rural-teachers.

Zhang, Laney. "Government Responses to Disinformation on Social Media Platforms: China." Library of Congress, Washington, DC, December 30, 2020. https://www.loc.gov/law/help/social-media-disinformation/china.php.

Zhang, Xing, You Wu, and Shan Liu. "Exploring Short-Form Video Application Addiction: Socio-Technical and Attachment Perspectives." *Telematics and Informatics* 42 (September 2019). https://doi.org/10.1016/j.tele.2019.101243.

Zhang, Z. Alex, Vivian Tsoi, Farhad Jalinous, Richard Burke, and Lin Li. "China Further Removes Foreign Investment Restrictions." White & Case LLP, 2019. https://www.whitecase.com/publications/alert/china-further-removes-foreign-investment-restrictions-0.

Zhang, Zongyi. "Infrastructuralization of TikTok: Transformation, Power Relationships, and Platformization of Video Entertainment in China." *Media, Culture and Society* 43, no. 2 (2020): 219–36.

Zhao, Yanan. "Research on the Consumer Finance System of Ant Financial Service Group." *American Journal of Industrial and Business Management* 7, no. 5 (May 2017): 559–65.

Zhao, Yuezhi. "China's Quest for 'Soft Power': Imperatives, Impediments and Irreconcilable Tensions?" *Javnost—The Public* 20, no. 4 (2013): 17–29.

Zhong, Raymond. "Ant Group Set to Raise $34 Billion in World's Biggest I.P.O." *New York Times*, October 26, 2020. https://www.nytimes.com/2020/10/26/technology/ant-group-ipo-valuation.html.

Zhongguo zhengfuwang. "Waiguoren juliu zhengjian qianfa fuwu zhinan" [Guide to service for issuing residence certificates for foreigners]. May 5, 2019. http://www.gov.cn/bumenfuwu/2019-05/05/content_5388755.htm.

Zhou, Kaile, Chao Fu, and Shanlin Yang. "Big Data Driven Smart Energy Management: From Big Data to Big Insights." *Renewable and Sustainable Energy Reviews* 56 (April 1, 2016): 215–25.

Zoom Video Communications. "Zoom 10-K Annual Report Which Provides a Comprehensive Overview of the Company for the Past Year." US Securities and

Exchange Commission, 2020. https://investors.zoom.us/static-files/09a01665-5f33-4007-8e90-de02219886aa.

Zoom Video Communications. "Zoom Video Communications Reports Fourth Quarter and Fiscal Year 2021 Financial Results." March 1, 2021. https://investors.zoom.us/news-releases/news-release-details/zoom-video-communications-reports-fourth-quarter-and-fiscal-0/.

Zou, Xiaolei, Lin Lin, and Fuzhong Weng. "Absolute Calibration of ATMS Upper Level Temperature Sounding Channels Using GPS RO Observations." *IEEE Transactions on Geoscience and Remote Sensing* 52, no. 2 (February 2013). https://ieeexplore.ieee.org/abstract/document/6504501/?casa_token=w-0KYcPgPV4AAAAA:BzYwvyII4EXPtq30YmSNbvF2jaCPTCIc5DM4CKsHDYI68WIXUdS5vgcb0bhsyLOyUBtYRB4dwA.

Zuboff, Shoshana. *The Age of Surveillance Capitalism.* New York: PublicAffairs, 2019.

Index

For the benefit of digital users, indexed terms that span two pages (e.g., 52–53) may, on occasion, appear on only one of those pages.

'Figures are indicated by an italic *f* following the para ID.'

US tech firms (*cont.*)
  time to market prioritized over data
    security by, 15–16
  as tool for expanding US influence, 2
  trade with China and illiberalism
    of, 18–20
  See also Silicon Valley
utility-privacy trade-off, 153
Uyghur Autonomous Region, China,
  technical surveillance in, 64, 79–
  80, 88–89

Vaidhyanathan, Siva, 100
Valve Corporation, 128
Venezuela, Chinese influence on digital
  infrastructure of, 74–75
Venmo, surveillance on, 12
Vietnam
  Chinese influence on digital
    infrastructure of, 74–75
  restrictions on TikTok in, 101–2
Virginia, data security laws in, 27, 35f, 36
virtual reality technology, and Chinese
  military, 8
Visa, obsolescence in China, 142–43
VPNs, ban in China, xvii

Walgreens, Alibaba and, 146–47
Wallach, Dan, xvii
Walmart, payments via WeChat, 107–8
Wang, Jun, 161–62
wangluo qiangguo (strong internet power),
  Xi Jinping's pursuit of, 69
wangluo zhuquan (cyber sovereignty)
  as network sovereignty, 78
  Xi Jinping's vision of, 53–54
  See also cyber sovereignty
Wang Qishan, 143
WeChat
  and AI tools, development of, 108, 109
  as "app for everything," 94, 107–
    8, 140–41
  ban in India, 115
  censorship of content on, 80, 96,
    112, 113–14
  and China's data-gathering efforts, 6, 62
  and China's transactional community,
    expansion of, 148

  Chinese government and, 96
  Chinese ownership of, 96, 99
  and data trafficking, 107
  economic role in US, 109, 189
  electronic IDs offered by, 156
  essential role in US-China digital
    communications, 94, 95–96, 97,
    99, 111
  extraterritorial oversight by Chinese
    government, 96, 111
  fintech services and increased user base
    of, 140–41
  growth of, xvii, 3, 70
  health codes in, 56, 156
  mobile payment systems linked to, 61
  network effects of, 94, 107, 114
  parent company of (Tencent), 94, 96–
    97, 107, 109, 120
  requirements for establishing
    account on, 62
  Silicon Valley practices as model for, 6
  and social credit system, 61–62
  stories of anti-Asian hate on, Chinese
    government actors promulgating, 5
  terms of service on Chinese-based
    phones, 111
  Trump administration's ban on, 94, 113,
    115, 122
  US companies' reliance on, 107–8
  used to track Uyghur
    dissidents, 79–80
WeChat Pay, 61
  Chinese bank account required by,
    61, 140–41
  and consumer spending outside of
    China, 146
  data gathering by, 141, 148
  data trafficking enabled by, 147
  and network sovereignty, 138
  reliance on Chinese banking
    system, 140
  social credit system and, 139, 141
  surveillance resources provided to
    Chinese government, 141
  terms of use of, 147
  US operations of, 146, 148
  worldwide operations of, 141–42, 146
WeChat Users Alliance, 94